GW00500836

A GREAT LIFE IF YOU DON'T WEAKEN

Robert Edom

MINERVA PRESS

ATLANTA LONDON SYDNEY

A GREAT LIFE IF YOU DON'T WEAKEN
Copyright © Robert Edom 2000

ISBN 0 75410 910 0

First Published 2000 by
MINERVA PRESS
315–317 Regent Street
London W1R 7YB

Printed in Great Britain for Minerva Press

A GREAT LIFE IF YOU
DON'T WEAKEN

*In memory of my dear old mum
who, in the face of each new misfortune to befall
the Edom family, would shrug her shoulders and say,
'Ah, well, it's a great life if you don't weaken.'*

Contents

Introduction

Edom's essays record the life and times of Robert Edom, born in total obscurity in West Wickham in 1933 without any hint of the complete anonymity that was to follow. However, for the record, amongst his major achievements was to fail his School Certificate in woodwork and to be second best recruit at RAF Padgate in August 1951. Since then his career has been mostly downhill.

Despite a life distinguished by repeated cock-ups he never doubted that one day he would discover the meaning of life or find true happiness or make the world a better place to live in or even, perhaps, win the spot the ball contest in *Titbits*. The plan was that some day he would be famous, admired and feted, and desired by women – although preferably in reverse order. He is now resigned to the fact that he may have to go round for a second time but, knowing his luck, he has an uneasy feeling that next time he may be a frog, or a hedgehog.

Edom's most unfortunate characteristic has been a nasty tendency to tell the truth – or most of it anyway. The trouble with telling the truth is that it is sometimes rude, often boring and no one ever believes it. Edom has stumbled over more blocks, missed more buses and been up more creeks without a paddle than anyone else he knows. Could Edom's life really have been such an unmitigated shambles and so littered with misadventures, unfulfilled aspirations, missed opportunities and anticlimaxes I hear you ask? The dreadful and truthful answer is yes.

Oh, by the way, the individuals and organisations described in these essays have been heavily disguised to protect the guilty. The innocent should have nothing to sue about anyway. If anyone does recognise him or herself it can only be because Edom's affectionate memories overrode his discretion.

Edom's collected essays are not recommended for people of a tetchy disposition, pimply young persons, pregnant ladies, members of the armed services with access to firearms or for elderly spinsters living in Leamington Spa. However they may be beneficial to members of the Self-satisfied Classes who will see in them yet more reason to feel pleased with themselves.

It is also possible that they will prove a comfort to the also-rans of this world who may be reassured to know that there is absolutely nothing so bad that it can't get considerably worse.

DANGER: HM GOVT HEALTH DEPARTMENT'S
WARNING –
THINK ABOUT THE HEALTH RISKS BEFORE
READING EDOM'S ESSAYS

The Rich Promise of that Dear Little Bobby Edom

Personally I blame it all on Hitler. Him and the Blitz. I was born in 1933 in a world that was just becoming optimistic again. Well, the First World War was then fifteen years gone and the League of Nations was going to make sure that there were no more wars. The General Strike was well past and the Bolshevik revolution had run out of steam before it reached my home town of West Wickham. Just as well really because my old dad couldn't tolerate the Co-op, let alone the Bolsheviks. The recession looked as if it might be over, there were more jobs about and prices were actually falling. Oh, and the Southern Railway had just electrified the Brighton line.

I still have the birthday card that my Auntie Molly gave me on my first birthday. It has a big 'ONE' on it surrounded by flowers and a little verse: 'BABY'S FIRST BIRTHDAY. Dear, this loving greeting brings a loving kiss. May your birthday hours be filled with happiness and bliss.' I don't even know who poor old Aunt Molly was and the verse was a bit excruciating, still it was very civil of her whoever she was.

So little Bobby Edom seemed to have arrived on the crest of a wave. As the song said, the sun had got its hat on. Hip, hip, hip, hip hooray. I have a picture of me on my summer hols at Herne Bay in 1937. I am proudly presenting arms with my shrimping net and have a sunny smile and an air of confidence. I am wearing my one-piece woollen bathing costume which clings to the body somewhat and highlights my little fundamentals to remarkable effect and seems to bode well for the future. To complete the sartorial effect I have my sunhat on at a jaunty angle and am wearing a pair of rubber beach shoes.

The photographs seem to have run out after 1938. This is probably in part because our 1939 summer holidays were rudely interrupted by Mr Chamberlain having his little tiff with Mr Hitler and partly because you couldn't get any 620 film for our Kodak box camera after the war started.

Well, reverting to my favourite subject, I too am puzzled to know what became of that dear little Bobby Edom. There are these stories of me swinging on the garden gate and chatting to everybody as they passed by. I was, I am told, always happy and smiling and had a very sunny disposition. Now, you have to admit something very strange must have happened.

Of course, there were all the usual disillusionments of childhood. First of all I discovered that Larry the Lamb on *Children's Hour* wasn't a real lamb at all. Then when the tooth fairy stopped coming I was not well pleased and when I discovered that Father Christmas didn't really exist I was totally pissed off. I swore that I would never believe anything an adult told me ever again. By and large this has proved pretty sound thinking. Mind you, I still hung up my stocking just in case I got lucky.

It was at about the age of five or six that I was made aware that there were some very nasty people about. Adults were very vague about the details of such nastiness but so far as I could gather they were mostly perpetrated by nasty Nazi spies who did you no good at all. As I understood it they either offered you poisoned sweets or kidnapped you and put you in a concentration camp. Of course, you also had to look out for Nazi paratroopers who might be disguised as nuns.

Overall, it remains my view that things began to go seriously downhill after 1939. Of course, it might have had nothing to do with the Blitz but if you emerged from the air raid shelter every morning never sure if the house was going to be there and even less sure that you or the house were going to survive until the following morning, I suppose it must have had some effect on one's outlook and personality. Not that they gave you any stress counselling at the time.

There is one further photo of little Bobby Edom. This is a studio portrait taken in Croydon and dated 31st May, 1941. I often wondered why my parents splashed out on a bus ride to Croydon and a studio portrait. Subsequent research fifty years later revealed that it was just two weeks after the worst night of the Blitz when about twenty thousand Londoners had been killed. More to the point, six bombs had fallen in Springhurst Avenue and five of our neighbours had been killed. I suppose that the photograph was a celebration that we were still around to be photographed. At this time I still looked fairly angelic in my best suit and a Burton House school tie but, not surprisingly, I appear to have a somewhat thoughtful expression.

Of course, my regular readers will know that I bang on quite a lot about the Blitz but you have to admit that it might have been a bit unsettling. Mr Göring and his chums had begun by bombing the High Street and then they had a go at the railway station and then the Tudor Parade and then they dropped one in the railway cutting at the back of our house. It was towards the end of the Blitz when they dropped all the bombs down our road that they blew up the Lennard family at number 120.

I took this a bit personally because I had always regarded Mr Lennard as a mate of mine. Besides, blowing people up in their own beds seemed a bit extreme to me. Mr and Mrs Lennard were killed instantly but their son was blown out of the house on his mattress and landed at the bottom of the garden. He lived for about five years but he never came out of hospital. I remember going to visit him. He looked like a broken doll and he was all parcelled up in a plaster jacket. It put me off hospitals I can tell you. In 1948 they endowed a bed at Beckenham Hospital in his name. They raised £430.

Then there was a landmine in Goodheart Way. Then they dropped a whacking great bomb on the New Inn at Hayes which did their trade no good at all since some of their customers were inside at the time. They also bombed the sports pavilion at Langley Park and then they bombed the railway stations at Hayes and at Elmers End. They really had it in for Elmers End station because they kept coming back and did it three times in all. There were landmines and oil bombs and big bombs and little bombs and incendiary bombs and then later on Hitler dropped pretty little butterfly bombs all brightly painted so that curious children would pick them up and get an arm blown off. Then there was the Focke Wolfe 190 that machine-gunned the High Street and then just when things seemed to be quietening down they dropped incendiaries all over Hayes. Then the Doodlebugs started. They came over more frequently than the 194 bus service (Forest Hill Station to Croydon via West Wickham). Then just when we thought it was all over the V2s started. I tell you that lot was enough to give anyone a nervous twitch and a pessimistic view of life.

While all this was going on I joined the Black Hand Gang. It may be that all my funny little ways are down to the influence of the Black Hand Gang. Mind you, the only members of the Black Hand Gang were Tony Lubbock and me although we did have his cat Blackie as our mascot.

In theory the gang was set up to protect us from the depredations of the boys from the Hawes Lane Council School. The Council School boys were thugs of a high order. They mostly wore hobnailed boots and had habits that would have embarrassed the Pioneer Corps. They were none too fond of us lot from Burton House School. I suppose it was because it was a private school and our parents paid money for our education. They showed their displeasure by throwing our school caps into the railway cutting and threatening us with Chinese burns or holding us down and gobbing in our faces.

The Black Hand Gang devised secret methods of defence that included hidden caches of weapons at various sites down Hawes Lane. The weapons consisted of bundles of nettles with newspaper handles and short lengths of rusty barbed wire. None of these weapons were ever used since whenever we sighted the enemy we always went the other way. Not that we were frightened, you understand; we were just making a strategic withdrawal before achieving ultimate victory.

As the war progressed I seemed to get more and more horrible. Our games became steadily more bloodthirsty and the back garden at Springhurst Avenue looked like the aftermath of the Second Battle of the Somme.

My toy soldiers fought in every theatre of war and inflicted horrendous injuries on the enemy. When I ran out of toy soldiers I chopped up the kerria bush and made pretend soldiers out of the stalks. Then I bayoneted them all to death with my school compass.

I totally gave up playing pretend games of bus conductors and ice cream salesmen and turned to garrotting German sentries and machine-gunning fiendish Japanese infantrymen. I also set up a concentration camp for captured earthworms.

I was also rather partial to building little model villages

and then bombing them to bits, and Calvin Sharp used to get a bit pissed off when I kept making him a prisoner in my Gestapo interrogation centre.

'I don't care if I am a spoilsport, I'm not having my fingernails pulled out for anybody.'

I got very destructive at about this time. First, Lionel Perrin from next door helped me flatten the sides of my little pre-war pedal car in order to convert it into a streamlined racer and then we stripped down my old pram so we could scoot up and down the garden path on it at high speed.

Still, it wasn't just me who was going a bit weird with the war. All the adults were so busy doing what adults do in wartime that they didn't have much time to notice that their offspring were going a bit odd. I used to have feuds with Lionel Perrin. He was older than I was and was also going a bit wild. Well, verging on psychopathic actually. He and his chums used to chase me up and down the garden hurling muddy Brussels sprout stalks at me. When they captured me they used to gob in my face as well.

Mind you, it was even worse if Bernard Dawkins caught me. He was going through a very funny phase and was best kept at a distance. Still, I have to confess that it was soon after this that Anthony Cohen and I became interested in naughty bits and conducted one or two strange experiments at the bottom of the kitchen garden.

Then there was a phase of throwing stones at trains, trespassing on the railway embankment and being chased by porters. One time a policeman joined in. I expect he needed the exercise. When we could get the elastic we were also inclined to fire our catapults at anything that moved. This was followed by trespassing in bombed houses, nicking golf balls from the Langley Park golf course and eating baked beans that Geoff Bragg had pinched whilst on his delivery round. I sometimes used to go round the shops with little Calvin Sharp who had a penchant for nicking things from Woolworth's. He didn't much care what he nicked, a packet of hairpins or a pill box of Beecham's pills; it was all the same to him. Personally I looked the other way and pretended that I wasn't with him.

I occasionally played games of long-range artillery by hurling stones over the railway cutting into Bill Oddy's garden, but I discontinued this when I discovered that he outranged me by a good ten yards.

I had a go at making incendiary bombs out of the waxed packets that the Americans sent our dried egg in, and I could produce a passable flame thrower out of a tube of lighter fuel. During this phase I incinerated the privet hedge at the end of the garden. I also re-enacted the bombing of Monte Casino on the mounds of earth protecting our air raid shelter.

I and my little chums often used to convene in Coote's field to plot some new mayhem. Bill Oddy, who was probably more sociologically disturbed than the rest of us, had a fondness for bombs made of calcium carbide and for high-powered catapults. Rubber and elastic were almost unobtainable during the war but Bill Oddy was a great improviser. His catapult was made from strips of old motor cycle inner tube. He used to terrify all potential targets, including me. Mind you, with that catapult I swear he could have taken out a low flying Dornier.

I also eventually obtained a catapult but it was a rather poofy affair. Whenever I could get hold of some elastic I was inclined to let fly at anything that moved. Fortunately, my aim was not good and I didn't have quite the same level of lunacy as Bill Oddy, nor the same access to strong elastic.

What I did find even at that early age was that I seemed to be drawn to the nuttier and more disadvantaged of the juvenile population. I think I was the only one in my social circle who had a mum and a dad as well as a permanent address. It was the war, you see. Well, that was what everyone said at the time. Still, it was all good training for my eventual career as a probation officer.

Perhaps our increasingly antisocial behaviour could have been put down to vitamin deficiency or malnutrition or something. There seemed to be so many things that weren't available. Take oranges or grapes or bananas or lemons or tomatoes or dates or figs or grapefruit or, or... Well, all you could actually have were cooking apples or rhubarb. And even then only in season. I can't pretend that the absence of figs was a great deprivation. In fact one of the few good things that came out of the Second World War was a marked absence of figs.

Still, I have never forgiven Mr Hitler for depriving me of toffee apples, proper ice cream, potato crisps, orange squash, tomato sauce and Fry's peppermint cream during my formative years. Could this be the reason for my nastiness in later life, I ask myself?

When the war came to an end I was about twelve and a bit. When the concentration camp at Belsen was captured the cinema newsreels showed what the troops had found. I saw it all on *British Movietone News*. There were mounds of emaciated corpses that they were burying in great pits with the help of a bulldozer. There were close-ups of mutilated corpses that had been tortured by the Gestapo and there were gaunt shambling living skeletons with vacant hopeless eyes and clad in filthy rags. Soon after that we saw pictures of those poor starved wretches who had been prisoners of war of the Japanese. More than fifty years later I still can't bring myself to buy a Nissan or a Honda and as for Mitsubishi, so far as I am concerned they have never built anything except torpedo-bombers.

Apart from the Germans and the Japanese I was coming to learn that there were a lot of other very funny people in the world, including the man in the one and threes at the

Plaza who put his hand in my lap and offered to augment my pocket money in return for certain unspecified favours. There was also the games master at school whose hand went up the legs of small boys' short trousers as if it had a life all its own.

Although I seemed to be getting nastier by the day I did my best to avoid violence and clearly had a highly developed sense of self-preservation and a low pain threshold. There was that humiliating occasion when I got into a fight with Clogger Spilsbury in the playground at school. This left me with a thick lip and in tearful retreat but even to this day I don't like to dwell on it. Beside it wasn't fair. He punched as if he really meant it.

I tried not to get into too many fights at school. My inherent cowardice usually kept me out of punch-ups. I did actually win a fight once. I take no pride in it though. Bodger Williams was much smaller than I was. I was sitting on him with my knees on his shoulders feeling rather triumphant when someone drew my attention to the fact that he had gone purple. Still, he did make a full recovery.

Ravensbeck Grammar School was probably the last straw. Everybody, just everybody, clonked somebody at Ravensbeck. Heads were smacked, bums were whacked and sometimes kicked, ears were twisted, hair was pulled and chalk and blackboard dusters were hurled. And that was only the masters. It was bully or be bullied at Ravensbeck. None of this namby-pamby peace-loving bullshit, I can tell you. Of course, the devotion to single sex secondary education led to a variety of other aberrations at Ravensbeck but I won't put you off your tea by telling you about those. In general, however, there is nothing like a grammar school education for making you feel inadequate, incompetent and useless. My time at Ravensbeck led me to formulate a survival package to make sense of the world. This philosophy has remained with me all my life. The essential components are:

(a)   Assume that all authority is mad or malign.

(b)   Treat with the utmost scorn anyone who tells you that your schooldays were the happiest days of your life.

(c)   Rapid retreat is the best form of defence.

(d)   Never get caught in a scrum.

By this time I had become tall, gangly and spotty and even worse I had discovered the opposite sex. Sadly, the opposite sex showed little interest in discovering me, partly, I suspect, because I had a natural facial expression resembling a constipated moose with toothache. Adolescence was not a happy time. In addition to spots I was troubled by embarrassing erections. Cold showers and regular doses of Enos Fruit Salts were supposed to be the answer. But things were going from bad to worse.

If Ravensbeck Grammar School wasn't enough, there was then national service. There was more bullying, more bullshit, and endless saluting, parading, polishing and grovelling. Two years in the Royal Air Works led to a further refinement in the Edom philosophy:

(e)   Per ardua ad asbestos, which roughly translated means, 'Blow you Jack, I'm fireproof.'

(f)   All authority is mad or malign and Station Warrant Officers are the worst.

(g)   Never trust an officer or a gentleman.

(h)   Never volunteer for anything.

(i) What can't be confronted may possibly be subverted.

(j) Don't let the bastards grind you down.

I don't think that I ever learned anything useful in the Royal Air Works but I did learn how to type at ten words a minute and I also learned how to bayonet a sandbag and how to score two outers and three ricochets off the side wall with a 1917 .303 Lee Enfield. You will gather from all this that I have never subscribed to the view that the reintroduction of national service would be good for the youth of this country.

Whilst I was in the Royal Air Works my dear old mum died. I was eighteen at the time. There is something very final about your mum dying. If you are six foot two and gangly and spotty and have the charm and personality of a temperamental dromedary, no one else is ever likely to give you unconditional love again, are they?

Then at age twenty-one I reached the age of majority and was given the vote and a pewter tankard and my social training was assumed to be completed. I was now a fully qualified adult.

The strange thing is that after all this lot I half-expected to end up a raving psychopathic bank robber but in my later years I have more inclined towards neurotic pessimism and melancholia. One thing is for sure however, and that is that I have never been able to fulfil the rich promise of that dear little Bobby Edom.

Burton House School

My entry into the educational system coincided with the Munich crisis of 1938. Personally I was more anxious about Mrs Sergeant than I was about Herr Hitler. Mrs Sergeant seemed much more of a threat to my health and happiness. Mrs Sergeant, it should be explained, was the headmistress and proprietress of Burton House School for Boys and Girls, aged five to eleven in brackets. She was a formidable woman; well, terrifying actually. When she played 'All things bright and beautiful' on the school piano she made it sound like a funeral march. Mind you, the piano was a bit past its best and a couple of the white notes just went 'clonk' when she pressed them. It was an elderly upright piano and had the distinction of having two double candleholders on the front. Mrs Sergeant was very keen on God, always going on about him. You would have thought that they were related. We did a lot of praying but kneeling on her hard wooden forms didn't generate much reverence although it probably caused a lot of housemaid's knee in later life.

The worst part of all was when we were required to sing 'Bobby Shafto'. I can't remember what the song was all about but it aroused great mirth and I had to become immoderately tetchy in order to avoid being called 'Bobby' for days thereafter because my given name was Robert and I was thus regarded as fair game.

There was also 'Oranges and Lemons' when the chopper always seemed to come down on my head and as for 'Ring a

Ring a Roses', I'm afraid the point of it all rather escaped me. I suppose that it just filled in time when Mrs Sergeant couldn't think of anything to teach us.

My ever-loving parents had bought me a school cap. It was for some reason the done thing. It was bright red with 'BH' emblazoned on it and it stood out like a beacon. All the lads from the Hawes Lane Council school homed in on it like Messerschmidts round a barrage balloon. They were a rough lot those Hawes Lane boys. They used words like bugger and shit and wore great clonking boots with hobnails in them. If they caught you they gave you Chinese burns or shoved you in the nettle patch by the railway cutting. Sometimes for a change they gobbed in your face instead.

I also had a little satchel and a pencil case. The pencil case had everything necessary for the academic life. There were two sharpened pencils, a pen holder and a little tin for spare nibs, a rubber, a protractor made of celluloid and a six-inch ruler made of tin.

Another feature of academic life after Mr Chamberlain had made his little speech on the wireless was Mrs Sergeant's air raid shelter. After the first excitement of the air raid warning it was a bit boring down in the shelter. It was damp and musty and there wasn't enough light to read my *Beano*. Big Eggo took quite a lot of concentration so you couldn't afford to miss anything.

The most momentous time, and perhaps the most gratifying, was when Mr Hitler, assisted by Herman Göring, plonked a 500 lb bomb just outside the school gate. It made a fascinating hole of impressive dimensions. At the bottom was a pool of muddy water and from its sides emerged severed pipes and wires of miscellaneous diameters like a giant's entrails. Over it all hung an interesting aroma of sewage, gas and damp clay. More importantly the bomb had removed most of Mrs Sergeant's roof tiles and all her front windows and school was closed for the week. I became very ambivalent about air raids after that.

Our school playing field was ploughed up for the dig for victory campaign; I think it was full of carrots for most of the war. I understand that they helped our brave fighter pilots to see in the dark. As a result we small grubby survivors (those who had not been evacuated that is) had to confine our playtime activities to Mrs Sergeant's back yard where the ultimate exercise opportunity was launching oneself off the air raid shelter into Mrs Sergeant's rockery. This led to both grazed knees and slapped legs – a painful combination.

I first fell in love whilst at Burton House. Her name was Ann Winterbottom and I loved her dearly. She had long dark hair and big round eyes and dimples. She used to tuck her dress into her knickers and do handstands up against Mrs Sergeant's fence. This drove me in to a frenzy of desire and I asked her to come to the Plaza Saturday Morning Picture Club with me. (We met inside because I couldn't afford two sixpenny tickets out of my pocket money.) In the end she betrayed me and started walking out with Donald Duxford, the publican's son, who always seemed to have unlimited sources of income.

There was also Jennifer, a blonde girl with blue eyes and a bow in her hair, but she got evacuated before our love blossomed. By the time I had discovered that playing mothers and fathers wasn't so cissy after all, it was far too late. Ah, the wickedness of war.

Gradually the school roll declined as families moved away, children were evacuated or people were bombed out. Mrs Sergeant got rid of her assistant teacher who taught the older children French and who knew about all sorts of other mysterious things like algebra and needlework. When Miss Buxom left the staff the range of subjects took a turn for the worse and as the number of little pupils dwindled lessons became more, well, innovative and spontaneous. Personally I concentrated on my joined up handwriting and hoped for the best.

Mrs Sergeant was very hot on handwriting and sums but the rest of the curriculum became distinctly unpredictable. She never taught me my alphabet for example. Whether she forgot to teach it or whether it all happened when Mr Hitler blew our windows out and I had to stay at home to help sweep up the glass I do not know and cannot say. It did cause me some later embarrassment. Even when I was working for the Flankshire Insurance Company in 1950 and was placed in charge of their filing system the files in the Ps and Qs tended to go astray and as for the Rs and Ss they are best not spoken about. I blame it all on the war.

My little friend Calvin Sharp attended Burton House for a while but it was not to last. Calvin Sharp was deemed to be a wicked little boy. You didn't get referred to the Child Guidance Clinic in those days. If you showed signs of oddness this was deemed to be a challenge to the system and got you seriously walloped. Most of us took the hint but poor old Calvin couldn't take a hint if it was delivered with a 500 lb bomb. Mrs Sergeant used to take his trousers down and whack his bare bottom with her horny hand. She did this with depressing regularity but with remarkable lack of effect. The more she whacked him the worse he got. In the end she gave up and he was moved to another school where they walloped him with a stick instead. He didn't take much notice of that either. Poor old Calvin, when he grew up he was admitted to a mental hospital which just shows that you can never buck the system, doesn't it? Still, it saved him having to do national service like the rest of us.

I never had a lot of time for school. It all seemed to be a bit unnatural to me. The only bit I really enjoyed was the gas mask drill. I discovered that if one breathed out very hard the gas mask could be persuaded to make exquisite farting noises. This used to infuriate Mrs Sergeant who could never locate where the noise was coming from.

At mid-morning break Mrs Sergeant produced mugs of hot milk. Children all had to have their milk ration in those days. There is nothing worse than hot milk with a skin on top. I used to pray for an air raid so that we would all go down the shelter and miss the stuff. Come to think of it, at that time child rearing was based on the belief that if little boys didn't like something it was probably good for them. Little boys were expected to be brave little soldiers, obedient to their elders and regular in their habits and there were homilies, whackings and syrup of figs to support this philosophy.

One day I arrived at school in tears. I explained to Mrs Sergeant that Johnny had died. When she discovered that Johnny was our cat she was very dismissive. 'It's only a cat,' she declared. 'Dry your eyes and don't be a baby; little men shouldn't cry anyway.' I wanted to explain that Johnny and I had grown up together, he had often shared my bunk in the air raid shelter and that we had been really good mates, but the subject was clearly closed. There wasn't a lot of time for sentiment at Burton House.

We seemed to be very short of materials at school. Whether it was Mrs Sergeant's inherent meanness or wartime shortages it was hard to say. We made lots of things out of wallpaper from a pre-war sample book and stuck them together with flour and water paste. All our little efforts came unstuck when the paste dried. Our art lessons were also inhibited by a certain lack of materials. Brushes were hard to come by and coloured crayons almost non-existent. I drew mostly air battles with lots of bullets flying about and bomb bursts and shells exploding in the sky. Mrs Sergeant didn't approve but even if she made me draw a fairy grotto it had a dog fight going on overhead and if I could squeeze a tank in, all the better.

What with Mr Hitler and Mrs Sergeant it was a funny old experience at Burton House. It taught me a few things: amongst others that most adults are a bit potty, and certainly all school teachers are, that life is uncertain and frequently tiresome and that just when you get used to something someone changes it. Thus I came to my entrance examination for the grammar school. The incredible thing was that I passed it. I don't know who was the more surprised, Mrs Sergeant or me. Mr Hitler didn't express an opinion although he did drop incendiary bombs all over Hayes High Street a few nights later.

Always Carry Your Gas Mask

'Hitler will send no warning – so always carry your gas mask.' That was what the posters said. I started at my junior school in the autumn of 1938 and one of the earliest elements of my formal education was how to put my gas mask on. Money sums and composition might have to wait but I was hot stuff with gas mask drill. I can't remember much detail about the initial fitting of the gas mask but it was a bit like going to Freeman Hardy and Willis for a new pair of shoes. It was, I gathered, important to have a good fit. I remember that much trouble was taking with adjusting the head straps of my mask so that it fitted snugly. I gathered that if the fit was not just right I might end up a bit dead.

At age five and three-quarters I was deemed to be too old for a Mickey Mouse gas mask and so I had to have the smallest size of a boring old adult one. I can still recall the pong of rubber when it was first pulled over my head. I was told that there were special contrivances for babies but my proposal that we should be supplied with one for our tom pussy was rejected out of hand.

The gas mask came in a government issue cardboard box but a new commercial window of opportunity opened up for the manufacture of carrying cases. My little fellow pupils at Burton House School, aged five to eleven in brackets, dutifully brought their gas masks to school in a multiplicity of carrying cases. My own case was a rather tedious cloth affair that was a depressing beige in colour. It was a bit like a small ladies' handbag which fitted round the government issue cardboard box. The case had a flap secured by a press button stud so that the gas mask was readily accessible. It had a cloth strap to match which kept breaking, probably because in my more exuberant moments I was inclined to whirl it around my head like a bolas. Some of my little chums had much more elaborate affairs that conveyed the status or affluence of their parents. Some had japanned metal cylindrical containers and others had cases in tartan or corduroy material. The less fortunate had home-made affairs made of old curtain fabric and one or two just carried the cardboard box with a loop of string threaded through it.

The best part was the gas mask practices. We all sat at our desks and had to see how quickly we could get our gas masks out and then we had to put them on in the approved fashion. In case you should ever need to know, I should explain that the key to good gas mask drill was to get your chin in first. I was very proud of my technique. The very best bit of all, however, was when I had my gas mask on. I discovered that by exhaling vigorously I could produce the most delightfully vulgar farting noises. This used to infuriate Mrs Sergeant who could never discover who was doing it. She never did have a sense of humour.

The whole of the country seemed obsessed with gas masks and once the war started we all knew it was only a matter of time before the gas arrived. They painted the tops of pillar boxes with some special stuff that was supposed to change colour when the gas came. Someone was supposed to come round with a rattle as well just in case you didn't have a pillar box handy.

I started to collect a series of cigarette cards about air raid precautions and I learned all sorts of things about gas attacks. Did you know that hanging a wet blanket over the door and stuffing the cracks with newspaper could make a room gas-proof? Well, that's what my cigarette cards said.

Of course, in the end Mr Hitler decided not to use his nasty old gas stuff after all but not before I had spent a good deal of time worrying about it. Forgetting your gas mask was for a long while a more serious crime than not practising your joined-up handwriting or forgetting to do up your trouser buttons. Eventually, however, people stopped bothering with gas masks. In course of time even I found that there were too many other things to worry about, including the Blitz, sweet rationing and my shrapnel collection.

Nonetheless, my gas mask case continued to hang on the hatstand in the hall throughout the war, gathering dust and plaster as well when Göring blew our ceilings down. The gas mask case was always a reminder that nothing was so bad that it couldn't get considerably worse. It had a powerful symbolism that may explain my lifelong pessimism. After all, now as then, you can never be sure what is going to happen next but it is best to be prepared for the worst. Always carry your gas mask!

Down Our Street

Springhurst Avenue runs all the way from West Wickham station to the Springhurst Arms in Hayes. It is about a mile as the crow flies but as a small boy walks it is the heck of a long way.

Springhurst Avenue is still there today but the time of which I write is long ago and, in a sense, far away. It is when I was a small boy back in the late thirties, a time when small boys had a greater sense of wonder and less access to hard cash, information or technology – a time when the ballpoint pen was still to be invented and a fountain pen was a longed for luxury.

Springhurst Avenue was my territory and the comings and goings of its inhabitants and its visitors were of supreme interest to me. Take, for example, the milkman. Old Ben was a real character, and he was only the horse. Old Ben was getting on a bit, in fact he was positively geriatric. Still, he had many virtues. For one, he was extremely regular in his habits and every morning he left a small pile of whoopsies precisely outside number four where Mr Cutler lurked to dash out with bucket and shovel to gather in nature's bounty for his floribundas. Old Ben knew every stop on the round and would wait patiently until Sid the milkman called him on. Mind you, Old Ben always had his nosebag on which kept him happy. When the oats got low in the bag he would toss the bag up to get the last morsels but once they were gone, by about number one hundred and twenty, he was inclined to get a bit tetchy.

Then there was Raybone's coal lorry. This had all the ingredients for making a small boy happy, being large, noisy and extremely dirty. The coalman was not Mr Raybone himself, but a minion who was nonetheless impressive in his own right. Like his lorry he was large, noisy and extremely dirty. We had two metal coal bins to store our fuel: one for anthracite for the kitchen boiler and one for the large lumps of shiny black stuff that were placed sparingly on the front room fire. When the coalman heaved each sack into the bin it made a noise like a thunderstorm.

I can still visualise that coalman with a leather cape affair that covered his head and shoulders, great clonking boots, string tied round his trousers to protect his vitals from coal dust, a blackened face and thick hairy arms bejewelled with small fragments of coal. He looked like someone in the employ of the devil.

I mustn't forget the egg man, Mother's favourite. He was a bit too smarmy for my liking but he had the added attraction of arriving on a strange motorcycle contraption that made a din far in excess of its performance. It really was a very weird vehicle, motorcycle at the front and little van at the back. Anyway, when the war came and eggs went on the ration the egg man disappeared for ever, together with his funny conveyance. I expect he joined the black market or something.

Now what else? Well, there was the mineral water man. He had a large lorry loaded with crates of bottles that made a cheerful jingling sound when it went over the bump where the Beckenham Borough Council had repaired the road. We only had a bottle of lime juice cordial once a fortnight but we were always under pressure to extend our drinking habits to include some improbably orange-coloured fizzy stuff.

I mustn't forget Carter Paterson, a less frequent visitor to the road and an even less frequent visitor to the Edom household. I always thought that Mr Paterson himself drove the van but I gather that it was just another minion. The van was open at the back with a rope hanging down for the van boy to swing up and down on like a miniature Tarzan. The van boy passed the parcels down to the driver who delivered the parcels to the doorstep, obtained a signature and waited, usually unproductively, for a tip.

The baker's man had a horse and cart as well but the horse wasn't a patch on Old Ben – no character, a young upstart who was a bit bored with the bakery business. If the baker took too long in chatting up number seven the horse would wander off up the road and try to chew someone's privet; he tended to forget that he had a cart and about two hundred farmhouse loaves lurching along behind him.

The most exciting thing that ever happened in Springhurst Avenue, before the Blitz that is, was when the Borough Council repaired the road. It was absolute magic. Tar lorries, great heaps of steaming tarmac, a steamroller with real steam and lots of large, noisy men in collarless shirts muttering interesting words.

The steamroller was the best. The driver had a little shovel and kept pushing shovelfuls of coal into its small firebox. The machine wheezed and panted and squirted steam and gave off a gloriously oily, sulphurous aroma. It had a large flywheel that spun round at great speed and when the driver moved the regulator the engine hurled steam from its chimney and made furious puffing noises as if it was about to throw an apoplectic fit.

I fear that until this moment I had forgotten the dustmen, a foolish thing to do since they did not take kindly to being forgotten, particularly at Christmas time. On Christmas Eve the head dustman would arrive on the doorstep to convey to us the compliments of the season on behalf of the corporation and the other members of his team who were lurking at the gate. This was the moment at which half a crown or, better still, five bob was pressed into the man's dusty palm; either that or most of next week's refuse would be accidentally scattered down the garden path. The dustmen were like a pirate crew: entrepreneurial, undisciplined, noisy, scruffy and riotous. At one stage in my early career planning I dearly wanted to become a dustman.

The postman did not make much impact on me except on my birthday or at Christmas. During the summer there was the occasional picture postcard from a neighbour depicting the pier at Eastbourne or some other far-flung place but otherwise it was just a succession of bills. My father ignored all bills until they were printed in red so we received quite a lot of reminders and final demands. It was best to keep a low profile when these arrived.

The paper boy was of little consequence except on Wednesdays when he delivered my *Knockout*. I was usually fairly anxious to see what Deed-a-Day Danny had been up to as well as Our Ernie. Well, you may scoff but it seemed important then. I expect that your own preoccupations will look a bit silly in fifty years' time.

Mr Handley, the grocer, employed a delivery boy for his high-class trade but this did not include the Edom family. The delivery boy was occasionally seen in Springhurst Avenue where he tried to conduct high-speed sliding turns like they did at the speedway. Mr Handley's delivery bike had a large basket fitted to the front and a metal plate suspended from the crossbar emblazoned 'Handley's Grocery Store, Devonshire House, Parties Catered For'. It was not ideally suited for high-speed sliding turns.

Mr Nutley's handcart appeared in Springhurst Avenue only occasionally. It was two-wheeled and had iron tyres that made a fine old din, a sort of grinding noise that set your teeth on edge. It was hauled by two overalled minions, the senior of whom wore a bowler hat. Everyone knew their place in those days. On the side of the cart was painted

'A.W. Nutley & Son, Builders, Plumbers, House Decorators & Undertakers'. Mr Edom senior was not a do-it-yourselfer but being of frugal disposition he was not a pay-someone-else-to-do-it-for-you either. In consequence I only remember Nutley's coming to us twice: once when the water tank burst and once to dig a hole for our air raid shelter.

Most of the other street users were of the pedestrian persuasion. There were very few private motor cars at the time. The only family in Springhurst Avenue who owned one were the Sharp family who owned the newest and biggest house in the road. They had a twelve horse power Humber and had a garage to put it in. They also drank ground coffee and were rumoured to have a machine that could keep butter hard in the summer. You really couldn't take a family like that seriously, could you?

At about eight every morning a migratory horde of black-coated, homburg-hatted, umbrella-toting office workers made their way down the road to catch the 8.15 or, if they were senior management or civil servants, the 8.30. In the evening at about six o'clock they all came back again like a flock of starlings. I used to swing on our front gate and watch them and wonder what working in an office was like. It sounded a bit important to me. I reckoned that you probably needed a Waterman's gold-nibbed fountain pen and a knowledge of your twelve times table to do a job like that.

Trailing along at the back of the homecoming horde was Mr Lennard. He was badly crippled and walked with a stick but he often paused for a few words so I regarded him as a personal friend. In 1941 Mr Hitler dropped a bomb on Mr Lennard's house and wiped out the whole family. I took the war quite personally after that.

I thought that I would end this little dissertation on a slightly poetic note. When dusk settled on Springhurst

Avenue in those long-gone pre-war days a man would arrive on his bicycle with a long pole over his shoulder. This was Mr Perkins, the lamplighter. The semi-detacheds in Springhurst Avenue were all built in mock-Tudor, half-timbered style and the gaslit street lamps were supposed to match. Mind you, I am not convinced that Elizabeth I had a supply of town gas and certainly this point was not covered in my subsequent historical studies. Anyway, the lamps in Springhurst Avenue were mounted on stout wooden posts and were shaped like lanterns with a finial on top. Mr Perkins would hook his pole into a ring on a chain, and 'pop' the pilot light would ignite the gas mantle. In the morning he came and pulled another little chain and the light went out again.

Mr Perkins cut a memorable figure with bicycle clips, his cloth cap and half-buttoned waistcoat and the half-consumed Woodbine dangling from his lips. Whatever happened to Mr Perkins? Did he have a distinguished career as an ARP warden or did he end his days painting out signposts so that when the Jerries came they wouldn't know where they were when they got there?

Anyway, in 1939 Mr Perkins put the gas lights out for the last time. When the lights went on again in Springhurst Avenue it was more than six years and a world war later and the gas lamps had been replaced by electric lights worked by time switches and mounted on distinctly non-Tudor pre-cast concrete posts.

World War II

I have come to the conclusion that the time is right to present to the world my own very special history of World War Two. I appreciate, of course, that other more illustrious personages have already published their contributions. However, I have to say that they were by no means definitive accounts. For starters none of them ever mentioned me. I accept that my version may be regarded as a trifle belated, but then I've been a bit busy, haven't I?

Mr Chamberlain and I declared war on Mr Hitler whilst I was on my summer holidays at Herne Bay in September 1939. I was only six and seven-twelfths at the time so some of the broader issues may have escaped me. However, I knew that Mr Hitler was partial to bayoneting small babies and I was quite clear that God was not on his side.

Mr Chamberlain told us all about it on the wireless although I don't recall him specifically mentioning the baby bayoneting. Anyway, everyone knew all about that already. Shortly after his little speech the air raid sirens sounded. My ARP cigarette cards had advised me that in such an event we should all stay indoors with a wet blanket over the doorway (to stop the poisonous gas) and sticky tape over the windows (to stop the flying glass splinters). Instead we all trooped out into the street to chat to the neighbours and to see the German bombers and parachutists.

The lady next door was leaning over her gate, arms folded across her ample bosoms. 'Don't worry,' she said, 'our brave Tommies will never let them get here.' Anyway, it turned out to be a false alarm which was just as well since there wasn't a brave Tommy anywhere in sight. We did hear a solitary aeroplane droning away in the distance and steeled ourselves for rape, pillage and sudden death but nothing happened so we all went indoors and ate our Sunday dinner. I remember that runner beans and marrow were in season at the time.

Important decisions now had to be made however. Father had to return to work for reasons that I did not fully grasp. His firm made office equipment and filing cabinets which scarcely seemed essential to the war effort. Still, come to think of it, war is an extremely bureaucratic business, isn't it? Mother loyally decided to return with him. My brother and sister would stay on to complete their holiday. I could stay as well if I wished.

It was my first big decision and served as a template for most of the other decisions in my life. I opted for comfort and security. I would return with Mum. At age six and seven-twelfths I was not ready for adventurous decisions. Besides, my relationships with my older brother and sister were distinctly strained at the time, just because I had destroyed the beach ball. I had only been trying to convert it into a hot air balloon with the help of the Primus stove in the beach hut. Finally, and so far as I was concerned irrefutably, I just had to go home with Mum because I was still having trouble with tying my own shoelaces.

By the time we returned to West Wickham the town's war preparations were well advanced. The street lights had been turned off, our chestnut tree which jutted out on to the pavement had been painted with a white stripe to stop people bumping into it during the blackout, and the name boards at the railway station had been painted out so that when the Germans came they wouldn't know where it was they had got to.

As the weeks passed other curious phenomena occurred.

An obsolete corporation dustcart appeared in the railway station approach road. Funny things like that were constantly happening and people just shrugged their shoulders and said, 'Oh, it's the war.' I eventually discovered the dustcart was to block the road so that enemy gliders couldn't land in it. The only practical purpose it served throughout the war was to act as a prototype adventure playground which I exploited to the full. It had no engine in it but I used to pretend to drive it and I provided suitable inventive engine noises of my own. Sometimes it also served as a Wellington bomber.

Another enthusiasm was sandbags. It was felt necessary to protect all public buildings with sandbags. I'm not quite sure why. Anyway, we were a bit short on public buildings in West Wickham but the entrance to the National Provincial Bank in the High Street was surrounded by sandbags and also the entrance to the public bar of the Railway Hotel. Sandbags were not, in my view, a great success. The local dog population took to them immediately and peed up them at every opportunity. By late 1941 most sandbag emplacements were not in good order. The hessian sacks had rotted and the sand had spilled out and they were a bit niffy too.

Concrete tank obstacles sprang up all over West Wickham. I never saw anyone erect them; they just suddenly appeared like giant mushrooms. Then the authorities directed a flock of evacuated sheep on to the Langley Park golf course. Here they nibbled in the rough, gambolled on the greens and widdled in the bunkers, much to the chagrin of the local golfing fraternity who already had a barrage balloon unit to contend with. The sheep were driven on the hoof down Springhurst Avenue and right past my house, much to my delight. Our little suburb was not used to sheep. In fact, I had never met one at close quarters before. All the local children turned out to assist with the herding which added to the novelty, not to say chaos. A number of extremely bewildered sheep ended up in suburban back gardens facing equally bewildered residents.

Soon after this the Local Defence Volunteers took charge of the defence of West Wickham and their Sunday morning manoeuvres helped to fill the gaping void that Sundays presented to the younger generation. Remember this was in an era when buying a stick of liquorice on a Sunday promised to bring down the wrath of God.

Week by week the LDV gained more equipment and honed the cutting edge of their military might to ever keener incisiveness. They used Coote's field for their training. This was a small plot that also served as our playground when it wasn't being used for goat grazing. Each week we noted the new additions to the LDV's equipment. First came the khaki forage caps, then the haversacks useful for keeping elevenses in. They were followed by dummy wooden rifles and a tin filled with small bits of metal which when shaken vigorously sounded vaguely like a machine-gun. For a brief period, before he was called up into the RAF, my brother was placed in charge of the machine-gun section so I had an opportunity to examine the tin and contents. It was a bit boring at close quarters and, patriotic little boy though I was, I was not convinced that it would have struck fear into the Waffen SS.

Reinforcements were on the way however, and our valiant defenders acquired heavy artillery. It was a curious device mounted on two wheels which was towed behind Mr Walpole's Morris Eight. (When he could get the petrol that is.) The gun could be tipped on its side, one wheel flat on the ground, the other forming a sort of metal umbrella beneath which the gallant gunners crouched. They drilled incessantly every Sunday. Well, until the Railway Hotel opened, but I never saw the gun fire. Perhaps they were waiting for the ammunition. Or the earplugs.

The LDV developed some very nasty habits. When they couldn't think of anything better to do they dug a slit trench. These appeared all over West Wickham and in the blackout they did nearly as much damage to the local citizenry as the Luftwaffe.

Then came the Battle of Britain. I know that it was our finest hour, but for a small boy with his feet on the ground in West Wickham, patriotic though he was, it was a bit of a swizz. It was just vapour trails in the sky and the distant rattle of real machine-guns. The rest I learned from my mum's *Daily Express* or the nine o'clock news. (Alvar Liddle or Bruce Belfridge used to rattle on about the numbers shot down as if they were cricket scores.)

Things livened up when a Focke Wolfe 190 machine-gunned our High Street, for reasons which the pilot kept exclusively to himself. What he had against the Home and Colonial Groceries I cannot imagine. My mum much preferred them to the Co-op. Anyway, there was I looking out of our dining room window when this Focke Wolf 190 flew down Springhurst Avenue at rooftop height. It seemed a bit cheeky to me. I was very proud that not only did I identify the plane without recourse to my aircraft recognition book but I actually saw the helmeted head of the pilot. It was the first enemy I had ever seen. Come to think of it, it was probably also the last. I was pretty convinced that he had an evil grin on his face. Still, at that time all Germans were assumed to have evil expressions on their faces so I suppose that I may have imagined it.

My father was appointed street warden and took charge of the official street stirrup pump and two buckets, one of sand and one of water. These were kept in an state of instant readiness on our front doorstep and a white post was nailed to our front gate to indicate their location. I was very proud of this since the Edom family were a bit short of status symbols. Father was issued with a special tin hat with a 'W' on it but it made his bald spot sore so he wore his trilby hat instead.

We never used the stirrup pump on national service but it did come in handy for watering the carrots during dry periods.

Then a man came and dug an enormous hole in our garden just beyond the hazelnut tree. It made a nasty mess of our back lawn I can tell you. The man dug out enormous clods of thick yellow clay which I modelled into German soldiers who were then summarily executed with my catapult. Then more men came with bricks and concrete and built an air raid shelter in the hole. Old clever clogs next door built his shelter on the surface and turned it into a garage after the war. The Edoms being pessimists by nature thought that (a) there wouldn't be an after the war, and (b) that even if there was they would never be able to afford a car. They were proved fifty per cent right.

Air raid shelters became as popular in the forties as patio sets in the eighties. It was interesting to see how other families adopted shelters according to personal taste. The Sharps, who had a very elegant garden with rose arbours and an ornamental pond, made their shelter look like a rockery whilst Mr Dawkins, who prided himself as a handyman, built his himself with great balks of timber, sheets of corrugated iron and six-inch nails.

The Luftwaffe began to bomb West Wickham before our shelter was completed. This, I thought, was typically inconsiderate of Mr Göring. The grand piano and the cupboard under the stairs were our main places of shelter during air raids for this interim period. Neither was ideal for a family of five. Even to this day however, whenever I see a grand piano I tend to judge its quality by the stoutness of its legs and I have never been in favour of open-plan staircases.

Happily, by the time that Göring had grasped the full strategic significance of West Wickham, we were able to take to our now completed shelter. In later years whenever I told people where I came from they invariably enquired, 'Where on earth is that?' I always used to point out with some irritation that it seemed that the entire bloody Luftwaffe could find us in the blackout without any difficulty so I didn't see why it should present any problems for anyone else.

I could never puzzle out why the German bombers were so keen to unload their bombs on West Wickham. It was on a direct route to nowhere in particular and there wasn't a factory of any kind for miles. The railway only went one more stop along the line because the South Eastern Railway had run out of money and enthusiasm in 1882 and no one in their right mind could have regarded the Amalgamated Dairies Depot at the bottom of the High Street as being central to the national war effort.

In the air raid shelter the conversation often turned to when the war was over. Little Mrs Braybird, the meek and mild lady from number fourteen who sometimes used to share our shelter, was in no doubt about what should happen to Mr Hitler. She would personally cut a half pound of flesh out of him each day and rub salt in the wound. She did hint darkly at where she would start although the significance of this was lost on me at the time. I have to say, however, that I did not meet any humanitarians or pacifists during the war. Perhaps they only flourish in the luxury of personal safety. If someone had suggested that it was wrong to want to bomb the Germans to perdition we would have thought that he was either shell-shocked or a member of the Fifth Column.

My own dreams of life after the war were not wildly ambitious. They revolved around what bananas would look like and how real oranges would taste. The idea of going into a sweet shop and seeing Fry's Peppermint Cream above the counter and buying it without sweet coupons spurred me on to make all sorts of short-term sacrifices, like putting up the blackout screens every night and taking round our potato peelings to feed the Sharps' chickens in the hope of an occasional eggy reward. (I learned here about market forces, viz. one egg equals a hell of a lot of potato peelings.) Another duty was to empty the bucket kept in our shelter for urgent calls of nature when a dash to the indoor loo at the height of an air raid could have proved highly imprudent.

My shrapnel collection grew steadily but some of my contemporaries far surpassed my own acquisitive efforts. Human nature being what it is, even shrapnel collectors had their own elitist hierarchies. Bill Oddy's incendiary fin was far superior to mine, being both unbent and unsinged – a fact that he frequently pointed out. (All my life I seem to have been plagued by the Bill Oddys of this world asserting their superiority with their own equivalents of his undented incendiary fin.)

Our little gang quickly gave up collecting the long lengths of metallic strip that the Jerries kept turfing out of their planes. It came in such quantities that it had no scarcity value at all. Its purpose was obscure to us. Something to do with deflecting our wireless rays it was said, but whatever its purpose it was dead boring. By contrast, Donald Duxford gained much local prestige amongst his peers by his ownership of a complete and very shiny steel shell cap. Rumour had it that he had not actually found it himself but had bought it from someone else. He was the son of the local publican and received two shillings pocket money every week. He also had a tin plate revolver that used to fire percussion caps in pre-war days when they still made caps. This weapon qualified him as our platoon commander whenever we played soldiers. Money always buys privilege, doesn't it?

The Ministry of Information said that we all had to dig for victory and I purchased little packets of seeds from Woolworth's. Sadly, they never grew like the pictures on the packets. My carrots grew all knobbly and spindly and the slugs came in great battalions to eat my lettuces. As if that wasn't enough, the local cats started pooping indiscriminately on my radishes.

I redoubled my war efforts. There was a poster that told me that careless talk cost lives and I desperately wanted to know a secret just so that I could not tell anyone about it. I collected waste paper and took it down to the depot in the garage of the bombed house at the end of Springhurst Avenue. There were different sections in the depot marked 'Paper' and 'Bones' and 'Rags'. But meat rationing meant that there were precious few bones, and make do and mend meant that there were very few rags either.

I was also very busy keeping number eighty-two under close observation since I was convinced that a German spy was living there. The occupants had moved to Paignton at the beginning of the war but I and my little school friends were convinced that someone had moved the curtains and we were highly suspicious. By this time I was devoted to total victory, just like Mr Churchill said. I even practised harder with my gas mask and at one stage of patriotic fervour even refrained from making those exquisite farting noises with it that so infuriated my teacher and had disrupted every school gas mask drill to date.

Unfortunately, my efforts were not enough to deter the Luftwaffe. They bombed the railway station, dropped something nasty through the roof of the Plaza cinema (much to the consternation of those in the one and threes) and blew the front out of the Tudor Library. This unprovoked assault on our literary heritage was a grave blow to me because they destroyed all the *William* books that I used to borrow for tuppence a week. I realised that it was going to be a long, hard and cruel war.

A bomb splinter gouged a lump out of our dustbin and gave Johnny, our tom-cat, a nasty scare since he was inclined to pee up against the dustbin when he couldn't think of anything better to do. Johnny resented the Germans deeply. They interrupted his nocturnal activities and he wore a permanent scowl throughout much of the Blitz. Then a refugee pussy cat of the opposite gender arrived from some other war zone and, uninvited, took up residence with us. She remained with us for twelve years, rewarding us for our hospitality by producing regular broods of fluffy kittens that replenished the decimated moggie population of West Wickham. I think that she had something going with Johnny who eventually cheered up no end.

For a while the air raids became distinctly nastier. I still get a disturbing sinking sensation in my tummy to this day if I hear a siren start up although these days they are only used in my part of the world to call out the volunteer fire brigade to put out some brush fire on Chobham Common. In those far-off days they were the prelude to all sorts of nastiness. We would troop down to the shelter bearing blankets, torches (if we had been able to get the No. 8 batteries), hot water bottles, a paraffin lamp and our emergency bucket, and then we would await events. First would come the distant drone of the bombers, gradually getting louder and more menacing – a nasty guttural, throbbing noise sounding just like you would expect nasty German planes with nasty German accents to sound. Then the guns on Hayes Common would start banging and woofing. They made a great din but I don't believe they ever hit anything. It was said that they fired just to keep up our morale but they played havoc with my nerves I can tell you. Whenever anyone complains about my irascibility these days I just blame it on the anti-aircraft guns on Hayes Common in 1941. Fat lot of good it does me.

One night a bomb hit the railway line at the bottom of our garden. It was a distinctly largish bomb. Fortunately, the railway line was in a cutting just there. Anyway, large lumps of the Southern Railway showered into our garden. There was a goodly length of signal wire (useful for stringing up the runner beans), miscellaneous bits of fishplates and bolts and a splendid lump of railway line that landed a few yards from our shelter and that was so heavy that I could scarcely move it. It was ragged at each end as if giant fingers had plucked it out of a sixty-foot length of railway line like a piece of soft plasticine. I used it as a sort of anvil for some years, that is when it wasn't serving as a part of the Maginot Line for my toy soldiers who had been defending the rose bed since the outbreak of hostilities.

Most nights the bombers droned over us on their way to London. One night the whole sky to the north-east was a red glow. 'That's the docks,' someone announced authoritatively. Some nights the bombs would whistle down on West Wickham. We used to try to gauge the degree of danger by the sound of the whistle but when they all came together we had to give up. My father used to stand uncertainly just inside the shelter door muttering, 'Don't panic, don't panic,' to no one in particular. Many years later it became a catch phrase in a comedy about the Home Guard but the copyright was indubitably my dad's.

Then the Luftwaffe dropped bombs all down our road. Our end of the road copped the little ones but they seemed to get steadily bigger as they progressed towards Hayes. I was quite glad that they started at our end. They reserved an enormous one for just outside our school which was about a quarter of a mile up the road and the final bomb despatched the Lennard family at number 120 to eternity. I had been very fond of Mr Lennard. He was crippled and walked laboriously with a limp and a stout stick. He was a kind gentle man and no great threat to the German military machine. He used to stop to chat to me on his way back from the railway station whilst I swung on our garden gate. His wife was killed instantly as well but his son lingered on with terrible injuries and then died quietly when most people had forgotten all about him. I never forgave the Jerries for what they did to the Lennards.

When we crept out of the shelter in the mornings there were two priorities: first a check to see if the house was still there and which bits had fallen off, and secondly a brew of tea. The Edom family ran almost entirely on tea in the Blitz. It was just as well that it was rationed or we would all have died of tannin poisoning. If I had to go through the Blitz again I would do it on Scotch whisky but at that time the Edom family was virtually teetotal and anyway Scotch was in very short supply.

Our house was between the wars jerry-built – mock-Tudor with artificial half-timbering and leaded lights. The leaded lights went in an early air raid, never to be restored. I picked the broken glass from the tangled remains and used the bits of lead for creative therapy. A few deft twists and a good deal of imagination used to produce a rough semblance of a Mauser pistol which was very useful when playing Gestapo and torturing Calvin Sharp.

In due course all the plaster ceilings in our house were blown down, the front door was blown open and the lock torn off, most of the tiles came off the roof and the gas, water and electricity came and went depending on the state of the road outside. At one stage it resembled a ploughed field. They dug long trenches to relay the shattered drains and other services and I used to run along the trenches pretending to be a steam train in a cutting. Unfortunately, on one occasion a jagged lump of paving stone was sticking out at knee height and when I ran into it it gouged a large lump from my kneecap. I have the scar to this day. I tell my younger, more impressionable friends that I got the scar in the trenches during the Second World War. They don't seem all that impressed.

After each air raid teams of Council workmen came around with tarpaulins to cover holes in roofs and tarred paper to stop the rain coming in the broken windows. Shattered ceilings were eventually restored with a sort of thick cardboard stuff, supported by battens. Some of the houses in the street were beyond first aid. Whole fronts were blown out, revealing the intimate details of our neighbours' domestic lives. I noted that some of them had execrable tastes in wallpapers.

When I drive down Springhurst Avenue these days I picture the houses as they were in 1941 and wonder if the present occupants have any idea of the battering and shaking that their homes once endured and how much they have been reconstituted. I don't think that they would thank me for telling them, not with twenty-nine years of a thirty-year mortgage still to go.

By this time I was an extremely warlike little boy and not very nice to know. With my little friends I fought battles in every theatre of war. My preference was for jungle warfare conducted in the shrubbery behind the chicken run in Calvin Sharp's garden. According to all the theories prevailing at the time I should have become a bank-robbing psychopath when I grew up but theories are notoriously unreliable and I leaned much more towards neurotic cowardice in my later years.

I thought that the bombing would go on for ever. There were high explosive bombs of all shapes and sizes and there were delayed action bombs; there were oil bombs and land mines and incendiaries and later on little bombs painted brightly and shaped like butterflies so that when you picked them up to take a closer look they blew your arm off. I used all the names with great authority although some of the technicalities were lost on me. The house across the road copped an incendiary but the householder managed to put it out without calling for our stirrup pump or our bucket of sand. My father never forgave him.

About the time that I took my eleven-plus, or what passed for the eleven-plus in those chaotic days, the Luftwaffe dropped incendiaries all over Hayes. I have no idea what sort of strategic logic influenced that decision. I suspect that the raiders got lost or panicked or just got bored and wanted to get home to their Bierwurst, or whatever passed for breakfast in that benighted country of theirs. Anyway Hayes, like West Wickham, had the strategic importance of a dried cow-pat. It was a very dull commuter suburb of private semi-detacheds (all mod cons, two recept, three bedrms). In happier times the most disturbing event would have been the late departure of the 8.10 to Charing Cross. Anyway, Hayes burnt merrily that night. I suppose that the German air crews reported that they had destroyed yet another armaments factory or Bomber Command Headquarters or something. In reality their score was roughly forty semi-detacheds (all mod cons) burnt out, approximately one hundred (ditto) seriously scorched and several thousand motley civilians distinctly off their shredded wheat and late for work. The next day we made a pilgrimage to the spot where it was alleged that a young girl had been killed by a shell splinter. The whole of Hayes smelt like bonfire night. We looked at a messy stain on the pavement. It could have been blood or brains or someone might have made the whole story up. The stain could have been the result of a spilled bottle of Wincarnis. I don't know and can't say.

Horror stories were rife at the time and fiction mingled with reality and it was hard to tell which was the more improbable. A lady in Langley Way was said to have been taking a bath when a bomb blew out her bathroom wall and she had to be rescued in the noddy by an enterprising ARP warden. The story had too much appeal not to repeat but I don't know whether it was true. For a while I resolved to be an ARP warden when I grew up. I didn't tell people that it was because I quite fancied the idea of giving firemen's lifts to distressed ladies in their birthday suits.

The war dragged on and I grew older and more horrible. I was in a sort of no man's land, too old for orange juice or a Mickey Mouse gas mask but too young for the pleasures of the fighting men. I wasn't clear what the pleasures of the fighting men were but I was aware that pints of bitter and packets of Players were much in vogue and there were certain goings-on behind the lecture hall after the Saturday night dances that led to a good few nods and winks as well. By this time I had started taking surreptitious glances at my brother's *Lilliput* magazine which had patriotic pictures of ladies wearing tin hats and not much else. It was getting to be a funny old war.

My pre-war toys had disintegrated and for a while I devised my own from wood or paper but toys did not hold the fascination they once had done. Empty dried egg packets were still quite fun. Set alight and hurled into the air they produced a vaguely pyrotechnic effect as they flared up and their melted wax dropped in spirals to the ground. But it was no good; childhood was coming to an end and the world was moving on. My sister had been called up to do factory work and my brother went off to Canada to train to fly Lancasters and my mum was still putting up with familiarity from the butcher in the hope of some off-the-ration offal. My father meanwhile was fire-watching somewhere in Islington to protect his firm's filing cabinet factory. Business apparently was very good.

Eventually the Blitz was over. No one blew a whistle and Hitler didn't announce that he was packing it in; it just sort of fizzled out. For a while life was just incredibly dull, like Stowmarket on a Sunday. Then it all started up again. There was this dreadful night with sudden inexplicable explosions. Rumour had it that several planes packed with bombs had crashed. Then all was revealed. It was the dreaded Doodlebugs. West Wickham got more than its share of these pilotless planes. Although aimed at London the stupid Krauts kept getting their sums wrong and they were all dropping short. They came over in droves throughout the day.

The air raid alerts lasted all day. These things rasped their way across the sky, stopped suddenly and then dived to earth. They made the hell of a bang and did my nervous twitch no good at all. First a large gap appeared in the Station Road, then they did Elmers End bus garage with a resultant fire that was said to be as good as when the Crystal Palace burned down. They also dropped one just round the corner, on the edge of Langley Park golf course. Fortunately, the sheep had gone but it made a hell of a mess of the fairway leading to the sixth hole, and there wasn't a tree for a hundred yards that had a leaf on it. Or many with branches either, come to think of it.

I was later told that seventy-four Doodlebugs exploded in the Borough of Beckenham during this phase of the nastiness. It felt to me that most of them flew over number eight Springhurst Avenue. Still, I suppose that even that was distinctly better than them stopping there.

There was worse still to come. Hitler had his V2s all ready to launch apparently. Blissfully unaware of this new variation, I was more preoccupied with the reduction in the sweet ration and the saccharine tablets that we were now using in our tea. I used to pretend that they were depth charges. You dropped them in and they sunk to the bottom and then after a few seconds they exploded and pushed a frothy white excrescence to the surface.

Of course, the war was still far from over and worse horrors were still to come. There was fish and potato pie and carrot fudge and ice cream made with soya flour. Still, by this time I was no longer in any doubt that this was total war, to the bitter end, and that nothing would ever, ever be the same again – not even ice cream.

Finally came victory. Much has been written about VE Day but I have to tell you that for a twelve year old boy living in the suburb of West Wickham it was a bit of a swizz. I had spent half my life waiting for victory to come and when it did it was dead boring. It wasn't nearly as exciting as when they dropped the V2 on St Stephen's church in Eden Park.

My mum had been keeping a tin of pre-war peaches in the larder to celebrate ultimate victory but I seem to recall that when we actually opened them they were off. We also got out our flagpole left over from the 1937 coronation but the Union Jack had got moth in so a patriotic display at number eight Springhurst Avenue was ruled out.

They did have a VE Day street party in Turpin Lane but they were a common lot in the council houses in Turpin Lane and I wasn't allowed to go. I believe that all the kids who did go were supplied with a spam sandwich, a paper hat left over from Christmas 1939 and some fizzy lemonade.

Mind you, that was just for starters. In the evening there was a bonfire and dance in the sports ground in Springhurst Avenue. However, I have to concede that once the bonfire had gone out and they had let off all the Home Guard's thunderflashes it all went downhill and when they started playing the Vera Lynn records I went home. I gather that in Piccadilly Circus things were a bit more exciting with people climbing up lamp posts and ladies kissing complete strangers and doing Knees Up Mother Brown and showing their knickers. There was nothing remotely like that in West Wickham I can assure you.

Herne Bay

Herne Bay played an important part in my formative years. The Edom family invariably spent the last week in August and the first week in September at Mrs Little's boarding house. In those distant days before frozen foods, such establishments served vegetables strictly in season so my holiday memories are irretrievably linked with thoughts of runner beans and marrow. I still remember my sense of outrage in Marrakech in 1983 when they served me couscous without either vegetable. Even a belly dancer with a jewel in her navel cannot compensate for a total lack of runner beans and marrow.

Herne Bay holidays were symbolised by Herne Bay pier, a magnificent Victorian structure which marched out eight-tenths of a mile into the sea as if it knew exactly where it was going. It was the Herne Bay UDC that claimed that the pier was eight-tenths of a mile long. I never measured it myself. I did think about it but I had concluded that it would be a bit boring crawling along on my hands and knees with my mum's tape measure. Some things are best taken on trust. I never queried the distance to the moon either. I preferred to rely on the mileage quoted in my brother's *Modern Boy's Annual* for 1938. Sometimes I used to wonder how they measured that but it made my head hurt to think about it. Anyway, no one would ever get there, would they – except Flash Gordon.

Never mind, Herne Bay pier was eight-tenths of a mile long, give or take a barnacle or two; that is until war threatened and they took two sizeable chunks out of it, when it became two-tenths, three-tenths and three-tenths approximately. This, I understood, was to stop Mr Hitler landing his Panzers on the end and driving them down the pier to occupy the clock tower and the Winter Gardens.

I had this fantasy of Mr Hitler's storm troopers playing oom-pa-pa music in the Winter Gardens whilst goose-stepping and Heil-Hitlering around the assembled UDC deckchairs and potted geraniums. These days, no doubt, the UDC wouldn't say no to a few goose-stepping Germans, provided they brought their Deutschmarks and their Bundesbank credit cards with them.

Now, back to Herne Bay pier again. It was never quite the same after they took those chunks out of it. After the war they replaced the gaps with narrow austerity gangways but the little electric tram all lit up with fairy lights never ran to the pier head again and the visits of the SS *Rochester Queen* were spasmodic and distinctly half-hearted. The *Rochester Queen* wasn't a patch on the pre-war paddle steamer which, according to legend, was sunk at Dunkirk. I expect that it sprung a leak in Deptford Creek really, but have you no sense of romance?

As I said, the pier was symbolic – a bit like my life. There was the pre-war bit (all happy and bathed in a rosy glow) and then the messy gaps that the war created and then, somehow, nothing was ever quite the same again.

I have visited Herne Bay in recent years but it isn't even a shadow of its former glory. I struggle to conjure up the full flavour of those childhood memories (were there really red sails in the sunset like the song said and did the sun really have his hat on?) but it becomes harder with every passing year, like remembering what toffee apples used to taste like.

What, I wonder, happened to all those buxom ladies of the Women's League of Health and Beauty who cavorted in the Esplanade Gardens? They were, I think, probably more healthy than beautiful but I was much impressed by the large acreage of sun-pinkened flesh and all their rhythmic arm-waving and knee-bending and stretching and leaping about. They did it all to music provided by a small bald-headed man seated at an upright and slightly out of tune piano. The piano had yellowing keys that matched the pianist's teeth. The ladies attracted a considerable following but I was a little surprised that so many gentlemen showed such intense interest. I assumed that they must all have been supporters of women's health and beauty or were loyal husbands. (Well, I was very young at the time and had yet to learn that there were more powerful passions than stamp collecting and French cricket.)

Then there was the red speed boat that used to hurtle the more affluent holidaymakers round the bay although at a shilling a go it was not on the Edom family's agenda. Still, it was good fun to watch it set off from its little rickety platform on the pebble beach near the outfall sewer. There was an exciting roar when the engine was revved up and the grey-green water and seaweed was whipped up into a mixture that reminded me of Mrs Little's cabbage soup. When the boat returned from its trip there was usually someone looking distinctly pukey which all added to the fun of the occasion.

I gained the same sort of vicarious pleasure from looking through the windows of the Cornucopia Ice Cream Parlour and keeping surveillance on the fortunate few who were dipping into tall glasses of Knickerbocker Glories or nut sundaes or slurping up their banana splits. Personally I gave my custom to the Eldorado Ice Cream Company whose salesmen were mounted on tricycles with a box on the front and who wore peaked caps. (Stop me and buy one, ting-a-ling.) Those white-coated entrepreneurs dispensed ice cream wafers or cones but my special favourite were the cardboard tubs thoughtfully augmented with a little wooden spoon. I especially liked the strawberry and vanilla, not least because it always seemed a wonder to me how they got one side white and one side strawberry. Science is wonderful, isn't it?

The tricycle brigade set off each morning from their depot on the seafront next to the pin-table saloon and in a series of skirmishes with ice-cream-crazed holidaymakers penetrated as far as the West Cliff Sun Lounge and the East Cliff Bandstand. 'Special attraction next week: Douglas Boothroyd (Pianoforte) and Ethel Spasm (Soprano) "We bring you our world of melody and song."'

Now, where was I? Ah yes, the ice cream. Those little waxed cardboard tubs and wooden spoons; there was something distinctly aesthetic about the whole marketing operation. I recall that I desperately wanted to be an ice cream salesman at that stage in my career planning. Being an acquisitive little boy I collected discarded ice cream cartons to take home so that I could play ice cream salesman to my heart's content in the back garden of number eight, Springhurst Avenue. When we packed to go home, always a tricky operation because I had usually taken a fancy to an odd boulder or two and a few lengths of dried seaweed, I had an exchange of views with my ever-loving mother about the degree of priority to be given to the inclusion of twenty-three slightly festering empty ice cream cartons and a somewhat disproportionate number of well licked wooden spoons.

There were other holiday pleasures at Herne Bay, collecting groundsel for Mrs Little's canary, for example. Mind you, I always found the canary a bit boring; all it ever did was go bloody tweet, or at very best, tweet, tweet.

Another amusement was the motor boat lake beyond the West Cliff. The lake was full of these splendidly solid wooden boats that made slow phut-phutting noises and reeked of oil and petrol. The lake had a delicious sheen of oil all over it and the edges were draped with old motorcar tyres to prevent small boys from re-enacting the first voyage of the *Titanic*. There wasn't a bit of fibreglass anywhere and there were none of those nasty little Yamaha outboard motors making horrid oriental snarling noises. If I had ever heard of Yamaha I would have thought that it was something out of the Mikado – if I had ever heard of the Mikado.

There was Crazy Golf as well but I usually got over-excited and whopped my ball over the cliff so I wasn't encouraged in my enthusiasm for this pursuit.

The concerts in the Central Bandstand were another attraction and the Herne Bay Town Band's renditions of 'Roses of Picardy' and 'South of the Border' and selections from *The Yeoman of the Guard* were quite electrifying. I particularly appreciated the euphonium player who used to turn puce just through going 'pharp' at fairly rhythmic intervals. There were concert parties too, who always sang 'The sun has got his hat on'. In the evenings there were dances in the East Cliff Bandstand but public dances were considered a trifle 'fast' at the time. Anyway, at age six and seven-twelfths I couldn't conceive how anyone would want to waste a perfectly good evening walking around to music holding some soppy girl; it seemed a funny sort of pastime to me and I couldn't see the pleasure in it.

Watching the other holidaymakers was all part of the seaside fun at Herne Bay. My special secret was that I had discovered that the Germans had already occupied Herne Bay before the declaration of war. (This is not recorded in any of the official histories so you are the first to know.) There was this group of square-headed blonde young men who made guttural noises and flexed their biceps and wore rude swimming trunks. They swam all the way out to the diving raft anchored in the bay. I expect that they were signalling to their U-boats because they were obviously spies although they claimed to be students from Utrecht. A likely story. There was also a sort of holiday home for nuns, next to the Crazy Golf course actually, so the town was full of old ladies in black habits strolling about in pairs. Everyone knew, of course, that this was the favourite disguise for German stormtroopers so I kept a fairly close eye on them as well. (You could tell by their jackboots, you know.)

Down by the pier each morning the East Kent Road Car Company marshalled its resources for the day's excursions. They went to places of interest like Canterbury (time to see the cathedral) or Tankerton (shrimp teas). There was also an afternoon Mystery Tour that always went to Ramsgate with a stop for tea and scones at the Tudor Tea Rooms near the roundabout on the arterial road. There was also a funny little single-deck bus that for five pence would take you up the winding cliff road to the Reculver Towers on the east headland. Mind you, it was so bleak up there that all there was to do when you got there was to come back again. Family funds ran to two excursions in the fortnight but the major investment was seats for all the family for the show in the Pier Pavilion.

The shows at the Pier Pavilion had titles like 'Startime' or 'Sunny Days' or 'Follies of 1939'. You could go twice in a fortnight because the crafty management had two different programmes; same cast but different costumes, sketches, jokes and songs. They alternated these programmes each week to try to persuade the two-weekers to go twice during their stay but Mr Edom senior was made of sterner stuff. 'When you've seen them once you've seen enough,' was his stated position and it was not negotiable. The show was a bit of swizz I suppose, although since I wasn't taken to pantomimes and hadn't even heard of television it was my one chance in the year to actually see entertainers and it was much more exciting than listening to *Music Hall* on our all wave mains wireless. (Buzz, buzz, crackle, crackle; it's interference from Hilversum again or a pigeon sitting on the aerial.) Still, you had to admit that the leading boy was a bit frayed at the edges and he became distinctly breathless when he did his little tap dances. The leading girl, who also graciously assisted the Great Marvo, certainly wouldn't see fifty again (not even from a distance) and she was struggling a bit when she hit (or only just missed) the top notes in 'Some Day My Prince Will Come'. I liked the funny bits best like 'Run Rabbit Run' and 'Siegfried Line'. I could never understand why they didn't invite Mr George Formby down (with his ukulele, of course) to give us his rendition of 'Chinese Laundry Blues'.

Of course, there were lots of other interesting people at Herne Bay – the 'Kwik Snaps' man, for example. He lurked with his Leica camera between the Central Bandstand and the pier and leapt out on unwary promenaders and thrust little vouchers into their hands. 'Results on the board in the morning.' It was quite fun to look at the results of his previous day's marauding. The proofs were displayed on boards outside his little wooden hut with the 'Use Ilford Selo for all round snapshotting' pennant flying from the roof. There were all those promenaders captured for posterity with funny expressions on their faces. The 'Kwik Snaps' man caught my dad once and he looked as though he had toothache.

There were many cheaper pleasures than buying a 'Kwik Snap.' There was walking along the promenade and there was watching the man who set himself alight and jumped off the pier (11 a.m. and 3 p.m. weather permitting). There was a silver collection if you stood too near. Sometimes he did it all on a bicycle for reasons that were none too clear to me.

Then there was looking for crabs and deploying my

shrimping net when the tide went out. The tide went out a very long way at Herne Bay revealing acres of muddy seabed but remarkably few shrimps. (Well, none actually.) I think the shrimps knew better than to hang around waiting to be netted and the beach was covered with disgruntled small boys with shrimping nets full of mud.

I also had a very small sailing boat but this was very boring; it kept blowing over and behaving like a submarine. I kept hoping that it would float away but it never did. What I longed for was a Triang clockwork motor boat but clockwork motorboats were low on my parents' spending priorities. In fact, they seemed to go deaf whenever I launched into the investment potential of clockwork motorboats.

Still, there was also skimming flat stones across the sea or knocking old tin cans off the breakwater. Sandcastles were out, despite my new Mickey Mouse tin bucket and wooden spade from Woolworth's (6d and 3d respectively). There was only one small patch of sand at Herne Bay, down near the pier, and you would have needed a medium-sized Bren gun carrier and a detachment of Grenadier Guards to have taken that over from the battle-hardened elite who occupied it for all the daylight hours.

Sometimes there were Punch and Judy shows although I never did quite grasp the storyline. (Where did the crocodile come from, I ask myself?) Then there was a row out to the end of the pier, accompanied with any luck by a playful porpoise trying to turn the boat over. There was also trying to get tar off my swimming costume or trying not to set the beach hut on fire with the Primus stove. I don't know who this fellow Primus was but he certainly had a sick mind and showed little love for his fellow men. Until they invented flame-throwers there was nothing more lethal than a Primus stove.

Of course, we had to send all our neighbours picture

postcards. 'Having a lovely time, wish you were here.' It was important not to forget number ten who looked after Johnny our tom-cat whilst we were away. We sent cards with slogans like 'Good Luck from Herne Bay' and vignettes of a fluffy black pussy cat surrounded by pictures of the pier by moonlight and stormy seas by the clock tower.

Perhaps the greatest pleasure, though, was the amusement arcade. If my mother gave me threepennyworth of venture capital I felt like Lord Nuffield himself. The sights and sounds of the amusement arcade were totally seductive. There was the regular clang, clang of the rifle range as little battered moving ducks were mowed down over and over again and there was the electric crackle and thump of the dodgem cars and, of course, the rattle and ping, ping of a host of pin tables. A pennyworth at a pin table was incredibly good value. It was a bit like a gobstopper; with skilled conservation you could make it last a very long time indeed and extract the maximum pleasure. Of course, you seldom won anything but you could make five balls last for ages and all those flashing lights and free balls and bonuses and scores that went into hundreds of thousands made me quite dizzy with power. Then there were the little pictures that lit up on the scoreboard; spaceships and racing cars and trains and things. Personally I liked the lady in the bathing costume who leapt off a diving board and got stuck in improbable positions when the machine indicated 'Game Over'. It was all pure ecstasy; even the 'tilt' light was an extra challenge. I have to warn you though that the haunted house was a swizz; even before you put your penny in you could see the skeleton peering out of the cupboard and the ghost looked more senile than ghostly when he appeared at the top of the stairs. Oh, I mustn't forget the 'Allwin' machine; in went your penny, round and round went the little metal ball, past all the little scoops marked 'Win' and straight into an unmarked hole at the bottom that we veterans knew meant 'Lose'. There were more esoteric machines that I did not waste my money on, like the 'Test Your Grip' machine and the punch ball with a dial to show how hard you could punch; these were mostly used by young men to impress their girlfriends. Having no punch and no girlfriend they offered very poor value to me. There were also a couple of those infuriating crane machines that always lost their grip on your prize just before it got to the delivery chute.

All good things come to an end. I seemed to sense that once the first air raid siren had wailed its eerie song over Herne Bay on that summer Sunday morning, life would never be the same again; and of course it never was. Seven years and a world war later, when the family returned to Herne Bay it was a different place and I was a different boy.

The east cliff was covered in barbed wire and there were strange bits of khaki-coloured militaria littered about, and there were holes everywhere as if a breed of giant mutant rabbits had been on the rampage. The poor mutilated pier was a shock to the memory buds and the Cornucopia Ice Cream Parlour had only mock Knickerbocker Glories in the window. They were, I think, made of plaster of Paris and poster paints and there wasn't a banana split to be had for love or money.

There were bullet holes in the glass of the West Cliff Sun Lounge and there were some very odd bits of old iron and concrete down by the outfall sewer. There was a concrete pillbox where the Crazy Golf had been, the 'Kwik Snaps' man (and his hut) had disappeared without trace and the Eldorado ice cream depot was bricked up and looked as though it had been used as an air raid shelter.

They had built some anti-aircraft gun towers far out to sea and I rather enjoyed keeping these under observation through my father's binoculars which he had unpatriotically refused to hand in for the war effort in 1939. To add insult to injury they were German. I used to stand by the esplanade railings scanning the sea with the binoculars and pretending to be the captain of a destroyer like a character from *In Which We Serve*. Mind you, I got some funny looks from passers-by as I muttered my orders to the engine room.

Of course, by this time my interests and preoccupations were changing and most of my holiday pocket money was spent on surreptitious visits to the bookstall near the seafood restaurant which sold paperback books with titles like *Dead Dames Don't Talk* and pictures on the covers of ladies, living or dead, who were invariably showing their legs almost up to their armpits. The text was always a bit disappointing and printed on brownish paper 'in complete conformity with the authorised economy standards'. Still, there were usually a few pages worth lingering over when Nick Donnelly, ace detective, crushed some broad into his powerful arms and pressed his throbbing body against hers... (These bits always ended in dots as if the typesetter had gone into a spasm.)

I liked looking at the rude postcards too. (You can tell he likes you, Gladys, it sticks out a mile; Oooh, doctor, that's a funny sort of stethoscope, etc.) Most adults tended to sniff disapprovingly at these cards but I was puzzled because the shopkeeper had to keep restocking his shelves. I used to watch to see who was buying them but I never caught anyone at it. This was when I first made the astounding discovery that sex and hypocrisy were not new phenomena and that there was a great deal of both about.

Then there was Miss Reid from Grove Park, who was staying in our boarding house with her mother (not Mrs Little's establishment because she had retreated to the Cotswolds at the beginning of the war and had not been heard of since). Anyway, Miss Reid was a rather moon-faced young woman who sniffed a lot and drooped a bit in places. However, she had the virtue of being frequently observable if not particularly sociable and since she clearly did not regard me as any sort of threat she had an endearing carelessness with her skirts that made my spots get worse. I used to follow her around hoping for a quick flash of her silken thighs, just like Nick Donnelly, ace detective, in *Dangerous Curves*. There was one happy occasion when, by peering through a knot-hole in the back of our beach hut, I was able to keep Miss Reid under sustained observation whilst she sat on the grassy slope behind the huts. She was trying to get her knees brown whilst, unbeknown to her, I was acquiring a crick in my neck through trying to imagine what mysteries lay concealed by the double gusset of her sensible knickers.

The age of innocence was passing swiftly and, as I said, neither Herne Bay nor I were ever really the same again...

Just a Small Cog

I was desperate to do my bit for the war effort. I had already dug feverishly for victory. Sadly, my carrots had grown all spindly and I've already told you what the cat had done to my radishes. I had also been trying to discover some state secret just so I could not tell anyone about it just like Mr Churchill asked us to do but it was all to no avail. I had also been keeping an eye open for German spies and whenever I saw a nun I always looked at her feet to see if she was wearing jackboots since it was well known that the Jerry paratroopers liked dressing up as nuns.

Then a little chum told me about the COGS. It was run by an eccentric but very determined lady who lived in Ravenswood Avenue. She organised teams of small boys to scour the neighbourhood gathering scrap. I was admitted to membership and was rewarded by an enamel lapel badge in the shape of a small cogwheel. The name of the organisation was, I learned, an allusion to the importance of small cogs in large important machines.

My chum Bill Oddy was the owner of a self-built soapbox cart made with four old pram wheels nicked off the Council tip at Hayes and a bit of six by four from the bombed cottages opposite the Tudor Parade. With this equipment we plagued the civilian population of West Wickham. There was a depot in the abandoned garage of a bombed house at the bottom of my road. Here were fixed to the wall neat notices marked 'Rags' and 'Waste Paper' and 'Metal' and 'Bones.' In the Edom family we hadn't seen a piece of meat large enough to have a decent bone in it since 1939. And not often then. Still the 'Bones' sign struck a suitably positive note. One day perhaps I would find a really big bone for the war effort.

Rags were a bit of a problem too. What with clothes rationing and make do and mend very few rags made it on to the scrap market and when they did they had more holes than material and they were usually a bit niffy I can tell you.

Sadly, as with most human institutions, the COGS became highly competitive. Sometimes Bill Oddy, always an entrepreneur, would take things for scrap even before the donor knew he had donated them. Bill took the view that if it wasn't actually nailed down with six-inch nails it was fair game. On one occasion I had to dissuade him from taking a metal air raid shelter sign for scrap. His argument was that everyone knew where the air raid shelter was anyway.

In my desperation to do my bit I even surrendered my shrapnel collection. I only retained the almost complete shiny metal nose cone from an anti-aircraft shell and my bent incendiary bomb fin and I even felt guilty about that.

Then all of a sudden the eccentric lady disappeared. Whether she had eloped to Gretna Green with an ARP warden or evacuated herself to Chipping Norton I cannot say. The house in Ravenswood Avenue was locked up and deserted and the lady was gone. The depot was full of scrap that the Council had stopped collecting and with no one to liaise with the Council or to organise us we lost our drive and direction. In no time at all the little COGS stopped turning.

Despite this loss to the military machine you will be pleased to know that we did eventually win the war. I redefined my own personal war aims and began taking our potato peelings round to our neighbours who kept chickens. In many ways this was a more satisfying contribution. Very occasionally I got lucky and our neighbours rewarded my efforts with an egg. I think that they call it enlightened self-interest.

Doodlebugs

Those amongst you who have had the benefit of reading my war memoirs will know that I have made more than passing reference to Mr Hitler's secret weapons. In 1994 we commemorated the fiftieth anniversary of the launch of his V1s and this encouraged me to launch my own little treatise on the subject. Whilst Hitler liked to call them his vengeance weapons we locals used to think of them as Doodlebugs or buzz bombs. It made them sound more friendly somehow.

I seem to recall that it all started in about June 1944. The most important event up to that stage of the year was that I had passed the Grammar School entrance examination. Oh, I forgot, D Day had also arrived and the fighting in Normandy was, according to my mum's *Daily Express*, going well. The air raids had more or less packed up and we were getting quite used to sleeping in our own beds rather than in the bunks in our air raid shelter. Then one night Mr Hitler's nastiness all started up again. That man really was a pain, I can tell you. When the sirens went we all hoped that it was a false alarm but once the anti-aircraft guns began their woofing and plonking and general banging about we made our way down to the shelter. During the ensuing shindig one plane seemed to zoom down very low and then there was a massive explosion. We couldn't really make out what was going on but it wasn't what we were used to. Life is like that, isn't it? No sooner do you get used to something than some silly sod changes the rules. Hitler was no exception. The bombers seemed to be flying lower and instead of a series of explosions as they dropped their sticks of bombs there were just these single large explosions every now and again.

The anti-aircraft guns had a fine old time and the shrapnel flew around like confetti at a pre-war wedding. (I thought that you might be interested to know that they didn't make confetti during the war.) Anyway, the general opinion in our shelter was that a bomber had been shot down with a full bomb load. This did not explain all the other big explosions unless our anti-aircraft gunners had suddenly got lucky. Still, it was nice to think that after five years of total war they were at last actually beginning to hit the enemy planes. That was certainly a novelty. Perhaps they had extra special magnetic shells or something.

Eventually morning came as morning is prone to do. In our street it was reported that a fully loaded German bomber had crashed on Chez Nous in the Station Road. As soon as I decently could I made my way to observe Chez Nous. For those who are unfamiliar with the environs of West Wickham I should explain that Chez Nous was a large detached house on the corner of Links Road and Station Road. Chez Nous was not looking its best that morning. In fact it was extremely horizontal. The gateposts were still upright but that was about it. On the other corner of Links Road had been Trudgers Nursery. I use the past tense with good reason. Not only had all the glass from the greenhouses gone but all the greenhouses had gone with it. The houses on the other side of the Station Road weren't looking all that good either. Not unless you preferred a house with a sun roof and the windows like jigsaw puzzles. It was said that an AFS fire engine was passing at the time. A case of being in the wrong place at the wrong time if I ever heard of one. Still they gave them all a very nice funeral with a guard of honour and all.

At first the authorities wouldn't tell us about Hitler's new toys but eventually even the papers were allowed to report on this new weapon. A pilotless plane the newspapers called it. I suppose that the censors thought that this sounded a bit less scary than calling it a flying bomb.

The Doodlebugs began to come over during the day as well as at night. They came with increasing regularity until the authorities gave up sounding the 'all clear'. We had wall to wall air raid alerts from breakfast time to teatime. Eventually the Doodlebugs became more reliable than 194 buses. (Forest Hill Station to Croydon via West Wickham, you will remember, and only five standing inside.) We even became accustomed to their funny little ways. The Doodlebugs I mean. No one *ever* got used to the 194s.

The spirit of free enterprise was not dead and I managed one or two nice little earners by standing on top of our air raid shelter and shouting a warning to the neighbours each time I heard a Doodlebug coming. They had a nasty rasping noise like a lorry with a broken exhaust or the devil farting. When they came into view they were nasty squat little things with stubby wings and a dirty great tube mounted over the tail that shot out a flame at the back. Mind you, all the time it kept rasping and flaming it was all right. When you had to worry was when it stopped rasping and flaming. Then it just went into a steep dive. This was the time to hop a bit smartish into the shelter and hope for the best.

Of course, nothing in this life is ever certain. Occasionally one of those dratted Doodlebugs would have a funny turn and dive into the ground at full throttle. This was considered to be grossly unfair. Not cricket in fact. Still, I don't think that Hitler was ever heavily into cricket.

I remember particularly well the one that did for Elmers End bus garage. The engine cut out just after it had passed over our house so that I knew that it was some other poor bugger's turn. In fact, it went into a dive and landed two and a half miles away. It actually flew through the doors of Elmers End bus garage much to the consternation of the firewatchers on the roof. It is the hell of a way to go, being bombed from underneath. The buses and the tyres and petrol burnt for hours and I could see the columns of black smoke from my vantage point on top of our shelter. We hadn't had a fire like that since the Crystal Palace burned down.

The next one to fall close to home came down one day at about elevenses. This was very convenient because I was on my school hols and could hop on my bike to see the results. I and my little chums had got a bit blasé about Doodlebugs by this time but they did add a bit of interest to the school holidays. This particular one had fallen on the edge of Langley Park golf course which was only just down the road. It made the hell of a bang I can tell you so I knew that it must be close. I hopped on my bike and followed the column of dust and smoke. When I arrived several of my little chums had beaten me to it. There was also a motley collection of officials. There was a policeman complete with tin hat, a number of auxiliary firemen and several ARP persons. They all stood around conversing earnestly but there didn't seem much for them to do and they seemed a bit frustrated. After all, you can't really ARP a golf course can you?

The whole event was a bit disappointing really. The hole in the ground was not all that big. Göring had made bigger holes down our road in 1941. The Doodlebug had landed in the fairway on the approach to the sixth hole. The Doodlebug itself was reduced to small bits of bent metal scattered as far as the eye could see. Some of the bits were still steaming slightly. The surrounding trees had lost all their leaves. Come to think of it, they had lost most of their branches as well. It was very quiet. There was not a bird song to be heard. I expect that they had all been despatched to that great ornithologist in the sky. Still, as an example of Hitler's terror weapon it had not been a great success. Thirty odd deceased sparrows and a dozen rabbits with hearing difficulties was scarcely likely to hinder the second front. Mind you, if a hopeful golfer had driven a Dunlop 65 into the debris I wouldn't have fancied his chances of a birdie at the sixth.

By this time in the campaign all the anti-aircraft defences seemed to have disappeared. There was no explanation from the authorities and at first I thought that perhaps all the anti-aircraft gunners had gone off on their summer holidays. It eventually turned out that they had moved all the guns down to the coast to try to stop the Doodlebugs before they reached London.

I am told that the V1 offensive only lasted about eleven weeks but it seemed considerably longer to me. West Wickham copped quite a few more during those months but in the end I began to lose count. When I went to an unfamiliar part of West Wickham I would often find another gap in the houses that I hadn't noticed before but I was getting a bit absent-minded and sometimes I couldn't tell if it was a new gap or one dating back to the Blitz.

Of course, a lot of the Doodlebugs flew over us and we just heaved a sigh of relief and waited for the next one. The trouble was that every now and then one didn't fly over. It would have been easier if they had displayed destination boards or something, then we would have known where we stood. Still the fact that most of them flew over wasn't a lot of consolation to the people at the other end of Springhurst Avenue who copped one or to the shopkeepers of West Wickham when one fell in the middle of the High Street. Oh, and another one made a bit of a mess in the Blake Recreation Ground and there was also the one on our school playing fields at Langley Park. Then I discovered a pile of rubble on the edge of a sports ground over the other side of the golf course. It had obviously been a rather splendid brick-built sports pavilion but by the time I found it the only thing surviving was the gentleman's urinal which stood like a porcelain headstone amongst the debris. I took the opportunity to have a pee in it. It seemed the least I could do.

Where all the others fell in the neighbourhood of West Wickham I didn't discover then and certainly can't remember now. All I can tell you is that there was a hell of a lot of buzzing and banging before it was all over.

It was only fifty years after these events that I discovered that those naughty old Jerries were not nearly as clever as they thought they were. The Doodlebugs were programmed to fall on Central London but Jerry got his sums wrong. Apparently our Government fed them false information that made them think they were wiping out important places in the centre of London when most of the Doodlebugs were actually falling in South London. Now this, of course, was fine so long as you didn't happen to live in South London. Apparently the very worst place to be according to the statisticians was about six miles north of my home town of West Wickham.

This meant that many of the Doodlebugs flew over us and quite a few fell on Penge which was about four miles away. I was due to start at Ravensbeck Grammar School later in the summer but luckily by that time the pesky things had stopped coming. Mind you, when I first saw Penge High Road it was not a pretty sight. It had more bomb sites than buildings. Amongst other things the police station was looking very lopsided, only half the Co-op was there and as for David Greig's, well it just wasn't. It wasn't only Penge, however. The residents of Bromley and Beckenham were none to pleased at having their towns rearranged either.

Shortly after that the launching sites were captured by

our soldiers and the Doodlebugs stopped coming. Then old Hitler started up with his V2s. At least you could have a relationship with a V1 but V2s were different. You couldn't even hear them coming. There was just a bloody great bang and then the whoosh came afterwards. Fortunately they mostly missed West Wickham and the nearest one fell outside St Jeremy's Church in Eden Park Avenue which was about a mile away. I nipped down on my bike to see it. It had made the hell of a mess of St Jeremy's but it wasn't the same somehow. I mean, I was never going to earn any money out of spotting bloody great supersonic rockets, was I?

Our Air Raid Shelter

The Edom family didn't go in for a lot of status symbols but, even if I say so myself, our air raid shelter was quite impressive. For the first part of the Blitz we used to shelter in the cupboard under the stairs, and then for a brief while under the grand piano but once it became apparent that Mr Göring was going to persist with his nasty little habits a longer-term sheltering strategy was called for.

Mr Edom senior decided on a shelter in the garden. I was not consulted about the design but I carefully oversaw the works and offered occasional helpful advice. First a man came with a spade and dug a hole. This was no ordinary hole. He dug and dug until I thought he was going to break through to Australia. It was the biggest hole I had ever seen although later on Göring made some even bigger ones down Springhurst Avenue.

Then other men came with bricks and a concrete mixer. They were fascinating men with collarless shirts and rolled sleeves and waistcoats. They wore big boots and string round their trousers and they smoked Nosegay cigarettes and said things like 'Shit' and 'Bugger' when they thought I wasn't listening.

When they had finished it looked like nothing that I had ever seen before and I brought all my little chums round to see it. They were visibly impressed. Ron Cardigan said, 'Blimey!' which was praise indeed since he normally didn't say anything at all. The shelter was half below ground and half above. It was brick built with a thick solid concrete roof and the spoil from the hole was stacked round the walls. We grew nasturtiums on the side nearest the entrance but the other side was out of the sun and nothing grew there so I used it to train my toy soldiers in mountain warfare.

I could clamber up on to the flat top of the shelter and I used it as an observation platform. Later in the war I used to spot Doodlebugs from up there but at this initial stage it was usually the bridge of HMS *Hood* or the launching point for my parachute jumps.

Once the shelter was completed the Edom family's Blitz routine was significantly modified. If the siren had not sounded by bedtime we all went up the stairs to bed. I was sent first so I usually got a bit of shut-eye before Göring got started. When the siren sounded we wrapped ourselves in blankets and trooped out to the shelter, each carrying what we considered to be essential equipment. I usually took my army ambulance complete with stretcher bearers, nurse and wounded soldier on a stretcher.

Sometimes the all-clear didn't sound until morning so we stayed down in the shelter all night but occasionally the Jerries packed it in and went home for an early breakfast – Bierwurst and sauerkraut no doubt – in which case we trooped back to bed. You couldn't leave much down the shelter because it went musty or soggy and no one could pretend that it was comfortable perching on those bunks. Still, it was better than the alternative.

Heating in the shelter was by a Valor stove that burned paraffin. Its oily smell and the reassuring pattern that it shone on the ceiling remain vivid memories. Paraffin always reminds me of air raid shelters. We also had a paraffin storm lantern for lighting. Originally the shelter was to be lit by electricity but this was not to be. A lead-covered cable ran from the French windows to the shelter but the lead covering split when Mr Edom senior put it up and the rain leaked into the cable and when we switched the light on in the shelter it immediately went 'phut'. We never dared try it again and new lead-covered cable was not an option at that stage in the war.

The shelter was furnished with two double bunks. They were solidly built and webbing straps were hung between the sides to support the occupant. Those webbing straps tended to cut into you after the first half hour and if you were in the bunk all night you had flesh markings like a zebra in the morning.

I was assigned one of the top bunks. It was quite nice up there but there wasn't a lot of headroom. I used to lay there looking up at the concrete roof about eighteen inches from my nose. The concrete had nice wood-grain patterns on it imprinted by the timber supports that had held the concrete in place whilst it was setting.

It didn't pay to have too much imagination during the Blitz but occasionally I used to lie in my bunk looking up at the concrete ceiling just above my nose and reflect that there was only about twelve inches of concrete between me and all the nastiness going on outside. Personally I didn't think that it was enough.

Occasionally when the guns or the bombs paused one was aware that quite a lot of little bits of ironmongery were dropping out of the sky. This was mostly shell splinters that came down with a hell of a clunk. They did your tiles no good at all – assuming that you still had a roof. Although it used to make me blink a bit when I heard all these miscellaneous thuds and clunks I used to console myself that in the morning I would be able to go out and augment my shrapnel collection.

The shelter had a wooden door but no door frame. It was commonplace for things in the Edom family to remain unfinished. Whether the man who made it was called up before he could build the frame or whether Mr Edom balked at the additional cost, I do not know and cannot say. What I do know is that throughout the Blitz the last one into the shelter had to drag the door into place, and if a big bomb dropped anywhere nearby the door fell over in the blast.

The shelter was quite sophisticated by the standards of the day. At one end was an emergency exit. One layer of bricks in the emergency hatch was laid in sand and only the outer layer was embedded in mortar. This was to make it easier to break out if the doorway was blocked. We had a broken garden spade down there to dig ourselves out with. The trouble was that the sand around the bricks used to get in the tea from our thermos. This problem was solved when I dropped the thermos. Thermos flasks were something else you couldn't get during the war.

Other essential equipment was the candle holder and the Bryant and May matches. We left the candle down the shelter permanently but you couldn't leave the matches down there or they went damp and wouldn't strike. Between the bunks was our card table on which the essential equipment was stored. This included a small tube of Horlicks tablets which was the nearest you could get to off-the-ration sweets during the war.

The shelter had a small lobby with a sump hole covered by a couple of small planks. The lobby was where urgent calls of nature were attended to with the help of a galvanised iron bucket.

My old dad used to take charge in the shelter during the air raids. He would stand in the lobby of the shelter wanting to do something useful but uncertain what. I remember the time they dropped bombs all down Springhurst Avenue. Each one made a whoosh and a bang and each one made a bigger whoosh and a bigger bang than the last. The shelter door blew down and gusts of warm dusty air rushed in. Dad stood there muttering, 'Don't panic, don't panic.' But the rising note in his voice made me realise for the first time in my life that there were some things that even dads couldn't sort out. A Dornier with a full bomb rack was one of them.

Sometimes when the raids were particularly bad, neighbours would come in to share our shelter. Mrs Braybird from number fourteen was our most frequent visitor, that is until she evacuated herself to Godalming in 1942. She was always going on about what it would be like after the war but up in my top bunk I had trouble following all that. I was having enough difficulty remembering what it had been like before the war. She also had this thing about Mr Hitler. She wanted to do things to him that I wasn't supposed to hear and which I won't repeat. I will say, however, that they involved a very sharp knife and a pound of salt.

Ah well, the old shelter served us well. It saw us through the big Blitz, the little Blitz, the incendiary raids and then through the Doodlebugs and the V2s. After the war it served as a coal bunker and at one stage we grew mushrooms in it as well. It was a very solid bit of civil engineering and so far as I know it may still be there to this day.

In later more peaceful times families were to go in for barbecue areas and patios or swimming pools to enhance their gardens. Before the war the Edoms' only garden furniture was the clothes prop but the air raid shelter was without doubt our finest ever status symbol – and really useful too.

Toys

I suppose that memories of childhood are inevitably associated with toys. Since my own childhood was interrupted by Mr Hitler's inconsiderate bid for world domination most of my toys and childhood games had a distinctly warlike flavour. My favourite toy circa 1939 was a rather handsome military ambulance with red crosses on the sides. It had a nurse, permanently in a kneeling position to tend the injured (women knew their place in those days), two stretcher bearers and a wounded soldier. The wounded soldier was somewhat flattened to lay on the little metal stretcher but the effect was a trifle disappointing because he looked as if he had been run over by a tank. Anyway, this humanitarian phase in my war was not to last. I next acquired twelve lead marching soldiers in tin helmets with rifles at the slope. Unfortunately they were decimated in a secret operation on the back lawn. The enemy secret weapon in the form of my dad's lawnmower caused heavy casualties. There were two survivors but they fought the rest of the war with their heads wedged on with matchsticks and were regarded as only suitable for light duties because their heads kept falling off.

Like all conscientious parents, my mum and dad spent much heart-searching trying to decide whether it was right to give their little Robert warlike toys. Meantime Herr Hitler blew our windows out and I used the lead from the leaded glass to fashion a rudimentary Luger pistol. What I really wanted was a wooden tommy-gun that had a round magazine and made a satisfying clattering noise when you turned a small ratchet. However, only Donald Duxford, the publican's son, acquired one of these. I never really forgave him. Every time I stood up he clattered his tommy-gun at me and I spent most of our war games being dead or wounded or running for cover.

I did recover my position to some degree as the result of some shrewd transactions on the toy market in the playground at school. By selling all my *Beano*s and *Knockout*s and my twenty-niner conker (which had a crack anyway) I was able to acquire a pre-war Woolworth's cap pistol. Of course, I couldn't get any caps but I could make a nasty noise at the back of my throat which was the next best thing.

Of course, Hornby and Meccano were significant names for young boys in those long-ago days but I rather missed out on all that. I was six and eight-twelfths when the war began so I was too young for all but the most junior of the Hornby train sets and far too young to appreciate the joys of Meccano. Building the Forth Bridge with little strips of metal and tiny nuts and bolts like the boy on the box seemed a bit boring to me.

I don't know what Mr Hornby did during the war but he certainly didn't make many toy trains. Perhaps he was building bits for stirrup pumps or gas rattles or Mickey Mouse gas masks. However, at Christmas 1938, it must have been, my Hornby M1 Passenger Set arrived fully boxed. The picture of the Flying Scotsman on the lid did create somewhat unrealisable expectations. Still, it is just as well to learn at an early age never to trust the picture on the box.

Anyway, my train set comprised a green four-wheeled clockwork locomotive with tender, two four-wheeled coaches marked 'Pullman' and an oval of tin plate track. Later on I acquired a cardboard tunnel, a signal, a platelayers' hut and a level crossing. Not that the gates on the level crossing actually opened, but you can't have everything in this world, can you? Later I acquired a Royal Daylight oil tank wagon and a flat truck with an LMS furniture container. The goods wagons proved over-ambitious since I never acquired a siding to put them in.

The train was a bit disappointing too. It hurtled round the track and kept flying off on the place where my dad had trodden on the rail. It used to knock chips off the leg of the dining room table. When I realigned the route it knocked chips off the sideboard instead. The locomotive had a stop and start lever in the cab but once you moved the lever to 'start' it went off like a rocket. The reverse lever was a joke and was only used if you wanted to pile the two coaches into a heap on the hearthrug.

My older brother had a superior train set with a Great Western locomotive that had a brass dome. It also had coaches with doors that really opened. I was not allowed to play with this under threat of serious nastiness. I've never quite forgiven my brother, or the Great Western Railway, for this denial of human rights. Bernard Dawkins had two train sets. They were electric and the locomotives had little electric lights on the front. The Dawkins were a bit like that: real show-offs. It used to take hours just to set it all out. At Christmas 1941 it went all round the Christmas tree, the sofa and the Morrison shelter.

Some time after they sunk the *Scharnhorst* I went into my nautical phase and acquired a number of small grey-painted wooden battleships and minesweepers and destroyers and submarines. Well, actually I only had one of each but this was a military secret. I fought the Battle of the North Atlantic on our front lawn. I left my fleet out one wet and stormy night and the rain dissolved the glue. In the morning my fleet looked like a re-enactment of Pearl Harbour.

Because toys were in such short supply during the war there was much trading and swapping. My trading instincts were not always sound and I was sometimes vulnerable to a persuasive sales pitch. I remember that I acquired half a Wellington bomber's wing in full camouflage, a Southern Railway third-class coach in 4 millimetre scale but without any wheels and a Gauge O clockwork Royal Scot locomotive with a broken spring, no tender and a bent cab. They seemed good investments at the time but they did demand a good deal of imaginative play to get the best out of them.

By the middle of the war the toy situation had become very serious indeed. Most toys were made of scrap wood but even screws, nails and glue were hard to come by. I did have a rather handsome wooden tank but the turret fell off and I never found anything to stick it back on with. In the end I eliminated it with a flame thrower made from a tube of Ronson lighter fuel.

It was still possible to buy a few rather poorly moulded metal soldiers but they were curiously flattened specimens, like silhouettes, to save metal presumably. We used to conduct amphibious landings with them in Calvin Sharp's goldfish pond. The frogs used to become very aggrieved at our interpretation of the Battle of Midway. There's nothing more disconcerting than an angry frog under your landing craft.

Another little friend, Ian McDougal, had several pre-war Dinky Toy tanks. These were used to re-enact the Battle of El Alamein until I knelt on the barbed wire entanglements and drew blood. War is a messy business, isn't it?

During the very worst phase of toy deprivation in about 1943 someone gave me a second-hand box of wooden bricks. When put together they made up a picture of a large 1920s limousine complete with chauffeur. I preferred to use the bricks to build little houses. Then I played air raids and bombed them to bits with the brass handle off our broken poker.

I feel this urge to record for posterity that at one stage I was also the proud owner of a fort. It was made of wood and papier mâché. It could be dismantled and packed away, but here was the rub. The pieces tended to, well, disperse. The drawbridge went first. This was extremely inconvenient for the garrison who were never able to take any leave thereafter. Eventually I was left with only one solitary papier mâché tower with a pinnacle on top. Even my kneeling soldier from the Indian Rifles complete with pith helmet and bent bayonet was unable to perch on it so in the end it disappeared into obscurity. In its place I acquired the 1940s version of fortifications: a model machine-gun emplacement mounted on a square of plywood and comprising an imitation rock, four nails entwined with wire and a small hut with a corrugated cardboard roof painted silver to look like corrugated iron. Not even my Indian Rifleman would fit in the hut, let alone a bloody machine-gun team. That's the trouble with military planners, they never consider the troops.

There were temporary toy enthusiasms. Marbles, for example, but I lost all my large glass alleys in competition and the small ones all ended up down the drains. Then there was five stones, but I lacked the manual dexterity. Worst of all was the dreaded yo-yo craze. I could never make the bloody thing climb up the string again; it seemed unnatural to me. I never actually owned one and the one I borrowed got severely knotted. As for roller skates, pogo sticks, hoops and skipping ropes, I avoided them all like the plague.

There were a few innovatory home-made toys. The best was two bolts secured together with one nut and with two or three red match heads compressed between them. Dropped on the ground this produced a satisfying bang sufficient to convince the ageing citizenry that Jerry was at it again. Then there were the waxed boxes in which the dried egg powder came all the way from the USA (God bless America). When these empty cartons were set alight and hurled high in the air it was like the Battle of Britain in miniature. Little spirals of melting wax flew in all directions like Messerschmidts being shot out of the sky.

At one stage I and a little friend acquired some saltpetre, some sulphur and some iron filings and tried to manufacture some fireworks. The effects were not impressive and the project came to a sudden end when I dropped some molten sulphur down my fingernail and in my panic set George Sodbury's kitchen table alight.

Some misguided relative gave me a board game somewhere around 1942. It had two teams of footballers and a little football all made of primitive wooden shapes. The rules were totally incomprehensible. I threw the board away and used the little wooden figures to conduct the Burma campaign. The football acted as the wicked Japanese commander.

For a while I tried to build model aeroplanes from the kits then available. Again the pictures on the boxes were deceptive. There was this box with a picture of a Spitfire hurtling out of the clouds and firing streams of tracer on an unsuspecting Focke Wolfe 190 and then when you opened the box there were several lumps of balsa wood, a tube of balsa cement, a tin propeller and a blueprint that was totally incomprehensible. I gave up model-making shortly afterwards.

When the war finally ended I was twelve but by the time there were any toys worth having again I was nearer fifteen. Whilst I still yearned for all the toys that I had missed out on this was seen as perverse. 'You're too grown up for Dinky Toys. What do you want them for? You should be concentrating on your homework.' There were all sorts of things that Mr Hitler should have answered for but without doubt one of them was for making me feel guilty about sloping off to buy a surreptitious Dinky Toy GPO van in 1948 just before my mock School Certificate examinations.

Coote's Field

Coote's field has a central and almost mystical place in my childhood memories. It served as the social centre for the more nonconforming and underachieving youth of West Wickham. There was, of course, the Yew Tree Youth Club but none of my associates would have been seen dead there. It was run by a consortium of middle-class Mafia led by the father of Tichy Twyford. Tichy Twyford was clever at everything from Latin to table tennis and Tichy Twyford senior ran the club as a platform for Tichy's unrelenting cleverness. My associates and I preferred Coote's field.

The gathering point in Coote's field was a long-abandoned hundred-gallon water tank. I don't know where it came from originally. It just appeared. Coote's field was like that. It had a sort of magical quality; you never knew what was going to happen next. The hundred-gallon water tank was a bit like the round table except that it was oblong and at the time we knew little of King Arthur and his exploits.

Somewhere around 1943 a four-foot length of two-inch galvanised pipe complete with elbow joint appeared in the field. This, applied with vigour to the side of the water tank produced a most rewarding tribal drum effect. We received a spirited complaint from the old boy in the bungalow next to the field, and he had been as deaf as a post since the First World War.

Someone, many years before, had dumped several loads of clinker in the middle of the field and this, now half covered in coarse grass and thistles, made quite a satisfying assault course especially if we had been chased out of the bombed cottages opposite the Tudor Parade and were looking for other ways to draw blood and risk life and limb.

During the war the Home Guard used Coote's field for their Sunday morning exercises. The best bit was their strange artillery piece towed behind a 1936 Morris Eight. I never saw it fire. I think that they were frightened it might blow up or else no one had given them any cannonballs. Still the rehearsals were good entertainment, better than *Bandwagon* on the wireless. The best bit was when the gallant gunner said 'Bang!' to let everyone know that the exercise had been a success.

At some stage during the war they built a little brick and concrete Air Raid Warden's post in the corner of the field. Later in the war it became a haunt for courting couples. It had few amenities but perhaps if you are doing ARP or courting you are prepared to rough it.

There was a hard-core membership of the Coote's field gang. There was Bill Oddy and Brian Huddle and Ron Cardigan and Norman Frange and Geoff Bragg and me. Others came and went and held associate membership but full voting rights rested with the aforenamed.

Bill Oddy acted as the quartermaster for the gang. He had contacts and know-how and could provide almost anything at a price, no questions asked. He produced, for example, the white paint to paint the cricket stumps on the water tank. You may think this unremarkable but producing white paint and a paint brush in the middle of World War Two required qualities of initiative better suited to the Marine Commandos. I am quite sure that Bill Oddy went far. Probably to Parkhurst.

If you didn't know where else to go or what else to do then it was always a good idea to head for Coote's field. There was usually something going on. Numerous games were in the repertoire of the Coote's field mob but most of them had to be adapted to the very special features of the terrain. Over the years so many loads of rubbish had been dumped in the field and had then slowly become overgrown that the field had the contours of a tank-testing ground. Or a graveyard. Some of the mounds looked distinctly sinister.

One game highly suitable for the terrain was 'Bad Eggs'. This was played with a tennis ball and with every player assigned a number. It had all sorts of desirable features like hurling the ball as high as you could, calling a number, running as far as possible, then indulging in hops, skips, jumps and spits. The exciting culmination to the game was when someone earned three bad eggs and was deemed the loser. This poor unfortunate had to bend over the water tank to suffer the indignity and discomfort of the other players hurling the tennis ball at said loser's bottom. This became particularly interesting when the loser was little Josie Higgins. Poor little Josie often found herself losing to some sort of Coote's field conspiracy and the view of her tightly stretched navy-blue knickers frequently raised the spirits of the other competitors.

At one stage a goat appeared in Coote's field. Like I said, you were never sure what was going to happen next. It did make Bad Eggs difficult to play because the goat could not be dissuaded from trying to have the tennis ball for his afters. Fortunately the goat was not with us very long. He disappeared as rapidly as he had arrived. Poor goat. Goat meat was off the ration I believe. Anyway, I suspect that there was insufficient sustenance in Coote's Field for an animal of his considerable appetite.

We also played 'Kick the Can'. Kick the Can was best played in the twilight. It was a sort of hide-and-seek and release with much cheating and accusations about who had been captured and who had been released. Donald Duxford used to disappear altogether much to the chagrin of the other competitors especially when he was found to be hiding in the shrubbery with Josie Higgins.

The painting of the cricket stumps on the water tank was a major event in the history of Coote's Field. The stumps lead to the creation of Bottle Cricket. Bottle Cricket was devised (a) because there was insufficient flat ground for a full length pitch (b) because we had no cricket ball (Don't you know there's a war on, sonny?) and (c) because we didn't have a cricket bat either. We did have an empty lemonade bottle and a bald tennis ball. Thus Bottle Cricket was born. It had the added virtue that when you had become bored with it and had also become hot and thirsty you could get your tuppence back on the bottle and by clubbing together a further fourpence could share a full bottle of lemonade. The custom of passing the lemonade bottle round for regular swigs until all was gone was part of the Masonic ritual of Coote's Field. Of course, etiquette required that you wiped the bottle with your sleeve before passing it on.

Coote's Field was never known by any other name but we never saw Mr Coote, Mrs Coote, or indeed any little Cootes. Perhaps they had all been evacuated to Chipping Norton or maybe they had been blown up by a landmine. Despite the absence of any Cootes flapping about we knew that someone must be in control. Remember, however, that we were children of the Blitz and had been brought up to be surprised at nothing and to expect a smack round the ear for asking awkward questions. Anyway, we used to just assume that anything odd that happened was something to do with the war and leave it at that. Sometimes the field was used to store things or to dump things but this only added to the magic. We treated it all as a contribution to our adventure playground and assumed that it was all available for our use.

Geoff Bragg worked as a delivery boy for Handley's the grocers and sometimes used the field as a short cut on his delivery bike. He paid his dues however and occasionally dropped off an illicit can of baked beans as he passed. These, with half-raw potatoes cooked over a camp fire provided us with highly indigestible refreshment breaks.

During the Blitz they set up a static water tank at the far end of the field but we never found much use for this so we were inclined to ignore it. I suppose that we could have swum in it but there were some very mysterious things lurking in the bottom and the pong was a bit pungent, particularly in the hot weather. We did try sailing model boats in it but they used to drift into the middle and become becalmed so there was little future in that.

The shrubbery in the far corner was probably the best value: ideal for hiding during games of Kick the Can or as a place for trying to persuade Josie Higgins to play Doctors and Nurses.

Originally there was a large timber hut in one corner of the field but providence (gale or bomb blast, I remember not which) blew it away. This enabled us to have a useful concrete base for hopscotch or anatomically correct drawings made with large lumps of chalk that Bill Oddy nicked from a local quarry.

In the topmost corner was the Old Hut Café (good pull-up for carmen, the notice in Station Road said.) The footpath that cut diagonally across the field gave access to the rear entrance to the Hut Café and also to the static water tank and to the bus stop in Station Road – if you were of an adventurous disposition that is. The Home Guard had dug a slit trench up there in 1941 although why they were prepared to defend the Western Approaches to the Hut Café to the death is beyond me.

Coote's Field also served as a sort of Woomera, a test site for our experiments with home-made fireworks and our innovative experiments with calcium carbide. If you have never experienced naked fear then you never saw what Bill Oddy could do with half a pound of calcium carbide and a couple of old milk bottles.

There was no doubt that Coote's field had a mystical quality about it. Once the field was closed up with barbed wire but if ghostly hands had been at work they were very ineffectual because we made short work of those obstacles to our single-minded pursuit of pleasure and leisure. Once, a load of timber arrived mysteriously and was stacked in one corner. At first we were affronted because it covered our hopscotch area but then we realised that it gave new opportunities for mountain-climbing exercises. In the end we were quite cross when it disappeared as suddenly as it had arrived. Not before, I am sad to relate, Bill Oddy had nicked several good lengths of six by four to use for the main frames of the soapbox carts he was building for sale or hire.

Of course, the times of which I write are now ancient history. Coote's field has long disappeared under the urban sprawl of Greater London. They built a swimming bath on the site in the early 1970s and swept away the last vestiges of our assault course and the shrubbery and all that I have described. I doubt however that municipal water sports provide any greater fun than bottle cricket. Still, if you do visit the baths and if you are of imaginative disposition and listen really hard you may still hear some ghostly voice from the past muttering, 'It's not bloody well fair. I wasn't out and anyway I'm taking my ball home now. So yah boo sucks to you all.'

Summer Holiday – 1944

These days people seem to be desperate to find more and more exotic places to spend their summer hols. During the war the choice was a bit more limited. The only people who saw any sand were the Eighth Army. However, I thought that I might enthrall you with my description of a wartime summer holiday. In fact, it was the only holiday I had during the war since I didn't even get evacuated.

I suppose that any holiday in the middle of a world war is likely to be a bit weird. Still, looking on the bright side, I won't be showing you my snapshots since you couldn't get any film at the time. If you had walked around with a camera during the war they would probably have shot you as a spy.

It was in July 1944 that my father announced that we were going to have a week's holiday in Newbury forthwith. There was no consultation or discussion and there were no holiday brochures to study. I must have been about eleven at the time. I don't really know why we went to Newbury but I have one or two theories. Well, three actually: (a) it would give us a break from the Doodlebugs, most of which seemed to be routed over our home in West Wickham; (b) you weren't allowed to go to the seaside because of the barbed wire and the landmines; and (c) the digs were recommended by a friend of my father's and he probably got a discount.

These days, of course, a holiday in Newbury would be regarded as a bit boring but if you hadn't had a holiday since 1939 and during that time had never travelled much more than about five miles from home you will appreciate it was a bit of an event. ('Is your journey really necessary?' the posters used to ask.)

The journey itself passed in a bit of a blur. We had only got about six miles up the line to Lewisham on the electric train when the siren went. South London was copping all the Doodlebugs at the time so we were glad that the train driver didn't hang about. In fact, it is not an exaggeration to say that his acceleration was extremely brisk and we reached Charing Cross ahead of time.

I can't remember anything about the train journey out west from Paddington which is a bit sad because it was the only time I ever travelled on the Great Western Railway before they nationalised it. I understand that before the war the GWR livery was a rather romantic chocolate and cream but during the war all train liveries were a sooty grey with rust streaks.

In those distant days Newbury station was a busy junction and you could get to all sorts of places. These days, of course, it is best known as a place where most trains don't bother to stop on their way to somewhere worth going to.

Our digs turned out to be a tall Victorian terraced house just off the Andover road. The best that could be said about the accommodation was that it was homely. Of course, we had to take our identity cards and ration books with us and also our own soap and towels. Our landlady thoughtfully provided toilet paper although this consisted of small squares of the *Daily Mail* threaded on a string. It was generally considered unpatriotic to use more than five pieces.

In the early summer of 1944 Newbury was in a bit of a turmoil. It was jam-packed with American troops waiting to move off to Normandy and the roads were full of lorries and tank transporters and other military hardware. To a small boy it was blissful. All this transport was directed by American military policemen who wore white belts and gaiters and roared about on noisy Harley-Davidsons or bounced about in jeeps. They herded the traffic with all the panache of the cowboys I had seen at the Plaza cinema.

When I wanted a change from watching the troop convoys I went down to the station and hung over the railway bridge. I had never seen so many steam trains before. At home our trains were mostly Southern Electrics with just a solitary steam engine on a goods train a couple of times a day. But at Newbury there were enormous Great Western express locomotives pounding through and goods trains of prodigious length hauled by large grimy many-wheeled locomotives puffing about in all directions and a goods yard with a little tank engine that never stopped pottering about. The station seemed to be permanently busy and the stopping trains were constantly disgorging and ingesting hordes of passengers, mostly servicemen loaded down with kitbags and military paraphernalia.

At age eleven and not being widely travelled, everything was an adventure and a new experience. For some reason we caught a train to Lambourne. This was when trains still went to Lambourne. It was a most unusual train. It was neither electric nor steam. It was a single coach pointed at both ends and it made a noise like a bus. The driver had to change gear and could be observed at work in his little driver's cab. I can't remember what we did when we got to Lambourne. I expect that we got on the train and came back again.

They were holding a Spitfire Week in the park in Newbury whilst we were there. The main feature was an American Army band, a netball match between the ATS and the American soldiers and a tour round a Horsa glider. The Horsa glider was a bit of a swizz. It was made of tubular metal covered in canvas. No wonder the airborne troops won medals. I would rather have gone to war in a cardboard box.

The whole fund-raising event was rather boring. Personally I preferred watching the army convoys. The participants in the netball match seemed to have a good time although I wasn't convinced that all that hugging and squeezing was strictly necessary.

The family we stayed with had a rabbit with whom I became very friendly. I came to the conclusion that he was the best part of the holiday. He was a very amiable rabbit and had long ears, big eyes and a soft nose that never stopped sniffling. I had never met a rabbit before. He was very partial to being hand fed lettuce leaves I remember. Then one day my new friend was not in his hutch. They told me that he had been rushed to hospital for an operation but I was not convinced and I couldn't eat dinner that day. All of a sudden rabbit stew had lost its charms. Gradually it dawned on me that during the war people who kept rabbits just couldn't be trusted.

All in all it was an educative week but it was quickly over and it was more than fifty years before I saw Newbury again. And then I wished I hadn't bothered. In some ways it was a relief to get back home to the Doodlebugs. There was something reassuringly familiar about them and I had never been one of an adventurous disposition.

The Entrepreneurial Spirit

I have always envied innovators, exploiters, opportunists, market manipulators, speculators, captains of industry and entrepreneurs. Through the media I gain vicarious excitement from each new commercial success story. Exciting too are the occasional plunges into penury which leave some poor tycoon down to his last Rolls Royce and forced to sell his ocean-going power boat and his personalised helicopter.

My own efforts to achieve commercial fame and fortune may seem somewhat puny by comparison but as a beginner I tried to be sensitive to the vagaries of the market and to take those few opportunities that came my way. The traditional ways for a young lad to earn a copper or two were denied me. I couldn't be a choirboy (voice like a frog with laryngitis) or even a newspaper boy (not considered respectable in Edom family circles at the time – what will the neighbours say and besides who would get me up?).

My first commercial opportunity came at junior school where I went into partnership with Tony Lubbock in the mass production of paper cut-out models of Centurion tanks, landing barges, armoured cars and similar military transport, all carefully crayoned with appropriate camouflage and insignias. Appropriate, that is, if they were brown, green or blue because they were the only crayons we had. (The manufacture of children's crayons was not as high a priority as we would have wished but we regarded this as just one more of those wartime little inconveniences like lentil cutlets and dried split peas.)

Anyway, we charged a penny or tuppence each for our paper creations and the demand was not inconsiderable. Despite our success in identifying this window of opportunity we had to abandon our Flying Fortress model because the wings tended to curl up so that they looked more like camouflaged seagulls with machine-gun turrets. Still all our other models were very successful and in great demand.

We exploited the market further by producing models of increasing sophistication and began to charge threepence each for our deluxe range that included the landing barge with a ramp that came down. At this stage our revered headmistress Mrs Sergeant (headmistress and proprietress of Burton House School for Boys and Girls, aged five to eleven in brackets) intervened. What would the parents of our customers say when they discovered that we were extracting such vast sums from their offspring? Apparently she didn't dare to think. 'They are only bits of paper after all,' she snorted in her usual dismissive way. We felt aggrieved. Our utility crayons were worn down to stubs, our patriotic creations were being belittled and we were to be denied the profits from our creative ingenuity and our labours. Not the last time, I think, that the dead hand of government was to stifle private enterprise and the free market economy.

Hitler's Doodlebugs gave me my next opportunity to fill an unmet need. It must have been in the school summer holiday of 1944 when there was often a perpetual air raid alert and Doodlebugs arrived erratically throughout the day rather like the 194 buses (Forest Hill Station to Croydon via West Wickham and no spitting by order).

I used to perch on the top of our air raid shelter and shout a warning to our neighbours when I heard the approaching snarl of the next V1. Number four gave me a shilling after my first day's duty and number ten contributed sixpence and a packet of off-the-ration Horlicks tablets. Old Mrs Fitch at number six let me down rather badly. She was as deaf as a post and contributed nothing at all. If they had dropped a landmine in her front garden she would probably have thought that it was only the dustman. When I shouted and waved from my vantage point to indicate that death and destruction was imminent she just waved back cheerily and went on hanging out her washing. Her drawers, I recall to this day, could only be described as voluminous like barrage balloons.

Nepotism played little part in my entrepreneurial activities. Mr Edom senior was organist and choirmaster at our local church. (C of E of course, there being nothing unorthodox about the Edoms.) Sadly, my father was not prepared to put his musical reputation on the line by giving me any share of the action. However, once, in desperation when his regular organ pumper went sick, I was enlisted to provide wind for the church organ during a wedding. My plea that the standard fee of half a crown should be augmented by a small bonus to compensate for the Doodlebug raid that was going on at the time was arbitrarily dismissed and I was never asked to perform an encore.

Then there was my brief career in pornography or what passed for pornography in those long gone prudish days when, if I had heard of fellatio, I would have thought that it was the name of an obscure Italian general. For a small investment I acquired a somewhat mutilated, much-thumbed copy of *Health and Efficiency* and showed the busty lady on page fourteen to any little school chum who could be persuaded to contribute one penny to the Edom Benevolent Fund. It was a bit of a swizz really; the busty lady's nipples had been airbrushed out of existence and she was posing behind what looked like a gooseberry bush so that there was not a single pubic hair in sight. From my limited experience I can only assume that prior to about 1950 ladies' pubic hair did not exist – not in *Health and Efficiency* anyway.

I also worked the second-hand comic market for a while but business was never better than sluggish. *Hotspur*s and *Wizard*s moved well enough but *Adventure*s and *Champion*s were a bit of a struggle. Personally I rather liked Rockfist Rogan but I suppose that he must have been an acquired taste (rather like dried egg omelette). *Beano*s, *Dandie*s and *Knockout*s were extremely tricky to shift and you had to find a rather specialised market for *Film Fun*s and *Radio Fun*s. As for my *Sexton Blake Library*, these were a glut on the market much to my chagrin. You couldn't even sell them to a first-former using threats of Chinese burns or grass cuttings up the trouser legs. I think that Dick Barton on the wireless finally put paid to Sexton Blake... I wonder what happened to Tinker, his assistant. With a name like that his hopes of a second career couldn't have been high. Anyway, the second-hand comic market wasn't worth all the trauma and effort and since I split my satchel with the weight of all the comics and missed all the playground football to boot (forgive the pun, I couldn't resist it), this particular enterprise was not to survive all that long.

The luggage delivery service was an interesting example of a nicely timed new service industry. In 1947 the great British public was ready to resume holidays again after a long and mostly holidayless war. Mr Attlee promptly announced that he was going to nationalise the railways and some obscure Labour politician declared that this would mean coal fires and comfortable wicker chairs in every railway waiting room. All the train services were immediately cut because there was a coal shortage and I never did see a coal fire or indeed a single wicker chair in West Wickham station. Apart from anything else the waiting room on the down side had been obliterated by a

250 lb. bomb in 1940. Undeterred by all this, the residents of West Wickham went off on their hols. They nearly all used the railway since hardly anyone had a car and anyway there was a petrol shortage as well. When they returned looking pink and clutching large quantities of luggage we leapt into action to transport their luggage from station to home.

It was Bill Oddy's expertise that made it all possible. He had this obsession with soapbox carts. He almost had a production line at one stage and would supply custom-built models for his cronies – if the price was right. The principles of construction were well established: a main beam of six by four, two cross beams for the axles, two pairs of old pram wheels, a bolt to pivot the front axle, a piece of rope to steer with, a soapbox for the coachwork and a quantity of miscellaneous nails pinched from his uncle's toolbox to hold it all together.

With this sort of transport all sorts of entrepreneurial activities were possible. When I first met Bill Oddy he was heavily into collecting and redistributing horse manure but I persuaded him to diversify and we set up the luggage delivery service. Of course, you had to be a bit discreet, a bit like an undertaker – servile and unobtrusive. No returning holidaymaker wanted to be accompanied home by two scruffs hauling their luggage in an old cart, especially if it was the one that still had bits of dried horse manure adhering to it. So we had to walk a respectful distance at the rear but not so distant as to engender anxiety that we might abscond with their fortnight's dirty washing and damp swimming suits.

We positively coined it in for a couple of months. There were no taxis to be had at West Wickham station so it was use the luggage delivery service or hump it up the station approach yourself. The going rate for a delivery was about sixpence a trip although some meanies would make you haul their luggage all the way up Springhurst Avenue and then only give you fourpence. Still, you had to take the rough with the smooth, or so Bill Oddy sententiously declared.

Then disaster struck in a series of what seemed like malevolent blows. First, our reserve truck came to a disastrous end during a sporting run down Corkscrew Hill, and then the back wheel of the flagship of our fleet finally collapsed under a particularly heavy load – a trunk and two suitcases returning from two weeks in Swanage, I think it may have been. The wheel buckled and the tyre came off. Finally, the unthinkable happened: Bill Oddy's seemingly inexhaustible supply of old pram wheels came to an end and no amount of cannibalising could recover the position. A cart with four different-sized wheels is not a viable transport facility, particularly when two of them are buckled.

But Bill Oddy had other irons in the fire. He had a concession on treasure trove at the Council tip at Hayes although he never offered me a partnership in this particular enterprise. He knew where they tipped the sludge from the drain-cleaning lorry and by careful sifting he could extract all the marbles that had fallen down the street drains throughout the Borough of Beckenham. A quick wash in a bucket of cold water and they were marketable again and Bill made steady profits, particularly from the big pre-war glass alleys with the whorled coloured insides which were much in demand.

Bill also had an unofficial arrangement with the golf professional at Langley Park Golf Club. Bill would patrol the rough of the golf course with all the expertise of a truffle hound and he could sniff out lost golf balls in rich profusion. He used to sell them to the golf professional who no doubt had an assured market for them. Bill could get half a crown for a mint Dunlop 65. I became Bill's apprentice in the golf ball recovery business but I finally gave up my indentures when in a panic I realised that sometimes, in his enthusiasm no doubt, Bill was finding the balls before anyone had lost them. One of them, I recall, he recovered when it was within a short putt of the ninth hole and only our fleetness of foot and our knowledge of the terrain saved us from the vengeance of an enraged golfer.

Bill was the very stuff of which true entrepreneurs are made. I would have expected him to have made his mark in the competitive post-war world but he seems to have been lost without trace. Every time I find a twenty-ton gravel lorry bearing down on me I half expect to see the inscription 'Oddy's Haulage' or 'Wm Oddy Transport Enterprises' but it is never so. Whatever happened to the rich promise of the young Bill Oddy?

Another example of commercial opportunity was that rather embarrassing incident in the one and threes at the Plaza in about 1946 when a rather seedy-looking gentleman in a distinctly shabby raincoat sat next to me and suggested with some persistence a way of considerably augmenting my pocket money. Whilst I recognised that this could have been a window of commercial opportunity it was one that I decided was better left firmly closed. The seedy gentleman shuffled off to put his business proposition elsewhere.

Mrs Frange had the contract for the provision of teas for the West Wickham Cricket Club. She prepared all the sandwiches in advance but on Saturday evenings she liked to adjourn to the Wheatsheaf with Mr Frange for several gin and oranges as a prelude to their Saturday night connubial rituals. In consequence she delegated responsibility for serving the sandwiches, brewing the tea and washing up to her son Norman. What she received for the contract was regarded as commercially sensitive information but Norman received five bob and split this fifty-fifty with me.

It wasn't a bad job as jobs go and it had certain fringe benefits. We got to eat up all the stale sandwiches and Mary Waggett, the daughter of the first wicket down, used to hang around to entertain us whilst we washed up. Mary was a stringy flat-chested but sex-crazed girl about whom I was extremely ambivalent. Her legs were the same diameter all the way up, like bean poles in fact, and even the closest scrutiny could scarcely identify her bosoms. Nature compensated, however, by granting her a fantastic repertoire of sexy innuendo which threw me into great confusion and made my ears go pink. Whilst I was still trying to work out how to react, Norman, ever the opportunist, had usually coaxed her out of the back door whilst I was left washing up the last of the cress sandwich plates and wondering what they were doing somewhere round the back of the heavy roller.

Anyway, the whole enterprise, perks and all, came to an abrupt end when one afternoon Norman and I conducted a weightlifting competition with a small barrel of best bitter. This, according to the barman Peg-Leg Sam, seriously disturbed the sediment. Disturbing the sediment of the West Wickham Cricket Club's Saturday evening best bitter was a heinous offence, worse even than standing in front of the sight screen. It was, we discovered, punishable by immediate termination of contract. There was no industrial tribunal to appeal to in 1948 and if there had been, knowing my luck, I expect that they would all have been devoted best bitter drinkers.

That's about it really. I rather gave up on entrepreneurial activity after that. If you have ever wondered why the *Financial Times* never features an in-depth article about the commercial achievements of Robert Edom, the foregoing may give you some sort of rationale for this unfortunate and conspicuous omission.

Mac the Barber

I have always found having my hair cut a bit of a pain. When I was small our neighbour's son was training to be a hairdresser and on one or two memorable occasions my parents allowed him to practise on me. Fred Cutler did his best but in my view it was not enough. He used a pair of hand clippers that gave you a little nip when you were least expecting it and occasionally tugged a tuft of hair out by the roots. Fred was nothing if not enthusiastic. He would snip away like crazy and hair would fly about in all directions. Much of it seemed to go in my ears, up my nose, in my mouth and down my neck.

Eventually I rebelled and was allowed to attend the hairdressers in the Tudor Parade. The men's department was entirely separate from the ladies' salon. This was in about 1943 and there was none of this ambiguous his and hers nonsense in those days. Men's hairdressers were very masculine establishments with discreet advertisements for Durex and conversation that consisted of football or cricket according to season.

The window of the men's side of the hairdressers was adorned with two aerial views of Dennis Compton's head showing highly glossy, Brylcreemed hair and a parting as straight as a Roman road. The outside of the establishment also had the mandatory red and white striped pole although its significance was happily lost on me at the time.

Inside the men's department was bare lino with a heap of multicoloured clippings swept up in the corner. It was a small steamy room but it did have a few amenities. There were six coat hooks on the wall and five bentwood chairs crammed tightly together along one side for the waiting patrons. If there were more than five waiting you leaned against the wall. On a table in front of the chairs was a stack of well thumbed *Picture Post*s and *Illustrated*s and the occasional copy of *Lilliput* or *Blighty* if you were lucky.

On a Saturday morning every fortnight I attended for my short back and sides. When I first attended I had to sit on a plank placed across the arms of the barber's chair but eventually I was tall enough to avoid this humiliation.

There were actually two barber's chairs and two mirrors and two sets of equipment but usually only one hairdresser. The chairs were wooden with leather seats padded with horsehair. Other equipment included a chromium-plated gas-fired device that made a gentle sizzling noise and produced hot towels and contributed to the steamy atmosphere.

Big Mac, the resident hairdresser, was, as you might have guessed, a large Scot. There was normally quite a long wait for his services since there were usually, at the very least, three or four customers waiting. You had to be careful to remember who was there when you arrived and who came after you because there was always some clever clogs trying to jump the queue. It never occurred to Big Mac to have an appointment system like the ladies' department and he seemed to take pride in how many were waiting for his attention.

When your turn came there was a theoretical discussion about how you wanted your hair cut but Big Mac only recognised one style which was short back and sides and a bit off the top.

Big Mac generally used hand clippers but occasionally he produced an electric pair which made a harsh rattling noise and reminded me of a film I had seen about sheep shearers in the outback. Big Mac used a cut-throat razor to tidy the stray hairs from the back of your neck and when he stropped the razor on his leather razor strop it made my teeth all on edge.

At the end of all this he would show you the back of your neck in the mirror for approval. Woe betide you if you did not express total satisfaction. Then finally you were offered brilliantine and a strange-smelling spray. You could get away with only one but certainly not with neither. The older men were also asked if they needed anything else for the weekend and packets of Durex and half crowns were surreptitiously exchanged. Young unmarrieds were not offered this service.

I was never entirely at ease with Big Mac. I think he had been in the Navy and you know what they say about sailors. Apart from his rather intimidatory use of a cut-throat razor there was something too manly to be true about his persona and his establishment and I was never sorry when the moment came to pay up, with mandatory sixpenny tip, and depart.

The best part of each visit was a chance to read the *Picture Post*. Much of my knowledge of post-war current affairs came from the *Picture Post*. I was never quite so keen on the *Illustrated* but a furtive glance at the photo of the nude lady in the middle pages of *Lilliput* was a bit of a bonus. *Blighty* was also very popular but you had to wait your turn for a look at that. I remember that it had lots of cartoons that involved leggy ladies with skimpy blouses and well developed bosoms.

Of course, these days there is no option but to attend a his and hers hairdressers where they drape a floral pinny round you and you look at yourself in a gilt mirror but on balance I think I would still prefer Big Mac's establishment. But only just.

The Blake Recreation Ground

The Blake Recreation Ground played a very significant part
in my teenage years during the late 1940s. In those days
other social venues in West Wickham were somewhat
limited. I always felt that my knees were too knobbly for
the Boy Scouts and as for the Yew Tree Youth Club, this
was out of the question. It was run by a middle-class Mafia
led by Tichy Twyford's dad. I and my scruffy mates would
have been blackballed without hesitation.

Although the Blake Recreation Ground was so important to me it was not until half a century later that I
discovered that it was named in honour of a leading light
on the Beckenham Borough Council. You must be very
important to get a recreation ground named after you. It
even had ladies' and gents' toilets and during the war an air
raid shelter and allotments as well.

I used to be on terms of moderate intimacy with Albert,
the head keeper of the Blake Recreation Ground. Come to
think of it, so far as I can recall, he was the only keeper.
Single manning, it seems, came considerably earlier to the
Beckenham Borough Council than to British Railways.
Albert would occasionally hold court in his groundsman's
hut and in my circles an invitation to join him had all the
social cachet of an invitation to a Buckingham Palace
garden party.

Albert brewed tea in an old enamel saucepan and
reinforced it with sticky sweet condensed milk from a tin.
Tea was not usually provided for visitors but occasionally

he would offer me a cup. It was a mixed blessing; surreptitiously spitting out the tea leaves was quite difficult especially since Albert slurped the lot with relish, grouts and all.

Seating was sparse in Albert's hut and I usually found a perch on a broken park bench. A strategically placed cricket pad minimised the pain. We sat, he in his rickety deckchair, me on my cricket pad, surrounded by the equipment of his trade: a large motor mower, oozing oil and petrol fumes, the nets for the football pitch and a motley collection of bats and balls that he loaned to us on occasions when we sought athletic pursuits.

My conversations with Albert were wide-ranging and educative. Albert's main dislikes were the entire staff of the Town Hall, our local MP (a Conservative with a 23,000 majority) and any lady who let her poodle poop on his cricket square.

Albert was a north-countryman and I never discovered how he ended up in West Wickham. I expect that it was the war. In those immediate post-war days anything inexplicable was blamed on the war. I found his candid and pithy views on human behaviour quite comforting and he even helped me to keep my sense of proportion about my English master, who was the current, sarcastic and irascible cross that I had to bear. Albert couldn't take seriously anyone who threw the chalk at you with bulletlike velocity just because you couldn't remember what came after 'Earth has not anything to show more fair...'

It made me feel very grown up to listen to Albert's sardonic observations delivered in his northern accent. Up to then the only northern accent I had heard was Wilfred Pickles in *Have a Go* and he had no sense of humour at all.

Albert enlarged my knowledge in curious directions. His brother, he told me, was suffering from a rodent ulcer. He pronounced it roaaa-dent and made it sound very nasty indeed. It was gnawing its way into Albert's poor brother. Apparently there was no cure and the doctors had given up. It was my first encounter with diseases that attack you like fierce, sharp-teethed little animals. It wasn't the sort of thing that you learned about from the *Wizard* or the *Hotspur*. They were more disposed to give snippets of information about the weight of the steel in the Forth Bridge or how if all the railway sleepers in the country were placed end to end they would reach three-quarters of the way to the moon. This was at a time when the moon was still an improbable destination for anyone – except Flash Gordon.

Albert taught me lots of other things. Like how to bind a split cricket bat and how to operate the clanking little machine that he used to mark out the football pitch and how to fill in a Littlewoods football coupon.

In his gruff and taciturn way I think that Albert had a soft spot for me. Apart from the man in the hairdressers, about whom I had my suspicions, he was the only adult who showed much interest in me. It was reflected in the way in which he would usually find a still spherical cricket ball for me to borrow in the cricket season or a football that didn't deflate on impact for our winter kick-abouts.

In those austerity days sports equipment was well worn and hard to come by. Cricket balls, for example, were made of compressed cork and tended to crumble with use so that one could produce some fairly spectacular leg-breaks with a suitably worn composition ball. When proper leather balls returned again some of us felt completely de-skilled.

In about 1948 the Council introduced a Games Warden who was supposed to encourage the local youth to aspire to great sporting achievements. The local youth were unimpressed and apart from organising a curious game that was a cross between football and tennis his impact was marginal. Albert was particularly dismissive when he discovered that the Games Warden was not going to help with marking out the pitches. 'Lazy bugger!' was his assessment.

Albert had a set of rules that were quite distinct from the long list of bye-laws on the notice board at the entrance to the Rec. No one read the bye-laws but everyone was pretty clear about Albert's laws: No girls in the hut when he wasn't there (and not very often when he was). No balls to be kicked, hit, bowled or thrown at the tennis court fence. (It was in an advanced state of decay and wire fencing was still not obtainable. Nothing got the man in the Town Hall in more of a tizzy than the appearance of yet another hole in the tennis court fence, said Albert.) No hard balls to be used near the kiddies' playground and, most important of all, no hanky-panky in the Rec.

It was an implicit rule that if the skylarking between the genders became too purposeful and likely to disturb the ratepayers, then the parties concerned would leave the Rec and head for Langley Park golf course. It wasn't that the golfers were more tolerant, just that Langley Park was famous for its rough and was heavily wooded. Thus an invitation to your intended to 'come for a walk across the golf course' had connotations that in later more sophisticated days were encapsulated in phrases like 'come back to my place for a cup of coffee'.

There is no doubt that the Blake Recreation Ground played an important part in my social education during adolescence but I find it necessary to write carefully. Sadly, as we grow older we seem to have great difficulty in acknowledging the urges and indiscretions of our youth. It could be, of course, that my own little social circle was so abnormal that it does not mirror the amorous interests and activities of other respectable citizens during their teenage years. I doubt it, however. Cast your mind back to your own youth – if you dare.

114

The Rec was full of characters and it was our regular meeting place, a sort of teenage Athenaeum Club. There was always someone there whom I knew and who would tell a joke (invariably obscene), kick a ball about, share a drag on a Woodbine or discuss the relative merits of Norton, Triumph, AJS or Ariel. Foreigners did not make motorcycles in those days, or if they did we had never heard of them. We would have thought that Yamaha was a ju-jitsu throw or something you did with a geisha girl. (Ju-jitsu and geisha girls we had heard of.)

Daft Jim was usually in the Rec. He was a lank-haired, dark-eyed giant of a lad, gentle and naive and about as bright as a Toc-H lamp. In the way of the world he was teased unmercifully, not that Daft Jim seemed to notice. Anything less than a four-pound hammer on the skull was likely to elude him.

Daft Jim was an amiable soul without an ounce of malice in him but he had a very literal turn of mind and subtlety was lost on him. He longed to impress the local girls. (But then, didn't we all?) He was also singularly proud of his phallus (with good reason, for nature had been generous to him in this respect at least). At the slightest encouragement he would display it rather like a gardener showing off his prize cucumber, sometimes at highly unsuitable moments. Daft Jim running round the Rec with his large member on display was not a sight for the faint-hearted. It had been known to bring a cup match of the West Wickham Wanderers to a complete standstill.

On long summer evenings a crowd of us would usually gather in the Rec. Most times we would fool around with a tennis ball or a football. With luck some of the local girls could be persuaded to join in some ill co-ordinated piggy in the middle type game. This would give opportunities for much chasing, grappling, groping, falling over and lying on top of activity. As the light began to fade we would flop down under the trees and recover our breath. There would be community singing. 'Roll Me Over in the Clover' was a great favourite, as were local variations of 'Colonel Bogey'. There was also one that began, 'Ain't it a pity she's only one titty to feed the baby on,' but the rest of the words escape me. Then there was that old favourite, 'Christmas Day in the Workhouse'. I am sure you know the words. Between songs there was much backchat and rolling about whilst the boys cast lecherous glances at the girls and the girls feigned indifference.

We were a sex-besotted lot at that time and Daft Jim was just more simplistic in his approach than the rest of us. Poor Daft Jim. I am glad to report that despite his lack of grey matter he eventually obtained a job with the Water Board and dug holes all over West Wickham. I like to think that Daft Jim ended up in charge of his own team of hole-diggers and pipe-layers. It would be all the same to Daft Jim. He had no airs or graces.

In later years, I learned about Maslow's Hierarchy of Needs. Put simply it propounds that man is a wanting animal and that as soon as one need is met he seeks to achieve the next. It holds, however, that until basic needs are met he is unlikely to give much attention to higher thoughts. Maslow defined the basic needs as food, rest, shelter and sex. Satisfied more or less on three of the four counts, you have an interesting theoretical base to explain why we were such a randy lot. If you don't approve, write to Mr Maslow.

Norman Frange was experienced. He had recently moved from the poorer part of Penge where they seemed to get down to basics at an earlier age. He had very high status in our group because he had a girlfriend in East Penge who allowed heavy petting. His descriptions were much more graphic. I would have said pornographic but I was unfamiliar with the word at the time and if I had heard it I would have probably thought that it was a new photo-graphic process.

Anyway Norman knew all about these things and he was pleased to enlighten us. We hung on his every word. Unfortunately, it seemed that the maidens of West Wickham were more cautious than their counterparts in East Penge. Perhaps the outer suburbs have a suppressant effect on the female hormones. I longed to emulate Norman but didn't know how to start. I had no hope of actually doing it, you understand – that was beyond my wildest dreams – but just, as it were, to get within striking distance.

I did manage to persuade little Sarah Jacobs to go for a walk over the golf course with me. It turned out that she kissed like an enraged ferret and had a penchant for being bent backwards to be kissed like Clark Gable did it. I was allowed to grope her pert little bosoms but my attempts to venture beneath her skirt were repulsed. She hinted that next time it might be different but by then I had lost my nerve. There was no next time. She was rather ugly anyway and I couldn't face a repetition of all that biting and back pain and the ridicule of my mates if the mission proved a failure yet again.

Back in the Blake Recreation Ground the youth of West Wickham spent hours in serious deliberation and debate. The North Koreans had crossed the 38th Parallel, the bacon ration had been increased from four to five ounces, Attlee had a majority of only six and Klaus Fuchs was on trial. There was little discussion about such subjects amongst the cognoscenti of West Wickham youth. There was considerable interest, however, in one international issue. Was Jane Russell really in the noddy when she climbed into bed with that lucky cowboy in the film *The Outlaw*?

Maslow's theories were vindicated by the subject matter

of our conversations: Pamela Ashwell, it was alleged, would kiss you in the most original ways, whilst Maureen Glumm, it was rumoured, would, if she took a fancy to you, permit liberties that closely approximated to the real thing. Some of these claims sounded both improbable and uncomfortable but it was not done to question the local mythology.

Norman Frange would join the group later after his evening foray to East Penge. He would provide a detailed report on how he had spent the evening. He would proudly explain his technique to an attentive and respectful audience. Paraphrased and much abbreviated it consisted of lots of kissing and neck-nuzzling and protestations of love accompanied by persistent stroking. Persistent stroking was the key, in Norman's view. The critical zone, he explained, was the inside of the thigh. It was, I understood, like crossing the Rubicon. Chance, I thought, would be a fine thing. At that stage in my life I only had two ambitions. One was to earn five hundred a year, the other to cross the Rubicon. The likelihood of either seemed remote. Norman also gave us a detailed description of what we could expect to find when we crossed the Rubicon and his analogies were certainly inventive.

Our study group spent a lot of time telling jokes as well. They were rather torturous affairs, mostly about ladies of easy virtue, commercial travellers, farmers' daughters and nancy boys. Gay was still an expression reserved to describe the West Wickham Operatic Society's presentation of *The Pirates of Penzance*.

Then I met Mary Whitley. She was fair-haired and pretty and had magnificent bosoms for a fifteen year old. I was astounded to discover that she quite favoured me. I have no idea why. I usually went pink when in the company of a strange girl and could never think of anything to say. It was a curious courtship. Mary wanted to be loved and cherished and I wanted her body. I regret to say that my adolescent urges made me see her more as a challenge than a companion. Don't blame me. Blame it on human nature and Maslow. I expect that Freud had something to do with it as well. He usually has.

I did eventually cross the Rubicon with Mary Whitley. In conformity with Albert's requirements the event took place in a field of long grass on the edge of the Langley Park golf course.

I suppose that it could be said to mark my graduation from the nursery slopes of the Blake Recreation Ground.

I wonder what happened to Mary Whitley? She must be drawing her pension by now. As for poor old Albert, the head keeper, I expect that he went to join his unfortunate brother (he of roaaaa-dent ulcer fame) many a long year ago.

The 'H' Stream

My admission to the Ravensbeck Grammar School for Boys in 1944 came as rather a surprise, particularly since my father, even in his most sanguine moments, regarded me as something of an educational disaster area and expected me to end up at the Hawes Lane Council School where the boys all wore boots, punched hell out of each other and swore like the Pioneer Corps.

Although I passed the entrance examination I was not deemed to be scholarship material and my father had to pay a grudging four guineas a term for my education at Ravensbeck. That is until the 1944 Education Act relieved him of that particular burden. Education then became free although my own view was that they ought to have paid me handsomely to attend Ravensbeck Grammar School for Boys.

According to my reading of the *Magnet* and the *Gem* scholarship boys were supposed to be looked down upon but it was just my luck that at Ravensbeck the situation was reversed. It was the unscholarshipped who were patronised, although in an egalitarian society, why either a birthright of wealth or intelligence should be regarded as a virtue was beyond my comprehension, particularly since my own inheritance on both counts was somewhat frugal.

I always felt that Ravensbeck Grammar School was a microcosm of society, although when I was in Form 2H I might have put it somewhat differently. Form 2H was a case in point. It reflected the proletariat of the wider world, the heavy residue that had dropped through the sparkling waters of intellectual society and was lurking at the bottom of the bucket.

In the first year at Ravensbeck we were allocated to our forms according to our performance in the entrance examination. Here the subtle graduations of school society began. At Ravensbeck everything had to be measured and counted and there had to be winners and losers. Come to think of it, people have been trying to put me into little slots and compartments ever since. (Sorry, Edom, you really won't do to represent the Lawful and Gentle Insurance Company. You are not personable enough. You don't even belong to your local rugby club. Edom? He's not really officer material, is he? etc.)

At Ravensbeck they were a little uncertain about me at first. There were four first forms graded A to D and I was slotted into 1C. After a spectacularly disastrous first year there came a further sorting of the wheat from the chaff and I had assisted them to their conclusion that I was unadulterated chaff. (I think that I came thirtieth out of thirty-two in the end of year results and the comments on my school report by Madame Donchard, our French mistress, have left their wounds to this day.)

I was unhesitatingly assigned to 2H and thus committed to the 'H' stream for the rest of my Ravensbeck days. The 'H' stood for Handicrafts. Whilst the elite in the other three forms went on to study a second foreign language – Latin, Spanish or German – the 2H mob confined themselves to French and were set loose in the woodwork and metalwork shops. Whether this was a wise decision on the part of the authorities is debatable. Having watched Tony Doncaster take the top off his thumb by trying to file his nails on a high speed grinding wheel, I was inclined to think that he might have been better off doing Latin.

My own efforts at producing a tin plate pastry cutter (a

whole term's work, I recall) reduced me to deep depression. Not only was I considered too thick to learn Latin, Spanish or German, but even my ever-loving, ever-forgiving mother refused point blank to subject her pastry to my blunt misshapen pastry cutter. (Who wants jam tarts the shape of broken paving stones?)

Most of us in Form 2H nursed similar feelings of failure and all the oddballs of the second year found their way into the form. There was Wally Wetpants, for example, whose misfortune was, at some stage in the distant past, to have wet himself in response to some unknown trauma and thus to have earned an appellation that stayed with him until the fifth form at least. For all I know it may have haunted him for life. Somewhere there may be a retired middle-grade civil servant still trying to live down his unfortunate nickname. The moral may be to never let anyone know your funny little ways.

Personally I felt some sympathy with Wally. 'There but for the grace of God' and all that. I often felt like wetting myself, or worse, during my time at Ravensbeck Grammar School, particularly when subjected to the biting sarcasm and ridicule of 'Dan' Daley, the personality-disordered second English master. Still, he has given me a lifelong alibi for my poor literary style. Would you, I wonder, have done any better if you had suffered 'Dan' Daley in your formative years? He could also get very nasty during English grammar when a moment's inattention or a split infinitive could earn a blackboard cleaner or a piece of chalk hurled at high velocity. I still flinch when people correct my grammar.

Then there was a small, freckle-faced and very smelly little boy who hoarded all sorts of undesirable oddities in his desk and used to disappear for weeks on end for no known reason. He was slightly mad; indeed, when I think about it, mostly mad. He used to smell of what I called 'tink' (tink, for tinkle, as in chamber pot) and usually had at least one lizard in his desk.

I also remember Gabby Arbuthnot, large, morose and taciturn. When he managed to speak or smile he was transformed like the sun emerging from a cloud, but he only did this about twice a term so it was easily missed and everyone thought that he was a two-planker. He did not fit our beloved headmaster's expectations that all his boys should be lively, intelligent, articulate, athletic and well endowed with the social graces. Gabby in fact had the appearance and social graces of an amiable but heavily sedated cart horse.

Of course, it was wartime and most of the social casualties of the Blitz or broken marriages or similar wartime disasters ended up in the 'H' stream. It was a bit like the Foreign Legion and no one asked why you had joined. My contemporaries could tell the most improbable stories and I would believe them, partly because I was a trusting lad and partly because after five years of being buggered about by Hitler almost anything seemed possible.

Terry Ryde, for example, had been bombed out from Southampton and having for some inexplicable reason come to live in Penge had promptly had a close encounter with a V1. I remember going to his flat for tea and finding a semi-derelict building full of wet plaster and broken glass. He had a pre-war Hornby train set, however, and that made up for everything. Anyone who owned a Schools Class 4-4-0, No. 900 'Eton', even if its smoke deflectors were a bit bent, carried very high status in those disadvantaged days. I met Mrs Ryde but she is only a vague figure in my memories and as for Mr Ryde, whether he was fighting a glamorous war with the Marine Commandos or having it off with a WREN officer in Hamble, I neither knew nor cared.

Then there was Pugh. He was another displaced person

and arrived in the middle of the Christmas term. He came from we knew not where but he didn't stay with us very long; he was not 'H' stream material, it transpired. He was a good-looking young man, pleasant, friendly and modest. I admired Pugh from afar. He proved to be highly intelligent and, more importantly, a good scrum-half, an excellent swimmer and runner and, in the right season, a pretty fair batsman. I believe that there was something that he didn't shine at but I can't remember what it was. Our esteemed headmaster, 'Oxo' Brown, so named because he was built like an ox, had clearly made a mistake. Pugh was manifestly university material, officer material and destined for some high office. He was quickly removed from 2H before contamination set in and was placed in the Spanish stream where he became a leading figure.

At some stage I took Pugh's wicket in an inter-form cricket match. I was aided by a much chipped composition cricket ball and the fact that they had been grazing sheep on the junior school cricket square. (Sports facilities at Ravensbeck Grammar School just after the war left a little to be desired.) Getting Pugh's wicket gave me some brief status but caused me much ambivalence. Who, after all, wishes to diminish his hero? Anyway, my fame was short-lived and I soon sank back into obscurity.

The transfer of Pugh from 2H was most unusual. Oxo Brown had never reversed a decision before. We thought that, like God and the BBC, he was infallible. The headmaster was a remote, threatening figure to the denizens of Form 2H. His name was printed in gold at the top of the school nameboard: J.A. Brown MA (Oxon) Headmaster. I didn't know what 'Oxon' meant but I couldn't believe that they would have dared to put his nickname up there so it remained a mystery to me for some years. Oxo was a great one for the proprieties; he always wore his gown although most of his staff wore tweed sports jackets with patches on the elbows and trousers at half-mast and the rest of us looked like refugees with school caps.

Although I don't think it was official policy, the 'H' stream seemed to get 'H' stream teachers. Our form master changed each year. First we had the senior geography master (irascible and well past his best), then the art master (eccentric was the kindest word that one could use), then the senior science master (brought back from retirement and nursing a pathological hatred of all schoolboys). The 'H' stream expected no better. Anyway, we had more important things to think about. There was the Dinky Toy long-distance run down the slope of the air raid shelter (won by Grey with his pre-war Bugatti filled with lead to make it go farther). Then there was the five stones' championship, the stuffing grass up new boys' trouser legs season and the season for sneaking round to the girls' school to chat up Valerie Sylvester who, it was rumoured, had been more than a little friendly with Mortenson, the stallion of the 'H' stream.

I found the first three years in the 'H' stream the worst. After that I became battle-hardened, capable of surviving in hostile territory and quick to turn any situation to advantage. They say that you can get used to anything in time, but it was a markedly violent sort of environment. I expect that the depravity of the 'H' stream and the unpredictability of the teaching staff was all down to the war. All the staff were too young or too old for military service or were unfit or were aliens. Of course, no one explained this at the time so we assumed that all teachers were congenitally weird.

The paradox of all this was that if you weren't fit enough for Tobruk or Normandy, you were certainly going to have trouble with the 'H' stream. There was scarcely a member of the 'H' stream who didn't get cuffed, slapped, whacked or generally clonked at fairly regular intervals. Face-slapping, ear-cuffing and chalk and blackboard cleaner-throwing were rife, as was ear-twisting, hair-pulling and kicks up the bum. The teaching staff attacked us with rolled up newspapers, sticks, gym slippers, horny hands and anything else that didn't actually draw blood. We retaliated with noise (the most powerful weapon was the anonymous fart, real or impressionistic), paper darts, inky blotting paper and rude inscriptions on the blackboard augmented with the occasional stink bomb when these were available. There was also Epsom salts in the ink wells which was a useful diversionary measure.

Mr Wickford, the eccentric maths master, had to be handled with some circumspection since he was prone to erupt into sudden rages. When he slapped faces with a chalky hand a sort of white haze hung in the air and if he ordered someone out of the classroom he would urge them on their way with a few energetic but fortunately ill-directed kicks.

The first English master, Mr Macbeth, had a flat piece of wood from a vandalised desk with which he whacked deviants and malcontents. I have this memory still of his stick descending on some poor unfortunate's haunches and a great cloud of dust arising that lingered in the sunlit air. We watched in awe, the suffering of our compatriot forgotten in the fascination of how much dust there is in the average schoolboy's trousers.

The art master, Wobbly Walters, odd enough to make Van Gogh look normal, wasn't so much malicious as bloody unpredictable, like an unexploded bomb. He could move from somnolent inertia (his usual state) to blinding, hair-pulling, bum-kicking, ear-cuffing rage in the time it takes to say, 'Well, who was Rembrandt anyway?' I could draw a bit which did ease my teacher–pupil relationship with Wobbly, but I had learned enough about survival techniques in the 'H' stream to know not to press my luck.

Basically, my guiding principles were to keep my head down and maintain a good point on my utility HB pencil and hope he would pick on someone else.

Then there was Mr Lemaitre. He taught French but he had a shaven head, a bull neck and looked as though he was on leave from the Gestapo. He made me excessively nervous, and I didn't even attend his classes. He used a rolled up copy of *The Times* or the flat of his hand round the face or just bellowed pupils into submission. He had a bellow with a decibel level that would have made a Stuka bomber in mid-dive sound like a lullaby.

I have already acquainted you with the ways of 'Dan' Daley, the second English master, and his quaint combination of chalk-throwing and sarcasm. The third English master was always threatening us with 'welts on your bums'. Still, he was Welsh and rather poetic so we didn't take a lot of notice. He does have the dubious distinction of once being quite enthusiastic about one of my essays so you can give him some of the blame for all this rubbish.

The history master, Mr Martinson, looked and spoke like Montgomery but lacked the leadership qualities. He just bored us into total surrender. He could drone away about the Corn Laws or the Enclosure Acts for hours on end without the class having the remotest idea of what he was on about. We just lapsed into a mass catatonic trance until the bell went and then trooped out like zombies. I don't know why Mr Martinson hadn't been called up. He could have bored the enemy into unconditional surrender with his dissertation on developments in the woollen industry in the late eighteenth century.

The Spanish master was crippled, ill-tempered and Spanish which is enough handicap for any man. He threatened everyone with his walking stick and lurked in a gloomy classroom at the end of the corridor. Since we didn't study Spanish we just kept our distance and blamed it all on Franco.

The first geography master was a face-slapper, particularly if you were ill-informed about the match-making industry in Sweden, whilst the second geography master just eroded any last remaining vestiges of our self-confidence by carping criticism. He told me (frequently) that if I really worked hard I might aspire to become a second-class lavatory attendant (but only just).

Our beloved headmaster, Mr Oxo Brown (he of the MA Oxon), set the whole tone for his establishment by his innovative use of a size ten gym slipper and 'Jimminy' Knight of the 'H' stream was the undisputed record holder for slipperings with an unchallengeable average of one slippering every three weeks during the 1947 summer term. For much of the remainder of the time he was truanting which was understandable and at least gave both Oxo and Jimminy a bit of a breather.

The participants in total war are primarily concerned with personal survival but, like all wars, ours involved long periods of boredom and, although I find it hard to recall any, some light-hearted moments too. I've spent forty-five minutes trying to think of any light-hearted moments and the best that I can manage are Mr Ben Grudge, the Neanderthal gym master being bowled first ball in the School v Masters cricket match and the wheel coming off Mr Wickford's motorcycle combination when he was trying to make his usual fast getaway after the four o'clock bell.

During the lulls in the battle one became aware of the casualties and one's personal wounds too. At one stage I deserted in the face of the enemy, the enemy being the acerbic 'Dan' Daley. I had failed to learn off by heart the fourteen lines of Masefield which had been assigned as the English homework task. Not that I hadn't tried; it was just that I had a memory like a sieve and my grasp of what the poet was going on about was, to say the least, tenuous. 'Quinquireme of Nineveh from distant Ophir…' What the hell did it all mean? Anyway, the thought of having to stand up in class to demonstrate my failure to remember it all and then to be subjected to 'Dan' Daley's clever sarcasm and whatever other punishment he could devise was all too much. At the morning break, immediately before the English lesson, I turned tail and fled home. My ever-loving mother dealt with her twelve year old battle-fatigued son sympathetically and, after a telephone call to the school in which she no doubt perjured herself, the crisis was resolved. Next day I was ordered back to the front never to desert again. Although, God knows, I was often severely tempted.

There were other casualties. Mr Caterham walked out on us in the middle of a chaotic lesson in which we all shuffled our desks forward until he was driven out of the door. On reflection, it was very cruel. He never came back. Rumour had it that he went off and had a nervous breakdown. I think that he was probably one of the most well intentioned of all the motley teaching staff but he was far too nice to cope with 3H and clearly lacked the moral fibre. He would probably have been okay at lion taming or polar exploration but 3H – it was asking a lot.

The senior biology mistress frequently dissolved into tears which left us thwarted and confused but the expression of uncertainty on the face of the junior biology mistress when the lewd and lascivious 3H surrounded her desk during her dissertation on the reproductive habits of the frog lingers with me still.

The results of four years in the 'H' stream were odd and inconsistent, although I suppose that there is a dreadful sort of logic in that I did achieve a moderately good School Certificate result. In those days you had to pass in at least five subjects in one go including English and maths before they could be persuaded to give you one of their bloody certificates at all. I refused point blank to stay on for the Higher Schools Certificate and as I walked out of the gate for the last time I swore that I would never, ever, claim that my school days were the happiest days of my life. It remains one of the few resolutions that has never caused me any difficulty.

Surprisingly, I did not become a delinquent – a dissident possibly, but not a delinquent. However, I have an implacable distrust of the National Union of Teachers and I never believe anything that I am told about our educational system.

These days my intellectual friends try to persuade me that the solution to all the nation's ills rests with education but then, they never had to survive in the 'H' stream.

The Gymnasium

Until I went to Ravensbeck Grammar School I had no idea what a gymnasium was. It sounded to me like one of those shapes that you studied in geometry although, truth to tell, I was pretty hazy about geometry as well.

When I started at Ravensbeck I was fearful about many things and physical training was one of them. The gym master at Ravensbeck had held the post for many years and had a fearsome reputation. My one and only encounter with him was when I attended the school in early 1944 to sit the entrance examination. He was the bellowing wiry old man who bullied us into order in the school playground before we were marched off to the various exam rooms.

I was not looking forward to resuming this acquaintanceship when I started at the school in the autumn. Rumour had it that Tarzan, as he was called, had a nasty habit of whacking small boys on the seat of their gym shorts with a cane that he fondly called Little Jimmy.

Happily when I arrived at the school Tarzan and Little Jimmy had just retired. The bad news was that while the headmaster sought a permanent replacement our gym classes were taken by a succession of ex-army PT instructors who seemed to have been demobilised early on medical grounds. They tended to be a bit twitchy but they all seemed to have large well muscled arms decorated with tattoos and they were invariably endowed with parade ground voices.

These temporary instructors were not noted for their

imagination. They were heavily into arm stretching and trunk bending and other cavorting about by numbers. However, to my mind this was slightly less traumatic than trying to hang upside down on the wall bars like a bewildered fruit bat in blue shorts. For light relief one of these temporaries liked to set us to games of chase in which if you caught your opponent you whacked him across the backside with a gym slipper. Fortunately, my long arms and long legs gave me some advantage and I quickly learned the law of the gymnasium. (Whack or be whacked.)

After about a year of the itinerant ex-army PT instructors Mr Grudge arrived. No one explained at the time but eventually we discovered that Ben Grudge, the original Neanderthal man, was to be on the permanent staff. Unfortunately Ben Grudge was also ex-army and was obsessed not only with gymnastics but with boxing and swimming as well. It quickly became apparent that things were going to get nasty.

The gymnasium itself was a vast echoing hall that looked to me like a medieval torture chamber. The school had been built in 1930 and the gym had been fitted with the state-of-the-art equipment of that era. Everything was on a massive scale and had obviously been built to last, although by 1944 it was well worn. The floor was of highly polished wood and walking on it with outdoor shoes would probably have got you expelled, if not worse. All the equipment was made of solid wood and padded where necessary with horsehair and leather. One side of the gym was covered in wall bars, another with window bars. Ropes hung down from the ceiling and great beams could be pulled out from the walls and set in place. These were for balancing on, vaulting over, falling off, and for other similar atrocities.

The gym always had a distinctive stale sort of aroma that would have served well as the before section of an advertisement for Lifebuoy Soap. The smell alone made me feel pukey and that was before we even started all the cavorting and leaping about.

My main problems were that I did not like heights and I certainly abhorred being upside down. This did restrict somewhat my gymnastic achievements. Being upside down seemed against nature. If the Great Creator had intended us to hang upside down he would have made our essential parts dangle upwards. As for heights, any distance more than three feet off the floor made me distinctly dizzy.

Lurking in the corners of the gym were various appliances waiting to be hauled out to increase the pain and suffering. There was a set of parallel bars, a long box, a vaulting horse with pommels and a vaulting horse without pommels. There were also great rolls of padded mats and a number of great hairy mats like a giant's doormats. The hairy doormats brought you out in a rash if you were silly enough to fall on them. There were also a number of leather-bound medicine balls that could bowl you over if they caught you off balance.

Of course, this was wartime and rubber-soled gym shoes were almost impossible to come by. The school supplied some well worn ones on a communal basis. When you entered the gym wearing just your blue utility shorts and your everyday vest you were confronted by a great pile of well used plimsolls. In theory they had been tied in pairs by the previous users with a quick release bow. Life being what it is they were usually not tied at all or were tied in a granny knot or were tied in an unmatching pair. The struggle to find a matching pair of the right size always ensured a fairly frenzied start to each gym lesson. The thought that the shoes you were wearing had already been worn by a number of other sweaty young feet that day did not make the exercise any more pleasurable.

It is hard to assess which part of the gym lesson I found most horrific. Sometimes we had to pair off and thump each other with boxing gloves or hurl the medicine balls at each other, but hanging upside down on the wall bars or climbing the ropes were probably the worst traumas for me. Some of my classmates could shin up the ropes like monkeys but I found that I tended to slip back one foot for every two feet climbed. The process wasn't helped by the fact that I didn't really want to get to the top anyway; from the top of the ropes the floor looked a very long way down and extremely hard.

The only bit of gymnastic activity that I found tolerable was vaulting. This was because I had long legs and long arms which enabled me to vault things with greater ease than my dumpier classmates. So whenever I got the chance I vaulted away like a rabbit on LSD and hoped that it would make up for all my other gymnastic inadequacies. In my efforts to please I would vault anything that stayed still long enough. I expect that if our beloved headmaster Oxo Brown (MA Oxon) had come in and bent down to tie his shoelace I would have vaulted him as well.

After it was all over and we were sufficiently hot and sweaty we had to put all the equipment away and then conduct the ritual of removing the shoes and tying them. Then there was the barefoot rush down the cold stone floor corridor to the changing rooms. The showers hadn't worked since 1941 so no one availed themselves of that facility. Anyway, so little time was allowed for changing that we were in peril of being late for the pleasures of algebra which always seemed to follow. Being late for algebra was nearly as bad as PT since the maths master was prone to erupt into blind, face-slapping, bum-kicking rages when displeased. I sometimes wondered if his evil temperament was attributable to an excess of PT in his youth.

Swimming

Sadly, I did not learn to swim as a small child. My parents were not overly fond of the water and my older brother, who was a good swimmer apparently, felt it beneath his dignity to teach me.

As a consequence it was my misfortune to arrive at the Ravensbeck Grammar School as a non-swimmer. Now I would have been quite content to remain in that happy state but unfortunately in 1946 the school appointed a new PT master. Sadly, Mr Ben Grudge, our very own Neanderthal man, felt that one of his missions in life was to ensure that every pupil at Ravensbeck should be able to swim.

Without doubt swimming was the greatest trauma of all my sporting experiences. Ravensbeck boys were not only expected to be young gentlemen but aquatic as well. Non-swimmers were treated as if they had a serious social disease. Once a week in the summer term our form shambled down to Beckenham Public Baths where one of the swimming pools was set aside for our use. Until you could swim a width of the baths you were deemed to be a non-swimmer and subjected to all sorts of depravities. I still have nightmares about Beckenham baths. Having a tooth pulled was more fun. My first defensive gambit was to forget my swimming trunks but they just loaned you a municipal G-string which set my teeth on edge when my mind dwelt on all the previous little privates it must have held.

Beckenham baths were pretty traumatic before you even

got into the water. There were the waterlogged changing rooms and the slimy duckboards for starters. Then there were the small metal cages in which you put your clothes and valuables in the blind hope that this would stop people pinching your cap and your dinner money. Next came the heavily disinfected footbath through which you had to pass in case you had some horrid foot disease. Finally there was the vast echoing hall containing the pool which ponged of chlorine and echoed with the joyful shouts of those smug lunatics who actually enjoyed swimming.

There were a series of techniques for teaching non-swimmers to overcome their deficiencies all of which tended to be a bit punitive. They didn't actually say 've haf vays of making you svim ' but I doubt if training to be one of Mr Hitler's frogmen was much worse. The teaching techniques were ingenious. There was the 'grab this piece of waterlogged cork and thresh around until you have swallowed at least three pints of chlorinated water' technique. Then there was the 'jump in and hang on to this long bamboo pole' technique. ('Oh dear, did that hit you on the head? How sad. What a pity. Never mind.') Finally, when the instructor became bored or impatient there was the 'we will just tie this rope round your middle, chuck you in the deep end and pull you along under water' technique. I am sure that those instructors will be pleased to know that I never did take to swimming and these days I can't swim more than about eight strokes of frenzied dog-paddle before sinking to the bottom.

Although I didn't know it at the time, all this misery was because Mr Grudge had set himself a performance target to eliminate all non-swimmers from the school. The best he achieved was about ninety-five per cent of swimmers but since he eventually included me amongst his successes you can see that like most statistics, the figures were somewhat suspect.

When the swimming lesson was over the next problem was what to do with my wet swimming trunks and towel for the rest of the day. If I placed them in my locker they turned my *World Atlas* and *Hymns Ancient and Modern* all soggy whilst if I carried them around all day I tended to squelch a bit myself.

When I finally managed to swim the width of Beckenham baths I was adjudged a swimmer and thus improved Mr Grudge's statistics. Sadly, I was naive enough to think that because his statistics recorded me as a swimmer I really was one. Thus at Herne Bay on my summer hols in 1948 I launched out to sea convinced that like the *Titanic* I was unsinkable. It was only when I went to put my feet down for a rest that things got nasty. My older sister managed to haul me out before I went down for the third time. By the way, your whole life does not, in my experience, flash before you but large quantities of salt water do make you feel extremely pukey.

The Manly Art

It all started when our venerable gym master retired. Not that the inky members of the first form at Ravensbeck Grammar School shed many tears. If you have been paying attention you will recall that Tarzan (as he was nicknamed) was a small, wizened, ill-tempered man. His nasty predilection for whacking small boys on the seat of their gym shorts with 'Little Jimmy', his swishy cane was not greatly appreciated, most certainly not by me.

When Tarzan left we hoped for better things, only to learn for the first of many times that there is nothing so bad that it can't get considerably worse. Tarzan's eventual successor was Mr Ben Grudge, straight from a no doubt distinguished career at Aldershot as an army PT instructor and destined to become Ravensbeck's very own Neanderthal man.

Mr Grudge was very devoted to boxing. It made, he averred, a man of you. So, I concluded, in course of time would nature, but I saw no good reason to provoke it. I gained the impression that Mr Grudge would have probably liked to teach us bayonet drill and hand grenade hurling as well on the basis that these would also prepare us for a manly future.

Anyway, there seemed no escape from boxing. We had all these little sparring tests in the gym and he was delighted with me. I had, he said, a good natural style. In fact, what I really had was a low body weight, long arms and legs, a streak of cowardice and a low pain threshold. My technique was to back-pedal rapidly whilst keeping my opponent at arm's length by prodding him on the forehead with my left. Everyone thought that I was just waiting for the opportunity to deliver a lightning right hook but in reality I was merely longing for the bell to go.

By misfortune (mine) and misjudgement (the Neanderthal gym teacher's) I was selected for the school boxing tournament. The competition itself was a nightmare. There were all these little squat thugs with bent noses and beetle-brows who were obviously delighted to have their psychopathic tendencies legitimised. The bout before mine was particularly messy. The lad in the red corner (I can't remember if he was one of ours or one of theirs) received a thump on the nose and spent most of his three rounds bleeding all over the ring. Very inconsiderate, I thought. It made an awful mess and made me feel distinctly pukey.

After they had mopped up the ring it was my go. I adopted my usual back-pedalling, left-prodding technique but the audience, roused by all that blood no doubt, was not pleased. They wanted more; either my non-existent lightning right hook or some more blood. At the end of three rounds I was out of breath and my opponent and the audience were thoroughly frustrated – positively miffed in fact. I can't remember if I lost on points or if it was a draw. I really can't remember anything except my overwhelming relief at getting out of that ring. Happily they didn't ask me to box in the tournament again and if they had I would have volunteered for the Foreign Legion.

French Lessons

My regular readers will be aware that amongst my other
distinctions I failed my School Certificate in French. My
junior school had a French teacher but about the time I
might have started French lessons (seven and six a term
extra I think it was) we fell out with Mr Hitler. As a
consequence we had a bit of a war and many of my little
school chums were evacuated and the school could no
longer afford a French teacher. Thus it was that Miss
Buxom left the teaching staff of Burton House School
taking her knowledge of French and algebra with her. I
understand she was also a dab hand at needlework. As a
result of all this I arrived at Ravensbeck Grammar School in
1944 knowing not a word of French. I was also worried that
I couldn't speak algebra either.

There were several handicaps to my French studies.
First of all, I was not particularly keen on the Frogs. After
all, surrendering to the Jerries and declaring Paris an open
city was scarcely cricket was it? Not even French cricket.
On top of this I couldn't see any value in learning French
since I was never likely to go there, was I? Except perhaps
in an invasion barge, in which case a Sten gun would
probably have proved rather more useful than a knowledge
of French grammar.

I don't think that the standard of French teaching at
Ravensbeck was very high but since I never had much of a
clue about what was going on in our French lessons I was
in no position to form a considered judgement. In any

event, giving an opinion on the subject could easily have led to a serious whacking.

My first French teacher at Ravensbeck was Madame Donchard. She was on loan from the girls' school because the regular French teacher was doing something terribly brave with the French Resistance. At the time I started French lessons France was still occupied by the Germans. I frequently wished that they had occupied Madame Donchard. She was a pain. She always insisted that we spoke nothing but French in her classes so that I seldom understood what was going on. When she walked into the classroom we all had to stand up and chorus, 'Bonjour Madame Donchard.' She would reply, 'Bonjour mes enfants. Asseyez-vous, s'il vous plaît.' After that it became even more difficult.

We had a text book about the escapades of a little French boy called Toto. If I had ever met bloody Toto I would have strangled him with my bare hands and done him a serious mischief with the plume of his aunt. In my jaundiced view he was un petit prat. Madame Donchard was knocking on a bit but she put on all these airs and graces rather like a high-class French courtesan. She had a rather skeletal head and a smile that really wasn't. After a year of Madame Donchard's tuition the war ended and she returned to her girls' school but by this time I was going down for the third time in the deep waters of French grammar and French conversation.

After the departure of Madame Donchard we had a succession of French teachers but none seemed keen to make a long-term commitment to the members of my form who had already been adjudged unsuitable to learn a second foreign language and most of whom, like me, were not all that enthusiastic about learning a first foreign language. Apart from anything else I never really grasped the reason why the rest of the world couldn't just speak English. After all, if I could learn it, then it couldn't be all that difficult, could it? Furthermore, no one ever explained to me why it was necessary for a table to be a boy, or was it a girl? I never could remember. That was another thing about the French, they seemed obsessed with sex. Well, there were French letters and French kissing and French knickers and what on earth did they do with those bidet things?

For a time we were taught by Mr Wilfort who held his lessons in a wooden hut located on the other side of the playground and round the back of the coke heap. We assumed that this was some sort of punishment. In the wet weather the whole class got soaked trudging over there and in the power cuts of 1947 the hut was bloody freezing. Mind you, I have never forgotten the French for cold. Mr Wilfort started up the French exchanges with a school in Nancy in about 1947. Now there was a daft name for a town; only the French could have thought of that. Anyway, none of my lot were ever invited to participate in these exchanges. For one thing you had to be able to conduct an intelligent conversation in French and I think it helped if you actually liked them. Personally I always thought that General De Gaulle was a bit of a show-off and as for all those frogs' legs and snails, it didn't bear thinking about.

Then we had Mr Caterham. I think he was probably a well-intentioned man but I never discovered if he could teach French or not. His classes were usually so chaotic that if it hadn't said French on the timetable we would have been hard put to tell what he was teaching. In the end Mr Caterham walked out of the classroom one day and never came back. Rumour had it that he had decided to have a nervous breakdown.

Then there was another master who taught French and games. Our form never attended his French lessons which was probably a blessing. He wore elegant pre-war tweeds and a neat military moustache. He liked little boys, particularly first formers with short trousers. The persistence with which his hand went up short trousers was quite breathtaking, particularly if they were your short trousers. No one ever shopped him because he was quite a pleasant old trout but if you were wearing short trousers and he came to sit beside you to watch the cricket it was best to keep your legs crossed.

Then there was Mr Lemaitre who taught French as well. Mind you, he didn't look like a Frog. He was a massively built, bull-necked man with a shaven head. He looked like a member of the Gestapo to me. Particularly when he wore his leather overcoat. His bellow carried from one end of the school to the other. He told dirty jokes to his class. If they didn't laugh he gave them extra homework. Everyone was frightened of Mr Lemaitre, even Oxo Brown, and he was the headmaster. Mr Lemaitre was a face-smacker. He once whacked me round the face with a rolled up copy of *The Times* because, he said, I had stared at him. *The Times* always was a supporter of power. Years later the paper ran an advertising campaign. 'Top people take *The Times*.' It always made me think of Mr Lemaitre.

I think we must have had some other French teachers but they were no more memorable than their lessons and things went from bad to worse. Homework usually consisted of memorising verbs or translating huge lumps of French prose. I even bought a small French–English dictionary but it didn't help much, not even as a doorstop. Dictionaries always seem to tell you what you don't want to know.

After five years of not learning much French I was faced with the School Certificate examination. I can't remember anything about the written paper but to add to my humiliation there was an oral examination as well. The awful part was that even if I knew the right word I could never pronounce it. The examiner had a large picture of a rural scene complete with farm and animals. We were supposed to have an intelligent conversation about this. I rambled on about brown cows and green fields and blue skies but it was evidently not enough. The examiner seemed to have difficulty in understanding me. But not nearly as much difficulty as I had in understanding the examiner.

Well, as I said, I failed my School Certificate in French and I have to tell you that I still consider the Channel Tunnel a most grievous mistake.

Woodworking

My regular readers will be aware that I failed my School Certificate in woodwork, but no one has ever asked me why. Part of the reason must be Mr Waterspoon. Wally Waterspoon was our woodwork master. To be fair, he was not deliberately malevolent and by the standards of Ravensbeck Grammar School he was almost human. I don't know how you become a woodwork master but Mr Waterspoon seemed to have much in common with two of his own very thick planks. Apart from anything else, although we knew each other for five excruciating years, he was always under the impression that my name was Ebdon which didn't lead to a great deal of empathy or mutual understanding.

It has to be faced that I was only doing woodwork because I couldn't be trusted with German or Spanish, let alone Latin. In consequence Mr Waterspoon knew that I had been adjudged an academic dead loss. What was unclear was if Mr Waterspoon had given thought to what this might say about him.

I went through a funny phase after I was allocated to the 'H' or Handicrafts stream which had consigned me to five years of unrelieved woodwork and metalwork. I decided for a while that my career lay in becoming a carpenter. I was prone to extravagant but short-lived enthusiasms of this kind. In fairly rapid succession I decided to commit my life's work to captaining England at cricket, playing right wing for Arsenal, being a press photographer, a Meteor pilot, a bus conductor and a milkman. Somewhere in there came being a carpenter and joiner. At Christmas 1945 my ever-loving parents, at my earnest request, bought me a saw and a claw hammer but being short of things to saw, hammer and claw the enthusiasm soon wore off.

Anyway, five years' hard woodwork followed. The woodwork shop at Ravensbeck Grammar School was in a separate building from the main school as if the school was slightly embarrassed about woodwork and wanted to be disassociated from it. I knew the feeling.

The large tiled porch of the woodwork shop was taken up by a large tree trunk sawn into planks and separated by small fillets of wood to facilitate the curing process. I assumed that Wally Waterspoon had acquired this tree at the beginning of the war in anticipation of the timber shortage. Mind you, it was still there when I left the school in 1949 so it was obviously a long-term investment. Either that or he had forgotten about it.

Woodwork itself was tiresome enough but Wally Waterspoon made it totally, irrefutably and indescribably tedious. Wally was a droner. He could have won medals for droning. Once he started on about front elevations and side elevations and plans you could get seriously brain dead, if not worse. It wasn't that he was a bad carpenter and joiner. If I had wanted someone to knock up a sideboard or a log cabin Wally Waterspoon would have been an obvious choice but as for teaching same, forget it.

Mind you, the teaching environment was not ideal. The woodwork shop was a large factorylike building with rows of workbenches, a woodturning lathe, a circular saw and a glue pot. The whole place was covered with a film of fine sawdust and the fishy smell of glue permeated the air. Mr Waterspoon wandered around in a khaki overall with a pencil behind his ear and a folding boxwood rule in his top pocket. He always seemed to have a slightly bemused air and he usually had a wood shaving or two in his thinning hair. When he wanted to lecture us about coniferous woods and deciduous woods and similar mysteries we had to sit on the woodwork benches. If you had a vice handle between your legs or were sitting on a bench stop this did not contribute to one's concentration.

Charlie Sloan had his own way of coping with the boredom of Wally Waterspoon's little lectures. He used to sit right at the back and what he used to do under the concealment of his war surplus respirator case which doubled as a school satchel I will not embarrass you by describing.

My other little school chums were also pursuing their own special hobbies in the woodwork shop. 'Jimminy' Knight was secretly working on his own private project. He was building a B29 in balsa wood from a kit he had been given for his birthday. As for Ritchmuller, he was carving a nude lady from a banister rail he had acquired from a bombed-out building in Penge High Road. I have to say that Ritchmuller was a bit funny like that. He was obsessed by women and some of his drawings in the art class bordered on the pornographic. Wobbly Walters, the nutty art teacher, really didn't know what to make of Ritchmuller.

Mr Waterspoon lived in an old-fashioned world of his own where all woodworking tools were treated with reverence and all joints fitted hand-tight. The harsh realities of teaching the 'H' stream were a great trial to him and as far as possible he tried to pretend that we were not there. He used to wander among us muttering little homilies like prayers: 'Wood to wood and metal to metal,' or 'Always cut on the waste side.' In the meantime members of the class would usually ignore him and go about their business. Tony Doncaster would continue to hammer an ill-fitting joint together with the help of a large hammer whilst

Wandsworth would absent-mindedly saw right through his wooden bench hook.

Each workbench in the woodwork shop was equipped with two vices and two sets of tools, one set at each end of the bench. There was a wooden jack plane and a tenon saw and three chisels, a mallet, a small hammer and a bench hook, a metal rule, a marker gauge and a set square. At the end of each lesson the tools were checked since there were always some missing. One of the central activities in a woodwork lesson was to sneak around nicking someone else's tools so that at the end of the lesson one's own set was complete. It was a bit like a complicated game of musical chairs or pass the parcel.

The most appalling bit of equipment was the dreaded wooden jack plane. First we had to draw all the component parts, then we had to learn how to set it and sharpen the blade and then we had to plane bits of wood for what seemed like for ever. When the wood was absolutely flat and absolutely square we had to mark the face side and the face edge with special marks. Mr Waterspoon was very hot on this. It was as important as a Masonic handshake.

One of the ways of relieving tedium during a woodwork lesson was to carve one's initials somewhere. With the range of chisels available some of the carvings were on a grand scale. The woodwork shop was at risk of total disintegration as more and more of the fabric of the building was carved away.

Occasionally as a special treat, Mr Waterspoon would allow someone to use the woodturning lathe. Personally I avoided it like the plague. The golden rule at Ravensbeck so far as I was concerned was never to draw attention to myself. No good ever came of it. However, Mortensen, who was a raving psychopath on the rugby field and was a bit of a stud in his spare time, was allowed to make a wooden bowl. He became quite obsessed with the bloody thing. It kept him quiet for a whole term. I think that this was a crafty move on Mr Waterspoon's part to divert Mortensen from consorting with his cronies, Hopkinson and Doncaster, who were usually plotting mayhem in the timber store. Hopkinson's favourite trick was to let the glue pot boil dry which ensured a forced evacuation of the whole woodwork shop until the smell subsided.

The final phase of my woodworking career was the fiasco of the practical woodwork exam for my School Certificate. The set piece of work was a rather complicated bracket with a dovetail joint and a mortise and tenon joint and various bits of bevelled edges and flimflammery. The joints were supposed to fit flush and hand-tight but mine wobbled about if you so much as breathed on it. Even with illicit wedges and a mixture of glue and sawdust as camouflage my set piece was clearly not a success. Oh, very well then, it was a bloody disaster. So that, you see, is how I failed my School Certificate in woodwork.

The Ravensbeckian

Perhaps I should explain that *The Ravensbeckian* was the magazine of the Ravensbeck Grammar School for Boys. The authorities moved the school to a new site in 1968, changed its name and eventually turned it into a comprehensive so in effect the old school no longer exists. I have to say that whilst I had no particular love for the place I do resent those in authority mucking about with my memories. They would never dare do that to Eton, would they?

In 1996, however, I was able to borrow a very dog-eared bound copy of the school magazine which covered the years that I attended from 1944 to 1949. Reading through those faded pages repaired with browning and peeling sellotape and annotated and decorated by succeeding generations of seditious schoolboys I was able to relive all the pain and trauma of those years of long ago.

Inevitably I looked for traces of my own school career but these were somewhat sparse. The tradition was that each issue of the magazine recorded the most recent arrivals and departures. However, to my chagrin the year that I arrived in 1944 was the exception. It was never explained to me at the time but in the early part of 1944 the school had been evacuated to avoid the flying bomb raids that had demolished a significant portion of Beckenham and Penge. The Doodlebugs had missed the school itself. With hindsight this was a great pity. When I arrived in September the school had only just reconvened so it was in a state of some disorder. I had assumed that this was the way it always was.

The first edition of the school magazine following my arrival was not published until the summer of 1945. It was a rather thin edition and had a distinctly austere appearance. It lacked photographs and appeared to be printed on medium grade lavatory paper. By the time it was published the authorities had already forgotten all about my intake and the magazine was full of news of the doings of old boys. At that time it helped to have gained a commission, won a medal or to be dead if you wanted your doings to be recorded.

I looked in vain for some acknowledgement that I was now a pupil. The headmaster's letter in the summer 1945 edition observes, 'The first forms which were at first unsteady have recently settled down to much better work and behaviour.' Just to set the record straight about one hundred and twentieth of those remarks refer to me although honesty forces me to acknowledge that I came thirtieth out of thirty-two in form 1C at the end of that first year. I had indeed settled down. Down being the operative word.

I recalled that I had been a member of Beaver House and I searched for any reference to my membership. The house report in the 1945 magazine observes that, 'By a supreme effort on the part of the more conscientious of our regular slackers Beaver has once again been reduced to sixth out of six in the audits. It seems a pity that these academic fifth columnists should remain anonymous and efforts will be made to give then publicity.' I have an uneasy feeling that whilst I struggled for survival in that first year I was deemed to be a member of the Fifth Column. Come to think of it, there were times when I was made to feel more like a member of the Hitler Youth.

But then came the first editorial recognition that Edom

existed. He is recorded as having come second in the junior
high jump in the school sports of 1946. I had forgotten all
about this but my sporting achievements were so sparse that
even after a period of fifty years reading this induced a
warm glow of pride.

Most of my other efforts at Ravensbeck go unrecorded
primarily because like all grammar schools it was only
interested in winners and I didn't do a lot of that. I did find
that I was recorded as having won a form prize in 1947 and
another one in 1948 but these achievements were
somewhat tarnished because I was in the non-academic
stream and our beloved headmaster had little time for
anyone who couldn't say something intelligent in Latin,
Spanish or at least in German. Personally, I had enough
trouble saying something intelligent in French. Or English,
come to that.

Of course, I risked life and limb every Wednesday
afternoon in the inter-form sports and games. The only
person excused games was Bradley and he had a club foot.
Rugby, hockey and cricket were each played in season but I
was never trusted to represent the house, let alone the
school.

The old school has a lot to answer for. It did not take me
long to learn that Ravensbeck Grammar School was all
about winning and losing. The first competition was to pass
the exam to get in the place at all. The entrance exam was
held during the firebomb raids of early 1944. Just to deter
any faint hearts, I assumed at the time. Anyway, that was
only the beginning. There were inter-form competitions,
inter-house competitions and inter-school competitions.
There was nothing it seemed that could not be turned into
a competition. Even the Junior Ornithological Society had a
bird identification competition.

The school magazine recorded all the competitions but
noted that the Air Training Corps was unable to hold a

shooting competition for lack of the necessary number of rifles. Still, there were proficiency certificates and aircraft recognition contests and other challenges so all was not lost. Although it is not recorded in the magazine I was in the ATC for a while. I remember I had great difficulty in learning the Morse code: 'dit dit dit, da da da, dit dit dit...' Or was it the other way round? You will have gathered that I was not awarded my proficiency certificate. Apart from anything else you needed to know your dits from your das.

The magazine has nothing to say about my efforts in the inter-house cross-country races. Participation was compulsory, of course. I came ninety-second out of one hundred and eleven in 1945 and seventh out of one hundred and ten in 1946. The worst part was that after my improved performance I was asked to join the school cross-country team. I would rather have gone for a swim in an alligator swamp.

There is also no mention of my one and only appearance in the school boxing competition. It is probably just as well that there is no record of my stark terror on that particular occasion although the magazine records the gym master's question: 'Do we realise how plucky are the few who go in the ring for the first time?' Plucky was not the word I would have used. Anyway, I didn't know I had any choice.

The school magazine is full of exhortations for everyone to do better and has a distinctly moralistic tone but it makes no reference to my constant struggle to survive in that hostile environment. The bullying left me in permanent fear and that was just of the masters.

The headmaster's contributions to the magazine were all about achievement and success, punctuated by glowing comments about the devotion of his staff. 'That the school life has retained its vigour is very largely due to the staff,' he wrote in the 1945 edition. I remember the vigour of the staff very clearly.

The headmaster set the tone by his innovative use of a size ten gym slipper but that was just for starters. There was 'Dan' Daley's sarcasm and chalk and blackboard cleaner-throwing, Mr Lemaitre's bellowing and ear-smacking, the art master's ear-pulling and hair-twisting, the geography master's repeated assertions that I would be lucky to achieve the status of a second-class lavatory attendant and the maths master's sudden rages accompanied by face-slapping and bum-kicking. Oh, and there was Mr Macbeth who whacked small boys' haunches with a flat piece of a vandalised desk. There was more, but you will have grasped the general ethos. Believe me, it was not a fun environment. At the time I was inclined to blame it all on the Blitz.

As for the master who had a fatal attraction for first formers in short trousers, no hint of any of his funny little ways appeared in the school magazine which should make you a trifle sceptical of what is published in official records.

Everything about Ravensbeck was about competition but, sadly, what I learned very quickly was that in order for there to be winners there inevitably had to be losers. I also learned, although rather more slowly, the role that had been assigned to me.

There was an elite amongst my contemporaries who seemed to be good at everything and who basked in the headmaster's favour. There was Pugh, for example, who played in most of the school teams, won a succession of events every sports day and was always winning form prizes. If this was not enough he was disgustingly modest about it as well. Then there was Tichy Twyford who was never modest about anything. He had a nasty habit of appearing in the school plays and singing duets with the headmaster at the school carol concerts and nearly every year he won a form prize. However, the individual who really brought home to me the winning principle was Hollytree, S.J. From the start it was clear that he was a winner. In the first year he won one of the first form prizes and this set the tone for ever after. The same thing happened in the second year and the third year and, yes, you've guessed it, in the fourth year as well.

By 1948 Hollytree was also awarded his colours in the cricket first eleven and each time he played he seemed to take five or six wickets and was frequently the highest run scorer as well. Each edition of *The Ravensbeckian* was littered with his successes. In the 1948–1949 season he was in the school rugby fifteen and he also became vice-captain of the school hockey first eleven. Oh, hell. I have just noticed that in 1949 he was in the school tennis team as well and he and Pugh became the senior house prefects of Beaver House.

The final magazine I looked at was for 1950 which recorded the doings of my last year. By this time Hollytree was totally out of control. His name and photograph were appearing all over the place and he was winning prizes that I had not even known existed. That was the year he won a prize for 'outstanding merit' in the School Certificate examinations. Oh, and I forgot, he was a school prefect as well. He also won a number of events in the school sports but I took some consolation from the fact that he only came second in throwing the discus.

The editorial in *The Ravensbeckian* for the spring term 1949 records: 'During the last few terms the recovery of the school from its wartime disorganisation and in particular the revival of the school spirit has become more and more apparent and we would say that the most difficult period has been passed.' It all seemed a bit late for me since I was leaving the following term. Perhaps that was what the editor meant.

The editorial continued with a homily about school uniforms that gave no recognition to the consequences of eight years of clothes rationing: 'The majority of boys, particularly in the lower school now wear blazers, although

there still seems to be a reluctance to wear school caps –
unless, of course, the owner happens to be discharging his
duty as a butcher's boy, or selling bargains at a stall in
Maple Road, when it is quite imperative that he should
show the world where he received the training for this lofty
and noble calling.' Well, you certainly knew where you
stood at Ravensbeck, didn't you?

For my part the Spring 1950 edition of the magazine
recorded that I had passed my School Certificate in July
1949 and then under the heading 'Valete' that, along with
about fifty others, Edom R.F. of 5H had left at the end of
the summer term 1949. Not a lot to show for five years'
blood, toil, tears and sweat, and with the old school gone
and most of its records destroyed even those brief traces
will soon be lost in the dusts of time.

Speech Day

Speech days at Ravensbeck Grammar School were not my most favourite occasions. Designed as they were to mark achievement and success I found that I could not relate to them. My regular readers will vouch for the fact that Edom is something of a stranger to achievement and success. The fact that there are very few regular readers to do any vouching only proves my point.

There were, of course, other school atrocities like the first form Christmas party and the annual carol concert and the school play and the al fresco concert given by the school orchestra but these were all out of school hours events and could with judicious excuse-making be avoided. Unfortunately, only a serious attack of bubonic plague could get you excused from Speech Day.

Anyway, with a horrible inevitability came each March the annual Speech Day. From 1944 until 1949 I endured speech days at Ravensbeck. It is hard to decide what the worst part was. Perhaps it is best just to review the whole dreadful process. The music master who, even at best, was as temperamental as Tchaikovsky started to go funny about three months before Speech Day. This was because music was deemed to be a special feature of the event. The whole school had to stay behind after prayers twice a week for a month in order to rehearse 'Jerusalem'. I expect that some years it may have been some other hymn but in my memory it was always 'Jerusalem'. Mr Smythe made us go over it again and again until we were all word perfect and every syllable and every emphasis was to his liking. It took me twenty years to forget the words to 'Jerusalem' after all that. Even now I still twitch a bit when I hear the tune.

The school orchestra and the choir had extra practices because they had to perform some additional little delicacies. Happily, I can't remember what they were. I always found the school orchestra a bit of a trial. Not that I knew much about music but the orchestra always had too much of a thin, scraping, wailing, reedy sound for my liking. Still, I expect that they meant well.

The actual day itself had an air of the paranormal about it. All the masters wore suits and gowns. Their normal attire was sports jackets with patches at the elbows and cuffs and utility grey flannel trousers that hung at half-mast. Our beloved headmaster, Mr Oxo Brown, he of the MA (Oxon), had a special furry coloured cape to his gown. Still, he always was a bit of a show-off. Even the school caretaker put on his uniform but the boilerman was kept hidden in the boiler room because there was absolutely nothing that could be done to prevent him from looking disreputable.

Once we were all assembled in the school hall the waiting began. Mr Lemaitre, the French master who looked as if he was on leave from the Gestapo, always took charge of discipline in the hall. Even he, however, was on his best behaviour and only smacked a couple of token ears.

Eventually the platform party of dignitaries made their way into the hall and up on to the stage. They all twittered about for a while until Oxo Brown showed them which chairs to sit on and then eventually we were allowed to sit down and the proceedings began.

The dignitaries were a bit of a disappointment really. There was Oxo Brown, of course, larger and more mountainous each year. There was also the chairman of the governors who also turned up every year. He was a small, white-haired, rosy-cheeked little man who looked like a benign garden gnome in his Sunday best.

The ceremony began with a bit of singing and praying and then the orchestra and choir did their special bits and then came the prize-giving.

Each year someone slightly important was invited to present the prizes. My own view was that no one really important would have been seen dead at Ravensbeck. One year it was someone I had never heard of who had a knighthood and was described as a world traveller and a diplomat who had once been a friend of T.E. Lawrence. At the time I thought it strange to claim to be a friend of someone who wrote dirty books. Another year it was our local Member of Parliament. He was Harold MacMillan but he wasn't famous in those days or he wouldn't have come either. I won a form prize that year. I was gobsmacked and assumed someone had made a mistake. I didn't query it however. Querying things at Ravensbeck could get you seriously whacked.

After the prize-giving things got really nasty. This was when you discovered why it was called Speech Day. First Oxo Brown presented his annual report. It was all about Bright of the Upper Sixth who had won a scholarship at Magdalen College, Oxford, and Smart who had won a special entry to Dartmouth Naval College and Blessed who had obtained a high place in the examination for the Executive Grade of the civil service. Then we had to hear about how the first fifteen had trodden the opposition into the mud every Saturday since early November. Then there were the achievements of the school cricket team, the hockey team, the boxing team, the cross-country team, the swimming team... Oxo Brown succeeded in making it sound as if he had personally led every single team to victory.

Oxo went on for a very long time. He praised the efforts of staff and pupils in maintaining the fine traditions of

Ravensbeck but was saddened that these efforts were undermined by a small minority who were wasting the opportunities that they had been given. He always seemed to be looking in my direction when he said things like that. Oxo concluded by thanking the school caretaker and his staff for their fine work during the year. I noticed that he didn't mention the boilerman.

When we were all sufficiently numbed Oxo sat down and the important dignitary gave his little speech. The important dignitary was usually quite modest about his own schooldays but he was always anxious to assure us that they were the happiest days of his life and he had learned that it wasn't the winning that mattered but the taking part. There was usually more along the same lines... importance of team spirit... everyone has something to contribute... value of fair play... preparing for the great adventure of life... always do one's best... etc.

Then it was the turn of the chairman of the governors. He tended to ramble a bit. Sometimes he seemed to be under the impression that he was addressing a meeting of the County Council Civil Defence Committee. He always ended by telling everyone how well they had done and what a splendid year it had been and asking the headmaster to grant an extra day's holiday. Since this was already included in the half-term holiday arrangements no one was all that excited but Oxo insisted that we give him three rousing cheers anyway. Even cheering at Ravensbeck was carefully co-ordinated. None of your foot stamping or whistling or any of that old proletarian nonsense. We were, after all, being educated as young gentlemen. The school captain resplendent in his new school blazer would call, 'School, three cheers for Alderman Jelly. Hip, hip, hip...' and we all called, 'Hurrah!' in a gentlemanly fashion. We did this, of course, three times which was a bit tedious, but we sensed that we were on the last lap which cheered us up no end.

The grand finale was when we all sang 'Jerusalem'. Mr Smythe was on a little rostrum with his baton and his hair slicked down like a Brylcreem advertisement. The orchestra did its scraping, reedy, wailing introduction and then we all started off together. 'And did those feet in an-cient time/Walk up-on Eng-land's moun-tains green?...' We progressed through the routine that we had practised for the last month. We sang like little automatons and old Smythe jumped up and down and thrashed his baton about like Malcolm Sergeant at the Albert Hall. No one ever explained to me what the song was all about but eventually we got to 'Till we have built Je-ru-sa-lem/In Eng-land's green and pleasant land.'

We all managed to finish together and there was a moments stunned silence. It was a great relief I can tell you. Of course, the day had to finish with the orchestra playing 'God Save the King' but that didn't count because in those days no public event was complete without everyone standing rigidly to attention for the national anthem. Finally, the whole thing was over until next year. Whilst we stood respectfully the important personages filed out and went and had tea and fishpaste sandwiches in the headmaster's study. The rest of us were left to go our separate ways. My own overriding concern was whether I would be in time to catch the four fifteen home. If so I might be able to get my algebra homework finished before *Dick Barton* started.

School Dinners

Current thinking suggests that we ate more healthily during the war than we do at the present time. Personally I am not convinced. Although I hesitate to challenge conventional wisdom I wonder if anyone took school dinners into account? Not that I wish you any harm but the awful truth must be revealed.

I started at Ravensbeck Grammar School in the autumn of 1944. These, of course, were stirring times with the Allied armies storming across Europe and Mr Hitler firing off his V2s in all directions. But there was another darker side to the closing stages of World War Two. You've guessed it: Ravensbeck school dinners.

Every Monday morning I had to take a half crown to school to purchase five sixpenny tickets for my week's school dinners.

'Dan' Daley the sadistic English master collected the dinner money and issued the tickets and there seemed a dreadful sort of logic in that.

The meals were eaten on the stage of the school hall. I seem to recall that there were two sittings to fit everyone in. For some reason a canteen or dining hall had never been provided. Don't ask me why. Asking why at Ravensbeck Grammar School in 1944 could get you seriously clonked. Anyway, the kitchens were located at the side of the stage and the folding dinner tables were set up centre stage as soon as morning prayers were over.

The hall was located in the middle of the school so it

followed that there was a permanent aroma of stale cabbage throughout the establishment. On Fridays it was a blend of stale cabbage and stale fish.

The whole system of eating was hierarchical. The masters had a separate table and were waited on. The rest of us sat at tables headed by a fifth-former aided by two lieutenants in the fourth form who went up to the servery to collect the food for the table. There was no choice. You got what you were given and were expected to be grateful. The fifth-former and his two lieutenants doled out the food and those at the bottom of the table received their food first. The portions had to be judged so that there was sufficient left for the seniors. In consequence juniors tended to get the smallest portions. Sometimes this was a blessing in disguise.

The head of our table was Ross, P.J. I secretly rather admired Ross, P.J. Not only did he play for the cricket first eleven but he also had a sense of humour. Anyone who could keep smiling whilst serving our school dinners would clearly go far.

The main course was usually a tray of incredibly thinly sliced cold meat with warm gritty gravy poured over it. I assume the meat must have been hot at some time but certainly not when it reached us. The origin of the meat was uncertain. It could have been mutton or it could have been goat. The only thing for certain was that it was invariably striated with fatty tissue. The vegetables were usually mashed potato and swede or mashed potato and cabbage. For a change it was sometimes mashed potato and turnip. It seemed to be a point of honour with the cook to mash the potatoes only partially and to leave the eyes in them. The eyes always seemed to glare at you malevolently. Occasionally the second vegetable was pithy carrots or, even worse, reconstituted dried peas that could have penetrated armour-plated steel at two hundred yards. What

I desperately yearned for was a baked bean or a chip but the consequences of nearly six years of total war was a complete absence of chips or baked beans.

On Fridays we had fish. A piece of fried fish would have been welcome but boiled cod in a runny parsley sauce was the only fishy meal ever provided – apart from fish pie, of course. I shall not comment on the fish pie. Some things are best left unsaid.

Sometimes we had stew or meat pie. I always yearned for a dumpling with my stew but dumplings needed suet and that was rationed. The meat pie was a bit of a misnomer. It actually comprised a square of pastry made with minimum fat and a ladle of stew. The special feature about stew or pie filling was that if you found any meat in it you treated it with suspicion.

If anything the puddings were even worse. Although I think we called them afters in those days. There were hard pieces of pastry smeared with artificial raspberry jam. The pastry was almost fat-free and the jam was actually made of date and apple augmented with raspberry essence. There was also lumpy unsweetened custard. Occasionally, as a treat, we had unsweetened tapioca pudding or unsweetened pink blancmange instead. Sometimes there was stewed apple or stewed rhubarb or stewed prunes. The only defence against stewed prunes was to ask to be excused and not to come back. When you thought things could get no worse they served you with a lump of cold stodgy bread pudding. If you found any raisins in it you kept it quiet in case they asked for them back.

The portions were invariably very small, particularly if the food on offer was remotely edible, but you were allowed a slice of bread and there was unlimited water to drink. The bread was from a National Loaf which was neither white nor brown but a medium shade of grey. The water seemed surprisingly normal.

There were other joys to school dinners. The duty master said grace before we sat down to eat. We dutifully thanked the Great Provider for his beneficence and then the general mayhem began. One of the advantages of lumpy potato was that it could be flicked surreptitiously with a spoon to provide a diversion from the horror of the food itself. Mind you, if you received an earful of mashed potato it did tend to leave you a bit deaf for afternoon lessons. When real potato was in short supply we were sometimes served with a synthetic variety called Pom. This was of gluey consistency and had the distinction of being neither edible nor flickable.

In the summer we sometimes had cold meat with mashed potato and diced beetroot. The meat was just the same as usual but without the hot gritty gravy. There didn't seem to be much salad about in those days and as for salad cream, well forget it, but the moment the weather became hot out came the diced beetroot. Occasionally there was a bit of lettuce or watercress but things like onions and cucumbers and tomatoes were just things you read about in books.

However, I must not forget the condiments. Sauce was out of the question, even OK Brown Sauce. We sometimes had this at home because tomato sauce had disappeared altogether but at school brown sauce or any other sauce was regarded as an unnecessary luxury. Occasionally, as a special treat, there was a dollop of yellow mustard pickle to go with the cold meat but sweet pickle had gone the way of tomato sauce. How I yearned for a dollop of Branston! Where did Branston go during the war?

For some strange reason there were flasks of vinegar on each table but since we could never find much use for it the flasks served as a sort of table decoration. Oh, of course, there was also a pepper pot (invariably empty) and a salt pot (always clogged with condensation).

By the time I reached the fourth form I gave up on school dinners altogether. One can only endure so much suffering. This must have been about 1948. Just to put things into context, in 1948 the Ministry of Food were publishing a recipe for herring fritters and describing them as 'a special treat for Sundays'. Food, you will have gathered, was still very scarce but I and my little chums either had a cheese roll in Tiny's Café or went down to the Empire Café. Here they specialised in sausage meat patties fried in nauseous-smelling oil which we saw being delivered in unlabelled five gallon drums. Still, if you didn't breathe in too deeply the sausage meat patties weren't all that bad.

Never mind, always look on the bright side I say. Grammar schools always claimed to prepare you well for the future. After Ravensbeck school dinners I coped remarkably well with the two years I spent eating in RAF cookhouses.

Penge High Road

When I was packed off to Ravensbeck Grammar School in 1944 I made my maiden voyage with my leather satchel on my shoulder and my pristine school cap nestling down over my ears. (He will grow into it, madam.) I felt like many a new boy before me, apprehensive but hopeful, conscious that a new era was starting and not yet at that advanced stage of pessimism where one realises that a new era is only an old era in embryo. In my new leather satchel, still smelling of dead cow, was all the equipment deemed necessary for a grammar school education. I had a pencil case and a nine-inch austerity ruler and, wrapped in greaseproof paper, two Digestive biscuits and a small cube of cheese for elevenses. Firmly clipped in my top pocket was my new Golden Platignum fountain pen which had cost the best part of five shillings and must surely further my academic career. One or two of my more affluent form mates turned up with slide rules and tended to whip these out at strategic moments to impress me. I can't think why they bothered; I was far too easily impressed to make it worth the trouble.

Anyway, I was in effect as well equipped as my parents could manage. Now it was up to me; that was the problem. It was a challenge and I have never been all that keen on challenges. My junior school teacher, Mrs Sergeant, had told me with lip-smacking relish that at my new school I would encounter the ritual of what she called 'the bend over'. She seemed to think that this was as desirable a ceremony as the Changing of the Guard but personally the thought of being whopped on the backside with a stick did not fill me with instant enthusiasm for the traditions of the Ravensbeck Grammar School. Nonetheless, Mrs Sergeant was very keen on it. It would make a man of me and anyway, I would probably deserve it; in her jaundiced view most small boys did. There was also, I was informed, a tyrannical gym master nicknamed Tarzan who beat small boys with a stick he affectionately called 'Little Jimmy'. Fortunately, this particular threat to my health and safety retired just before I arrived, much to my relief. He took 'Little Jimmy' with him and, no doubt, mounted it over his mantelpiece as a reminder of his sporting achievements.

One of the few compensations for all the anxiety and trauma of attending the Ravensbeck Grammar School was Penge High Road. It wasn't exactly Oxford Street or the Champs-Elysées but it had its own special charms. I travelled by train to school; three stops on the Southern Electric to Clock House. Yes, I know it is a silly name for a station. Don't blame me. Blame the Southern Railway. From there to school there lay a walk of about a mile along Penge High Road.

There was a funny little single-decker bus that did that trip but small boys were expected to walk. In any event if three-halfpence was available it was better spent on a second-hand copy of *Adventure*. (Thinks... would Wilson the wonder runner still win the ten-mile race even though the evil conspirators had put a tarantula in his running shorts?) The buses were fascinating contrivances though. They had bonnets that stuck out in front and large mudguards that vibrated in sympathy with the engine and headlamps that perched each side of the bonnet, heaving like Carmen Miranda's bosoms. There was none of this modern streamlining nonsense; there were bits sticking out all over the place; great leaf springs and mirrors and sidelights and a starting handle held in place with a leather strap.

The buses rested and turned round at the Weary Traveller in East Penge so sometimes we would venture up there to inspect them as they stood taking a breather and leaking oil and petrol fumes before they turned round and went all the way back to Bromley. The drivers stood around taking a breather too. They all used to wear white coats like doctors or ice cream men and they displayed their PSV licences in leather holders hanging from their lapels like medals.

Mind you, Penge High Road was not what it had been. Mr Hitler had been bombing it, on and off, since 1940 with a motley selection of ironmongery so that by the time I began my pilgrimage along this highway in 1944 it was a bit past its best. Of course, in some ways this all added to its fascination. There were all these gaps in the High Road fenced off with old floorboards, stair railings and floor joists. You could peer down into open cellars and basements that were exposed to daylight for the first time since the Victorian and Edwardian artisans built them. (Don't worry about the pointing, Alfred; no one will ever see it.)

It was funny really because directions in Penge tended to be based on well known non-landmarks: 'Walk down past where the Co-op was and turn left where the police station isn't.' It was exciting though; there were tiled entrances to shops that no longer led anywhere and steps that ended in mid-air. I particularly liked one splendid tiled doorway that spelt out 'H&C' in an ornate monogram. Beyond it nothing remained of the Home and Colonial Stores apart from half a wall at the back and a metal rail where they used to hang the prime streaky.

On some of those bomb sites enterprising traders had tried to re-establish their businesses. There was one middle-aged lady with hair drawn back by twin bone combs who lurked in a large wooden hut on a bomb site near Clock House station. She called her establishment The Cabin – unoriginal but succinct and descriptive. It was very gloomy inside because it had only one small window. (You can't get the glass, you know.) The proprietress didn't have electricity so on gloomy winter afternoons she conducted her business by the light of a solitary paraffin lamp. She was a formidable lady with steely eyes and a sharp nose and a chin that could have cracked walnuts. One was immediately aware that if Hitler couldn't get the better of her then the average Ravensbeck schoolboy stood no chance.

Her speciality was penny drinks for thirsty schoolboys. She sold highly diluted blackcurrant cordial in small screw-stoppered bottles that had previously held some higher quality pre-war beverage like ginger beer. The bottles stood in a rack; you served yourself, proffered your penny, swigged your drink from the bottle and returned the empty bottle for a perfunctory swish in a chipped enamel washing-up bowl. The proprietress refilled the bottles somewhere in the dark recesses at the back of the shop, probably from a cauldron. I never hung about in there in case she was in a funny mood and turned me into a frog.

There was another shop that pioneered ice lollies. There, diluted cordial was poured into shallow tin trays and placed in a pre-war refrigerator. When it was frozen it was brought out and broken up with a pair of rusty steel tongs. The misshapen pieces were placed in the half page of an outdated London telephone directory. You paid according to size. It was a bit of a swizz really because one good healthy schoolboy suck and all the cordial was drawn out leaving a rather boring lump of ice rapidly melting in a soggy piece of the A–D section.

That shop also sold off-the-ration sweet substitutes.

These were mostly curious rootlike bits that you sucked and chewed until your mouth and tongue went bright yellow. There were also some unsweetened brightly coloured little lozenges that tasted like talcum powder but these had the undesirable side effect of making you want to puke so they were best avoided unless you were a first-former and didn't know any better.

Sometimes the shop had liquorice which was also off the ration. It came in little reels like hosepipes or in straplike pieces or in coiled lengths like a bootlace. Personally, I never liked liquorice and no matter what shape it came in I still regarded it as one of the nastier aspects of Hitler's bid for total world domination. However, that particular shopkeeper taught me an important wartime principle: if it isn't rationed and it is not under the counter be prepared for disappointment. The principle was reinforced for me when I first tried whale meat, and as for snoek, least said soonest mended.

Unusually, that particular shop still retained its large pre-war plate glass window; unshattered but grimy and with a window display of nothing but empty boxes. Stacks of empty cigarette packets and signs that were more declarations of faith and hope than advertising, such as 'Players Please'. (Chance would have been a fine thing.) There were lots more signs and empty packets: De Resque and Du Maurier and Capstan Full Strength and Nosegay and Churchman's Number One – just empty packets and condensation-streaked cardboard signs. I expect that they had a few fags under the counter for their regular customers but apart from the occasional Woodbine I wasn't much into cigarettes at the time. Anyway smoking, or more accurately being caught smoking, was at Ravensbeck Grammar School only a slightly less heinous offence than putting the junior biology mistress in the pudding club. I remember that this shop also sold real sweets but since no one I knew ever had any sweet coupons after the first Saturday in the month we took no notice of these other than to observe them in an aesthetic sense, rather in the way one regarded the cardboard wedding cakes in the window of the Penge Bakeries.

After the war finally ended the long awaited 'peacetime' that everyone had been going on about seemed a bit slow to take effect but eventually another shop in the High Road came into its own. Theoretically it was a bicycle shop and it did have the odd (and I use the word with precision) second-hand bicycle for sale, but mostly it sold puncture repair kits in little oblong tins and penny lengths of valve rubber. (How that man made a living I can't begin to imagine.) For years we had become used to a standard set of responses to any request to buy almost anything: (a) it was on the ration, (b) it was unobtainable for the duration, (c) it was needed for the war effort. And finally, and irrefutably, (d) don't you know there's a war on?

Anyway, came this incredible day in about 1947 when the word went round the school that the unbelievable had happened. The bicycle shop was selling Dinky Toys – new Dinky Toys. For the ill-informed Dinky Toys were small die-cast models of contemporary motor vehicles and since none had been made since 1939 any few remaining in schoolboy hands were not only in need of maintenance but had a distinctly dated look.

By the time I got to the shop I found a queue all the way down the road to the Queen's Hall cinema, known to us as the fleapit (change of programme Mondays and Thursdays). When I eventually reached the counter I found the owner drunk with power and positively coining it in. You got what you were given. No choice, no questions asked. Hand over your one and threepence and be grateful. It was pure chance whether I received a red post office van, a Vauxhall Vanguard, a taxi cab or a small van with a loudspeaker on top. (I got a post office van.) I was never able to augment my collection because never again did I reach the head of the queue before the stocks ran out. Still, it was a memorable day. Better than the street bonfire on VJ Day really, and that had set the tar in the road on fire.

There were other shops in Penge High Road although some of these were a bit boring. There was the school outfitters, bombed but still open. 'Business as usual' they proclaimed, but there were no clothing coupons to spare for a school blazer, not unless your dad was something pretty big in the black market. Our caps came from there however. War or no war, school caps were de rigueur at Ravensbeck. The headmaster clung on to this last vestige of school civilisation so that we could be pinpointed by the local citizenry when we committed our après-school misdemeanours. Oxo Brown, our beloved headmaster, went his usual puce colour when denouncing the latest depravities of the lower orders in Penge High Road. Evilness was rife: apple core throwing, whistling at the pupils of the girls' grammar school or Woodbine smoking on the Co-op bomb site. These evil miscreants, if identified, would see him after assembly. I dutifully wore my Ravensbeck cap up and down Penge High Road for five excruciating years and never grasped what the little motto under the badge meant. It said 'Mores et studia.' I assumed that this was probably some obscure exhortation to do extra homework.

Mr Oxo Brown's predecessor had been blown up in his semi-detached in Beckenham during an earlier phase of Mr Hitler's nastiness and there were days (most Mondays to Fridays) when I half hoped that a similar fate might befall Oxo. Well, at least a little bomb just to stop him turning so sickeningly puce and going on about the good of the school. Once the war was over even this faint hope was denied me and I had to try to devise some convincing scenario in which Oxo, bearing a striking resemblance to Captain Bligh, was cast adrift in an open boat by a mutinous and cut-throat Form 3H. This alternated with a fantasy of him being strung up from a lamp-post in Penge High Road à la Mussolini.

Some of the pupils of the grammar school for girls cycled down Penge High Road and past our playground on the way to their school. It was only years later that I realised that there was a much more direct route that bypassed our school altogether. I can only assume that ours was the more scenic route. One or two of the more sporting girls seemed to have trouble in controlling their skirts as they pedalled by. It was only when I was in the third form that I became aware of this curious phenomenon. Valerie Sylvester was the most disturbing. She seemed to have no control over her skirt at all but she had an enthusiastic following waiting to cheer her as she pedalled by on her Raleigh each morning.

There were other less regular delights to be savoured. A number of seasonal vendors vied for the schoolboy trade in Penge High Road. There was the hot chestnut man in the winter term and the ice cream man in the summer term. Well, ice cream was perhaps a bit of a misnomer but we knew no better. It was a sort of utility ice cream, a yellowish watery substance with little chunks of ice embedded in it that was dispensed with a flourish from tins loaded on an old hand barrow with a tattered piece of bunting wrapped round it. The barrow leaked ominously from underneath and stood in its own pool of unidentifiable excrescence like an incontinent donkey. Wafers and cones were not available and I think that the ice cream man sold his wares in little paper cups; however my memory may be faulty since it was not the sort of confection that it was wise to dwell upon for too long.

Then there was the Penge Bakeries. It was a vast

cavernous shop full of empty display cases. Sugar rationing was the death of a thousand cuts to the bakery trade and the average Ravensbeck schoolboy was none too pleased about it either. The bakery did sell sticky buns and these were much in vogue because they filled a lot of space at minimum cost. However, once you had bought a bagful you were faced with the reality that they were a bit of a gastronomic disaster area, a bit like gnashing one's way through several old bath sponges. Those buns were excessively short on currants. In fact, if you got more than one in each bun you boasted about it. The top of the bun was smeared with some sugary substance to make it go brown but, I promise you, sticky they might have been but sweet they were not. In these affluent days I am prone to go nearly as puce as Oxo did when some trendy dietician lectures me about my sugar intake. Don't they realise that I have a lot of catching up to do? You had to eat a lot of penny buns in those days to do much harm to your teeth, arteries or colon, although your tummy did tend to swell up a bit after the third one.

Of course, I mustn't forget Tiny's Café. Tiny provided alternatives to school dinners. There just had to be an alternative. His cheese rolls were a distinct improvement on the wafer-thin slices of cold meat striated with fatty substances that were the main component of school dinners. In fairness, they tried to camouflage the depravity of it all with hot and gritty gravy essence but even those who got free dinners sometimes turned and ran. Perhaps it was the lumpy mashed potato with its eyes leering malevolently or maybe the pithy carrots that even Bugs Bunny would have spurned. Anyway, Tiny's establishment was much in vogue. He claimed to be an ex-racing cyclist of some repute but since he was only about five feet nothing I found it hard to imagine him in the Tour de France, unless he did it on a fairy cycle. Still, his apple pie wasn't bad.

One other memory lingers. There was this corner bomb site where one crowded boozy lunchtime a motley collection of Penge citizens from the local factory had been suddenly despatched to never-ending overtime in the sky. It was one of Hitler's buzz-bombs that did it. It gave me a funny feeling just to look at that silent vacant plot. Just a bit of rubble and some wild flowers, and to think that only a few months before it had been a pub full of people slurping mild and bitter and wolfing spam and pickle sandwiches and then... whoosh. At least it helped to put Oxo's inanities into some sort of perspective.

So Penge High Road had a special sort of significance for me; it was my foothold on reality. It might have been the road that led to educational serfdom but it was also the road to freedom and leisure... it was just a question of which way you were facing at the time. Most of all, however, it was what Oxo Brown seemed to resent about it most. It was a place where boys could emphatically be boys – and invariably were.

My First Sweetheart and After

My first sweetheart was Ann Winterbottom. I must have been about nine at the time. She had long dark hair and dimples and I was besotted with her. She used to wear conspicuously short gym slips and white ankle socks and patent leather buckled shoes. In those days children were not encouraged to be curious about love and loving. *The Children's Newspaper* was a bit short on information of this kind and as for the BBC, well forget it. All you got on *Children's Hour* was Larry the Lamb, and he was found under a gooseberry bush. Even finding out how men and women kissed each other was a problem. Well, where did their noses go? You see there was no television, no videos and 'U' pictures at the cinema were a bit short on essential information of the reproductive kind.

There used to be a rather knowing clique at our junior school who used to play mothers and fathers behind the hawthorn bushes at the top of our playing field but by the time I began to get interested in this the playing field had been dug up for the Dig for Victory campaign.

I was an avid reader of *Knockout*, *Dandy* and *Beano* but Pansy Potter, Desperate Dan and Lord Snooty and his friends were not heavily into loving relationships. Even when the characters in my comics had female friends the culmination of their relationships tended to be a slap-up feed in a posh restaurant with lots of fizzy pop and sausages.

There were, however, love songs that my older brother played on our wind-up gramophone. I learned a love song off by heart for Ann Winterbottom. I used to sing it to myself over and over until I was word perfect. I never dared sing it to Ann; you see I had a voice like a frog with laryngitis. The song went: 'Dearly beloved, how clearly I see, somewhere in heaven you were fashioned for me...' Sad, isn't it? I have forgotten the rest.

When Ann Winterbottom tucked her dress into her navy-blue knickers and did handstands against the school fence my passions used to become really inflamed. Mind you, I had a rival for her affections. This was Donald Duxford, the son of the landlord of the Springpark Hotel. On one occasion Donald invited all his little chums to play. We were allowed the run of the attic floor at the Springpark Hotel and we played soldiers. Ann was the nurse. I kept getting wounded so that I could get her to bandage me up. It never occurred to me to get wounded in any vital part. In fact, I don't think that I knew I had any vital parts. Then we got to play some kissing games and I kissed her all over her face. Actually, there didn't seem a lot of fun in it but it was obviously the thing to do when you were in love. There followed a torrid courtship which included several visits to the Children's Saturday Morning Cinema Club and a shopping trip to Croydon with her and her mum. Sitting next to her on the bus all the way to Croydon was absolute bliss. The half-fare was tuppence ha'penny so you could tell it was a long way. Sadly, Ann eventually transferred her affections to Donald Duxford who got regular pocket money.

The next woman in my life was Josie Higgins. She was a very forward little girl. Our small gang used to play games of hiding and chase in Coote's field and occasionally little Josie would honour us with her presence. She was very pretty with blonde hair and she also wore disturbingly short skirts. She would sometimes become exasperated if she didn't get her own way and would then say, 'Oh, I'll do you.' If she was in a more forthcoming mood she would vary this and say instead, 'Would you like to do me?' I didn't really know what she meant but I thought that it sounded quite interesting. These remarks would be reinforced with a jerk of her pelvis that was knowing beyond her years and made my neck go pink. I never had any moments of great intimacy with Josie but I used to think about her a lot. When we played 'Kick the Can' she sometimes hid in the bushes with Donald Duxford. Sometimes we couldn't get them to come out even when the game was finished.

Sometimes I used to go round to the home of the Dawkins family. There were three Dawkins girls around my age and we used to play a variety of games and have goes on their swing. I gave their older brother Bernard a wide berth since he was going through a funny phase at the time. I did once get locked in the pram shed with Vera Dawkins and we occasionally played games of truth and dare. Sheila Dawkins once dared Vera Dawkins to run round the garden with her skirt up and her knickers down but the dare was rejected, largely on practical grounds I suspect. After all, running about with your knickers round your ankles would be a bit tricky, wouldn't it? It could easily land you head first in Mr Dawkins's floribundas for starters.

The Dawkins girls had another little friend who used to come round to play. She was rather pretty and impressionable and she used to look at me admiringly whilst I recounted my knowledge of Harold Larwood and leg theory but I signally failed to exploit this brief period of hero-worship. Mind you, we had some very nice games of French cricket.

My group of little chums who used to meet in Coote's Field would occasionally have desultory discussions about where babies came from but these were curiously theoretical affairs and I don't think we had made the connection between babies and love, let alone lust. Bill Oddy had this theory that babies came out of ladies' belly buttons but this was generally regarded as more improbable than tooth fairies. My own secret and unexpressed view was that you probably saved up for a baby and then sent away for it and had it delivered by Carter Patterson rather like a Christmas hamper.

Ah well, after keeping Carter Patterson under scrutiny for some considerable time there comes a moment when you just have to consider other possibilities, no matter how improbable.

Learning About Love

It took me a long time to discover that there was more to love than kissing. Going to Ravensbeck Grammar School, however, provided education that was not in the official curriculum. At the age of twelve whilst queuing up, rather aptly for a French lesson, an inky young classmate told me my first dirty joke. (You are quite right, I was a late developer.) The joke was about the conversation of three secretaries. The first announced that she had found a 'Frenchy' in the boss's desk. The second said that she cut the top off it to teach the boss a lesson. The third one fainted. Yes, I do realise that this is not a very good joke. In any event it was totally lost on me. For starters I didn't know what a Frenchy was. My young colleague explained. Thus a whole new field of learning was opened up for me.

I began to give the subject considerable attention since it seemed to beat conkers or five stones which were the other crazes at the school at the time. I can't pretend that I approached the subject as methodically as might have been desirable. There was, as I have explained, only very limited source material available. I did manage to obtain a copy of *Health and Efficiency* but all the nude ladies shown in it had their backs turned or were hiding their most interesting bits behind what appeared to be gooseberry bushes.

Mortensen, the stud of form 2H, did have a postcard of a gentleman clad only in his socks and a moustache who was engaged in some form of close activity with two ladies with bobbed hair and suspenders but I only ever got a brief glimpse of this and I couldn't establish who was doing what to whom, let alone how.

At a much later stage in my education I acquired a little book entitled *Married Love*. I don't think that there were any books around at that time that acknowledged that there was any other kind. Even my new acquisition was a bit disappointing. The highlight of my little book, which was somewhat coy with a heavy emphasis on loving relationships and a certain vagueness about practicalities, was a diagram depicting a lady's naughty bits. The artist seemed to be into cubist impressionism rather than the old school of artistic realism. Personally, I have always preferred Constable or Landseer. With them you knew what it was you were looking at. Well, that diagram was the best that I could get. It looked rather boring actually and I couldn't tell what all the fuss was about. Still, I memorised it just in case.

Sometimes a group of us would stand outside the Black Cat Café at Elmers End. We couldn't usually afford to go in but we would stand and watch the girls go by and exchange strategic information. Pamela Ashwell was alleged to be very familiar with her boyfriends, so familiar that the thought of it made me quite twitchy. Then someone made a date for me. She lived in a bomb-damaged cottage near Elmers End bus garage. We went to the cinema and I braced myself to be ravished in the back row. It was not to be. Perhaps I should have invested in a quarter pound box of Milk Tray but sadly venture capital was in short supply at the time, not to mention sweet coupons.

They were exciting but frustrating years. All that yearning and pent-up energy! Despite all the talk and bragging my social circle seemed to have remarkably little success with the opposite gender. Norman Frange introduced a system by which we recorded our amatory successes. In essence this involved a scale of one to ten.

Average scores in my social circle were about three point four. Then there was a breakthrough. Norman Frange claimed a seven point five and described the achievement rather like the Normandy Landings.

My school chum Barry Quiller and I used to go out in the evenings after homework looking for girls. The convention of the times was that boys walked around in pairs and girls walked around in pairs, then boys followed girls, girls stopped and looked in shop windows or sat on park benches and boys tried some subtle conversational gambit. I could never think of anything to say but Barry Quiller was very good at it. You couldn't say anything too familiar since this would make the girls feel that they were being picked up. And that, of course, was considered dreadfully common. On the other hand, comments about the weather were clearly not going to advance the relationship very far.

One of my other school chums, Stuart Vigour, was a very self-confident fellow. He used to say outrageous things and the girls would just giggle and blush. His favourite chat-up line was, 'Can I book you a place in Sunnyfields?' Sunnyfields was the local maternity hospital and this approach was considered very naughty. Mind you, according to Stuart, he did very well out of it.

One evening Barry Quiller and I met Samantha Spinks and Diana Morton. Sammy went straight up one side and straight down the other. She would have made a beanpole look shapely. Diana was rather pretty with a shape that even her school uniform could not conceal. Her nose was a bit beaky but you can't expect everything. Anyway, sadly she favoured Barry Quiller. Sammy mostly giggled and clung to Diana's arm. Since I could never think of anything to say, I tried to convey that I was the strong silent type like Randolph Scott but it didn't seem to impress anybody. I used to carry a torch for Diana for about a year after this.

Her house was by the railway line at Elmers End. I used to hang out of the train window on the way home from school in the vain hope of catching a glimpse of her and in direct contravention of all the railway bye-laws. Eventually she did deign to go to the pictures with me but the event was a fiasco. Diana finally decided that she wished to engage in a spell of passionate kissing just at the moment that my nose started to run. It was all very unfortunate. We never met again.

The trouble was that there was so much to learn and not many places to learn it from. My chums and I used to spend endless hours standing around telling each other rude jokes about commercial travellers and farmers' daughters and ladies of the night and boasting about our experiences, real or imagined.

Our wanderings often took us to the Langley Park golf course where a Dunlop 65 could occasionally be found in the rough. Bill Oddy would buy them from us at two bob each and then sell them on to the golf professional for half a crown. However, as our interests broadened we became aware that other sports were taking place on the golf course and that there were products of another rubber company littered about in the rough. We found a vicarious thrill from locating the scene of these activities and pursued our interests with all the perseverance of forensic scientists. There, usually below a tree, we might find an area of flattened grass and a few cigarette ends. (Whatever the pleasure Players complete it, the advertisement used to say.) There too we would often find a shrivelled rubber thing rather like a colourless balloon left over from an austerity party. The instantly recognisable wrapper was usually round the other side of the tree and probably meant that the gallant but shy male had retired there to gird himself for the fray. We used to examine these scenes reverently.

These days, of course, even the BBC talks about

condoms but in my youthful years you could get seriously clonked for saying, 'Durex'. One day Norman Frange took Geoff Bragg and me into his parents' bedroom to see the reusable rubber thing that lay in their bedside cabinet. The thought that Mr and Mrs Frange did something like that quite shocked me. The thought of actually doing it oneself was frequently imagined and talked about but it seemed to be extremely hard to arrange. How did one get hold of the necessary accessories for a start? If you couldn't speak about Frenchies in public how did you buy them? I was very impressed in the barber's one day when a man came in and without a word spun a half crown in the air and was given a packet of Durex. He didn't even stop for a haircut. He just marched out as confidently as he had entered. I couldn't help thinking that if I had tried the same technique I would have probably ended up walking out with a large jar of Brylcreem or a hygienic steel comb. Eventually I did acquire a packet. I can't remember how. I suspect that I persuaded a braver spirit to buy them for me. I certainly didn't go into the chemist's. I would never have been able to look the lady assistant in the eye. The packet of little rubber goodies remained in my wallet for a very long time and was used to convince my friends that my intentions were serious. Sadly, all three little items remained untouched by human hand and only reinforced the harsh reality of my lack of success with the opposite sex.

In those days we wouldn't have known what a condom was. In my social circles they were usually referred to as Frenchies or French letters. Funny, isn't it, that anything a bit naughty is given a foreign name? There were Dutch caps and French letters and French knickers and French kissing. There was even a rumour in my social circle that the French used a special device for washing their naughty bits but I assumed that this was just fanciful rubbish.

Then I fell in love with a photograph. It was a photo of

Geoff Bragg's cousin. She was sitting in the garden with her pet dog on her lap. She had magnificent legs and the dog was a wire-haired terrier. Now Geoff was as ugly as sin but this girl was well, fantastic. She lived in Woodford Heath which was sixpence on the telephone. Geoff used to phone her sometimes and I would get to chat with her. Eventually I began to phone her every day. She used to say cheeky things to me that made my spots get worse. We only ever actually met once but we had lovely telephone conversations. When we did meet she turned out to be even more ravishing than her photograph but she was promised to another who turned out to be about ten feet tall and at least eighteen and with a mean expression like William Bendix in a bad mood.

In desperation I found a penfriend through the *Filmgoers Weekly*. She lived in Newcastle. She wrote nice friendly letters and we shared a common interest in Alan Ladd. Still, there is a limit to the number of letters you can write about Alan Ladd. Eventually she sent me a photograph. It showed two young women on a beach at Whitley Bay. One was very pretty. You've guessed it, mine was the one with the prominent teeth and the receding chin.

My desperate urge to have a more rewarding relationship with a woman was not helped by Norman Frange's constant claims of amorous achievement. Even allowing for a certain amount of exaggeration Norman was disgustingly successful with women. He had a close relationship with Mary Waggett who was the daughter of the first wicket down at the West Wickham Cricket Club. She was a spindly-legged, flat-chested girl with glasses but she had engaged Norman's interest by her graphic description of what she did with her Waterman's fountain pen. He passed on this information to the rest of us. He used to take her round the back of the cricket pavilion whilst her father was batting valiantly for West Wickham.

Norman continued to report to us on an incredible succession of achievements. There was the foreign ward orderly at Bromley Hospital where he had enjoyed being an inpatient and there was his childhood friend who had granted him an exploration licence when she was only fourteen and a half. Then there was a solidly built girl with thick ankles but willing ways who used to wear her mother's French knickers in order to captivate our Norman. Finally, Norman settled for Betty Huddle. She was a rather skinny girl who always looked as though she had been dragged through a hedge backwards. She had a perpetual sniff and adenoids but she quickly grasped the way to Norman's heart. It was at about this stage that I realised the secret of Norman's success: he was totally relentless and completely undiscriminating.

I can't tell you how jealous Norman made me feel. But into each life an occasional ray of sunlight must fall. I met Mary Whitley in the Blake Recreation Ground in the early summer of 1948. She was fair-haired, pretty and had outstanding bosoms for a fifteen year old. For reasons that I have never understood she took a considerable liking to me. I was overwhelmed by passion. It was like having Virginia Mayo as a girlfriend.

There followed a voyage of adventure for us both that included frequent walks around the Langley Park golf course and some passionate cuddles under the oak tree behind the British Legion hut. Don't misunderstand me. It was scarcely *Lady Chatterley's Lover*. Still, we did eventually get to about eight point three three recurring on the Frange Scale. Sadly, after a year we fell out. I was heartbroken. I tried to seek solace elsewhere but even a ride in the Ghost Train with Loraine Perch was not enough. Still, she did have a very tight sweater and extremely pert little bosoms. Then I went off to do my national service and life was never the same again. You didn't learn a lot about love in the Royal Air Force.

Mary Whitley

My first grown-up love affair was with Mary Whitley and I
have never forgotten her. I think the relationship lasted less
than a year but it left me more shell-shocked than the Blitz.
I met Mary in the Blake Recreation Ground in West
Wickham in the summer of 1948 when I was fifteen and a
half and she was just fifteen.

There was something quite mystical about the summer
of 1948. I expect that it was all to do with adolescent
biology but it seemed more magical than that at the time.
Each evening as the shadows lengthened in the Blake
Recreation Ground, drowsy May-bugs droned around like
slow, low-flying anti-submarine bombers. There was a
warm lazy somnolence and the sap was rising and young
hormones were doing whatever it is that young hormones
do whenever given half a chance.

As the light failed and the various sporting activities
ceased the local adolescents would flop down on the grassy
slope under the trees just upwind of the public toilets and
thoughts would turn to love and associated subjects. The
assembled youths told jokes and sang rude songs and
boasted about their achievements and the subject was
nearly always sex. Soon Albert the park keeper would ring
his bell and we would all obediently trek out of the Rec.
The lucky ones would disappear with their consorts and the
rest of us would have our dreams.

Most of my chums boasted about their amorous
achievements, real or imagined. It was often difficult to tell

which. Norman Frange was the most experienced. Mind you, he was totally unrelenting and quite undiscriminating. Bessie Braddock wouldn't have been safe if Norman had been within striking distance. He had a scoring system to measure his achievements. Ten on the Frange scale was the ultimate but even he did not claim that. Young women of our acquaintance did not surrender their virtue easily in those days – well, only a little of it. Norman did, however, consistently claim scores of between seven and eight which, even allowing for a measure of boasting, impressed us greatly.

Why is it, I wonder, that when people grow older they forget the powerful urges of youth? It is sad really that old people are forced to disapprove of the behaviour of young people and young people cannot believe that old folk ever did anything below the waist. When people are honest about their amorous activities, past or present, this old world will probably stop turning.

Most of my friends seemed much more successful with women than I was. Well, actually I didn't really know any women. Then one evening a crowd of us were fooling about with a bald tennis ball whilst a small group of girls hung around to watch our sporting prowess. As dusk fell the males and females merged into a single group and flopped down under the trees as was the custom. There was much banter and showing off and I watched with envy the chat-up lines of my more self-confident friends. Mary Whitley was amongst the crowd and was receiving a good deal of attention. I had seen Mary on a number of occasions before and I had secretly admired her but had assumed her to be unattainable. She had fair hair and was very pretty and had surprisingly large bosoms for a fifteen year old. Come to that they were surprisingly large for a seventeen year old.

That magical evening, for reasons that I could not fathom, it became apparent that she had taken a fancy to me. I couldn't believe it. This had never happened to me before. I was enraptured. Here was a girl, a real live girl with bosoms and everything, who actually seemed to like me. Perhaps she preferred older men. After all I was fifteen and a half.

I was a bit overwhelmed by Mary Whitley's growing devotion to me. I usually went pink when in the company of a girl and could never think of anything to say. It was a curious courtship. Mary was a nice, intelligent, loving girl but I regret to say that my adolescent urges made me see her more as a challenge than a companion. There was no doubt about it, I wanted her body, or at least as much of it as was feasible. Don't blame me. Blame it on human nature and Freud.

We used to meet in the Blake Recreation Ground and Mary would come straight across to where I was consorting with my mates. She would put her hand in mine and give me one of her long adoring looks. It was flattering but embarrassing and it made my neck go pink.

I can't remember much of what we used to talk about when we were alone. We must have said something to each other during all our long walks and cuddles. I was in my Alan Ladd phase at the time so I expect that when lost for conversation I probably limited my comments to 'Yep' and 'Nope' and tried to give the impression of being the strong and silent type. Enigmatic monosyllables had not gone down too well with the other local girls but it seemed that I could do no wrong where Mary was concerned. She even seemed interested when I gave my somewhat embroidered account of my cricketing achievements. I suspect that I also tried to impress her with a detailed report of my one and only flight in a Tiger Moth whilst in the Air Training Corps and by quoting the long bits of *Macbeth* that I was learning for my School Certificate examination.

Sadly, I never had a proper photograph of Mary. I did

once take a snapshot of her chubby little knees whilst a group of us were skylarking in the park shelter between the tennis courts. I am embarrassed to confess that the focus of the picture was indicative of my preoccupations at the time.

At Christmas 1948 Mary gave me a really nice present. This was the first time a girlfriend ever gave me a Christmas present. I was immensely impressed. It was two records. There was Mario Lanza singing 'Be my Love' and a piano selection by someone called Semprini which included a tune called 'Thinking of You' and another one with the lyric: 'Maybe I'm right and maybe I'm wrong, maybe I'm weak and maybe I'm strong, but nevertheless I'm in love with you.' It was all very romantic. There was a good twelve bob's worth of records there which was not peanuts out of a schoolgirl's pocket money. Slow on the uptake though I was, I then realised that Mary was in love with me. It was very scary. It made me feel sort of trembly. Apart from my dear old mum nobody had ever loved me before.

Sometimes when pocket money allowed we went to the pictures. My first experience of the magic of the back row of the one and nines was shared with Mary. I think the film was Betty Grable in *Mother Wore Tights* or it could have been Alan Ladd in *Whispering Smith*. When engaged in amorous activities I tended to neglect the film a bit.

When one of the first post-war travelling fairs arrived in West Wickham I took Mary for a ride on the dodgems. I felt very much in charge. It is a powerful sensation to take your baby for a drive. I felt like George Raft giving his moll a ride in his Cadillac. We had a cuddle on the big wheel as well but then my money ran out.

There was also one memorable occasion when Norman Frange's parents went out for the evening and Norman invited his current girlfriend Betty Huddle to spend the evening with him. Mary and I were invited to join them.

The Frange family had this Regentone radiogram. It was very modern and expensive and I think they were having trouble with the payments. Anyway, it played eight 78 records automatically which was the next best thing to having your own jukebox. With the lights out a good deal of serious hanky-panky could go on during the course of eight 78s. Betty sat on Norman's lap in one armchair and Mary on mine in another one. Sadly, the sounds of passion from the other side of the room were only partly replicated on our side. Nonetheless, Perry Como singing 'Far away places' still brings back some pleasant memories.

Despite her devotion to me Mary was a virtuous girl. Sadly, in those days most girls were, more or less. Mary defended her territory doggedly. Nonetheless, she was keen to please and she used to borrow her mother's high-heeled shoes to look more sophisticated. Another of Norman Frange's girlfriends, he claimed, had gone one better and used to borrow her mother's loose-legged panties. This avoided the problems that most of us faced in struggling with school knickers with elastic round the legs. These were known as Harvest Festivals. Oh, work it out for yourself.

When I first circumnavigated Mary's school knickers I knew how Captain Cook must have felt when he discovered New Caledonia. My success took place in the middle of a field of sweet-smelling long grass on the edge of Langley Park golf course in the late summer of 1948. It was one of the most exciting moments in my teenage years. I don't think that I said thank you to Mary at the time so a word of appreciation seems long overdue.

Our voyages of discovery continued during long evening walks to the more secluded and leafy parts of West Wickham. There were rapturous interludes during our rambles across the Langley Park golf course and some magical occasions when time stood still under the oak tree behind the British Legion hut. Whilst we never reached beyond eight point three three recurring on the Frange scale it all seemed pretty wonderful at the time.

Our relationship took us through the winter of 1948 at a time when courting for youngsters usually had to be conducted al fresco. This was in an era when teenagers didn't have much spending power so we could only engage in activities which were free, or at best which didn't cost more than about four bob a week.

There were all sorts of obstacles to a satisfactory love life in those days. For starters each of us had an hour and a half's homework each night and Mary's parents set a curfew of ten o'clock. We also used to fall out over the loss of Friday nights. Mary followed the advertisements and insisted that Friday night was Amami night. (Gives hair natural clean silklike sheen: fourpence and sevenpence-halfpenny each.) All this coupled with the vagaries of the weather demanded high degrees of perseverance and ingenuity.

Sometimes I would try to persuade Albert, the Blake Recreation Ground head keeper, to loan me the keys to his hut so that I could coax Mary in there after the Rec had closed and when inclement weather was restricting my amorous initiatives. Sadly, he was impervious to my pleas. Whether it was sour grapes or fear of the Parks Committee I cannot say.

Eventually we found a particularly accommodating oak tree on the far side of the Langley Park golf course under which we plighted our troth throughout the worst of the 1948 winter weather. I made a sentimental journey there in 1996 to see if the tree was still there. Not only had they chopped it down but ironically they had built a girls' school on the site.

Sadly, I was a Walter Mitty lover, high on fantasy but low on practical skills. There were so many unanswered questions. For example, why were bra straps designed like an initiative test and how did one go about French kissing? I couldn't find the right words of love or the right caresses. Surreptitious looks at *Health and Efficiency* were no help at all and there was little other source material available.

Mary was a modest girl and I didn't dare to admit to her that once her defences were lowered I was perplexed about how best to proceed. Making love leaning against an oak tree in deep midwinter is fraught with difficulty. There was also the unspoken fear that if things became too torrid Mary might end up in what Norman Frange called the pudding club. In respectable West Wickham this would have been the ultimate disgrace. I became more and more frustrated and confused. Sometimes I positively ached with frustration. Alan Ladd never seemed to have problems like this.

Sadly, in the early summer of 1949 Mary and I fell out. I had never really been able to cope with her devotion. It was a bit scary and, anyway, I was pretty sure that I didn't deserve it. I can still picture her pale face framed by her fair swept-back hair looking up at me with those gentle, adoring eyes. In the ways of love I suppose that I had taken her for granted. There seemed to be so much to worry about. There was my School Certificate exam and my plans to become a famous press photographer and whether my excessive use of Brylcreem was making my spots get worse. There was so much to do as well and sometimes I wanted to play single wicket cricket with my mates or spend Sunday cycling to Brighton and back.

The situation was not helped when Mary and I played tennis. I had never played tennis before but I imagined that you just whopped the ball over the net. Since I was bigger and stronger I assumed that it would be easy to beat Mary and to impress her with my prowess. Unfortunately, Mary played tennis at school and actually knew the rules.

Furthermore, the shortness of her tennis skirt played havoc with my concentration. She beat me soundly. Whilst I blamed my defeat on my sister's old tennis racket my excuses were not convincing, especially since I suspected that Mary, in her tactful way, had not been trying all that hard.

I became a bit huffy and sulky after that and then we had our big quarrel and stupidly I stomped off in a rage without making any arrangements to meet her again. I very quickly discovered that I missed her desperately. Sadly, it was too late. I must have been particularly horrible to her because she wouldn't have any more to do with me. I couldn't phone her because she was not on the phone. I didn't dare call at her home because Norman Frange told me her mum had called me a bugger for upsetting her daughter so. Norman seemed to relish my misery and I wondered if he had designs on Mary himself. I was also frightened of Mary's dad. I had been told that he was a fireman and I always pictured him in uniform with one of those hatchets in his belt ready to fight a fire or anyone who had taken liberties with his daughter. Even worse, it was said that he made all visitors sample his dandelion wine.

Desperate to re-establish contact I wrote Mary a note asking her to phone me and enclosing four pennies for the phone box. At the time this seemed a suitably masterful approach. Rather in the James Mason mode, I reckoned. I waited for a message or a phone call but none came.

Then I saw her with a group of friends at the grand Bank Holiday Fair in Beckenham Park. She sent an emissary over to see me. My heart surged with hope. Perhaps I was to be forgiven. There was no message. It was just the return of my four pennies. 'Mary asked me to give you this,' he said. I can still remember the pain and humiliation of that rejection. A football in the vitals was more fun. Sadly, Mary never spoke to me again and thereafter I only caught glimpses of her from afar.

For a very long time after that I used to haunt the district where she lived. I used to hang around hoping for a chance meeting or even to effect some miraculous reconciliation but it was not to be. I was too proud and too hurt to risk further rejection. I used to lurk in the shadows wearing my old raincoat with its collar turned up and smoking my cheap cigarettes just like that man in the cigarette advert. 'You are never alone with a Strand.' The reality was that I was extremely sad and lonely with a nearly empty packet of Players Weights. Sometimes I imagined I was James Mason in *Odd Man Out* instead.

Then came two years in the Royal Air Works with Sunday nights in the billet spent listening to the top twenty on Radio Luxembourg. All the records seemed to remind me of Mary: 'My Heart Cries for You', 'Unforgettable', 'Too Late Now', 'I Apologise'… I used to get so heartsick that in the end it almost came as a relief when they played 'How Much is That Doggie in the Window?'

Ah well, it was all a very long time ago. I wonder what happened to Mary Whitley. She could be a great-grandmother by now. I still have these pangs of regret that I did not treat her better. I wonder if she would be flattered if she knew I still think of her? Probably not.

The Wireless

I was a late convert to television, mainly because Mr Baird was a bit slow in getting around to inventing it. It's true that they started transmitting programmes about three years after I was born but they abandoned television during World War Two and I didn't even learn about its existence until after the war and even then I didn't believe it. I thought that it was one of those stories like Father Christmas. I was as sure that they couldn't send pictures through the air as I was that Santa couldn't get down our chimney. I was twenty years old before I actually saw a television programme and even then I wished I hadn't bothered. Reception was terrible and sets in those days seemed to have a lot of trouble with their horizontal holds so announcers often looked as if they were jumping up and down in a snowstorm. It did my nerves no good at all.

Anyway, in my youth there was only what we called the wireless to bring entertainment into our semi-detached in Springhurst Avenue. Incidentally, I never knew why they called it the wireless. What with the aerial and the mains lead and all the fiddly bits inside it positively sprouted wires.

By the time I arrived on the scene the Edom family had passed through the cat's whisker and headphones stage although there was some equipment abandoned in the garden shed that looked as though it was destined for the Science Museum. There was an elderly accumulator and a curious folding device for carrying it round to the wireless shop for recharging and there was an ancient wireless set the size of a small coffin with all its inner workings mounted on a block of solid wood. It looked like the inside of Battersea Power Station and had controls the size of doorknobs.

The sense of wonder about the miracle of wireless was beginning to wane by the time I began to take an interest in the air waves. Every garden in Springhurst Avenue still had a tall wooden pole for the wireless aerial but the Edom family pole had rotted and blown down in a gale. In fact, I didn't even discover what it had been for until about 1943. That was when we chopped it up for logs during the fuel shortage. Anyway, our new set could make do with a wire aerial draped round the picture rail. People still talked affectionately about 2LO and Savoy Hill and cat's whiskers and things but it all made my eyes go glazed, like when they talked about the Kaiser or the Battle of the Somme.

I did wonder about experimenting with a cat's whisker. Sometimes I would look speculatively at Johnny, our tom pussy, and wonder whether to utilise one of his accoutrements to build my own set but I never put it to the test mostly because he always drew blood when he was displeased.

Our new wireless bought in 1934 was the first one I can recall listening to. It was a large square wooden box and it had a small dial, three knobs and a large fretwork piece with fabric behind it that concealed the loudspeaker. The fretwork bit was shaped like a flash of lightning which was considered very modern. Electricity was still a bit of a marvel in those days. The wireless was, I was told, an all wave mains affair with exciting places on the dial like Hilversum and Geneva, wherever they were. Anyway, apart from the national and regional programmes there wasn't a lot to be heard except for a good deal of humming, buzzing and crackling and an occasional bit of screeching. It was linked to the mains supply by a frayed flex and a cracked Bakelite two-pin plug that would have brought the Health and Safety Executive out in spots.

When you first switched it on a little light came on behind the dial but this went out in 1938 and never worked again. It would have been more symbolic if it had gone out in 1939 but technology has no sense of timing or romance, has it? Our wireless took a terribly long time to warm up and seemed to lack concentration so that it kept wandering off the programme and lapsing into crackling and buzzing like an elderly relative. This was a bit vexing if you were trying to listen to the Western Brothers' funny lyrics or the football results. As for the King's Christmas message, what with his stutter and our wireless's lack of concentration it was a wonder we heard any of it.

During the war the Edom family became a two wireless family. We had a smaller set located on the shelf in the kitchen next to the pots and pans. It was a brash modern affair made of Bakelite; a lump came off it in 1940 when a nearby bomb brought the kitchen ceiling down but it made no difference. It still crackled and buzzed even worse than the one in the dining room. Still, it was cosy in the kitchen on winter's evenings. Saturday evenings were best.

Saturday night was fish and chip night if the Yew Tree Fish Restaurant had any fish. The best news you could hope for in those days was a chalked sign outside the Yew Tree Fish Restaurant announcing 'Frying Tonight'. A ninepenny piece of cod and threepenn'orth of chips was sheer bliss. Mind you, I never forgave Mr Hitler for denying me tomato sauce. For some complex military reason tomato sauce disappeared for the duration of the war and we had to make do with brown sauce. I shudder to think what that was made with.

Anyway, the kitchen was the venue for Saturday night fried fish and chips and it was not only nicely warmed by the anthracite boiler but it also allowed us a swift line of retreat out of the kitchen door to the air raid shelter when the siren went off.

The wireless was at its best on Saturday nights. First there was *In Town Tonight*. Once again we stop the mighty roar of London's traffic to bring you those interesting people who are... In Town Tonight. Then we got Eric Coates's 'Knightsbridge March'. It made you feel that you were really there. Who the interesting people were I really can't remember, but then fame is ephemeral, isn't it?

After *In Town Tonight* came *Music Hall* with people like Gert and Daisy and 'Mind my Bike' Jack Warner or 'The Day War Broke Out...' with Rob Wilton. Sometimes Teddy Brown had a go with his xylophone. After that came Alvar Lidell with the nine o'clock news. He usually had bad news to tell us but he did it with an impeccable stiff upper lip. Sometimes Bruce Belfridge did it instead.

The nine o'clock news during the war was a semi-religious event. Everyone stopped to listen. My old dad would get his *Daily Telegraph* war map out to trace the location of the latest military disaster. It was all a bit lost on me. Where the bloody hell was Singapore anyway?

I wasn't very partial to *Children's Hour* either; they all seemed a bit too posh for me. When you listened it always made you feel that you ought to straighten your socks and wipe your nose. Still, I liked the Toytown music and Larry the Lamb was all right but Uncle Mac was a patronising old pain. He always made me feel that he didn't really consider me a suitable member for his elite band of little listeners. *Children's Hour* didn't really seem to be designed for kiddiewinks with South London accents and a bloodthirsty taste for Red Indians and pirates. Mind you, his wasn't the only club that I didn't belong to. I never joined the Teddy Tail Club either, or the Ovaltinees and the Cubs certainly wouldn't have had me.

My brother, rather older and more sophisticated than me, was an aficionado of Henry Hall and his orchestra but I preferred Richard Murdoch and Arthur Askey in *Bandwagon*. Richard Murdoch used to say, 'You silly little man!' and Arthur Askey would say things like 'Aythangyow' and everybody laughed like billy-o. There was also Mrs Bagwash and her daughter Nausea.

Before the war it was mostly military bands and talks and theatre organs and Mr Stuart Hibberd telling us that Mr Chamberlain was convinced that 1939 was going to be more tranquil than 1938. Mind you, Mr Chamberlain seemed to have forgotten this when he gave us his little chat on 3rd September, 1939.

Never mind, there was always *Monday Night at Seven* which was more to my taste. There was Harry Waldron's 'Puzzle Corner' and it was all presented, as they told us every Monday, by Harry S. Pepper.

Then there was *ITMA* which appealed to me because of all the funny characters. There was Colonel Chinstrap: 'I don't mind if I do, sir,' and Mrs Mopp: 'Can I do yer now, sir?' but best of all was the German spy: 'Zis is Fünf speaking.' Our school playground used to be full of little urchins doing bad imitations of Colonel Chinstrap or Fünf and reading *Radio Fun*.

The BBC was a bit sniffy and self-righteous in those long-ago days. The Corporation clearly knew what was best for you. Some things don't change, do they? There always seems to be some self-righteous prat around to tell you what is best for you. Anyway the BBC wouldn't even mention the odds on the horse-racing results and wouldn't admit that most people wanted to hear the football results to mark them on their Littlewoods coupons. The announcer wouldn't tell you how many draws there were and as for mentioning the probable pools pay-out that would have been as unthinkable as saying something disrespectful about the royal family or using a naughty word like 'poop'. I believe they thought that encouraging gambling wasn't good for the lower orders and might lead to riot and civil commotion. When the BBC really wanted to assert its authority or didn't know what to do next it resorted to a carefully chosen gramophone record. Their best favourite was Ann Ziegler and Webster Booth singing 'Ah, Sweet Mystery of Life'. This usually reduced any malcontents to numbed silence.

During the war the BBC felt that it had a mission to improve our morale and to offer morally uplifting programmes. The result was a funny old mixture ranging from gardening hints (how to get the best out of your compost heap) to cookery tips (fish pie again). Then there was *Workers Playtime* which was intended to spur us on to even greater efforts although I have to confess it never did a lot for me.

Then there was *In to Battle*, introduced with stirring military music and telling a story of valour with full sound effects. (Rat-a-tat-tat-tat... boom, boom, etc.). '...then Sergeant Hemsley, severely wounded, stormed the machine-gun emplacement, armed only with a beer bottle opener and a tin of bully beef.'

In about 1947 the BBC came over all queer and introduced *Dick Barton*. It was very exciting. When the BBC realised how popular it was they panicked; they had obviously made a mistake.

I used to listen to *Dick Barton* whilst I did my home-work. It used to take my mind off my algebra. (Who wanted to multiply letters anyway? Figures were bad enough.) First of all there was this exciting music. Later on I discovered that it was called 'The Devil's Gallop'. Dick and his chums, Snowy and Jock, were always facing some fiendish plot and at the end of each quarter-hour episode Dick was always left in some tricky predicament: up to his neck in a swamp, hanging over a cliff by his finger tips or tied up in a cellar with a cobra down his trousers.

Dick Barton suffered all this without benefit of alcohol or thingy with his lady friend and he never said anything more rude than 'Demmed bad show' or 'By jingo'. Years later I discovered that the BBC had strict rules for Dick Barton's behaviour that excluded naughty words, violence (except in self-defence), alcohol and nookie. How that man survived, God alone knows.

I don't know when *Have a Go* started. Sometimes I think that it must have been going on for ever. Wilfred Pickles used to introduce the programme from somewhere improbable like Chipping Norton or Ashby-de-la-Zouch. It was all done in his dreadful over-emphasised north country accent: ''Ow do, 'ow are yer?' or 'Give 'im the money, Barney.' Wilfred's wife Mabel was also involved. I always had my suspicions about Barney and Mabel. Mabel, it was said, was at the table. But what, I asked myself, was Barney up to? Apart from giving out the money I mean.

Sunday lunchtime was a peak listening period just after the war. There was *Two Way Family Favourites* which even now makes me think of the Sunday roast gently sizzling in the oven. By the time we sat down to eat it was the *Billy Cotton Bandshow*. 'Wakey, wakey.' I went to see Billy Cotton and his band at the Croydon Empire once. During one of the novelty numbers the band pelted the audience with cotton wool snowballs. You didn't get the snowballs on the wireless.

Oh, God, I had quite forgotten; at some stage there was also Big Bill Campbell and his Rocky Mountain Rhythm. This was the BBC's idea of Western music. I think that the musicians were all meant to be cowboys but I was never really clear about why they were up the Rocky Mountains. After every rendition Big Bill Campbell would say, 'Mighty fine,' and someone in the background would shout,

'Yippee' in a BBC accent. The band seemed heavily dependent on accordions and violins and the music was of a distinctly jiggy nature. It all sounded the same to me.

Of course, there were other atrocities like Sandy MacPherson at the theatre organ and Edmundo Ross and *Victor Sylvester's Dancing Club* but they all pale into insignificance at the thought of Big Bill Campbell.

Still, even the Edom family had to move with the times. I remember feeling very proud when our new Murphy radio was delivered in about 1948. By this time it was considered modern to call your set a radio. Our Murphy was quite impressive if you didn't look too closely. It was floor-standing and very big although when you peered in the back it just had some valves and wires and things and a loudspeaker and a great deal of empty space. Anyway, it had a very shiny cabinet in mahogany veneer. Some people were buying radiograms after the war but the Edoms never had the cash for that sort of ostentation.

The programmes started to get better too. There was *Take it from Here* and *Ray's a Laugh* and *Educating Archie*. Mind you, having a ventriloquist on the wireless was a bit of a swizz. How could I be sure that Peter Brough's lips weren't moving?

These days people talk about the Goons and *Hancock's Half Hour* with nostalgic reverence but these are just modern upstarts as far as I am concerned. What, I want to know, happened to *Happidrome* with Ramsbottom and Enoch and Mr Lovejoy?

In my teenage years the BBC still had terrible hang-ups about jazz and popular music and felt it necessary to ration it and, as for rude words, it was absolutely terrified of them. Popular music wasn't described that way at all. It was referred to by the BBC as 'dance music' in a heavily condescending tone and was generally broadcast by a superannuated orchestra and late at night when the BBC hoped no one of consequence would be listening.

The BBC had still not come to terms with the hit parade by 1951. It just couldn't bring itself to play the records of the top twenty. Partly because most of the records were American but mainly because the BBC always panicked if the young started to enjoy themselves. You had to try to find a foreign commercial station for depravities like the hit parade. I can still remember trying to listen to Radio Luxembourg on the camp radio late on Sunday nights to hear if Nat King Cole was still number one with his rendition of 'Too Young'. Lying in my little RAF cot straining to listen to the wistful strings of a Nelson Riddle arrangement pulsing and fading over the air waves and echoing down the billet was something a homesick national serviceman was unlikely to forget. The BBC, however, was sure that it would do me no good at all. I expect that they feared that it would undermine the British way of life or bring on a mutiny or something. Like I said, the BBC always felt that it knew best.

A Matter of Record

I was heavily into gramophone records by about 1949. Prior to this the only system of sound reproduction in the Edom household was a wind-up portable gramophone that had been past its best before Hitler invaded Poland and had not been much improved when the front room ceiling fell on it in 1942.

Mind you, the Edom family did have a selection of gramophone records to play on the wind-up gramophone. I struggle to remember them all but we certainly had Paul Robeson singing 'Boots' and there were some tiny children's records that had nursery rhymes on them. Then there was a record with a humorous monologue entitled 'With His Head Tucked Underneath His Arm'. Well, don't blame me; I didn't buy it. During the war my brother and sister who were older than me brought home more interesting records like 'In the Mood' and things by Mr Glen Miller. There also seemed to be a lot of bird songs for some reason, like bluebirds over the white cliffs of Dover and nightingales singing in Berkeley Square and things.

Whilst my brother was in Canada learning to navigate Lancasters he sent home a recorded message on a wax disc. We had to use special fibre needles to play it but gradually the wax peeled away until he was reduced to a hiss and a whisper. Still, it was marvellous what could be done in the new world. Fancy being able to record your own voice like a famous crooner.

Then in about 1948 after considerable saving (nothing

came into the Edom household on HP) I acquired my Collaro record player. This was a state-of-the-art machine, fully electric with its own built-in loudspeaker. True, it only played one 78 record at a time but it had this very clever arrangement that when you pulled the arm outwards the turntable started revolving, which was the nearest thing to magic I had seen since the school epidiascope caught fire. Sometimes it also switched itself off at the end of the record but it was unwise to rely on this.

My first love, Mary Whitley, bought me two records for Christmas 1948. These formed the basis of my collection. There was Mario Lanza singing 'Be My Love' and a piano medley by Semprini (ault vuns, new vuns, luffed vuns, neglected vuns). There must have been a good twelve bob's worth there. If that wasn't love out of a schoolgirl's pocket money, then what was ?

Once I started work in 1949 I became a serious record collector. Once a week, on pay day, I purchased a new record. One of my earliest purchases was Mr Pee Wee Hunt's rendition of 'Twelfth Street Rag', a most satisfying piece of music. In those long-gone days the record companies issued catalogues and I would pore over the latest releases before making my selection. There were, of course, serious choices to be made. Decca records were about four and six each whilst Brunswick or HMV were around six and tuppence, or was it six and thruppence. Anyway, the difference was a Saxby's pork pie and a portion of chips. It was a problem, though, because Danny Kay recorded on Brunswick. On the other hand, Charlie Kunz recorded his piano medleys on Decca and you got about six tunes on one record (with rhythm accompaniment), even if they did all sound the same.

I took some pride in the sophistication of my record collection. There was also some satisfaction that much of the music that I played enraged my father since it often interrupted his communion with Chopin on his grand piano in the back room.

Another of my early records was Bill Snyder playing 'Bewitched' on the piano. Personally, I felt that it beat old Chopin hollow. Then I got a record of Harry James and his trumpet playing 'Muskrat Ramble'. I never did know who or where a muskrat was. I also had his recording of 'Flight of the Bumble Bee' and 'The Man I Love'. Then I discovered Stan Kenton. His version of 'How High the Moon' used to make the lid of my Collaro rattle.

I was also very proud of my record of Anton Karas playing the 'Harry Lime Theme' on his zither. There were many more novelty records in those days although 'I Taught I Taw a Puddy Tat' was an acquired taste.

There weren't any disc jockeys on the wireless and you had to settle for *Family Favourites* and Sam Costa playing some gramophone records of uncertain vintage. The BBC was a bit suspicious of anything popular, especially if the young liked it and they had a policy of restricting the playing of American records.

There was a record shop in Acre Lane, Brixton, which had little booths that you could go in to hear your choice before you bought it. Mind you, they got a bit sniffy if you decided against it after they had played it. It was here that I heard my first Les Paul and Mary Ford record. They had this incredible idea of making several recordings on the one track. All those voices and electric guitars all playing at once. Technology was going mad but I was certainly rather proud of being part of the technological revolution. Still, I didn't really think that electric guitars would catch on. They were far too twangy for my taste.

One of the few occasions when I recognised the benefits of new technology was when my friend Norman Frange demonstrated his new autochange radiogram. This played eight records automatically which meant he could snog with his girlfriend Betty Huddle in the front parlour for the best part of half an hour without getting up to change the record.

There was a technological revolution going on in the gramophone needle industry as well. At first I purchased little tin boxes of steel needles which you were supposed to change after each record. Then came fibre needles with a special sharpener. Then came needles that you could use up to sixty times that were called sapphire needles. Of course, every technical advance cost more than the last.

During the next few years my 78 collection grew and grew. Brunswick, Capitol, Decca, Columbia, even a few HMV although these were usually a bit posh. My favourite artists were Danny Kaye and Nat King Cole but I also had an Al Jolson phase for a while. (Evrybahdy lovesa baby, thas why Ahmin luv wid yew.)

It was while I was doing my national service that I went into an extremely sad and sentimental stage. My first love, Mary Whitley, had rejected me and my love life was as bleak as the Gobi Desert. This was when the first and lushest of Nat King Cole's records were issued. 'Unforgettable' and 'Too Young' were the most memorable of his early records. After that I bought each new Nat King Cole recording and I always got goose pimples at that mellow voice and those lush Nelson Riddle backings. Nat King Cole sang lyrics like: 'Are the stars out tonight? I don't know if it's cloudy or bright, 'cos I only have eyes for you.' My favourite was probably 'Walking My Baby Back Home' although sadly at this stage I was lacking a suitable baby.

From the early 1950s Nat King Cole produced a series of hits, all of them love songs, wistful and full of longing. There was 'Pretend' (Pretend you're happy when you're blue, it isn't very hard to do). The bit of the lyric that made me very sniffly went: 'You'll find a love you can share, One you can call all your own, Just close your eyes, she'll be there, You'll never be alone…'

Then there was 'Answer me' and 'Make Her Mine'. His songs were full of yearning and were a powerful influence on a lonely, lovesick young man suffering from a severe and prolonged attack of unrequited love. His were not the sort of songs you forget, even when you are old and crumbly.

Soon after I was demobbed in 1953 long-playing records became popular – not with me though because my record player wouldn't have anything to do with them. Anyway, you couldn't take seriously a record that went round so slowly, could you? This was I suppose the beginning of the end for me. I had been brought up in an era when if you wanted to hear a symphony you bought it on about eight twelve-inch records and kept jumping up to turn them over. Packing the whole of Beethoven's Fifth on to one bendy plastic record seemed to be positively disrespectful to me. Mind you, in those days I wouldn't have known Beethoven's Fifth if all eight records had dropped on my head.

By 1956 the record business was getting very confusing. There were people like Bill Haley on what were called 'Popular 45 Extended Play', 33 rpm LPs of *Carousel* and *Oklahoma* and *The King and I* and a motley collection of 78s starring people like Winifred Atwell.

In about 1957 my spouse and I bought a state-of-the-art radiogram. Our KB De Luxe three-speed auto-radiogram was nine-valve, eight wavebands, superhet with push–pull output, RF stage on all bands and high and low-level listening. No, I don't know what it all meant either. The cabinet was covered in high gloss walnut veneer and it had three loudspeakers which it was claimed gave it a stereophonic effect. It never seemed very stereophonic to me but it had sufficient volume to make the neighbours a bit tetchy when I played my Harry James 78s on it.

Of course, later in life I dabbled with LPs, tapes,

cassettes and CDs. I had speakers with tweeters and woofers and various other atrocities and hi-fis with enough technology to guide a rocket to the moon. Sadly, none of it ever recaptured the magic of my Collaro and my Nat King Cole 78s.

Let's Go to the Pictures

I suppose that I saw both the rise and the fall of the cinema industry. The Plaza in West Wickham opened in 1933, the year of my birth and it quickly became the entertainment centre of the town. Mind you, apart from four or five pubs, the lecture hall, the local dance class and the Yew Tree Youth Club there wasn't much else in the way of entertainment – not any that anyone would admit to, that is.

I was too young to attend the opening ceremony at the Plaza but I understand that the Breezy Babes danced, the Plaza Orchestra played selections and Stanley Evans, tenor, sang. I gather that they eventually got around to showing some films as well.

The cinema was the wonder of the age; Bernard Dawkins, his doting mother claimed, had made a model of the Plaza complete with little seats and lights that dimmed at the touch of a switch. I never saw this masterpiece but I was suitably impressed.

My first visit to the Plaza was a great treat. I saw *Snow White and the Seven Dwarfs*. My older sister took me. I thought the dwarfs were very funny, especially that old Dopey. Snow White was all right as well but the wicked witch and the poisoned apple made me duck down behind the seats although I pretended that I was just tying my shoelace.

I think that my next visit was to see *Rebecca*. The whole family went. The cinema was full and a gentleman in a black suit and bow tie who seemed to be in charge was very concerned not to be able to offer us seats. Eventually, he opened up the special box at the rear of the stalls and we all sat in there like royalty. I pretended that I was King George VI and smiled graciously at everyone. The film, I seem to remember, was a bit boring. There were lots of talking bits and a few slushy bits and some rather creepy bits. As for that Mrs Danvers, she was a really nasty one she was, and reminded me a bit of Mrs Sergeant, our headmistress.

Mind you, the cinema wasn't all good fun. I never forgave them for shooting Bambi's mother for starters and poor old Pinocchio had the hell of a time. On balance, I preferred Donald Duck. He was a bit bad-tempered but you knew where you stood with him.

When the war got under way I didn't get to the cinema much because I was too young to go on my own and everyone was too busy to take me. My brother went off to navigate Lancasters, my sister was doing war work in a factory and my father was busy firewatching. As for my poor old mum, she was mainly preoccupied with making the rations go round, seeing to the blackout curtains and cleaning up each time Mr Hitler blew our plaster down and our windows in.

I do remember a few wartime visits to the cinema however. I recall, for example, seeing the hole in the ceiling of the Plaza. Apparently a large lump of bomb debris had dropped through the roof and, folklore has it, had clonked some poor cinema-goer in the one and threes on the head. I bet that he went in the one and nines after that. I used to look up at the tarpaulin covering the hole and wonder what it must have been like the night the roof fell in.

There was another wartime occasion when I attended a Saturday afternoon matinee to see a special showing of the new George Formby film. I was much excited about this. Something, however, was wrong. The curtains parted but the screen remained blank. It was the man in the dark suit and bow tie again. The train bringing the film, he announced in grave tones, had been delayed by enemy action. I had all sorts of fantasies of teams of fierce-looking Germans with blackened faces paddling across the Channel in rubber boats just to thwart my passion for George Formby films. In the best tradition of the cinema there was a happy ending. The man in the bow tie announced that by means unspecified he had obtained another George Formby film and we would have to make do with that, even if we had seen it before. After all, he implied, there was a war on and it was our patriotic duty to grin and bear it, etc.

Another phenomenon of wartime picture-going was the unscripted interruptions. Suddenly a hastily written slide would be projected that cast an urgent message right across Ginger Roger's lumpy bits. AIR RAID ALERT. It was very distracting, particularly since I had started to get really interested in Ginger Roger's lumpy bits.

During the interval various other slides would be shown but these were usually more of a domestic nature: Norman Parker for all your wedding photographs. After the cinema why not visit the Yew Tree Fish Restaurant? (frying most nights, fish supplies allowing). Marcel, Ladies' Hairdresser for that personal touch. Etc.

The Plaza in West Wickham started a children's Saturday Morning Cinema Club in about 1943 and I was an enthusiastic member. It was pretty good value for sixpence: a couple of cartoons and a main feature (a 'U' certificate but never much more than twenty years old) and then the serial, mostly Flash Gordon and his cardboard rocket, usually nipping up to the moon I seem to recall.

I really cut my cinematic teeth at the Saturday Morning Cinema Club. I was indoctrinated into the wonders of the Marx Brothers and Laurel and Hardy and Charlie Chaplin. As for cowboys, there were shoot-outs and hold-ups and bank robberies and train robberies and cattle rustling and galloping up the gulch and down the gulch and singing cowboys and funny cowboys and a few cowgirls and lots of stagecoaches and chuck wagons and campfires with coffee and beans and redskins and wagon trains and black hats and white hats and, and…

You really got value for money in the cinema of long ago. Not only was there a 'B' film and a newsreel but if you were lucky you got Mickey Mouse and a travel documentary as well. '…and so we say farewell to the palm-fringed shores of Bangkahulu.'

There was also the ice cream lady with her tray of ices blinking in the spotlight like the pilot of a Junkers 88 caught in a searchlight. Ice cream took a distinct turn for the worse during the war. It was made of soya flour and had brown bits lurking in it. You had to use the cardboard lid of the tub to scoop the ice cream out. When the lid went soggy after the second lick and started to disintegrate you couldn't distinguish the ice cream from the cardboard.

The demand for cinema seats during and just after the war was fierce. More often than not one would arrive to find those ominous little boards: Queuing 1s. 3d., Standing 1s. 9d., seats at 2s. 3d. and 2s. 9d. Money always has bought privilege, hasn't it?

There was a uniformed commissionaire to keep order and he had a uniform that would have put General Eisenhower to shame.

In those days one did not worry about the starting time of the film; one just went. You went in during the middle of the film, picked up the story as you went along and then sat through until you got to the point where you came in. Then you got up and went out. It seemed to work perfectly well although sometimes you couldn't remember where you had come in. It was a bit like starting reading a book in the middle but once you got used to it there didn't seem to

216

be any problems. If you didn't grasp the story you just stayed in until you did. If it was a good film you could always watch it twice round.

Cinema technology was not so good in those days. Sometimes one suspected that the projectionist had gone to sleep or was drunk. Sometimes the talking was not synchronised with the actors' mouths or the film was so old that the cowboys looked as though they were riding through a snowstorm. Some of the accidental effects were more fun than the correct version. Deanna Durbin with a baritone voice was a distinct improvement.

Actually, all the technical hitches were part of the fun of the cinema in my view. When the film broke and the cinema was plunged into darkness or there was a problem over changing reels and the screen showed all the little numbers at the end of the reel we had legitimate reasons for much hooting and whistling and foot stamping.

Audience participation was very much in vogue and the hero's attempts to woo the heroine were accompanied by much enthusiastic if slightly improper advice from the one and threes. When the hero finally pinned her to the bed and kissed her the whistles and slurping noises reached a crescendo but the hero's feet never left the floor and the scene would fade out before the heroine had even shed her earrings. One was always hoping to see a naughty bit but films didn't have naughty bits in those days. I remember that Dorothy Malone did once say to Robert Stack, 'There is something you haven't said to me in a long time,' but it turned out to be a bit disappointing.

Slowly I learned the vocabulary of the cinema. Characters from Genghis Khan to the Count of Monte Cristo said thing like, 'Let's go,' in Brooklyn accents. Characters in films about explorers always said things like, 'I don't like it, it's too demmed quiet out there.' My own conversation became littered with cinematic clichés like, 'So long,' and

'You dirty rotten rat'. You couldn't make many trips to the cinema before someone said, 'I have an idea; it might just work…' or, 'It's been a long time.' Before anyone hit anyone they usually said, 'Take that,' and gentlemen were always saying to ladies things like, 'What are you doing tonight, baby?' or, 'This is bigger than both of us.' I always thought this latter observation sounded a bit rude but they kept on saying it, even in U films, so I suppose it must have been all right.

The experienced cinema-goer became used to all the conventions. The violins always introduced the slushy bits but when ladies and gentlemen clutched each other they always did it above the waist. There wasn't any recognition that anyone had any bits below the waist until about 1960. Not in the cinema anyway. Foreigners always had heavy accents and frequently carried knives as well. If they were French they were usually a bit naughty. People would break into a song or a dance at the drop of a baton and as for costumes, even the Roman slaves and the Russian serfs looked well dressed. There was always a balcony somewhere to appear from and a chandelier to swing from. There always had to be a chase on foot, on horseback, with a chariot, coach, dog sleigh, motorboat or on roller skates. Then in the end the heroine always got seen to, although the actual business was usually concealed by swirling clouds, lashing seas or a view of the ceiling. Finally, there was the mandatory happy ending. These involved people going off into the sunset, or sunrise, or long, lingering cuddles or kisses accompanied with a crescendo of music followed by… THE END. Then they started to play 'God Save The King' and everyone rushed for the exit.

Gradually I made the transition into an adult filmgoer. It was not an easy transition. 'Take me in, mister?' was a frequent request when an 'A' film was showing and the cashier was particularly vigilant. Then there was 'bunking in' through the emergency exit although I was not very adept at this. It demanded both speed and nerve and I was a bit short on both. Fortunately, time and nature was on my side and I began to grow tall and look as if I might be just about sixteen.

My tastes had changed now and I had gone off Tarzan a bit. Besides, he always seemed to be wrestling with the same geriatric lion. I wanted to see gangster films with George Raft and Edward G. Robinson and Humphrey Bogart. I also liked my film heroes to be tough like Robert Mitchum and John Wayne. If they were in the middle of some war and there was lots of blood and explosions so much the better.

By now I was seriously addicted. When I couldn't afford a cinema ticket I use to spend ages outside poring over the stills. One lot were labelled 'This Week' and some were labelled 'Next Week'. Mind you, the stills never seemed to appear in the actual film. It was the same in the trailers. 'Coming shortly to this cinema... Colossal, stupendous, nerve-tingling, throbbing with passion, never seen before on the screen...' etc.

By now the cinema became my spiritual home and my cinematic intake increased to two, three, even four visits a week according not so much to what was showing but more according to how much money I had available. My friends and I ranged the district in pursuit of more and more cinematic experiences. The Regal at Beckenham was at the very limit of our range since it involved two buses whilst the Odeon at Elmers End was better (one bus) and the Odeon at Hayes was better still because if you were hard up and couldn't afford the fare it was possible to walk the footpath beside the railway line all the way from West Wickham to Hayes.

On Sundays all the local cinemas were closed in recognition of the inalienable right of religious minorities to make life miserable for everyone else. A Christian Sunday in West Wickham in 1948 was a unique experience. Even buying a liquorice stick was regarded as the work of the devil. Anyway, all the cinemas in the Borough of Beckenham were closed on Sundays so that the devil wouldn't be able to get a foothold, or a liquorice stick. Hayes, however, was in the Borough of Bromley and they let the devil in after four o'clock in the afternoon. So all the local youth would trudge down to the Hayes Odeon. If we walked there and back a group of us could pool our spare coppers and buy ten Abdulla or Nosegay (all that was usually available unless you were a regular customer and we couldn't afford to be regular customers). Then we would queue to get in to the Hayes Odeon as soon as the doors opened at a quarter to four. The depravities of Sunday could then be blotted out whilst we watched some scratchy old gangster film and spluttered our way through our share of the Abdullas and kept an eye open for any girls who looked remotely friendly.

The Regal at Beckenham had a very special attraction – the Wurlitzer. During the war and for a while afterwards it remained shrouded under its dustsheet. Then one magical day some time around 1948 the mighty Wurlitzer sprang to life again. In the middle of the programme, right after the *Pathé News* and before the main film, up came the mighty Wurlitzer from its cavern in front of the screen. Its rainbow panels all lit up, its tailcoated rider turning to wave nonchalantly as he rose to the occasion. They projected the words of the songs on the screen and the bouncing ball showed you when to sing. Everyone roared away with gusto, 'Powder Your Face with Sunshine', 'The Woody Woodpecker Song.', 'I Want to Be Happy.'

Cinemas were like that really: womblike pleasure palaces. It was all magical. When the lights went down anything was possible and believable and the harsh real world was forgotten – even form 4H at Ravensbeck Grammar School.

There was more magic yet to discover – the magic of the back row. The older teenagers were the role models. They tended to arrive with girls on their arms and self-satisfied expressions and make for the back row of the one and nines. Usherettes with a judgement based on long experience knew precisely who to direct to the back row and those of us less privileged realised that there were often more exciting things going on in the gloom behind us than on the silver screen. Love on the screen was all long kisses and hugs but in the back row it was more French kissing and biting and groping with lots of giggles and the rustling of stealthily displaced nylon. These days when some elderly woman deplores the behaviour of the young I wonder if she was one of those who used to sit in the back row of the one and nines with her feet up on the back of the seat in front and her coat over her knees. Rumour had it that some of them had their panties in their handbags but I can't vouch for that.

My own experiences were less than triumphs. As you know, the time that Diana Morton finally agreed to come with me to the Plaza was a disaster and I suddenly got a runny nose just at the moment when she wanted to indulge in some passionate kissing. On another occasion I took a girl to the pictures and cuddled her all through the programme and my arm went numb and I had to have physiotherapy.

There were techniques for cinema courtships but I never really mastered them. Certain conventions had to be followed. No respectable girl would admit that she was going in the back row for hanky-panky. It all had to start with the casually draped arm along the back of the seat and then the accidental touch of hands and the film star-type kiss where lips stayed clamped firmly together. If one got lucky there would then be much stroking and squeezing whilst intently watching Gary Cooper. Hanky-panky never got talked about; it just sort of happened, very accidentally. There were quite a few accidents in those days.

Of course, some cinemas were an acquired taste. The Queen's Hall at Penge was known as the fleapit. They used to change the programme twice a week to coax you in but the films were old, the prices cheap and itching was hard to resist. Then there was the Astra Cinema at RAF Padgate where you stood rigidly to attention when they played 'God Save the King' on pain of being charged with conduct prejudicial. The worst film I ever saw was in the RAF. It was all about nasty diseases and festering parts.

Despite the traumas of national service I remained a devoted cinema-goer during another two decades, contributing vastly to the fortunes of Warner Brothers, Metro Goldwyn Meyer and Universal Studios. Over my cinema-going career I snuffled surreptitiously to *Carousel*, laughed uproariously at *Passport to Pimlico*, peered through green and red spectacles at three-dimensional things from outer space, chortled with Abbott and Costello and suffered stoically with Jack Hawkins in *The Cruel Sea*. If that was not enough, I sang with Jolson, thirsted with John Mills in *Ice Cold in Alex*, investigated with Alistair Simms in *Green for Danger*, kept a stiff upper lip with Alec Guinness in *The Bridge on the River Kwai* and rode with the US Cavalry and Dana Andrews. I flitted around the sewers of Vienna with Harry Lime and I struggled desperately to develop a suitably laconic style of speech in an amalgam of Alan Ladd in *Shane*, James Stewart in *Broken Arrow* and Gary Cooper in *High Noon*. I hummed all the tunes in *Pal Joey*, shivered at the ruthlessness of Rod Steiger in *On the Waterfront*, lusted after Betty Grable and Marilyn Monroe and envied Bogart his special relationship with Lauren Bacall.

But the cinema was changing. There was Vistavision and

Cinemascope and Supertotalscope and the screens became wider and wider until you went cross-eyed trying to see it all. Colour films were becoming the norm although some of them made the stars look green whilst others made everything look rusty-brown. Then they started putting in extra speakers and the sound came out of the walls at you. It didn't matter. I was besotted with all of it, totally undiscriminating. When the lights went down and the curtains parted I was transported to another world where anything could and did happen, but it would always come right in the end. It was magic... pure magic.

The Motor Age

The Edom family had difficulty in coming to terms with the motor age. My father never drove, let alone actually owned a motor car. He made his local journeys on a large upright bicycle whose Sturmey Archer three-speed gear made a dignified whirring noise as he progressed down Station Road, West Wickham, at a steady three miles an hour. There was something inexorable about it. West Wickham didn't have any traffic lights in those days but if it had they would never have dared to turn red in the path of my old dad.

The family did travel by car at least once a year. This was when we hired a taxi to our nearest mainline station at Bromley on our way to the annual holiday at Herne Bay (the last week in August and the first week in September). The taxi was a very imposing affair. It was a large Austin with broad running-boards and a luggage grid at the back on which were strapped our cases. The large family trunk had been sent luggage in advance, courtesy of the Southern Railway.

The taxi driver wore a uniform and a peaked cap and saluted deferentially. The Edoms weren't used to that sort of treatment. In any event, he need not have bothered. If he had known my father better he would have known that a tip was not a serious prospect. Mr Edom senior was not in favour of such frivolities and usually spent most of the holiday with an expression of acute pain at the thought of how much it was all costing.

I was most impressed by that taxi. I knew that it was fourteen horsepower and I used to sit in it wondering what it would look like if it was actually pulled by fourteen horses. How on earth did all that power come from under that small bonnet? I reflected that fourteen horses would take a hell of a lot of oats and their droppings would be a godsend to little Mr Cutler at number four who always rushed out with his bucket and shovel whenever a horse was caught short in our road. Fourteen loads all at once would have kept Mr Cutler's floribundas in fine fettle for a whole season.

In about 1947 something really exciting happened. We had a driver and car to take us all the way to Herne Bay. I never understood how this came about; to me it was quite mind-boggling and an extravagance that was totally unlike my dear old dad who, as you will have gathered, was not noted for his financial exuberance. Just after the war the railways were very short of coal so that travelling by train became a very uncertain and uncomfortable business. I can only assume that this car we went in was having to make the journey anyway and my father did a deal and paid for us to travel as a sort of human ballast. Anyway, it was very exciting. Herne Bay was about sixty miles from West Wickham and it had never occurred to me that the two places were linked by roads as well as railway tracks. I was so excited about the whole thing that I kept careful notes of the experience and wrote an article about it afterwards. It was called 'By Car to the Coast'. Sadly, the article has not been preserved for posterity but it was jolly exciting, I can tell you.

The thing that always struck me about motor transport was the way that in a few minutes it whirled you to places that took me a whole morning to walk. The idea of using private motor transport as a regular mode of conveyance struck me as ridiculous. It was a bit like those fanciful

artists impressions in my brother's *Modern Boy* magazines.
You know the sort of thing: 'Impression of spaceship
landing on the moon in the year 2000.'

It was true that there was one family in our road who
owned a car but they were very superior people. They had
an electric coffee percolator as well and Mrs Sharp played
the mandolin so you could tell they were a bit odd.

My father had a couple of rich friends who owned
motor cars and who very occasionally took us out for a
drive. One of them had this disconcerting habit of driving
us to some remote spot and then trying to light a campfire.
I always thought that Baden-Powell had a lot to answer for.
I was never all that keen on campfires but I suppose they
might have been ignited for my benefit. Mr Lockitt seemed
obsessed with them, nasty, smoky affairs. He was an
Australian so perhaps he imagined he was in the outback. If
that was all they did in the outback I couldn't help thinking
that Australia must be a bit tiresome. Smoky campfires and
hanging upside down didn't seem a lot of fun to me.

The last outing Mr Lockitt took us on was a bit of a
disaster. It was just after the war started and we were
stopped by a roadblock halfway across Mitcham Common.
There were soldiers with tin hats and rifles and bayonets. It
was quite exciting but the soldiers did not like Mr Lockitt.
It was probably his Australian accent. I think that they
suspected him of being a spy. Everyone in the least odd was
suspected of being a spy at that time. If they had seen Mr
Lockitt lighting his fires all over the place I expect that they
would have shot him as a saboteur.

My other close associations with motor transport before
the war were rather limited. There was a bus that ran
between Forest Hill and Croydon and some of them used
to turn and wait at the Railway Hotel at West Wickham. I
used to stand and watch these events. The bus drivers in
their long white coats used to sit outside the Railway Hotel

smoking their Woodbines and Nosegay and conversing about busmen's matters. They sat on the concrete bollards that had been erected to stop them driving their buses over the hatch covers of the Railway Hotel's cellars. With hindsight, if you will forgive the pun, those bollards could not have been a lot of fun. Piles in later life were probably a likely outcome. At the time I never thought of the drivers as being susceptible to mortal ills. They seemed like supermen to me, driving those great lumbering buses. I used to stand there for ages soaking up the magic. The buses leaked oil all over the forecourt of the Railway Hotel and made interesting creaking noises as their engines cooled down. Everything about those buses was on a giant scale. They had starting handles held secure with leather straps and great brass horns with a rubber bulb attached and when the engine started up everything vibrated and shuddered as if it were alive.

During my childhood I lived in Springhurst Avenue. This was just a mile of semi-detacheds that wound over the hill towards Hayes and Bromley. No bus went that way and it was too far to walk and even with a Sturmey Archer three-speed gear you still had to get off and push, although I expect that Messrs Sturmey and Archer would have taken that as a personal affront. Nowadays Springhurst Avenue is regarded as a short cut and lunatics in Volvos and Saabs hurtle along it at speeds that decimate the cat and hedgehog population. To add insult to injury, more often than not the cars have stickers in their back windows that say 'Mind that child' or 'Save the Whale.' Nothing about hedgehogs, you will notice. Ironic really that evolution took a few million years to help hedgehogs to devise that infallible defence of stopping still and rolling up in a prickly ball and then along came Henry Ford and – splat.

Before the war there was not a lot of motor transport in Springhurst Avenue. Cars were so infrequent that I used to collect their licence plate numbers. Then I turned to recognition exercises. Gradually I built up my repertoire and I could eventually tell the make of almost any car as soon as it turned into the road. There was a good deal of variety in those days: Morris and Austin and Ford and Rover; Sunbeam, Alvis, AC, Riley, Hillman, Jowett, Vauxhall, Standard, Singer, MG, Morgan BSA, Humber and Wolseley…

Most of my knowledge about cars came from my story books. In my Bulldog Drummond books Mr Drummond was always tearing off in his open-topped Bentley tourer and driving it at full throttle up the Great North Road, wherever that was. I can't remember why he was always tearing off like that but his petrol bill must have been something dreadful. It was another thirty years before I discovered where the Great North Road was. Mind you, my little chums and I were fascinated by the romance of the open road. When we eventually acquired bicycles we used to ride four miles to the Sidcup Bypass just to sit on the embankment to watch the cars go by. It was called the mad mile and some of those cars must have been doing nearly sixty miles an hour.

Of course, motoring was a much more relaxed business in those days. Delivery vans had messages on the back: 'Please sound your horn so that our driver may extend to you the courtesy of the road.' Imagine what would be extended if you did that today.

A number of the tradesmen still used horses to make deliveries in Springhurst Avenue in those days but even then the motor age was exerting its grip. The mineral water man had a motor van with no doors to the cab and sort of porthole things at the side with no glass in. Motoring in those days seemed to be a very draughty business. However, motor transport certainly had much more character. I suppose that it was still evolving. There were little three-wheeler motor cars with what looked like a motorcycle engine mounted on the front and there were motorcycles with sidecars that came in all shapes and sizes; my favourite was a sidecar that looked like a monster bull's eye.

One or two local residents favoured autocycles. These were strange machines with pedals but also little two-stroke engines that burned a special mixture. They were slow, noisy and pongy.

My chum Bill Oddy, who lived in one of the council houses in Turpin Lane, had several claims to fame. For starters he lived with his uncle and grandma. (All the relationships in the council houses in Turpin Lane seemed a bit strange to me but I never liked to enquire too closely.) Anyway, Bill Oddy's uncle owned an elderly motorcycle and sidecar. An AJS, I think it was, with a gear lever mounted on the petrol tank. Bill Oddy used to brag that he knew how to kick-start this machine into life, a very hazardous activity according to Bill who said that sometimes the engine kicked back and if you were not pretty nippy about getting your leg out of the way the machine could break your ankle. Motorcycling didn't sound all that much fun to me.

Sometimes Bill's uncle would take Gran out in the sidecar. They would both wear leather flying helmets and when Gran was hunched up in the open sidecar with her helmet on she looked like a geriatric kamikaze pilot.

Then there was our egg man who had a vehicle that was a motorcycle at the front and a small van at the back. I never liked the egg man, too smarmy by half. I think he had designs on my mum. It was a relief when the war came and eggs and the egg man disappeared. I expect he joined the black market.

Motor transport took on some original forms during the war. Some cars had little trailers that converted chicken droppings into methane gas, whilst others had gasbags on their roofs to power their engines. One snag, of course, was that you needed a car to start with. Mostly people walked. At least, most of the people that I knew did.

A motor transport company of the Canadian Army was stationed in West Wickham for a while during the war. They used Wickham Court as their headquarters. They had funny habits, those Canadians. They parked their three-ton trucks all over the stately lawns and used the oak panelling for firewood. There were always army lorries roaring about West Wickham, nose to tail like herds of elephants which made the elderly citizenry very nervous, especially in the blackout.

Motor transport got much nastier after the war. All sorts of abominations turned up. There was a thing called a Corgi which was a sort of motorised roller skate. It was said to be modelled on a device used by our brave paratroopers during the war. You'd have to be brave to ride on something like that.

My friend Clive had a father with a false leg which seemed to give him some priority when the first new cars went on sale after the war. I was invited round to view this new status symbol. It was a Ford Popular and it looked as though it was the same design as the ones made in 1939. Still, it was new and shiny. I had never seen a new car before. It smelled strange, like new boots and sewing machines.

Then there was the Bond Minicar, all 197 ccs of it. In icy weather it used to turn over with its wheels in the air like a stranded turtle. Then came bubble cars mostly made by our ex-enemies. They were three-wheelers of extremely curious and varied designs. The Messerschmidts and Heinkels were the worst. They were noisy, draughty and unreliable. I think they were just a way of paying us back for winning the Battle of Britain. There was also something called an Isetta which I think was Italian, but after Salerno who could take the Italians seriously?

After the war there also came a temporary interest in motorcycles. My little band of teenage associates couldn't actually afford to buy motorcycles but we could talk about them for hours. We discussed Nortons and Ariels and Royal Enfields and Triumphs. Then there was Matchless and AJS and BSA and Douglas and the Vincent HRD. There was a Velocette with a water-cooled engine and a little lightweight BSA 125 cc machine. There was also a very odd invention called a 'Winged Wheel' which was a small engine that fitted into the wheel of a pedal cycle. It was only 35 cc and was grossly underpowered. If you came to a drain cover you had to start pedalling to get over it.

All this talk about motorcycles began to put me under pressure. I rashly indicated that I would like to acquire one. It was mostly boasting but my chums took me seriously. When I was actually old enough to ride a motorcycle things got distinctly nasty. Secretly I didn't even like motorcycles very much – dangerous, noisy, oily, smelly things. Still, you can't say things like that to your teenage chums, can you?

When I had saved up thirty pounds I had no excuses left. I could scarcely believe that I had saved up so much money. Mind you, I had sold all my Biggles books to a dealer in Beckenham. I think that my *Boys' Book of Knowledge* and my stamp collection went as well but I can't quite recall. Anyway, I began protracted negotiations to purchase a 1936 250 cc OK Supreme from a deranged motorcycle enthusiast in Beckenham. He was a mechanic in Westerby's Garage. Motor transport was meat and drink to him. I think that it probably took the place of sex as well. It can't do you much good, can it, all that rattling and shaking around? His conversation was weird as well. He was obsessed with getting a special motorbike for speedway racing. 'Bloody hell, mass prototype dirt bike specially tuned by Westerby's back-room boffin boys,' he explained. He prefaced every remark with 'bloody hell' and 'mass' was his favourite superlative. He used to talk in short staccato phrases like a motorcycle backfiring. Half the time I didn't know what he was talking about.

When I actually saw the OK Supreme it filled me with fear. I had no idea how to ride it. It leaked oil from the most improbable places and made a most fearful noise. In the end I lost my nerve and put my money in the Post Office instead. I managed to save face with my friends by telling them that the spring-tensioned camshaft driving chain was suspect. They were very impressed and I didn't tell them that I got the words out of a book.

I first actually drove a motor vehicle whilst in the Royal Air Works. It was nothing very exciting – not a fire engine or an ambulance or anything dramatic like I had seen in *The Way to the Stars*. On our Wednesday sports afternoons a selected few were assigned to assist the officers' gliding club. Gliders fell out of the sky and were littered all over the airfield and we had to recover them. Officers are like that – too bone idle to do their own tidying up. We towed these gliders back to the launching point with 15 cwt Bedford trucks that had seen better days. Even in their prime they had only been used to transport the fire picket. I found them complicated and recalcitrant and that went for the officers too. The Bedfords were difficult to start, and to change gear you had to double declutch. I found this operation a great trial. I used to forget the sequence halfway through which made the gears grind with rage and pain. In the end I drove my Bedford mostly in first gear and gained a great reputation for towing the gliders so carefully.

Back home after demob I found that a number of my friends had become motorised. Bodger Williams, now a regular in the air force (he was always a bit odd), had acquired an MG. He had also grown a bushy moustache and kept saying, 'Whacko!' and talking about 'wizard prangs'. I felt that he went over the top a trifle since he was only an airframe mechanic. I learned that MG owners had their own special club. So far as I could tell from Bodger the rules were simple: you waved vigorously at every MG owner who you passed and every time you saw an attractive woman you yelled, 'Down with her drawers!' as you hurtled by.

My friend Clive Worst acquired a Lambretta scooter with a large plastic windshield. In windy weather it acted rather like a sail. We once tacked along Mitcham Common Road in a gale rather like something out of the *Onedin Line*. The only thing that I envied him about that scooter was all the girls who seemed to queue up to ride on his pillion. Lambrettas were not designed for modesty or aloofness. When I saw one of his girlfriends with her skirt hitched up and knees astride perched on his pillion I began to think that there might be some benefits in the motor age after all.

Fairs and Fetes

Fairs and fetes, garden parties and other open-air soirees are essentially for the young. I feel that I rather missed out on the best of these events because during my childhood years the most exciting open-air event was watching the Home Guard rehearsing their anti-tank strategy in Coote's field on Sunday mornings. Thank God the Germans didn't come; four lemonade bottles filled with petrol and two crowbars lent by Mr Raybone the ironmonger would, I suspected, have been insufficient to halt Hitler's Panzers in their tracks.

Other forms of wartime open-air entertainment included things like Spitfire Week or Navy Day when a Ministry of Information cinema van would appear in the Blake Recreation Ground and show rather blurred and shaky images of our brave boys performing deeds of derring-do in monochrome. Towards the end of the war there was another rather nasty development inflicted on the civilian population called Holidays at Home. Not that anybody I know went away on a proper holiday during the war anyway, but this was a device to make you think that you had enjoyed a holiday without anyone cluttering up the trains or otherwise getting in the way of the war effort. As if there wasn't enough pain and suffering around already, the authorities laid on good homely entertainment in the local parks. These often included exciting events like a display by the Boy Scouts or the Auxiliary Fire Service.

Holidays at Home brought out all sorts of other

frustrated entertainers in various stages of senility. Anyone who was any good was away entertaining the troops or had been called up themselves so that standing on a rickety wooden platform in the local park with a leaking piano accordion was an opportunity reserved for the senile, the slightly mad or the excruciatingly tone deaf. Holidays at Home were in my view considerably worse than a Doodlebug raid.

The next open-air excitement that I recall, apart from the V2 on St Jeremy's Church, was VE Day. There was a street party in Turpin Lane but I wasn't allowed to go.

Next came VJ Day. That was a bit boring. They had a street bonfire outside the council houses in Turpin Lane which set the tarmacadam on fire but that was about it. No thunderflashes, no spam sandwiches and no fizzy pop. Still, the burnt patch on the roadway stayed there as a permanent memorial until the Borough Council repaired the road in 1955.

The next post-war attempts at communal jollity weren't much of an improvement. Those community-minded people who had spent the war years dabbling in things like ARP and flogging savings stamps formed a committee and revived the West Wickham Fair and Flitch. This centred around a competition to find the married couple who had not had a cross word for a year and a day. The prize for this appalling piece of perjury was a side of bacon. However, in those early post-war years of meat rationing the successful couple received a supply of Mr Rosegood's best pork sausages. Of course, they weren't really pork but what did you expect in 1948?

The Fair and Flitch began with a procession round the town led by the West Wickham Sea Cadets drum and bugle band. The centrepiece of the procession was Mr Raybone's coal lorry suitably scrubbed down for the occasion and bedecked with bunting and greenery. This elegant chariot accommodated the Queen of the Fair and her attendants. I was expecting the Queen of the Fair to look a bit like Betty Grable but I can only assume that she was selected for her intellectual qualities or had friends on the selection committee. Her lumpy bits were a particular disappointment since I had become really interested in ladies' lumpy bits. I rather liked the attendants however who wore little short pinafore things that happily seemed to have shrunk in the wash. I deserved some compensation for having endured the Sea Cadet drum and bugle band in the awfulness of their opening barrage.

The fair itself was incredibly dreadful. There was a flower show in a big ex-army marquee and guess the weight of the cake, and there was an egg and spoon race and similar athletic depravities, and a baby show. All this was accompanied by music on gramophone records by courtesy of Mr Hodges's electrical shop. Mr Hodges, it seemed, had been unable to shift his pre-war stock of Paul Robeson records. Oh, and I have forgotten, there was also tombola, hoopla and coconut shies with wooden coconuts. At this stage in my development I really didn't believe in real coconuts. They couldn't really have milk in them, could they? There was also a raffle for a patchwork quilt made by the ladies of the St Mark's sewing circle but I had sloped off down to the Black Cat Café by then. The Black Cat Café had a juke box with Stan Kenton records. Not that I could afford to play it, of course, but it was the ambience, wasn't it?

The Fair and Flitch event was only surpassed in awfulness by the West Wickham Conservative Association August Bank Holiday Fair also held in the Blake Recreation Ground. There was a white elephant stall and a men's knobbly knees competition and a children's flower show... need I say more?

Never mind, better days were ahead. About this time

small travelling fairs reappeared. Mind you, West Wickham was not the most popular venue since the wasteland opposite the Wheatsheaf was somewhat cramped and uneven. The Beckenham Borough Council were reluctant to allow its public parks to be desecrated by dodgems and roundabouts, partly out of concern for the municipal football pitches but mainly because of a puritanical belief that fairs would corrupt the youth of the neighbourhood. Chance would have been a fine thing.

The first funfair to arrive opposite the Wheatsheaf caused a great stir amongst the youth of the town, most of whom couldn't even remember what a commercial fair was like. The first thing to get used to was having the outdoors lit up with hundreds of light bulbs. The years of the blackout had taken their toll and there was still a sense of great naughtiness about showing lights in public. One half expected the Luftwaffe to arrive or a warden to shout, 'Put that light out.' Not only were there all those lights powered by a war surplus generator but there was also a set of dodgem cars and one of those things that went round and round in a motion reminiscent of a rowing boat in a choppy sea. It was all very exciting. There was also a rifle range and hoopla and roll a penny down and coconut shies with the inevitable artificial coconuts. You couldn't have shifted those coconuts with a three-inch mortar, and even if you had you only won a framed picture of Winston Churchill. There wasn't room for much more on the Wheatsheaf site but there was a small stall providing cups of stewed tea and sticky buns.

The next fair to arrive was a step more advanced and they managed to squeeze in a big wheel. Well, actually even the most enthusiastic of us had to concede that it was a fairly small big wheel. Still, from the top you could see the pigeons roosting on the roof of the Home and Colonial Stores in the High Street. The extra thrill for me was that I had a few intimate moments with Mary Whitley whilst suspended on the big wheel at an altitude of forty feet above the Wheatsheaf.

Then came the grand Bank Holiday Fair in Beckenham Park in 1949. This was a threepenny bus ride and a long walk away but was considered a worthwhile investment. This was a much bigger fair and amongst a variety of rides there was a device called a Divebomber that hurtled you around in several different directions at once. I pretended not to notice it because I always felt that being upside down was against nature. My chums and I spent most of our money on a device called the Whip and another one called the Octopus which allowed us to show off whilst staying more or less the right way up. Sadly, the visit to Beckenham Park was spoiled for me because here it was that my first love Mary Whitley finally rejected me. In a state of hurt pride I persuaded Loraine Perch to go on the Ghost Train with me but although she wore a tight sweater and had pert little bosoms that protruded like upturned eggcups it was little consolation for the loss of Mary Whitley. Groping Loraine Perch in the Ghost Train was the finale of my al fresco pleasures before national service engulfed me in an eternity of assault courses, parades and guard duties. Open-air events never gave me the same pleasure after that.

Grundy and Bone

It was my first venture in employment. I had always wanted to be a photographer but jobs of that kind were, I discovered, hard to find. Eventually a friend of a relative, knowing my aspirations, put me in touch with Messrs Grundy and Bone. They were an unlikely partnership. Grundy was mercurial, taken by sudden enthusiasms, an opportunist and one keen to take a chance. He chain-smoked cigarettes and was informal to the point of occasionally calling me Bob which was pretty unorthodox for an employer in 1949. Bone was older, dour and taciturn. He never used three words where one would do and by inclination preferred no words at all. He smoked a pipe and took a cautious view of the world.

Grundy and Bone had formed their partnership to make their fortune in the world of document copying. They sold document-copying equipment and services in a era of blueprints and dyeline copying and before anyone had heard of the plain paper copiers that we know today. It was all photographic emulsions and wet developers and large copying cameras and great copying light boxes and darkrooms. They also acted as agents for a firm that manufactured photoprinters for drawing offices and planning departments. (Agents for the Gaunt Photoprinting Equipment Company, their headed notepaper proclaimed.)

I was their first employee. I like to think that they gave me the job because I was keen to please and they recognised my inherent worth. However, I have to admit that I was also the only applicant and I wasn't expecting much money. The local authority rate for a darkroom assistant was deemed to be appropriate – two pounds fifteen shillings and seven pence a week. They never got around to giving me a job description or a contract of employment. In fairness, I doubt if anyone had heard of such things in 1949. Anyway, with hindsight, I think that I was lucky that they stamped my card. Had I been unionised my duties would have provided enough demarcation disputes to give a full-time union official a real sense of purpose in life.

I was a sort of general assistant: some work in the darkroom, up to my armpits in gungy foul-smelling chemicals; a quick spell in the packing room; a bit of maintenance and repair work as bits of the second-hand equipment broke down or fell off; brew up the tea; demonstrate the Gaunt Super Copyline Machine to potential customers; sweep out the storeroom; unpack the new deliveries; lend a hand with the invoices; and hop on a bus to deliver an urgent order.

Sometimes my services were required to sit on the giant enlarger during a long exposure that coincided with a tram shaking the old building as it rattled by in the High Street. The sharpness of many a mural was preserved as the result of my timely intervention and if I sat on the old enlarger at the right time twice a week I had covered my wages.

I quickly realised that Grundy was the technical expert of the partnership whilst Bone was the tactician and the one who dealt with sales and worried about the overdraft. Grundy was a man of ideas and sudden impulses. He was always buying new pieces of equipment. I say 'new' but I only mean new to us. Most of the equipment he purchased looked as though it had come from the Science Museum. At one stage he acquired a massive ammonia developing machine. It had to be manhandled up two flights of stairs and when it was finally in place in the print room Grundy couldn't take his eyes off his new acquisition. He was besotted with it. It was an incredible piece of equipment. It had great oily gearwheels, a moving canvas belt and a device for warming the ammonia. We had to devise some primitive trunking sealed together with parcel tape to carry the fumes up through the trapdoor on to the roof. When we set it going it made a sort of squeaking, grinding noise and leaked ammonia fumes at every joint. When the first print was developed in it Grundy was ecstatic. Bone stood watching and puffing enigmatically on his pipe. I just stood there with my eyes weeping with ammonia fumes whilst Grundy extolled the blackness of the line on the print I had just put through the machine. When I complained about the ammonia fumes Grundy said that he expected that I would get used to them.

However, the most horrendous machine was the double-sided continuous photoprinting machine. It must have been built in about 1925. It is hard to describe and I don't expect you will believe me anyway but there is no need to make up anything about my time with Grundy and Bone. The machine had a continuous moving belt that carried tracings and photosensitive paper in close proximity round a curved plate glass screen. The arrangement was duplicated on the other side of the machine and between the two plate glass screens an electric arc lamp trundled up and down on rails to expose the light-sensitive paper.

The machine had a speed control but if I needed to run it very slow or very fast I had to change gear. Changing gear was about as difficult as the gears on a B-Type bus with a crash gear box. Then there was the arc lamp. The lamp glass would keep getting gunged up so that it had to be dismantled frequently and cleaned with methylated spirits. The carbon arc rods had to be manually adjusted to create the right gap. If the gap became too great the light went out. One time I went to adjust the rods and forgot the power was on. It gave me such a scare that I dropped the cast iron lamp cover on the lamp glass. Still, it saved me cleaning it.

Keeping that machine going brought me close to a nervous breakdown. Rushing from one side of the machine to the other feeding in tracings and paper, watching that the glass didn't need cleaning, or the arc rods adjusting, ensuring that the speed was giving the right exposure, changing gear when necessary. I tell you flying a Vampire jet would have been child's play after that.

Then one day when I was dashing about like a dervish I dropped a pencil down between the moving belts and one of the plate glass bends cracked. I decided not to mention the pencil to my employers.

Mind you, Grundy and Bone was like that. Trying to make a living out of superannuated equipment and with a distinctly make do and mend philosophy. Then there was the great washing tank disaster. We had an enormous galvanised iron washing tank. It had a hosepipe to fill it and swirl the water round to wash these 30″ by 40″ prints. One day the inevitable happened. The hosepipe was left on and the overflow wasn't up to the job. The next day the place looked like Niagara. I denied responsibility.

Then there were the great enlarger and camera. They ran on rails and everything about them was on a giant scale. The camera produced half-plate or even whole-plate negatives and the enlargements were seldom smaller than 30″ by 40″. We enlarged on to paper or linen or transparencies. When you took a photograph with those things you had to get it right or a day's profits went up the spout. Grundy used to spend ages focusing the camera with a ground glass screen and a magnifier like a jeweller's eyeglass. The enlarger had an electric cable to connect the lamp to the power supply. That lamp would have done credit to the Eddiston Lighthouse. For some reason the power cable had a plug at both ends. Thinking about it now makes me go tingly all over. If the factory inspector had seen it he would have wet himself with rage. There were more threats to health and safety working for Grundy and Bone than there were down a Victorian coal mine.

Developing a 30″ by 40″ print wasn't a lot of fun either. The sheet had to be looped and then drawn through a massive developing tray in one smooth movement to ensure that both sides were immediately and completely immersed in developer. The technique, if effectively applied, created a small tidal wave that landed several pints of developer down your trousers. Then the whole process had to be repeated in the fixing solution and that was even before one reached the dreaded washing tank. I acquired a couple of white overalls to protect me. The only ones I could get did up at the neck and made me look like a dentist. Even then the developer still showered down over my shoes and in the course of time the stitching began to rot.

Grundy wasn't cut out for commerce. He was never happier than in the darkroom. He would spend hours over a light box, carefully spotting all the blemishes out of some enormous negative with opaque spotting liquid. He was a bit possessive about the spotting liquid but if he was in a good mood he would let me have a go.

We also had this curious device called a photostat machine. I suppose that it was the precursor of the modern photocopier. It was a massive box with a glass top and lots of lights. I would place an opaque drawing in there with some photographic paper and then lay a rubberised sheet on top. Then there was a pump that was used to pump out the air to create a close contact. Then some test exposures. When the right exposure had been established a full sheet of paper would be used. Then there was the developing, fixing and washing processes. This produced a paper negative that when dry had to be printed as a positive. I can tell you, copying documents in those days gave you a real sense of achievement.

The year I worked for Grundy and Bone became more surreal as it progressed. Grundy became more and more maniacal with each new scheme, his eyes glinting wildly behind his heavy glasses whilst Bone puffed more deeply on his pipe and looked increasingly like Stanley Baldwin during the abdication crisis.

Grundy taught me a lot about photography. I was entrusted with the task of mixing up the developers from the Ilford book of photographic formulae. I had to use a chemical balance and lots of little brass weights. Sometimes I pretended that I was working at Harwell. I also learned which chemicals were most deserving of respect. A quick sniff at the glacial acetic acid could clear a hangover in a trice and if you were foolish enough to put a cut finger in even a dilute solution it could lift you a foot off the floor.

Then Grundy had a new idea. We were going to market our own photographic chemicals ready mixed. Salesmen were recruited to sell the chemicals and the photoprinting paper and the Gaunt Super Copyline Machine. A motley band of aspirant salesmen spent a couple of weeks training in the darkroom and were then sent out to make their fortunes on what I suspect was a commission-only basis. Grundy and Bone were now so busy organising all this that they recruited a manager who, amongst his other duties, supervised my work in the darkroom. Sadly, he knew considerably less than I did about the darkroom and all its works. Mind you, he demonstrated for me for the first but certainly not the last time in my life that bullshit baffles brains. He eventually disappeared as suddenly as he had arrived. I expect that he had talked his way into a job as a brain surgeon.

Every day with Grundy and Bone was different. Inexplicable things were always happening. Next they recruited another darkroom assistant and there was actually someone junior to me in the organisation. I made my very first managerial decision: I delegated the sweeping up duties and the tea making. Then Bone came back with a big contract from a large engineering firm to produce a hundred copies of each of their engineering tracings for the Monolithic all-in-one cake-making machine. For a while the print room was a frenzy of activity. The double-sided continuous photoprinting machine ran almost red hot for a fortnight. Grundy acquired another machine to deal with trimming all the prints. It was a foot-operated guillotine. Every time I used it my teeth were on edge. Once it took the end off my tie. My trouble was that I worried too much, Grundy said.

Then orders for photoprinting paper and Grundy and Bone ready-mixed developers began to flow in from our new salesmen desperate for their commission. I was reassigned to the packing department. In fact, I *was* the packing department. After that I never had trouble with Christmas present wrapping again.

All sorts of strange photographic jobs came in and another more senior darkroom technician was hired. I rather resented this but he mollified me by projecting some pornographic negatives in the enlarger. I shudder to think how he got those negatives. They would have made a gynaecologist blush. If Bone had seen them he would have bitten clean through his pipe.

The haughty lady from Carshalton who worked three afternoons a week in the office began to get a bit testy with all the extra invoicing and the commission cheques. I had always been required to price the photographic jobs from a well thumbed price chart but now I was called in to check the invoices as well. Grundy said that it would be good experience for me and to be sure not to get developer stains on the invoices.

Then disaster struck. I don't know what went wrong but the orders stopped coming in and Bone became more and more contemplative and even Grundy became quite subdued and preoccupied. Eventually the news was announced. Grundy and Bone were going out of business. The partnership was being dissolved. The Gaunt Photoprinting Equipment Company was taking over any remaining assets and would close down the premises. The remaining equipment was dismantled and loaded on to a lorry. Down two flights of stairs and on to a lorry went all the machinery, including Grundy's much-loved ammonia developing machine still exuding a defiant aroma of ammonia as it went. I never saw the machine again. I suspect that it went for scrap.

I was told that the Gaunt Photoprinting Equipment Company might be prepared to give me a job. I was interviewed by Mr Cohen who it transpired was the Gaunt Photoprinting Equipment Company. I could have a job in his darkrooms, he said. But the darkroom was a further ten miles away from home and it was a 7 a.m. start. As compensation he would round my money up to three pounds a week. Mr Cohen concluded this rather one-sided interview by observing that my face was very spotty and I ought to see a doctor about it.

The darkrooms of the Gaunt Photoprinting Equipment Company were in a basement below their showroom and workshop in a back street just off the Clerkenwell Road. They were presided over by a morose and bald-headed man of sallow complexion who gave the impression that he actually lived down there. I never saw him in the daylight. The darkrooms were even grimmer than Grundy and Bones's had been. I wouldn't have been surprised if gremlins had emerged from the darker corners. I gave my notice on the first day and left at the end of the week. My venture into the world of photography was at an end.

The Flankshire Insurance Company

It was all a terrible mistake. The last thing that I wanted to be was an insurance clerk. Everyone in Springhurst Avenue seemed to work in a bank, or a stockbroker's or as a shipping clerk or in the civil service or, even worse, as an insurance clerk.

Each morning droves of homburg or trilby-hatted minions in dark suits and brollies trooped down Springhurst Avenue to West Wickham station. (There were very few bowlers or pinstripe trousers; the lower middle classes knew their place in those days.) Every evening the same horde trooped back again just in time for the six o'clock news on the wireless.

The trouble is that my education had left me in a sort of no man's land: overeducated for a career with MacFisheries or digging holes for the water board but never likely to get a place at the London School of Economics. It was only rotten swots like Tichy Twyford who got places at universities and other clever places. Although I swore that when I left school I would never work in an office, the options seemed to be narrowing alarmingly.

I had no wish to conform to the norms of Springhurst Avenue. Somehow I was going to be different. I didn't realise at the time that it was the fond belief of every sixteen year old that he or she was going to be different; I thought that I was the only one. I decided that I was going to be a press photographer. This ambition was based mainly on a passable photograph I had taken in 1948 of the West Wickham Sea Scouts drum and bugle band marching at the head of the Fair and Flitch procession. Unfortunately, Fleet Street was not impressed so I had settled for my employment as a darkroom assistant in an industrial photographers in Croydon, an unfortunate choice since the partnership collapsed a year later with a flurry of final demand notices through the letter box.

These events faced me with the prospect of being even more different, i.e. unemployed. The prospect was unthinkable. Mr Edom senior had been none too pleased with the first streaks of my unseemly originality. Unemployment would have been the last straw. There were certain standards that had to be maintained in Springhurst Avenue and these did not allow for getting girls in the pudding club, putting a Labour Party poster in the window or getting oneself seriously unemployed.

My nerves badly shot to pieces, I went to an employment agency. They only offered me one job; as a junior insurance clerk with the Flankshire Insurance Company at their South London branch in Brixton. The pay was three pounds a week (first week's wages to the Acme Employment Agency by way of commission).

The interview for the job was a bit of an anticlimax. I had been very apprehensive. I had no idea what people actually did in offices but I assumed that it must be rather clever and complicated. However, my medium-to-good School Certificate, a dark suit and well polished shoes and my willingness to call everyone 'sir' twice in every sentence seemed to do the trick.

I was interviewed by Mr Worthington, the chief clerk, who then took me in to see the branch manager, Mr Jefferson-Jones, for a final blessing. Mr Jefferson-Jones didn't really seem to know what was required of him. He muttered a series of appropriate phrases. (All the time I knew him he never seemed to speak a complete sentence.) 'Excellent prospects... fine Company... assets exceed £12,000,000... hope you will be happy with us... work hard... sky's the limit for a young man...' The effect was rather spoilt by the fact that he had already forgotten my name but he smiled benignly, if rather toothily, as he terminated the interview.

I was now a junior insurance clerk for the Flankshire (established 1834). In addition to the three pounds a week there was a half-crown luncheon voucher each day.

Although I professed disdain for office work I was a bit intimidated by it. After all, they wouldn't pay you three pounds a week for nothing, would they? My immediate boss was Mr Worthington. He was the key man in the Flankshire's South London operation, a well nourished man in a slightly too tight grey pinstripe suit and with a plummy voice. He had a very good opinion of himself and adopted a rather lordly air and a sense of dignity far beyond his years. He was in his late twenties or early thirties but far too preoccupied with his status to allow any traces of youthfulness still to remain and he had a bum a little too big for his trousers.

The job itself turned out be a bit disappointing. The main essentials turned out to be doing the post, answering the phone and attending to the filing. However, there was the technology to master, primarily the telephone switchboard and reloading the stapling machine. In those days there were no adding machines, copying machines or addressing machines and if there was any adding, copying or addressing to be done then Edom was expected to do it.

Mr Worthington proved to be a pain. As the most junior member of staff the only relationship with him that proved tenable was one of grovelling sycophancy. I discovered that he was a leading light in the Surbiton Round Table which evermore made me distrustful of any organisation that professed to altruism.

Mr Worthington was a little uncertain about how heavily to patronise me. He would have clearly liked to address me as 'Edom' but didn't have the gall. First names were unthinkable. It just wasn't done in the Flankshire circa 1950. 'Mr Edom' would have given me far more dignity than Mr Worthington was prepared to allow so he either used no name at all or just addressed me as 'mister' with a lip-curling emphasis that left no one in doubt that it was not a term of respect.

The Flankshire's South London office was decorated in a sort of urine yellow but it was hard to determine the relative contributions made to the decor by the original colour scheme, the passage of time, the Brixton air and nicotine. Those were the days when non-smokers were viewed as distinctly poofy and just about everyone smoked. (Passive smoking would have been construed as smoking a Capstan Full Strength without coughing.)

The office was located in Brinkley's Bank Chambers. Brinkley's Bank occupied the entire ground floor and the first floor was occupied by Hingebury and Tucker, Solicitors and Commissioners for Oaths. The second floor was the preserve of the Flankshire and, to prove it, across the second floor windows looking out over the Brixton Road was emblazoned in gilt letters: 'The Flank... Insurance Company Ltd. (Est. 1834). To explain, one of the windows had been blown out in 1941 and had been replaced by plain glass thus reducing the impact of the company's PR initiative.

Every piece of woodwork in the office was a light brown with an imitation grain etched on it. I don't know when the Brixton office opened but I found an old document that showed that it was certainly before the General Strike of 1926. I think that was probably when it was last decorated.

The floor was plain linoleum, also brown, and although every room had a fireplace, the heating was by strange cast-iron gas-heated radiators which went off like cannons if you didn't get a match to them quickly.

The Flankshire was very proud of its insignia which portrayed a lady with spear, helmet and shield in defiant pose with what appeared to be a male lion with acute depression peering up her nightie. This insignia appeared on all the Flankshire's proposal forms, its letter heading and anything else they could find to stick it on. There was also a large papier mâché version on the counter in the general office but the effect was spoilt because the lady's spear had fallen off and she looked as if she was shaking her fist at the lion.

Mr Worthington was in charge of everything in the South London branch. He did all the dictation and somehow managed to keep three shorthand typists busy by dictating to each one in turn. 'Take a meemo to Head Office, Miss Trimble,' he would say. (For reasons I could not grasp he always called them 'meemos'.) I had a secret passion for Miss Trimble and would have dearly liked to have instructed her to take something down for me but this was out of the question. Mr Worthington kept his little harem of shorthand typists very much under his control and apart from when they emerged for dictation they were kept in purdah in an adjoining room. Woe betide any office junior who ventured in there without an extremely good alibi.

I used to listen to Mr Worthington's dictating technique with fascination. His plummy voice dominated the general office and when he got into his stride and dictated to all three shorthand typists in swift succession the air was full of meemos and ultimos and instants and proximos with a smattering of pro tems, pro ratas and assuring you of our best attentions at all times. His performance echoed around the general office and it was generally thought to be more entertaining than Cyril Fletcher at the Brixton Empress.

It was made clear at the outset that in the hierarchy of the Flankshire the office junior did not give dictation. In fact, he didn't do anything except what he was told. I did have to adjust the office calendar every morning first thing. It was a splendid affair in a large mahogany box with a series of roller blinds like the destination boards on the trams that rattled and ground along the Brixton Road. I also had to make up a folder for every new insurance proposal and make a copy of the form in blue-black ink in my best handwriting before the original was sent up to Head Office. Photocopiers didn't exist in those days; it was all down to my Golden Platignum fountain pen and my best handwriting. Then the details had to be entered into a metal-bound register that went back to 1931.

I was also the telephone operator and had total control over two lines and eight extensions. The switchboard was another mahogany box with flaps that fell down to indicate incoming calls and little numbered eyes that winked at me when an extension was picked up. There were also rows of little levers for me to cut people off with. The branch manager had a separate intercom system to impress wealthy clients and there was a separate sleek black telephone on my desk that buzzed and flashed a red light whenever my lord and master required tea, a twopenny halfpenny stamp or was just feeling bored. That bloody machine did my nerves no good at all. He always seemed to set it off just as I was adding up the post book or had a difficult caller on one of the outside lines.

There was no doubt that Mr Jefferson-Jones was very proud of his personal intercom. It had a Bakelite facia on his desk that looked very modern. With just a flick of a switch he could set off this howling banshee on my desk. If it caught me unawares I nearly wet myself. Sometimes I

would be subjected to all that trauma just so that he could
call me in there to fill his gold fountain pen with his very
special violet ink. Don't people in authority just make you
sick?

I was heavily into ink at the Flankshire. I also had to fill
all the inkwells from this large bottle of Stephens blue-
black ink that was kept in the stationery cupboard. There
was enough ink in that bloody bottle to keep the entire
insurance industry going until about 1960, I would have
thought. If you didn't lift it carefully you could have got a
double hernia. Then there was re-inking the date stamp
pad, sticking innumerable labels on with watery gum,
sticking on hundreds of stamps and sealing vast quantities
of envelopes with the help of a damp sponge.

But the ultimate in gunginess was the filing system.
Details of each policy issued by the Flankshire South
London branch was contained in an individual cardboard
folder and these were stored in open wooden racks. The A
to Ks were stored in the general office but the remainder of
the alphabet had overflowed into racks along the corridor
past the accounts department and almost down the stairs
leading to the lavatory. I reckoned that the Zs would be
under the lavatory cistern in a couple of years. The less well
used sections had collapsed into crumpled heaps and were a
very dusty adventure in time. Some of the files had
postcards in them with King George the Fifth stamps on.
The Zs were a particularly messy lot and made me feel like
an archaeologist. If I had the misfortune to be sent to find
Mr Zuckerman's fire policy issued in 1928 it was best to go
searching with a brush and dustpan, or better still, put it off
to another day.

I had another secret problem with filing. I always
blamed it on the war. No one ever taught me my alphabet.
At about alphabet learning time my education was getting a
bit disrupted. Hitler had plonked six 250 lb bombs down

our road with a couple of 500 pounders for good measure.
It did take my mind off my education somewhat so maybe
that's when I missed the alphabet. Either that or our
beloved schoolteacher, Mrs Sergeant, just forgot to teach it.
She was a bit like that. Anyway, by the time I realised the
omission it was too embarrassing to admit it. I knew the
first part well enough, the A to K bit but then it tended to
get a bit uncertain. L…? M…? N? and then like a train
coming out of a tunnel, lightness and clarity gradually
returned. R…? S…? T…? U…? V-W-X-Y-Z!

However, I have to confess that if you insured with the
Flankshire South London Branch around 1950 and you had
a name like Postlethwaite or Quincey there was a serious
risk that your file would never be seen again.

Mr Jefferson-Jones was a bit of a disappointment to me.
I had assumed that because he was the branch manager he
would do a bit of managing, but not a bit of it. Some days
he did not come to the office at all and other days he
arrived in the middle of the afternoon and caused a flurry of
activity as he demanded a cup of tea or a refill for his
fountain pen. He seemed to have all sorts of exotic contacts
and would produce strange new business like insurance on
a racehorse or a herd of pedigree Friesians or fire insurance
on a sixteenth-century thatched cottage or personal
accident insurance for an entire rugby team in Weybridge.

He never seemed to fit in to the rather seedy environment of the South London office. The furnishings were a
case in point. They left much to be desired. The chairs
were all different. The only thing they had in common was
that they were all about thirty years old with carved backs
and padded seats with the stuffing hanging out. The desks
were very old indeed, like leather-topped tables with brass
handles to the drawers. They looked as though you ought
to have been able to find Nelson's initials carved on them
somewhere.

One of the crosses that I had to bear was the post book. It was expected to balance and if it did not then this was attributed to incompetence or dishonesty. Since it never did actually balance there were three options open to me: (a) to put the money in or take it out to make it balance, (b) to record imaginary postings of large envelopes to Head Office to make up the difference, or (c) to confuse the issue with a large ink blot.

Weighing the larger items of post took one into the realms of higher technology. We had a little letter scale with brass weights and then once the letter was weighed I had to do rapid calculations using the book of Post Office postal rates. Even Mr Worthington deferred to my decisions over postal charges.

I was also responsible for the counter display of proposal forms held in a wooden rack of artificially grained wood decorated with the Flankshire lady with spear and voyeuristic lion. The Flankshire had a proposal form for everything. They insured things that I did not even know existed: anthrax, foot and mouth, consequential loss, fidelity guarantee, endowment, annuity, employers' liability, workmen's compensation, property owners' indemnity. The Flankshire, I quickly discovered, would insure anything that you were prepared to pay a premium for: your yacht, caravan, motorcycle, your life, your cattle, your horse, your plate glass, your boiler or your mink coat. You name it they would insure it – for a price.

When the proposal came in, the smooth efficiency of the Flankshire would take over. I would make up the file, copy the proposal in my best handwriting and enter it in the heavy register that caused a blood blister if you caught your finger in it. Then it was over to Mr Worthington. 'Take a meemo to Head Office, Miss Trimble' (or one of the other members of his little harem, Miss Lean or Miss Penny). Miss Penny had small pert bosoms and a sniffle whilst Miss

Lean was older and was never known to smile. She always arrived late for work but even Mr Worthington was a bit frightened of her and pretended not to notice when she arrived precisely ten minutes late every morning.

There were certain duties in the general office that were reserved for Mr Worthington. Opening and date-stamping the post, doing the dictation and winding the office clock were duties that came with high office and were his exclusive preserve.

Another of the nasty little duties delegated to me was to get out the files for all the correspondence received. Now this was not too difficult when the writer quoted a policy number or signed his name in a decipherable fashion but some of the pieces of correspondence gave no clue at all and I was left with all these odd bits of correspondence for which I couldn't find a home. One of my contemporaries who worked in a City office was faced with a similar problem. His solution was to cast the day's unlocated post to the winds as he walked over London Bridge on his way home each evening. I fear that I never had the stomach for such a radical solution – nor access to the River Thames.

The staff amenities at the Flankshire were rather limited. There was a gas ring in the typists' room where tea was brewed in the afternoon. There was also a lavatory which was along a dark corridor and down a flight of stairs and was part of the caretaker's flat. This meant that you sometimes had to be patient if the caretaker was having a bath. That was about the limit of the amenities really. Mind you, they didn't charge you for filling your fountain pen.

Mrs Parry presided over the accounts department, a small room off the back corridor. Three large desks were crowded in there and the other two desks were occupied by Miss Purley and Miss Bagshawe, a giggling duo who spent much time talking about their boyfriends, their marriage plans and their sex lives, although not necessarily in that order. They were all sling-back sandals and headscarves and stockings with seams. I found them very exciting although they did make me blush a bit. They were the first girls I had encountered who talked about thingy quite so blatantly. I proved a useful butt for all their jokes and innuendos. I secretly found all sorts of reasons to go to the accounts department. Checking if a claimant's premium had been paid was the best excuse. Mrs Parry did not approve of all this naughty talk although she seemed to listen fairly attentively. Whenever there was a pause after one of the girls had said something particularly rude Mrs Parry would say, 'Ho-hum,' or sometimes, 'Tsk, tsk.'

Gradually the insurance industry surrendered up its secrets to me. There were mysterious men known as 'Inspectors' who called in periodically to collect their commission cheques. They turned out to be a superior sort of salesmen who persuaded estate agents, solicitors and the like to recommend the Flankshire's policies. Mr Gear was the supremo of the South London inner suburbs whilst Mr Filbert and Mr Barker covered Kent and Surrey respectively. Mr Filbert was struggling a bit with his territory and had a permanently anxious expression. Mr Gear had been doing the job for many years and gave the impression of being on drinking terms with everyone of consequence in South London and of having one or two nice little earners on the side. Mr Barker dressed like a farmer, had a ruddy complexion and seldom introduced any business other than herds of cows, thatched barns and tractors.

When I returned to the Flankshire after an enforced absence of two years serving the colours in such diverse and exotic places as Lancashire, Oxfordshire, Wiltshire and Berkshire, I was welcomed back with deafening apathy. Long gone were the days when returning ex-servicemen were decorated with medals and welcomed with banners, bunting and female embraces.

I had still not forgiven Mr Worthington for my reception when I called in to the office whilst on leave to show all uninterested parties the photos of my passing-out parade. He glanced dismissively at the photos. 'The slope of the rifles looks a bit ragged,' he observed in his lordly way. The remark wasn't made any more acceptable by the fact that the superior sod was right.

Anyway, my eventual return was a bit weird. The Flankshire had to have me back. It was not an expression of their confidence in my intrinsic worth. It was just that the law said that employers must take back returning national servicemen. However, there was no law that said they had to be enthusiastic about it.

Lots of things had changed in my absence but some had not. Miss Purley was now married and lost no opportunity to let me know what an incredibly super married life she was having – every night apparently.

The company rules hadn't changed however, and I had merely changed one uniform for another. Dark suit, white shirt and sober tie. (None of your coloured shirts here; only art students wore those.) On Saturday mornings, however, concessions were made. A sports jacket and grey flannel trousers were allowed just so long as there was none of this nonsense with suede shoes or similar poofiness. Clothes rationing had only recently ended and both clothes and money were in short supply. Shirts were of the detachable collar variety and I used disposable cardboard collars that, with the careful use of a pencil eraser, would last for three days. Mind you, the pointed cardboard tips gradually drilled holes in my shirts. I did try the newfangled plastic collars which you could buy in Woolworth's but they just brought me out in a rash.

I have now reached that depressing stage in life where I am convinced that there is little new under the sun. When I returned to my duties after my service with the Crown I found that the Flankshire was in the throes of a major reorganisation. This involved something called 'mechanisation'. Apparently they were going to use machines to issue the Flankshire's renewal notices.

Reorganisation has convulsed every organisation I have worked for ever since (with very similar results on each occasion). I've always been a bit wary of reorganisations ever since the 1963 Beeching Plan promised profitability for the railways by 1970. I have also noticed a correlation between the frequency with which an organisation is reorganised and its decline.

Our beloved branch manager, Mr Jefferson-Jones, seemed to have become even more flamboyant whilst I had been away. He was now the manager designate of the soon-to-be-established Southern Counties Branch. He was at his best on Epsom racing days when he appeared in the office in outrageous checks, armed with large binoculars and a jaunty hat with a feather in it – a sort of Liberace of the turf. The only apparent benefits for the Flankshire were a further two proposal forms for livestock insurance and one of those was cancelled following a subsequent debacle in the three thirty at Wincanton.

Mr Worthington's star was also in its ascendancy. Since he did all the work, Mr Jefferson-Jones was happy to sponsor him as chief clerk for the new Southern Counties branch. He became even more pompous in consequence.

The company also had plans for me. Not that I was consulted about these. I was to become junior fire insurance clerk, drafting all the household policies and the fire insurance endorsements. To equip me for these onerous duties I was to be given a technical training – two months in the fire department at Head Office.

As a temporary expedient I was assigned to the accounts department where I cared for three enormous agency ledgers, using a steel-nibbed dip pen and ruling off the balances with double underlining and running up and down columns of pounds shillings and pence like a monkey up a tree.

The grand opening of the new Southern Counties branch was a memorable event. Mr Jefferson-Jones made a speech: 'Auspicious occasion, fine new office… increased business and new developments… Assets now exceed £13,000,000… New era, must pull together… Great opportunities, fine prospects for the future…'

After the speeches were finished and the local press and the Head Office dignitaries had left, the occasion deteriorated into an office party in the grand tradition of office parties. It was, in fact, the first office party I had attended. I was a bit surprised.

It was a very boozy event. The accountant who I had always suspected of being a bit poofy redeemed himself in my eyes by going to the aid of the new senior typist who had spilt a glass of sweet sherry down her dress and was seeking someone to sponge it for her. And for once Miss Lean smiled. Mind you, she was getting a cuddle from the accident underwriter at the time. Then Mr Worthington emerged from the staff toilet. He was puke green. 'Christ!' he said. 'I feel bloody awful.' It was the only time I ever saw him show human frailty. For a moment I almost liked him.

Cricket, Lovely Cricket

In my first year at Ravensbeck Grammar School a curious affliction beset me. Whilst aimlessly lounging around the playing field and reflecting on how to avoid retribution for not doing my French homework (who cared où est bloody Toto anyway?) something very strange happened. Some idiot hurled a cricket ball at me and to my astonishment I caught it. Even more to my surprise, when I wildly bowled it at someone (mainly to get rid of the bloody thing since I didn't like being the centre of attention) I hit the wicket. In a flash, or at least before a double period of maths was over, I had become the great white hope of Form 1C. I expect that statement is institutional racism, but remember this was 1945 when all foreigners were Dagos, Wops, Huns, Frogs or Yanks and anyone else was assumed to have a predilection for popping you in a stewing pot and eating you.

Never mind all that. I became the opening bowler for my form team. This was heady stuff indeed. I might have been thirtieth out of thirty-two in the Easter term exam results but now I was a person of consequence. Thereafter I gave my all to concentrating in the hot sun on Wednesday sports afternoons at our sports ground at Park Langley (or what passed for hot sun in July 1945).

Of course, once I began to take the wickets of the sporting pundits I became the subject of much criticism. My bowling action was suspect. Was my arm straight? Did I drag my foot? It was all a bit lost on me, far too sophisticated. I just used to hurl the ball down as fast as I could and every now and then a wicket disintegrated or an umpire said, 'Out.' It was all rather satisfying.

Batting, however, was an entirely different matter. I preferred to be number eleven in the batting order, then with any luck it would be raining or the light would fail before my turn came. If I did have to bat I would try to avoid the bowling and end up not out. I was usually nought not out but occasionally I made a scoring stroke (ball hit my bat whilst I wasn't looking and eluded first slip, or using my bat to protect my vitals the ball whizzed past fine leg). My batting average wavered between .01 and 2.2. Still, fast bowlers weren't expected to be good batsmen, I explained.

I began to see myself as a second Harold Larwood; fast but controversial. I acquired a pair of pre-war second-hand cricket boots. (Harold Larwood wouldn't have been expected to annihilate the Australians in a pair of worn-out gym plimsolls, would he?) The boots didn't have leather uppers, just rather worn canvas ones but with some white blanco they looked quite impressive and the hole where my right big toe stuck out didn't show all that much when I acquired my white socks. Mind you, the metal spikes kept falling out of the soles which made me skid about a bit. Sometimes I would slide halfway down the wicket in a less than graceful impersonation of Sonja Henie. The problem was I couldn't get replacement spikes. I got no sympathy in the boot and shoe repairers: 'Don't you know there's been a war on, Sonny Jim?' Eventually I did manage to get some large hobnails which I hammered in on my father's old shoe last. I wonder where all the cricket spikes went during the war. After the war I suppose they all went for the export drive, probably to the Australians.

Never mind, my cricketing fame was spreading. I was invited to play in one or two matches against local youth clubs. I lengthened my run up to thirteen paces and developed an impressive ritual of pacing out the run and digging a trench with my heel to mark my starting point. That trench was so deep that you could have sheltered from a Doodlebug in there but I had to let everyone know I was serious and didn't expect to be taken off once I had started.

I began to compile a secret notebook in which I recorded all my cricketing hints and tips. My notebook recorded all the secrets of my success. I had little notes and diagrams about yorkers and Chinamen and googleys and off-breaks and all the other great mysteries of cricket. Unfortunately, at some point when I had a crisis of confidence, I tore the pages out and used the remainder of the notebook for recording train numbers, thus denying posterity my very special cricketing secrets.

Nonetheless, I continued to study all the cricketing hints in my weekly *Adventure*. Here I learned that 'Swerve bowling is a science, linked up with a new ball, the atmosphere and other things'. Well, that was a great help; I was bottom of the form in physics, a new ball hadn't been seen at Ravensbeck since 1940 and as for atmosphere and other things that sounded suspiciously like black magic to me. However, on one humid afternoon in about 1948 I took six Form 4G wickets for twenty-two runs and my team mates, delirious with joy at winning for a change, assured me that I was swinging the ball in the air.

This experience was intoxicating. I lengthened my run to fifteen paces, began to wear Brylcreem like Dennis Compton, let my sleeves flap loose to distract the batsman and acquired a pullover just so that I could take it off and give it to the umpire. I spent ages deliberating about whether I needed a third slip or a silly mid-off and I could go on for hours about the special grip needed to achieve the famous Edom swerve.

I was invited to play in the scratch team that challenged the second eleven of the Yew Tree Youth Club. Now this was fame indeed. Playing against the Yew Tree Youth Club had the same social cachet with the youth of West Wickham as being chosen to play opposite Jane Russell in *The Outlaw*. I can't remember much detail about the game but it was a memorable occasion just to be performing on the sacred turf of the Yew Tree Youth Club pitch. They had their own pitch that lot, none of your hiring the cricket square in the Blake Recreation Ground (five bob for an evening match and seven and six for Saturday afternoons).

Anyway, even the officials of the Yew Tree Youth Club had to acknowledge that I was, as it were, in contention. Tichy Twyford's dad, who was one of the umpires and believed that only Godfrey Evans's wicket-keeping skills were superior to his son's, had to acknowledge that the third ball in my fourth over wasn't at all bad, although he redressed the balance by declaring the next ball a wide.

My batting still presented problems. Although I took guard in a style worthy of Cyril Washbrook (middle and leg please) and surveyed the field with all the authority of Len Hutton, things tended to get a bit tricky thereafter. I decided that some batting gloves might help. The ones supplied at school were curious affairs made of interlinked padded segments that looked like a string of sausages. I could never get on with these and tended to get the sequence all messed up so that I padded the palms of my hands or had two sausages on one finger and none on my thumb. In the end I bought a pair of more orthodox gloves with bright green spiky bits on the knuckles. From then on the best bit about batting was walking out to the crease pulling on my spiky green batting gloves. I developed all the other batsman's skills of patting down a bump or two with the flat of my bat or picking up and discarding the odd stray bit of rabbit droppings. I would have liked to have had the sight screen moved but the pitches we played on never had such refinements. Never mind, I always kept an impeccable straight bat and my green spiky batting gloves and my Walter Hammond autographed bat gave me an air of considerable distinction. Sadly, my batting average never rose above 2.2 although I did once score a four. (Hit the shoulder of my bat, wicket keeper was picking his nose, ball reached the short boundary before anyone noticed.)

I continued to take wickets with the Edom swerve. I had this iron determination and will-power you see, and I was at my peak. After 1949, however, my cricketing career began to go downhill. Even my acquisition of a new canvas cricket bag (32s. 6d. from Kennings Department Store's sports department, Croydon) failed to stop the rot.

Once I left school and was plunged into the adult cricketing world I rapidly found myself well out of my depth. (I couldn't afford the subscriptions and certainly couldn't compete with people who took their sport seriously to the point of torn cartilages, pulled Achilles tendons and imminent burst blood vessels.)

I had a number of cricketing revivals however. In 1959 I played for the Penworth Heath Prison Officers (B Shift) cricket team. It was a memorable season. (Well, have you ever attended a cricket practice with a truncheon in your trousers?) We played a full range of fixtures. There was the Wortfordshire Constabulary third team, the RAF Halwell second eleven, the staff and boys of an approved school in South Weald, a pub team in North Greenford and a number of other memorable teams that I have completely forgotten. We lost every game that season but we had a good deal of fun (or so we consoled ourselves). It wasn't that we didn't try. We practised every Thursday evening in some nets behind D Wing to the shouts of the hardened criminals therein who encouraged us with pithy observations like, 'All screws are bastards,' or, 'Hope your bails drop off.'

Our captain was a six foot four screw who presided over

the mailbag shop. He was an amiable giant who desperately wanted us to win at least one game. He used to field in the slips and on one occasion he hurled himself into horizontal flight in pursuit of a catch off one of my outswingers. It was like the maiden flight of the Bristol Brabazon. He missed the catch but when he came to earth I swear the whole of West Acton playing field vibrated and small cracks appeared near mid-wicket.

Then one day in about 1966 I became embroiled in cricket again. The senior probation officer at Peckham Magistrates' Court, who happened to be my boss at the time, decided to challenge the Police Gaolers to a cricket match. The challenge was issued at the back of No. 2 Court during some very boring committal proceedings, an affray outside The Belted Earl at closing time I suspect. (There were always minor riots outside The Belted Earl at closing time.) I suppose he couldn't think of anything else to say. We were appalled. Most of the probation officers got out of breath climbing into the witness box and I have to concede that personally I was distinctly past my best. It was just for a laugh, we all assured each other, just a beer match. Just in case, however, the probation officers sneaked off and practised diligently in Peckham Park every lunchtime.

The match was held at the Metropolitan Police Sports Ground at Hayes, specially booked for the occasion. The gaolers staff had told us not to worry about whites and assured us that the bar was very good. After all, it was only a beer match and just for laughs, wasn't it? Our motley team of probation officers arrived on the due date. Our only hope was Colin Simpleton-Hughes who, he assured us, had opened the batting in his last year at Eton (or was it Harrow?).

Well, I have to tell you that the match was an unmitigated disaster. The Metropolitan Police Sports Ground was as big as Old Trafford and totally intimidating. The pavilion was nearly as big as Buckingham Palace and the distance from mid-wicket to the boundary was a day's forced march. Believe me, you had to take rations when you went out there. Even worse, those devious gaolers had reinforced their team with some young and extremely fit cricketers from the Divisional Police first eleven. Reinforced is perhaps the wrong word; I only recognised four members of their team and one of those was twelfth man. Their lot were all clad in elegant whites whilst we wore a motley collection of grey flannels, shrunken jeans, yellow socks and footwear more suited to a pop festival or a CND march. Only Colin Simpleton-Hughes was sartorially correct, and he was out first ball. It was a slaughter. The splendid scoreboard couldn't keep up with the fall of our wickets. We scrabbled and poked and scraped together about forty-odd runs and most of those came out of sympathy. I don't like to tell you my score but if someone had quacked things could have turned very nasty.

Then it was their turn to bat. I opened the bowling. I mustered together every ounce of energy, every morsel of aggression, every fragment of expertise. The young bloods from the Police Divisional first eleven whopped me all around the ground. It was more dangerous on the boundary than anywhere else on the pitch. They were merciless. I went from bright red to puce. Little veins pulsed on my forehead. I feared a coronary. I bowled ever faster and they whopped them ever harder. They didn't seem to notice the Edom swerve, let alone have any trouble with it. I knew how Napoleon must have felt. It was the end – my swan song. Well, more of a croak actually. The humiliation of it all lingers with me still. My only consolation in retrospect is that by this time those young bloods must themselves be looking pretty decrepit and will have had the experience of being trounced by yet another generation of clever clogs.

I haven't played cricket since and nowadays even getting

out of my chair after watching the Test Match on television makes my back hurt. Still, it's a lovely game, isn't it?

Terpsichorean Skills

I had been led to believe that the key to social success was to learn ballroom dancing. In 1949 there was no other sort of dancing. The only social success I wanted was the sort that led to lots of bodily contact with those of the opposite gender. There were lots of dance halls around at the time and they seemed my only hope of achieving my amorous desires. It was rumoured that at the Regal Ballroom, Beckenham, the birds were positively falling over themselves to be invited to flutter. Thus it was that I decided that I must learn to dance forthwith.

I learned my initial dancing skills at the Monica Flinch Dance Academy in the winter of 1949. Monica Flinch was a blonde horsey-faced lady who held her dance classes at the Councillor Prendergast Memorial Hall in West Wickham every Wednesday evening. She was also available for private tuition. I attended one or two beginners' classes but the other pupils seemed to be learning much faster than I was and being shy and spotty I did not enjoy demonstrating to the other clever clogs that not only had I two left feet but I was also endowed with a complete absence of rhythm. I quickly decided that I would have to opt for the private lessons. They were seven and six an hour so I could only afford five lessons. Sadly, it was not enough.

Being locked in the arms of Monica Flinch was a terrifying experience for a young man of sixteen. 'Hold me firmly, I'm not made of glass,' she would hector. I was acutely aware that she was not so constructed; more whalebone corset and wired uplift bra it seemed to me.

We danced to very worn records of Victor Sylvester: waltz, quickstep and slow foxtrot. We never risked the tango. Our relationship began on a basis of mutual distrust and went steadily downhill from there. The last straw was when, in a vain effort to complete a double reverse turn, I ran out of floor and deposited us both across a pile of stacked chairs in the corner of the hall. Monica was not well pleased. I had laddered her nylons and ruffled her dignity. I didn't dare point out to her that she at least had the consolation of being paid for the experience.

I then tried a do-it-yourself approach. There was a series of books much in vogue at the time with the generic title *Teach Yourself*. There was *Teach Yourself Algebra* and *Teach Yourself Canasta*. For all I know there was probably a *Teach Yourself Basic Mongolian*. I bought the volume entitled *Teach Yourself to Dance*. It had very precise written instructions: 'Now move left foot to right foot…' These were reinforced by little maps of ladies' and gentlemen's feet trekking across the page. One pair of feet were black and the other set were white. I forget which were which but I don't think any sort of ethnic integration was being promoted. I bought a number of Victor Sylvester records. They had different titles but they all sounded much the same, apart from the tempo. All in very strict tempo they were. I played the records over and over again and waltzed and quick-stepped and slow-foxtrotted across my bedroom lino until my feet hurt. It didn't seem to help all that much. I kept muttering, 'Slow, slow, quick, quick, slow,' but I invariably lost the beat or forgot which way the diagram went.

I didn't do a lot of dancing after that. I came to the conclusion that I only had the courage to venture on to a dance floor when terminally drunk and by then I usually seemed to be functioning with three left feet. There were, of course, the monthly dances in the NAAFI at RAF White

Waltham but they were an experience apart. Monica Flinch wouldn't have stood much chance there, I can tell you that, whalebone corsets or not. There was also the dance to celebrate passing out from the Prison Officers' Training Course at Wetherby in 1959. Lots of nurses from the local hospital were invited to this event but I never dared to ask for a dance for fear of some further disaster or embarrassment.

In later years there the was the occasional office party where everyone lurched around the general office in an inebriated daze whilst somebody's record player churned out Beatles music. There were, of course, a few clever clogs who could do the twist or something else equally droll but I usually concentrated on trying to increase the alcohol content of the fruit punch.

I once lived on a small housing estate where the neighbours took it in turns to hold Saturday night parties but these were events where you took your own bottle of wine and groped your own wife and there was usually only enough space to revolve on one's own axis so the dancing skills required were minimal.

I mostly missed out on discos. By the time they were in vogue my slipped disc was exerting increasing influence. Still there were one or two holiday experiences. Everyone knows that holidays don't count and you can be as silly as you like when on holiday. I remember this nightclub in Madrid in about 1980. It startled me no end. I had never encountered this sort of scene before. The music came from hidden speakers and made my eardrums hurt and the lights were incredible. They flashed and twirled and twinkled and made my shirt look blue and my face look orange. It was worse than the Blitz.

Now that I am a pensioner everyone at any social event I attend expects me to break into a waltz or a slow foxtrot since it is well known that us oldies are partial to a bit of ballroom dancing. I always have to explain about Monica Flinch. She certainly has a lot to answer for.

The Amateur Photographer

I had always wanted to be a photographer ever since I discovered the wonder of producing my first contact print. In about 1947 I had discovered some pre-war contact paper and an ancient daylight printing frame in one of my old dad's cupboards. There was also some stuff called hypo which looked rather like Epsom salts. Photography was full of mysteries like that. The printing frame dated from my dad's interest in family photographs during the early years of parenthood. That must have been in about 1933 but thereafter he seemed to go off the whole idea. I try not to take it personally but I was a late arrival to the family and was born in 1933. By the time I arrived on the scene the urge to record the family for posterity seemed to have waned so the early years of Robert Edom have not been recorded extensively, photographically speaking. There is one studio photograph of me wearing my best suit and a pensive expression that was taken in May 1941 just after the worst night of the Blitz when my parents were motivated by the thought that there might not be many more photo opportunities.

Anyway, there I was in 1947 discovering the mysteries of photography. A book from the library, a tenpenny packet of developer from the chemist and my father's pre-war tin of hypo and some contact paper and I was ready to go.

The only negative I had available to print from was a pre-war holiday snapshot taken at Herne Bay in about 1938. It would have to do. After I had exposed the paper in my printing frame I plunged it into my mum's enamel pie dish full of developer. There was an exciting moment when the image appeared but then the print went totally black. For the first but certainly not the last time in my life I had overdone it. This did lead me into a few philosophical thoughts. For example, is all life a series of fleeting images that pass rapidly into darkness before they can be savoured? I get troubled by such thoughts occasionally. Where for example does all the sound go when you have heard it? Oh well, never mind.

Still I had definitely caught the photographic bug. Sadly, 1947 was not a good time to begin a photographic hobby. Everything was in short supply and this went for things photographic as well as most of life's other little comforts. It was a case of make do and mend.

Now that I was a serious photographer I began to subscribe to the *Amateur Photographer*. Gradually a range of new equipment became available for amateur photographers and I would wistfully peruse all the advertisements in my magazine and imagine what I would buy if only I had the necessary funds.

I acquired a number of cameras. First a small and very ancient folding camera of my father's. The bellows leaked light so that all my photographs had white fuzzy edges. My best effort was a picture of East Grinstead High Street that looked as though the whole town was on fire. Then I had a box camera that reduced everything nearer than ten feet to a blur and totally disregarded anything that was more than twenty feet away. Then I acquired a curious device in a plastic case that actually had a choice of shutter speeds (well, two actually). It didn't have a very sophisticated lens. In fact, it looked suspiciously like a piece of plain glass to me. Sadly, I dropped the camera and cracked the case and after that all the pictures it produced looked as though they had been taken in a fog.

For a long while after that I relied on an elderly box camera of my father's for my photographic efforts but I knew that I would never be taken seriously as a photographer until I had a more versatile instrument. My Kodak Box Brownie only had one shutter speed although the aperture could be adjusted to allow for 'bright' or 'dull'. At this stage there were very few new cameras around and they were not very impressive. The advertisements in the *Amateur Photographer* were full of second-hand pre-war cameras and I perused these covetously. There were Rolleiflexes and Leicas and Contaxes but the prices were all far beyond my reach. Then I saw an advertisement for a second-hand camera which I might just be able to afford. The camera was a pre-war Foth-Derby. Which war it was pre I was not sure but it had a focal plane shutter with a choice of speeds and an f3.5 lens. The camera was priced at ten guineas but I knew I had to possess it. I can't remember how I raised the money and I had to travel all the way up to London to buy it but at last the deed was done. The Foth-Derby was mine and I was immensely proud of it.

The Foth-Derby took 127 roll film but its most exciting feature was the focal plane shutter. I will not bore you with the details but that camera had a primitive life all of its own. You wound up the shutter and when you released it the device exploded into life with a ferocity unparalleled in photographic history. I produced a whole series of photos marred by camera shake and I developed a highly nervous disposition. Using that shutter was like waiting for an unexploded bomb to go off. The camera's highest shutter speed was one five hundredth of a second which in 1948 was a bit sharpish. It would have enabled me to take a picture of Sam Bartram in mid-air as he saved yet another goal for Charlton. Trouble was I couldn't afford both film and a trip to Charlton so I began by taking action pictures of my chums down in the Blake Recreation Ground. I was particularly proud of my picture of Ginger Watts diving for a low ball during a kick-about. Mind you, the goal comprised two heaps of coats and Ginger was wearing his long trousers and a pair of old tennis shoes so the dramatic effect was reduced somewhat. Still, there was dear old Ginger suspended in mid-air at one five hundredth of a second for posterity.

The only other action shot I can recall was when I managed to get a quick shot of Mary Whitley's chubby knees whilst she was skylarking with one of my compatriots and was manoeuvred into an inelegant position in the park shelter between the tennis courts.

By now I had become something of a photographic poseur. I began to talk knowledgeably about shutter speeds and aperture numbers and the benefits of using panchromatic film. I continued to study the *Amateur Photographer* every week and longed for the day when I could take pictures of naked ladies, very tastefully and artistically of course, just like the contributors to *Amateur Photographer*.

The magazine advertised all sorts of accessories and equipment and I became aware that I desperately needed more equipment. A tripod and some filters and a lens hood and an exposure meter for starters. And then, oh so much more that I yearned for and could not afford.

Then there was darkroom equipment. I wanted developing dishes and a developing tank and a darkroom light and a thermometer and masking frames and a printing box and most desirable of all, an enlarger. I saved prodigiously and managed to buy two Bakelite dishes and a pair of developing tongs. For a while I had the loan of a primitive enlarger but I never had a masking frame to go with it so the few enlargements I could afford to make all had my thumb marks in the corners where I had held the paper down.

In my pursuit of greater photographic knowledge I acquired a number of photographic books. My favourite was the *Kodak Book of Photography* for 1948. The best bit was a photograph of a nubile young woman posing on a beach in a short summer dress. The wind was blowing in her hair but more importantly it was blowing her very thin dress between her legs and her hands were up in her hair so that her bosoms stuck out. The photograph was intended to demonstrate what you could do with HP3 film at 1/200th of a second at f8. However, I have to admit that in my fevered imagination I was extremely familiar with that young woman for some months thereafter.

Looking back over the years my most successful photographs were Mary Whitley's chubby knees and the West Wickham Sea Cadet band leading the Fair and Flitch procession in 1948. I also have a photo of our pet pussy cat who is looking somewhat aggrieved at having been pursued all round the garden in order to achieve the right photographic effect.

Film was a bit of a problem in those immediate post-war years. None of the pre-war manufacturers were back in production for the domestic market but opportunists had bought up job lots of RAF reconnaissance film and had cut it down to size for private use. Unfortunately, their measurements tended to be a bit haphazard and the film often jammed in the camera or suddenly unrolled when you least expected it. I bought a developing tank and proudly began to develop my own films but loading out of gauge film into my special spiral developing tank with my head under a blanket was not a fun event since you didn't dare come up for air for fear of exposing the film. Grappling with an unrolling film was like fighting an obstreperous snake in the blackout.

I never tried processing colour film. Colour film was at an early stage of development in 1949. The film was very primitive and if your subject wasn't bright red, blue or yellow it was best to forget it. More to the point, however, I couldn't afford it.

Whilst I was in the Royal Air Works I took photos of all my service chums with a cheap plastic box camera. These were in true *Picture Post* style, showing my mates going about their everyday RAF business like polishing the window brasses on bull night or skiving round the back of the billet for a quick spit and a draw.

The final phase of my photo enthusiasm was the purchase of a new German folding camera just after I was demobbed in 1953. It cost £23. 0s. 11d. with its leather ever-ready case and I pushed the boat out and bought a film as well for 2s. 11d. The camera was called a Baldix. No, I have no idea why. The ever-ready case enabled me to wander around all over the place with my camera at the ready waiting for that photo scoop that would get me on the front page of the *Daily Mirror*. My new Baldix had 1950s state-of-the-art bits and pieces like a fitting for a flash gun and a delayed action device for taking your own photograph and a special fitting for a tripod and facilities for fitting different lenses. The thing I discovered was that the more sophisticated the equipment the more it created marketing opportunities for the photographic industry to sell you something else. There seemed no end to it. The camera had a f2.9 lens that was supposed to be specially suited for colour photography but there was no way I could afford that. Only rich people took colour photos in those days.

At about this time I became friendly with a slightly older fellow enthusiast who tutored me in the ways of serious photographers. Sometimes we would go out at the weekends to some photogenic location and earnestly take photographs of churches and country cottages.

I was very proud of the artistic photo of a church porch somewhere in north-west Kent taken in fading light on an autumn day in 1953 which created a mystical soft focus effect which I had not planned but for which I was quite happy to take the credit.

But it was my public persona that most needed enhancement. Then came the offer of a second-hand light meter. It was an impressive affair that hung on a cord round my neck. The readings were converted into exposure times by a calculating ring round the edge. I used to wander around taking readings all over the place and then doing my calculations. I liked to think that I looked a little like Alexander Korda or Carol Reed. As it happens, I didn't take all that many pictures using my light meter but I was convinced that it improved my public image no end.

I lost interest in photography sometime in the mid-1950s. By that time I was both married and poor. Young marrieds in those days didn't have much money to spare for hobbies. Well, in my case my main hobby was paying the rent. I understand that these days you can buy cameras that take the pictures for you and for all I know play your CDs as well but for my part I think I had the best of it and in my mind I can still hear the explosion of my Foth-Derby focal plane shutter. You don't get an experience like that every day.

The Football Fan

I first became a football supporter when my big brother took me to watch Crystal Palace at Selhurst Park on Boxing Day in 1947. I can't remember much about the game but I know that it was exceedingly cold on the terraces. You really kitted yourself out to watch a football match in those days. Overcoat, cap, gloves, scarf, a woolly jumper and two pairs of socks was the minimum kit required and even then you would have been warmer on a polar bear hunt.

The amenities at Selhurst Park were a bit basic in 1947. At the top of the terrace was a roofless corrugated iron screen behind which supporters relieved themselves in a cloud of steam during the half-time interval or when the Palace were more than three goals down.

The terraces were formed of old railway sleepers and here and there a railing was provided for supporters to lean on. Leaning on the railings, however, was considered a bit poofy. Hardened supporters were expected to be made of sterner stuff. However, it was acceptable to stamp one's feet, pound one's chest and shout abuse at the referee in order to generate some warmth. The only other concession to creature comforts was down near the entrance turnstiles where there was a tea stall with a communal spoon on a short string.

I expect that the Palace lost that day. They usually did. In those days they were acting as the foundations of the Third Division (South). My brother was a fervent supporter and remained so for many years. My mum had knitted him a scarf in the club colours and he kept a book full of newspaper cuttings about the team which made pretty desperate reading. There was better news in a Stafford Cripps's budget speech. My brother even went to some of the Palace's away games although I think he gave Millwall a miss. The Millwall ground was known as the Den and supporters of visiting teams could end up needing stitches.

Football supporting in those days of the forties and fifties was essentially a masculine occupation. Females didn't often venture on to the terraces. On the field too, players were expected to behave in a Jack Hawkins sort of way. There was none of this hugging and kissing and leaping about when a goal was scored. The scorer might receive a slap on the back but this was generally regarded as a bit too demonstrative and he would usually just hitch his shorts up and march back to the centre spot. The whole atmosphere reeked of Elliman's athletic rub, and a spit on the ground and a scowl were the limits of emotional expression.

In about 1949 I went to see Charlton play at the Valley. I walked down the hill to the ground behind their goalkeeper, Sam Bartram. In those days footballers earned about ten quid a week and used shanks's pony like everybody else. These days, of course, they are more likely to run you down in their Ferraris.

My football supporting has tended to be spasmodic and fickle. Over the years, apart from the Palace and Charlton I have made occasional visits to Leeds, Chelsea, Fulham, Gillingham and Hendon. Yes, I did say Hendon. There was also a team who played in the Blake Recreation Ground, West Wickham, whom I watched occasionally, even if I didn't know who they were, but the only team that ever inspired me to full-blooded supporting mania was Gravesend Amalgamated. I was living in Gravesend in 1958 and it just happened that Gravesend Amalgamated's ground was at the bottom of the road where I had found lodgings. Gravesend Amalgamated played in one of the amateur leagues, the Impecunious League or something similar. That was in the days when amateur clubs pretended not to pay their players.

The club had the benefit of a ground that was situated in a natural amphitheatre on the outskirts of Gravesend. The ground was eventually flogged off for redevelopment and a supermarket delicatessen counter covers one of the goal areas today. The ground was approached down a muddy lane where the directors parked their cars. Most supporters, however, walked or came by bus. On one side of the pitch was a small stand with changing rooms underneath and a room at the back for the directors to drink their double whiskies at half-time. On the other side of the pitch was a construction resembling a large bus shelter. You paid extra to watch under cover, unless you were a director or a distinguished visitor. Most of us stood on the terraces huddled together for company, warmth and moral support. Besides, it was considered distinctly poofy to have a roof over your head or to sit down to watch a football match.

There was a bloody-minded fanaticism about the typical Gravesend Amalgamated supporter that appealed to me. The underlying principle was that anything a Gravesend Amalgamated team member did was totally praiseworthy and demonstrated skill of a high order whilst anything an opposing team player did was pathetic, reprehensible and probably a foul. The referee, of course, was a short-sighted imbecilic bigot, or words to that effect. That is unless, of course, he awarded our lot a penalty. It was all extremely therapeutic. One could shout abuse and use threatening language for an hour and a half. And all for two shillings. Oh, and sixpence for a programme. The programme helped you to personalise the insults.

Gravesend Amalgamated weren't a bad team and they were about middle of the league table but even I had to admit that they were a bit thuggish and one of their half-backs would have received rapid promotion in Ghengis Khan's army. He had the build and grace of Desperate Dan and so far as I can recall he made it a point of honour to never kick anything below the kneecap.

I didn't have enough money to attend Gravesend Amalgamated's away games so on alternate weeks I watched their reserve team who if anything were even more psychotic than the first team. Gravesend Amalgamated played teams from faraway places like Harrow and Wealdstone and Walton and Hersham and Enfield Town and these visitors from afar brought a sense of romance to the Amalgamated's ground.

Then came the Cup. I can't remember what Cup it was but Gravesend were in it. The town went mad. Well, about two thousand of us did anyway. We were at home to a team in a different league and some of their players actually got paid a proper wage. The excitement was intense. We shouted ourselves hoarse. Perhaps we were on the verge of a magnificent Cup run. Who knows, perhaps it might even lead to Wembley. In the event we lost. Three–one, I think it was but I don't like to dwell on it. I never forgave Gravesend Amalgamated for losing to Tunbridge Wells. It just didn't sound right somehow. I left the town soon after that and never gave my wholehearted support to any team again. After all, it is only a silly old game, isn't it?

Taking to the Air

I have always fancied going up in a hot air balloon but I doubt if I shall ever manage it now. I still take a childish delight in those helium-filled toy balloons shaped like fish and parrots and attribute this to my childhood balloon deprivation. Don't you know there is a war on and the bloody Japs have nicked all the rubber? When I was a kid I used to think that discarded French letters were austerity balloons and that someone was holding secret parties in Coote's field after dark. It is not fair really. I have not had enough balloons in my life but a pensioner trailing a parrot-shaped balloon around Addlestone High Street does tend to attract a measure of adverse comment.

Orbiting the earth in a space capsule is neither an opportunity open to me nor one that I would wish to pursue. Taking giant steps for mankind is really not my scene. So, I prefer to turn my thoughts to more orthodox experiences of air travel.

Apart from falling from the lower branches of an oak tree in Hawes Lane in 1943, my first flight in space was in a war surplus Auster in about 1947. We were on our holidays at Herne Bay I recall and I saw this advertisement for pleasure flights at nearby Swalecliffe. Thirty shillings a nob was the going rate which, I can assure you, at that time was not peanuts. We took off from what felt like a ploughed field and only managed a single sweep across Herne Bay pier and a couple of circuits of the field before it was time to come down again. Mind you, in my imagination our

Fairey Swordfish had just torpedoed the *Scharnhorst*.

This brief experience was enough to change the direction of my life. I gave up all thoughts of a test match career for England and sold my Walter Hammond autographed cricket bat. No, my mind was made up, I must be an aviator.

The first step was to join the Air Training Corps, No. 572 (Ravensbeck) Squadron to be precise. The second maths master at Ravensbeck Grammar School was a flight lieutenant in the volunteer reserve following a distinguished wartime career in the pay branch of the Royal Air Works. Joining the ATC was a mixed blessing. The uniform buttoned up to the neck and was distinctly hairy and scratchy. I itched my way stoically through interminable sessions of footdrill, map-reading and morse code – dit, dit, dit... da, da, da... dit, dit, dit – and finally earned the privilege of a trip to RAF Biggin Hill for a flight in a Tiger Moth. It was all rather dramatic; we were equipped with Biggles-type flying helmets and jackets with furry collars and parachutes that strapped up under the crutch and made your eyes water. No wonder all our pilots won DFCs. The parachute itself hung down at the back so that it thumped you behind the knees as you walked. The only way to proceed was with a staggering gait like a mutilated crab. I'm sure that Rockfist Rogan never had such trouble and he wiped out a squadron of the Luftwaffe every Friday in my *Champion*.

Before you climbed aboard the Tiger Moth they handed you a sick bag. One clever clogs asked the pilot to loop the loop when his turn came. He looked distinctly pukey when he came down. Served him right, the silly sod. Personally, I prefer to do my flying the right way up. If the Good Creator had meant us to fly upside down he would have given us bits that hung up and not down.

I achieved several more flights whilst in the ATC. I flew

in an Avro Anson which was the RAF's version of a number nine bus. We also had a trip in a twin-engined biplane called a Dominie which was strangely exotic like a sail round the bay in the *Cutty Sark*. One of our number did puke on this occasion. I expect that it was the whining of the wind in the struts or maybe he had fatty bacon for breakfast.

As a treat we were also taken in the back of a three-ton truck to visit the newly established London Airport. This was in about 1948. The airport was in what can only be described as its formative years. It was mostly prefab huts and canvas hangers and a lot of mud and puddles. We were driven round in a canvas-topped lorry and visited various huts that housed the met and briefing rooms. The only other thing that I really remember was that it rained all day and my socks got wet. Still, I never did have a sense of history.

Number 572 (Ravensbeck) Squadron actually had its own aeroplane. It was a partly dismembered Fairey Battle bomber which I think became obsolete in about 1940. Anyway, the Air Ministry gave it to my ATC Squadron in the mistaken belief that it would encourage air-mindedness amongst the pupils of Ravensbeck Grammar School. Actually, all it encouraged was a serious outbreak of juvenile vandalism. It was parked, minus its engine, between the sight screens and the groundsman's hut. Every playtime the members of the first and second forms swarmed over it and removed anything that was in the least portable. In the end it looked like a turkey carcass on Boxing Day.

I was extremely air-minded by now. I had several aircraft recognition books and a book about the Royal Air Force that seemed to imply that if I joined, the very least that I could expect was my very own personal Spitfire. I borrowed books from the library that showed me how to fly a plane and I learned all about the theory of flight and spoke knowledgeably to my mates about ailerons and rudders and elevators. I worked hard on my map-reading and was pretty sure I could have found the marshalling yards at Hamm if Bomber Harris had called upon me to do so. I knew how to make a three-point landing and how to extricate myself from a spin and how many thingies a group captain had on his sleeve.

Then I was called up to do my national service. After my medical there was some delay but eventually I was notified that I would be assigned to the RAF. I was surprised and indeed a little hurt that there had been any doubt about it. After all my efforts I had assumed that it was only a question of time before I was allocated my own personalised Spitfire. I have to say that the RAF was a bit of a disappointment to me. It was really like the army in blue uniforms. RAF Padgate did not have an airfield at all. It had a decomposing Lancaster on the number two parade ground and a derelict Spitfire outside the main guardroom. I noted with disapproval that the Spitfire's tyres were flat but no one seemed very interested when I pointed this out. My flight was allowed to look in the Lancaster once just to remind us that we were in the air force. There was what looked suspiciously like a bird's nest in the tail gunner's turret but this time I decided to keep my observations to myself.

Then one afternoon we were ordered into a three-ton lorry without explanation and driven to the Royal Naval Air Station at Stretton and given a flight in an Avro Anson. This was at about the time that they were trying to get us national servicemen to sign on as regulars so perhaps it was intended as an incentive. Shortly after this I was told that I was too colour-blind to be entrusted with an aeroplane of any kind and would I like to be a clerk instead. It was the kind of offer that one was not expected to refuse. It appeared that my flying career with the RAF was over.

During the remaining eighteen months that I was with the RAF I did my best to take to the air whenever the opportunity arose but I have to say that I continued to be disappointed with what the Royal Air Works had to offer. Eventually I was posted to RAF White Waltham which actually had an airfield although it only had what was called a communications flight which meant in practice a few Ansons, a couple of Proctors and a number of super-annuated flying machines that lurked in the back of a large canvas hangar and were never known to move, let alone fly. There was one aircraft there that didn't even appear in my aircraft recognition book.

White Waltham's claim to fame was that the Duke of Edinburgh learned to fly there. Now he was given his own personal plane, his own personal hangar and his own personal RAF police guard and his own personal hut in which to change into his flying suit. It all comes down to who you know, doesn't it?

On Wednesday afternoons the officers from the RAF Staff College at Bracknell used to drive over to fly whatever planes they could get their hands on. This was so that they could keep their flying hours in and thus continue to receive flying pay. We erks used to hang around the flight office looking wistful and hoping to be offered a flight. Occasionally we got lucky. One afternoon a rather bleary-eyed flight lieutenant took pity on me. 'Want a flight, airman?' he enquired. He had been assigned one of the Proctors, a twin-seater single-engined training plane. When he had taxied it out to the perimeter track he drew out the instruction book. He turned and breathed a beer and pickle breath at me and chuckled. 'I had better just have a look at the book,' he said. 'I haven't flown one of these before.' It turned out that he was planning to buy a house in Dorset for his retirement so we spent much of the afternoon flying in ever-decreasing circles over Bournemouth.

Then we erks latched on to a particularly good wheeze. We became helpers for the officers' gliding club. In return for lots of saluting and glider-towing and miscellaneous grovelling we were occasionally rewarded with a flight in a dual-controlled glider. Once I was allowed to put a glider into a stall which was rather like the big dipper at Dreamland only with a better view. Gliding was quite exhilarating. There was only a piece of waist-high plywood between you and a thousand feet of space and this I found quite exciting, if a trifle thought-provoking. With the wind in my face and this sense of drifting in space I felt a bit like a drunken seagull.

After the Royal Air Works flying never had the same sense of adventure. For a while I retained my interest in flying by visiting the Farnborough Air Show each year but as the planes got faster and faster you saw less and less of them. It was all sonic booms and dots in the sky. It was also a bit disconcerting that more and more of our aeronautical hardware seemed to come hurtling out of the sky when it wasn't meant to. It came so fast that you didn't even know when to duck. In the end I stopped going. It was getting to be nearly as bad as the Blitz.

The first cheap holiday that I took abroad was in a superannuated Comet. Keen though I was to fly the flag I couldn't help thinking about those tiresome little past incidents when Comets had fallen out of the skies like grouse on the glorious twelfth. I also flew in an elderly Britannia whose rivets vibrated in sync with the engines. When the Britannia was first introduced it was called the 'Whispering Giant' but by the time I flew on one it was more asthmatic than whispering. But even those moments of excitement passed and soon package tour flights took on all the excitement of a Sunday in Stowmarket.

Mind you, there were a few flights that linger in one's

memory. There was the thirteen-hour flight to Nairobi in a Kenyan Airlines plane that had part of the internal fittings held in place with sellotape. Kenya Airlines seemed especially suited to those who like a little uncertainty in life. They once created a six-hour flight delay for me in Mombasa just for the fun of it. After much chaos they agreed to provide a free lunch for our flight in the airport restaurant. It was steak or steak on the menu. From the sounds coming from the kitchen it sounded as if they were killing the cow there and then. However, when the steak finally arrived I began to wonder if the cow had died of Alzheimer's disease. Just so that I don't sound racist, I can also recall a flight with Ozark Airlines where the pilot flew his light aeroplane in and out of a number of small airfields in Illinois as if he were a helicopter pilot in Vietnam.

I often think that I must be the albatross of the airlines. I must have flown on every airline that has ever gone bust: Laker, Court Airlines, Braniff International, Air Europe, Pan Am, you name it I've flown it. Fortunately, my reputation is not generally known or I expect that they would charge me extra. Thinks… I wonder what happened to Ozark Airlines?

I find that airports themselves are a great pain. The technology of modern flying depresses me and that's before I even get to the bloody aeroplane. At Dallas/Fort Worth airport (the biggest in the world, they claimed) in 1974 there was a driverless train that went in a circle round and round the airport stopping at each terminal and giving recorded announcements in an accent so Texan that it should have had a translation in English. I had to go round twice before I eventually discovered where to get off.

Modern airports take all the romance out of flying. These days you don't encounter real air from the time you enter the terminal. You move from the air-conditioned departure lounge down hermetically sealed corridors and enclosed gangways so that you are not even aware that you are in a plane until you see a sign saying 'Fasten seat belts'. Then you scarcely notice that the bloody thing has taken off until they start selling the duty free. After I have had my gin and tonic and discovered that they have run out of my favourite aftershave and don't stock litre bottles of Old Highland Moose there never seems much left to do except go and queue up for the toilet.

Of course, I blame it all on Biggles. Captain W.E. Johns really has a lot to answer for. He created all my expectations about flying. I was a great devotee of Biggles as a child and it never really wore off. Flying for me has always been about flying helmets and parachutes and flying jackets with fur-lined collars and the slipstream in your face and the whirr of the propeller and a sense of adventure.

These days the only wind in your face is the air-conditioning and the only adventure is a four-hour flight delay in Madrid or when they lose your luggage in San Francisco. Personally, I preferred my flight in the Tiger Moth.

Bicycling

When I was a boy, to coin a phrase. (Thinks... I suppose that even 'coining a phrase' is coining a phrase.) Anyway, when I was but a bonny youth the ultimate ambition was to own a bicycle.

There was a world war on when I was at the tricycle–fairy cycle phase and I was led to believe that all the tricycles and fairy cycles were needed for the war effort. I was a patriotic little boy and accepted this trustingly although I was a trifle uneasy about General Montgomery's chances against Rommell at the second battle of El-Alamein if he led the Eighth Army on a fairy cycle. Apart from anything else the sand would have played havoc with the bicycle chain.

Anyway, a lack of fairy cycles meant that I didn't even learn the art of pedal propulsion until I was allowed a go on my sister's pre-war bicycle when I was about eleven. That heady moment when I realised that no one was holding on to the saddle and before I fell off lingers with me still. I was immediately hooked. I yearned for a bicycle, a real bicycle with drop handlebars and a three-speed gear and cable brakes and lightweight wheels.

After several years of grinding attrition my father finally accepted the inevitable and bought me a bicycle. Unfortunately, the purchase was governed by my father's unique commercial precepts. First and foremost he believed in economy, so it was second-hand and cheap. Secondly, to him a bicycle was a bicycle and the subtle hierarchy of bicycles in my adolescent social circles was completely lost on him. Finally, he didn't believe in consultations, negotiations or joint decision-making so the bicycle just arrived. It was an uneasy moment. My father was still suffering the pangs of having parted with six pounds ten shillings, and I was trying not to show my disappointment. The bicycle was, well, just a bicycle. It had wide wheels, brakes controlled by metal rods, no gears and a saddle that would have accommodated Bessie Braddock. The handlebars did bend down slightly but they were not adjustable and the only saving grace was a bell that made quite a satisfying noise rather like the bell in the signal box at West Wickham station.

Still, it was a bike and it gave me a foothold, or pedal-hold, within the West Wickham cycling fraternity. I set to and made some cosmetic improvements. I abandoned the saddlebag. (Well, only old gentlemen, ladies and our curate went in for saddlebags.) I bought some new rubber handgrips and I swathed the handlebars in highly-coloured sticky tape which was the current fashion in sophisticated cycling circles.

My ingenuity and my savings exhausted, I settled down to being a serious cyclist. My friends, both of them, already had bicycles and we formed a exclusive group, a sort of cycling Mafia, dedicated to pedal power. Being a serious cyclist largely consisted of convening every evening in the Blake Recreation Ground and bragging to anyone who would listen about our cycling achievements. We muttered phrases like 'being on the bonk on River Hill'. This always sounded rather rude to me, like describing an adolescent erection but I was assured that it was true cycling jargon for needing a breather.

A key element in establishing cycling status was to cycle to Brighton and back. For some reason the Brighton Road at that time was to cyclists what the Long March was to

Mao Tse-tung. Girls didn't usually accompany us on our Brighton trips but there was one occasion when we were persuaded to take Belinda Rutland with us. She was a large, powerfully-built girl but inclined more to soft flesh than muscle. She had thick ankles but willing ways and she stuck with us. The memory of cycling behind her up Handcross Hill lingers with me still. She wore rather tight white shorts I recall, and the rhythmic oscillation of her ample haunches had quite a disturbing effect on me.

Our own sartorial efforts didn't normally run to shorts but we bicycle-clipped our trousers high on the calf to reveal a fleshy gap between short socks and trousers. Don't ask me why; I have no idea. It was the fashion and seemed quite important at the time.

One of our associate members was prone to tuck his trousers into his socks and to wear his school cap but he suffered a severe reduction in cycling status as a consequence. Ron Cardigan wore his school cap everywhere. I have this fantasy of him on his honeymoon, adjusting his school cap before settling down to perform his conjugal duties.

I recall a somewhat humiliating experience myself when I first acquired my bicycle. It had been decided that I should spend a week with some friends of my father in a caravan on Box Hill. I think that the merit of the plan was that it was cheap. I was to cycle down with these two older lads who, it transpired, were seriously superior mortals. I remember being carefully equipped by my mum who was anxious that I should be neat and respectable for my holiday with these important friends of my father. After all, they not only owned a caravan, but they also had their own ironmongery business in Hayes and were people of consequence in the district. As a result I arrived at the Hayes ironmongery on my heavy non-sporting bicycle wearing my tweed sports jacket and neatly pressed grey flannel trousers, with my heavy brown brogues and hairy utility socks. I had my father's old haversack on my shoulders and my mother's anxious admonitions ringing in my ears, '...and don't forget to clean your teeth.' To my horror my two companions for the journey were part of some elitist cycling fraternity. They wore sports shirts and very short shorts and ankle socks and canvas shoes and even looked quite suntanned in a pre-Benidorm sort of way (more in a two-weeks-in-Swanage sort of way actually).

The journey to Box Hill was excruciating. The route is not an easy one, especially in grey flannels and tweed sports jacket plus haversack, not to mention heavy brogue shoes and hairy utility socks. Even to this day I break out in a sweat just thinking about it.

My two companions were sympathetic in a patronising sort of way. They had to keep stopping for me to catch up and at each pause I found myself getting hotter and more sweaty and increasingly sulky. Tears, I am relieved to say, were just about averted. (Well, I had a fly in my eye, didn't I?)

It was, I suppose, my cycling Dunkirk. After that defeat I had to rethink my whole cycling strategy. I struggled on with my second-hand pre-war roadster for quite a while but I knew, with a steely resolve, that I would have to re-equip and fight my own particular Battle of Britain.

As a temporary expedient I acquired a bicycle dynamo set purchased from that Mecca of the West Wickham cycling fraternity, Topley's Bicycle Shop. The dynamo was not a great success. It cost twenty-two and sixpence but it was an austerity affair and looked as if it was army war surplus and had been torn off the front of a tank transporter. Just fitting the thing was a major trauma since Robert Edom has never been distinguished for his manual dexterity. I learned at an early stage that whatever I wanted to do to a bicycle I never had the right size or shape of spanner. However, having faced the challenge of fitting the dynamo, I decided that to improve my status as a cycling virtuoso I had to master the art of bicycle mechanics. My friend Geoff Bragg had a disconcerting habit of dismembering his bike whenever he felt like it and wherever he happened to be at the time. It was a marvellous conversation piece and impressed the girls no end. He was always upending his bike and adjusting the chain or tightening the wheels or something.

Anyway, in the privacy of my own home I began to teach myself cycle mechanics. I spent hours recovering all the ball bearings out of the pedal crank after I discovered how to undo it. (That required a spanner the shape of which I could scarcely believe.) Then I learned to adjust my brakes and had one or two nasty incidents when a touch on the brake lever could propel me over the handlebars like a rocket launcher.

The greatest art however was puncture repairs. The most difficult bit was getting the tyre off with my newly purchased tyre levers. (Old Topley was making a fortune from me at that stage.) Then with pumped up inner tube immersed in my long-suffering mother's enamel washing-up bowl there was the search for tell-tale bubbles. Then I deployed my puncture repair kit (more profit for Mr Topley). The kit was packaged in a small oblong tin and I usually got a nasty cut just getting that open before I really started. Still, it was all very scientific. There was a bit of indelible pencil to mark the puncture, a piece of sandpaper to rough up the surface, several little rubber patches, a small tube of rubber solution and a lump of French chalk which you powdered over the finished job with a little grater to make it dry. Soaked with water, cut fingers covered in rubber solution and French chalk up my nose, I would restore the inner tube and pump up the tyre. Often it would go flat again but I had to persevere because new inner tubes were hard to come by. It was something to do with the Japanese pinching all the rubber trees in Malaya. Mind you, the war had been over for years but I expect the Japs had forgotten to give them back.

By now I was saving furiously and studying the bicycle market most carefully. I remember inspecting a number of second-hand sports machines. I even discovered that you could have a bike made to measure like a Burtons suit but the cost was well beyond me. I scoured the world for my superbike (well, all the adverts in the *Beckenham and Penge Advertiser* anyway).

Then it happened. There it was in Mr Topley's window. It was love at first sight. It was called the Norman Invader. It had Reynolds 531 tubing throughout and GB alloy brakes and three-speed derailleur gears and pedals with toe clips and adjustable handlebars that enabled you to cycle with your nose almost on the front wheel. It had narrow lightweight wheels and lightweight mudguards and a racing saddle so narrow that only sheer fanaticism could give you the courage to sit on it. It was priced at seventeen pounds nineteen and six (or easy terms) but I had to have it.

If Box Hill had been my Dunkirk then the Norman Invader was my fighter command. With it I triumphed on the Hastings Road and stormed the heights of Bury Hill on the way to Littlehampton. (Well, everyone has to get off and push for the last bit of Bury Hill, but don't spoil the romance of it all.)

Our cycling fraternity extended its range appreciably as Norman Frange and Geoff Bragg also acquired new lightweight bicycles. Geoff Bragg went for a machine with a fixed wheel. He liked to show off by gaining momentum and then standing up on the pedals so that he went up and down like a galloping horse on one of those big roundabouts. Norman Frange bought a Hercules Kestrel. It had more chrome than mine but I consoled myself that my dull aluminium was much lighter. Demonstrating the lightness of one's bicycle by lifting it with one finger under the cross bar was a sort of West Wickham youth virility test.

We all pursued a series of cycling affectations including the acquisition of alloy feeding bottles mounted on our handlebars, just like the riders in the Tour de France whom we saw on *British Movietone News*. They all slurped lemon barley through a little plastic tube as they rode up the Alps or wherever it was that Tour de France riders indulged their masochistic tendencies.

I also acquired an expensive (7s. 6d.) tie with a racing cyclist hand-painted on it. I bought it through the post as the result of an advertisement in the *Wizard*, or was it the *Hotspur*? It was a toss-up between the tie or a postal course guaranteeing robust health, doubled strength and dashing energy (in thirty days or money back). It also promised iron will, perfect self-control, virile manhood and personal magnetism; surprise your friends! (It would certainly have surprised my friends.) Anyway, I opted for the tie and my family were suitably appalled at my bad taste and the tie gave me some small distinction amongst my friends. Geoff Bragg reacted by purchasing a pair of daffodil-yellow socks and Norman Frange retaliated by borrowing his father's white silk scarf which he thereafter wore on all occasions when he appeared in public.

At one stage we had a spasm of pedal-cycle dirt-track racing. We found an abandoned tennis hard court, suitably decomposing and gravelly, and marked out an oval of track with old bricks from a bombed sports pavilion. We practised standing starts and vied with each other to achieve the most spectacular broadside slides round the bends, foot extended, bike at forty-five degrees, just like we had seen Dirk Bogarde do it in *Once a Jolly Swagman*.

There was a sudden demand for old bikes and Bill Oddy came into his own because he was a great forager of rubbish tips and was handy with a spanner. The experts acquired cycle mutations with handlebars turned up, no brakes or mudguards and ridiculously low gears.

I had to make do with an elderly bicycle that my father had by this time abandoned. I felt sorry for that old bike which had faithfully carried my father at a leisurely pace to choir practice every Thursday evening for years and then, in its twilight years, was called upon to produce death-defying forty-five degree slides that nearly tore its tyres off.

The whole craze ended as swiftly as it had begun in a surfeit of torn trousers, scuffed shoes and gravel rashes. We all then reverted to more orthodox cycling behaviour and resumed our worship of Reg Harris who had just broken the British flying start quarter-mile record.

It is hard to remember the details of all our cycling excursions. In my memory they all blend into an amalgam. Geoff Bragg was a temperamental, volatile cyclist who liked to be the pacemaker, disappearing out of sight in furious bursts of speed and then collapsing on the hills complaining of mysterious leg cramps or problems with wheel wobble or an urgent need to adjust his calliper brakes.

Norman Frange was a more phlegmatic rider, heavily into his romantic cowboy phase. He could cycle for miles tonelessly crooning, 'East is east and west is west and the wrong one I have chose… drone, drone, drone, de da da da… in buttons and bows.' He did it in a dreadful imitation American accent that sounded like a Cornishman with adenoids.

Norman fancied himself as a cowboy, a cross between Alan Ladd, Randolph Scott and Howard Keel. Norman used to wander around West Wickham with a large Webley air pistol strapped into a home-made holster which hung low on his hip ready for a quick draw. He also wore his father's white silk scarf and a Woodbine in the corner of his mouth. I think that he believed that he was in Dodge City for much of the time. It's a wonder he wasn't arrested for possessing an offensive weapon but the war had only recently ended and people were used to much odder events than this. Norman didn't bring his Webley air pistol on our cycling trips but I suspect that he pretended he was riding the range on his horse for much of the time.

Our cycling aspirations had a momentum all their own. Brighton and Littlehampton were not enough. We devised a grand tour, a positive expedition – a weekend marathon – striking south-west to Littlehampton on Friday night and then along the coast to Brighton and on to Hastings before turning north-west to return to West Wickham by Sunday evening. We learned a lot from that trip, the value of contingency planning and meteorological reports, for example.

We arrived at Littlehampton in the small hours of Saturday morning. The romance of sleeping out on the sand dunes was somewhat less than we had anticipated. It was, not to put too fine a point on it, bloody freezing. I had thought that the sand would be warm and that we would be stretched out under the stars like something in *The Desert Song* but it turned out to be more like *Scott of the Antarctic*. Geoff Bragg, with uncharacteristic foresight, had brought a small blanket with him but it wasn't a lot of help and we spent most of the small hours running up and down the sandy beach trying to keep warm.

The rain started after we had eaten a cheese roll breakfast in a café by the harbour. It just kept on raining and we kept on cycling. By the afternoon we were very wet and saddlesore and somewhere near Hastings. A change of plan was called for. We had envisaged sleeping out on the cliffs at Hastings and then returning home up the Hastings Road on Sunday but this no longer seemed a particularly attractive option. It would have been drier in Beckenham swimming baths and Norman Frange's cycling cape (an army war surplus ground sheet) had sprung a leak, whilst my plastic mac was funnelling a steady stream of rainwater into my lap.

Rain always seems so much wetter when you have nowhere to go. We set our faces to London and kept on pedalling. Apart from being stopped in Tunbridge Wells by a bored policeman, who, at 2 a.m. wanted to point out to Geoff Bragg that his rear light wasn't working (thank you, officer, nice of you to tell us), I can't remember much about the return journey. I think that it stopped raining about midnight, but the gods always seem to relent after they have made life bloody intolerable, don't they?

We arrived home about five on Sunday morning just as the Amalgamated Dairies' milk carts were taking to the streets. We dispersed to our beds but by the evening we had reconvened in the Blake Recreation Ground for a debriefing in which our achievements grew in grandeur almost by the minute. Mary Whitley was positively adoring as she heard of my heroic struggle against the elements, a reaction which I tried to turn to my advantage later under the oak tree behind the British Legion hut.

We never repeated our grand tour, however, partly because it could only have been an anticlimax and partly because, secretly, none of us fancied re-experiencing all that pain and suffering. Nonetheless, as an exercise in uncomfortable futility it prepared us well for military service which was to be inflicted on us shortly. I have to tell you that Norman Frange signed on as a regular in the Royal Navy and substituted bell bottoms and an exaggerated sailor's rolling walk for his cowboy drawl and his Webley air pistol. Geoff Bragg, who had always been a bit of a show-off, joined the East Surrey regiment on a five-year engagement and went off to fight the North Koreans. All this offended my own civilian tendencies and I served my time in RAF Home Command in deepest Berkshire. I often wonder what happened to my cycling companions. Are they working out on their exercise bikes somewhere or have they already joined that great cycle track in the sky?

RAF Padgate

The time of which I write is long distant, positively prehistoric in fact. From the very first I had not been overly impressed by RAF Padgate. It was not at all like the *First of the Few* or the *Way to the Stars*. Even the reception unit was a bit of a trauma – those clonking great boots and hairy underwear and a haircut that made my head look like an electric light bulb. Then there were those innoculations for God knows what dire diseases that made me come out in funny bumps and finally the photo for my 1250 identity card that was a dead ringer for Göbbels.

After this first week of being kitted out and numbered and documented the powers that be decided that I should remain at Padgate for my recruit training. A little mob of us humping all our kit were marched across the camp to the Number One School of Recruit Training being shouted at all the way. I was assigned to Hut 100, Number Three Flight, A Squadron. In charge of Hut 100 was Corporal Bogley, a podgy, swaggering bantam-cock of a man, much given to obscene analogies. He introduced himself to me on that raw April afternoon in 1951. I remember it well. We had just been marched over to Number Three Flight for the first time and we stood by our beds in Hut 100. In swaggered this corporal with spotless blanco, gleaming brasses, knife-edge creases, and a self-satisfied expression. 'My name is Bogley,' he announced. 'They call me Bogley the bastard, and I am a bastard too.' Time was to prove him irrefutably right.

He had a crudity of expression that drew grudging respect from even his worst enemies, which certainly included every member of Number Three Flight. He likened our marching to that of pregnant pelicans, he threatened to climb to great heights in order to defecate upon us and generally he gave us the impression that he did not like us all that much. Personally I wasn't all that struck on him either.

Life in Hut 100 was a shock to my system. Nothing in my eighteen years until then had prepared me for Corporal Bogley or for RAF Padgate. True, I had endured the inanities of Ravensbeck Grammar School and had learned that authority was inconsistent, arbitrary and frequently downright nutty. I had survived the Blitz which had taught me that life is uncertain and unfair and makes little sense. Come to think of it, I should have been well prepared for Corporal Bogley but there we are – it was a shock.

The day began at RAF Padgate with the playing of reveille over the tannoy. The bugle call to rise and face the day was played on a cracked record in the guardroom nearly a mile away and relayed over hundreds of loudspeakers. The record was past its best and had, I suspect, not been renewed since VE Day. The trumpeter sounded as if he was suffering from a double hernia and the scratches on the record provided an erratic rhythm accompaniment. Corporal Bogley added to this by marching up and down outside, rattling his drill stick against the sides of the wooden hut and shouting encouraging remarks like, 'Wakey, wakey, get out of your pits, you dozy lot.' (For the benefit of the faint-hearted this is an edited version but conveys the general tenor of his observations.)

The day tended to go downhill from this point. First of all the hut was freezing cold and secondly the ablutions block was a ten-second dash away in blizzard conditions and when you got there it was even colder than the hut.

The next nasty surprise was that the hot water had run out (in about 1942, was my guess). In any event, the toilet habits of some of my compatriots left a little to be desired so there was a double threat to lingering over one's shave, (a) from frostbite and (b) from acute nausea.

Breakfast was a day's forced march away. We were not trusted to make our own way to the dining hall but marched in lines of three as if about to participate in the King's Birthday Parade. 'Swing those harms, 'eads 'eld 'igh, chests hout, lots of swank, dig those 'eels in.' There was only one thing more designed to put you off your breakfast and that was breakfast itself. Lumpy porridge with watered milk followed by soused herring, one, airman for the consumption of. Any lingering doubts about the quality of life at RAF Padgate were finally dispelled by the distinctive aroma of soused herrings that pervaded Number Two dining hall at least twice a week. On other days the main course was (a) rissole – small and obscenely wrinkled, (b) sausage – even smaller, curled and with unidentifiable filling, and (c) one rasher of burnt streaky bacon, all served with the chef's speciality, a scoopful of coagulated baked beans. After a Padgate breakfast one was well prepared for the pain and suffering of a quick dash round the assault course.

The Padgate assault course had been devised and built in the early days of World War Two and had been slowly festering since that time. It had been built on swamp land sold to the Air Ministry by an enterprising farmer who, no doubt, in the way of farmers had claimed that it was prime arable land. This, I would suggest, would only have been true if you had wanted to grow frogs. The course had been devised on the basis that the wetter the troops became the better. I fell in so many puddles, pools and ponds on that course that my boots squelched for days. The worst part was where you hurled yourself into space, grabbed feverishly at a suspended rope, lost momentum, hung helplessly like a monkey on a stick and then slid slowly down the rope into four feet of muddy water and aquatic wildlife. Then there was crawling through buried drainpipes (which did my claustrophobia no good at all), crawling along a rope twenty feet above the ground (played havoc with my vertigo) and scrambling over a brick wall (caused me some nasty moments when I became impaled astride it). Eventually we all managed to get round it in various stages of incapacity. Time flies when you are having fun, doesn't it?

Talking of fun, there were also twenty-four hour guard duties. Four hours on, four hours off, and a psychotic guard commander who turned out the guard at regular intervals throughout the night in the firm belief that it was only a matter of time before the Russian hordes arrived at Padgate. Personally, I would have given it to them.

I also attended the Astra Cinema at Padgate. For a short while you could almost imagine that you were in civilisation but once they started 'God Save the King' and everyone, by conditioned reflex and behaving like civilians, headed for the exits, things got nasty. The cinema seemed to suddenly become full of puce-coloured drill instructors screaming, 'Stand still, you 'orrible little men!' or words to that effect. George the Sixth, flickering on the screen with the Union Jack fluttering bravely behind him, appeared unmoved by these expressions of loyalty.

There were three NAAFIs at Padgate and they mostly sold blanco, Brasso and Cherry Blossom. There was little demand for much else except the inevitable tea and a wad and packets of Woodbines. Well, on twenty-eight bob a week minus barrack room damages and amenities you didn't go in for a lot of smoked salmon sandwiches. Thinks... I never did discover what the amenities were. Perhaps it was the trestle table in the middle of the billet.

We purchased prodigious quantities of blanco. We blancoed nearly everything and what we didn't blanco we polished. Except the coal; we whitewashed that. Then there was boot polish. The NAAFI probably had shares in Cherry Blossom. We polished our boots, our shoes and our gym plimsoles. When they were all polished to a high sheen Corporal Bogley convinced us that we should polish their soles as well. Nothing escaped polishing in Hut 100.

Kit inspections were part of the way of life at Padgate. Everything had to be laid out for inspection. If it was polishable it had to have a high sheen and everything had to be set out to a pre-ordained pattern. Things had to be folded in to squares and oblongs, blankets, sheets and towels. Smaller items like socks and PT shorts and vests and hairy drawers had to be fitted with little bits of cardboard so that they were square and symmetrical. Then they were laid out in predetermined patterns in an open ammunition box. Don't ask me why. Asking why was not encouraged at Padgate. I expect that there was a special department somewhere in the Air Ministry to plan it all. Like I said, it wasn't what I had hoped for. I had rather hoped that they were going to give me a Canberra to fly.

I went sick whilst I was at Padgate. It was a mistake. You needed to be one hundred per cent fit to go sick at Padgate. Pack all your kit and hump your kit bag round to the stores, then parade with your small pack and mug and eating irons outside the orderly room in the pouring rain. Then march to the sickbay half a mile away. It turned out that I had some mysterious lurgy. Once the MO had ordered hospitalisation there was another march to the hospital. If you weren't sick when you started out you certainly were when you got there.

Padgate Hospital was one of those memorable experiences that one would rather forget. The nurses were all of commissioned rank. Not only did they expect salutes and deference, they also conveyed the impression that being ill was at best excessively tiresome and probably dumb insolence. The only fantasies you would have had about that lot would have come out of a horror comic. I don't think that they would have known what a bedpan was if they had tripped over one. All the work was done by orderlies. The nurses just stood around looking important and, well, like officers. Even worse, they had legs like tree trunks.

After my spell in hospital I was sent on sick leave. No one told me what had been wrong with me but I must have been quite ill. You didn't get sick leave in the Royal Air Works unless you were close to death or festering or important bits were falling off you.

When I returned from sick leave I was re-flighted. This meant I had to join a junior flight so that I wouldn't miss any of the joys of a complete training. I had to make a fresh set of mates and learn to cope with a different set of lunatic instructors. 'That will teach you to go sick,' seemed to be the attitude of the authorities.

Well, all good things have to come to an end and eventually my training was complete. I was now a fully-fledged ruthless fighting machine. I could strip a Bren gun, even if I couldn't put it together again, and I had put the fear of God into my instructors with my performance with a 1917 Lee-Enfield on the firing range.

The passing out parade was the final comment on RAF Padgate. It was a shambles. Some relatives actually came to watch. Still, I expect that you could get some people to watch dogs pooping. We had rehearsed our passing out parade for weeks. Our uniforms were immaculate, brasses gleaming, blanco unblemished and boots bulled to perfection. Unfortunately it had been raining and the parade ground was under several inches of water. After we had marched to and fro a few times and had done a bit of the usual foot stomping we were all distinctly soggy. It was not a pretty sight.

At the end of my training I was somewhat shattered to discover that I was in the running for designation as best recruit. It was a bit unnerving, like finding yourself first in the queue for the knacker's yard, a distinction you could well do without. Anyway, that particular nasty moment passed. I was in contention with another equally bemused erk. We marched about in front of the drill sergeant, showed off our rifle drill and displayed our immaculate webbing and brasses. Finally, we had an interview with a slightly loopy squadron leader who was obsessed with the Japanese. He did not, I gather, like them all that much. Well, I blew it. I could not remember where it was we dropped the second atom bomb. This it seemed was serious and left me unfitted to be best recruit. By this stage I had begun to think that the competition really mattered. There was no prize for being second-best recruit at RAF Padgate in July 1951. Come to think of it, there was no prize for being best recruit either.

The dreadful thing was that having passed out and having thought that I would now be leaving Padgate for ever I was issued with my posting notice. It was to the pool flight at Padgate. I was distraught. It appeared that the vast RAF machine couldn't think what to do with me. I wanted to suggest that they could, if they wished, demob me forthwith but I lacked the moral fibre to propose this.

After some leave I returned to the pool flight at Padgate to await the Air Ministry's pleasure. Everyone in the pool flight was in a state of limbo, waiting to go somewhere or just having come back from somewhere else. Some were trying not to go anywhere at all. It was like a lost parcels office. We spent our time trying to dodge the orderly corporal who had a long list of fatigues and assigned us a little task every time he managed to catch us. The tasks ranged from cleaning the brass on the fire extinguishers to loading lorries with dirty laundry.

Finally, my permanent posting came through. I was assigned to RAF White Waltham as an AC2 Clerk Personnel (u/t). I hadn't a clue what it all meant but one thing was sure; it was unlikely to be worse than Padgate.

For King, Queen and Country

I can claim to have served in the armed forces of two monarchs. However, before you leap to any conclusions about my devotion to duty or ask to see my long service medals, perhaps I should explain. I was doing my two years' national service when King George the Sixth snuffed it and the new Queen, Elizabeth the Second, decided to continue my contract. She didn't actually communicate her decision to me personally but I continued to receive my five shillings a day so I knew that I was still required to do my duty. (They had started me on four shillings a day but I had bettered myself by the time my new employer took over.)

I never understood the logic behind peacetime national service and it wasn't something that I was invited to have a view about. (National service came at age eighteen but the vote arrived rather later at twenty-one.) It was apparently important to our national leaders to have large numbers of young men clad in prickly serge uniforms and able to fire a First World War Lee Enfield. Volunteers, it appeared, were hard to come by. Also expensive because for some reason they paid the regulars more for doing the same jobs. So you see, national service had some interesting dimensions. Not only was it undemocratic but it had connotations of sweated labour and social injustice. You will, no doubt, be surprised to hear that no one, apart from the conscripts, seemed to give a monkey's.

Personally, I kept my sense of injustice to myself since Corporal Bogley, my beloved drill instructor, gave no indication that he wanted to discuss anything other than the quality of the blanco on my webbing and my failure to bull my boots to the ultimate in perfection, if not better. Corporal Bogley likened my performance on the drill square to that of a pregnant pelican and threatened to climb to great heights in order to defecate on me (or words to that effect). Thinks... at some stage I really must attempt an in-depth psychological study of Corporal Bogley.

Anyway, after some months of arm-swinging, foot-stamping and rifle-slapping, Corporal Bogley, on behalf of the Air Ministry, decided that I was as near to a ruthless fighting machine as I was ever likely to be. The Royal Air Force was then faced with a dilemma. What the on earth were they to do with AC2 Edom, R., for the remaining twenty-one months that I was to be with them? I had suggested that they might like me to fly one of their Canberras for them but they declined firmly, indeed, rather rudely I thought. Their refusal seemed to be based on the fact that they were a bit short of Canberras at the time. They had also discovered that I couldn't read all the numbers on the pages of little coloured dots that they flipped under my nose when I had my medical. Their aeroplanes, it seemed, could not be entrusted to young men who could not tell their greeny browns from their reddy browns.

We attended the Personnel Selection Centre where they had a display of all the jobs that the RAF had to offer. They explained that if we signed on for three years the range of choice would be much greater and we would be paid more. Furthermore, if we signed for ten years then the sky was the limit. Not quite literally, however, because as I had already discovered they were very choosy about who they let play with their aeroplanes. The problem was that if you signed on they gave no guarantees. I later discovered a very disgruntled erk who signed on for three years in the belief that he would be trained as an armament fitter and who ended up an officer's batman. The general consensus was that it served him bloody well right.

My first posting was to what they called the pool flight at RAF Padgate which was where they sent erks who they didn't know what to do with. Here lurked the detritus of the conscript force, the bottom of the barrel. Some were trying to work medical discharges, some were on their way to somewhere and some were on their way back from somewhere else. Some of its occupants spun out a substantial portion of their national service in the pool flight, living on their wits and trying to avoid the fatigues that the corporal in charge allocated each morning to keep them occupied. Sadly, I had no chance to learn the ropes, because on the morning after I arrived my permanent posting came through.

To digress briefly, I would be interested to hear the views of Amnesty International, the Council for Civil Liberties and the Howard League for Penal Reform concerning my two years' deprivation of liberty. Unfortunately, they had nothing to say at the time. Perhaps they were all doing their national service. As for the trade unions, not usually noted for their reticence, they had nothing to say either, despite the fact that my pay was minuscule, my hours of work unlimited and my conditions of service bloody awful. I suppose that the women's liberation movement was also in its latent period since I heard of no demands for women to have equal opportunities to be conscripted for two years. Shame really. With all the women between eighteen and twenty in uniform my contribution could have been reduced to one year and might have been considerably more pleasurable.

Anyway, my posting came through and I was despatched, together with large pack, small pack and kitbag, to RAF White Waltham where I was assigned to clerical duties in the Home Command Headquarters drafting office. Command Headquarters, being deemed an important sort of place, was full of commissioned officers. At the end of the day my arm used to ache from all the saluting. You are no doubt familiar with the old adage: If it moves salute it, if not whitewash it, and if all else fails use Brasso.

When I first arrived at White Waltham the regime was quite relaxed and benign. Indeed, after the lunacies of recruit training at Padgate it seemed almost like normal. Then we acquired a new station warrant officer. There was nothing normal about Station Warrant Officer Nutkins. SWOs were to COs what Himmler must have been to Hitler, only this one was worse. He initiated monthly Cos' parades and weekly kit inspections and extra bull nights and billet inspections and all sorts of other depravities. The veteran conscripts on the camp wandered around in a shell-shocked daze. There hadn't been a kit inspection at White Waltham for nigh on a twelve-month. The old-stagers disconsolately tipped out heaps of mouldering webbing from cobweb-strewn kit bags and gazed without hope at the green brasses on their best blues. Those of us who had recently arrived from square-bashing gained our own back for all those jokes about our virgin-white kitbags and the improbably high service numbers stencilled on them. Our kit was already in that ridiculous polished, blancoed, scraped, folded and pressed condition so beloved of drill instructors and obsessional SWOs.

There was a desperate market in chitties to avoid the parades and kit inspections but the SWO refused to accept them. It was like the Wall Street crash. There was nothing to put one's faith in any more. We turned to the opium of the masses. Everyone resorted to incantations of, 'Roll on demob!' or, in more fatalistic mood, 'Roll on death, demob's too long!' We resorted to devoted poring over our demob charts which showed precisely how many days, or in some cases even hours, we still had to serve. We could tell, within a few days, a fellow airman's demob date by a glance at his service number. Gradually my own number moved from being the object of hysterical laughter to one of limited respect.

The drafting office remained a small island of sanity in the general nuttiness of RAF life. Even the regulars in the drafting office did not take the RAF too seriously, apart from Warrant Officer Crimm that is. But there was little hope for him since he had been in the service for thirty years and came from Accrington.

Apart from the kit inspections and Cos' parades and bull nights there were other little amusements like fire picket or being duty clerk. The duty clerk had to go around in the evening putting all the lights out and locking all the offices because the officers were too idle to do it for themselves. Sometimes there were fire drills and then there were special guard duties when we had to patrol the WAAFery to protect them from molestation by mysterious prowlers.

In our leisure moments we cultivated those near to demob in the hope of swapping cap badges. A vintage cap badge carried considerable social prestige and, because they were worn so smooth, had the added advantage of requiring very little polishing. The night before demob was celebrated by a riotous boozy party at the Coach and Horses on the Bath Road. The landlord reserved a barn-like room for us where we could do no harm to his furnishings, the locals or the passing trade. The evenings usually ended with someone being thrown into the static water tank or by all the folding beds in the adjoining billets being adjusted to collapse when their drunken occupants fell into them. There were biscuit fights too: pitched battles with the three squares of mattress which formed a bed for erks in those days. When held by two corners and then skimmed from one end of the billet to the other they could easily bowl over an opponent. Most of the lampshades went as well and barrack room damages were high at White Waltham but it was a small price to pay for such cathartic activity.

Skiving became a pure art form at RAF White Waltham. Great respect was shown to those who demonstrated the greatest originality. The clerks who worked for the senior officers in the Command Headquarters were the elite. They could produce chitties signed by an Air Commodore that not even the dreaded SWO would dare to counter-mand. Such chitties reduced him to apoplectic rages when their bearers sloped off from his interminable parades to undertake urgent unspecified duties. He knew very well that they were in the comfort of the Command Headquarters with their feet up leering at the pin-ups in the *RAF Review*.

I would like to tell you that if war had been declared we would all have rallied behind the SWO in the face of the common enemy. But *Boys' Own* stories can only be found in old copies of the *Boys' Own*. The truth is that we would probably have shot the SWO before we shot the enemy, preferably with slow, blunt bullets. The Swoman, as he was called, became public enemy number one. We played endless Swogames, mimicking the strutting, pompous little man. Taffy Morgan imitated him to perfection and we played endless games of foot-stamping, saluting and general grovelling.

Slowly I passed through the system as a clerk personnel. First as an AC2 then AC1, and LAC and then SAC. Finally I was promoted to the elevated status of senior aircrafts-man/acting corporal (paid). The last word was the crucial one. I ended my service days as corporal clerk personnel earning two pounds ten shillings a week.

My promotion brought its own snags. Being a corporal was a bit like being a factory foreman; you had responsibility without power. You just did the dirty work for the senior management. All my life I have longed for a job where the principle is reversed. Sadly, the Great Computer in the sky programmed me as a middle-management dogsbody and the RAF recognised my dogsbodying potentiality before anyone else did.

On the domestic side I was placed in charge of a decomposing wooden dormitory hut. I worked out the rotas for bull nights and accompanied the orderly officer on his inspection of the billet and tried to stand in a strategic position so that he wouldn't notice the one idiot who had forgotten to polish his window brasses. The RAF had this obsession for polished brasswork. Anything that was brass had to be polished to a high sheen. The coming of aluminium must have broken many a Swoman's heart, assuming that they have them, of course. The fabric of our well polished billet was in a sorry state. I suspect that if we had scraped all the polish away it would have fallen down. There was a two-inch gap between the wall and the floor. It made for good ventilation in the summer but in the winter the water in the fire buckets froze solid and we all went to bed in our socks and greatcoats.

Once a fortnight I was orderly corporal, engaged on duties of the highest importance, making myself instantly available if war was declared outside office hours and locking the NAAFI after they closed the bar. I also remember that I had to wear my blancoed webbing belt to denote my orderly corporal status but the rest of my duties are lost in the mists of time. I think that basically it all meant that if anything went wrong then it was all my fault. Thank God I wasn't on duty the night someone nicked the CO's geraniums. I am sure that the orderly corporal was charged with gross dereliction of duty.

You will have gathered by now that the RAF gave me many opportunities for rich new experiences but one that I hankered after was denied me. I had this unrequited passion for the blonde nursing attendant in the station sickbay. I had a fantasy of attending the sickbay after some dramatic accident and being devotedly nursed back to health whilst I told her of the very important mission I had just accomplished. In fact, I seldom found good reason to attend the sickbay and my most dramatic attendance was for a sore bum. Fortunately, she was not on duty at the time. She did feature in other fantasies of mine but these always faded out at the crucial moment because I was never sure if WRAFs actually wore air-force-blue knickers under their air-force-blue skirts. That is an item of ignorance that I have never declared before. Well, I was shy and spotty and there were only about thirty WRAFs to about five hundred airmen so someone had to go without this kind of learning experience.

RAF White Waltham tended to ignore the local community but once a year a small party was despatched to parade at the local war memorial service. I remember the occasion on which I attended. We did our best but it was a typical RAF cock-up and we were completely outshone by the local Boy's Brigade who provided the drum and bugle accompaniment for the occasion. The only other links with the community that I was aware of were forged by two of the lads from our billet who established a very liberal relationship with a mother and daughter in Maidenhead. Our colleague's accounts of this *ménage à quatre* roused us to greater, but generally unfulfilled, social aspirations.

Periodically the Command Drafting Office fell into a panic when it discovered that its records bore even less resemblance than usual to the personnel in post at the stations for which we were responsible. On such occasions I was detached on temporary duty to check our personnel records against those of the chosen unit. Thus it was that I was sent on detached duty to exotic places like Netheravon and Lytham.

The RAF was prone to sudden panics. At another stage I was packed off on what they called a ground combat course. It was a week of nightmarish proportions full of assault courses and exercises involving thunder flashes and the firing of blank rounds. I don't know if my colleagues would have scared the Russkies but they certainly scared me.

My two years' service dragged on, seemingly never to end. I remember the weekend passes when the moment I got home someone said, 'What, you home again! When do you go back?' The civilian population would have been much happier if we had been away fighting a war somewhere and getting ourselves killed. Some were, of course. There was a war going on in Korea. I only met one RAF bod who had been out there. When he was posted back to our unit we all queued up to look at his Korean War medal.

Leaves were a drag. All the local girls were fixed up with lads whose national service had been deferred and who were thus earning civvy rates of pay. My pay and personal charm were insufficient to achieve any changes of loyalties. There was one nasty contemporary of mine who had achieved a national service commission and swaggered around with his adoring girlfriend trying to find some erk on leave in uniform to salute him. He caught me once and I never forgave him. Eventually he became a bank manager so I expect that he spent his life trying to make people grovel.

I remember the return to camp after weekend passes. We delayed the evil moment to the very last. We caught the last train out of Paddington on Sunday nights. It was full of servicemen. When we arrived at Maidenhead we waited outside the railway station for whatever conveyance the MT Section decided to send to collect us. It was usually a curious utility buslike vehicle much beloved by the RAF authorities but viewed with some reserve by those who actually had to travel in them. The driver usually drove the station coal lorry during the week so he was not noted for his finesse. We hurtled through the country lanes and back into the bosom of the RAF where we were met with the sour looks of the guardroom sergeant. He resented anyone having a weekend pass and resented even more the wearing of civilian clothes since it denied him the opportunity to find fault with buttons and badges. He resorted to generalised comments about national servicemen and the state of haircuts and tended to turn very nasty to the two corporal policemen on duty with him, a manoeuvre that always delighted us.

But all bad dreams come to an end. In course of time my demobilisation process began. Conscripts prided themselves on beginning this exercise at the earliest possible moment and spinning it out until the magical demob day arrived. The process involved carrying a card around from section to section getting one's name knocked off everyone's registers. There was the armoury, the sickbay (she wasn't on duty and I wouldn't have dared ask her that still burning question even if she had been), the postal unit, the part-worn stores and so on. The tour culminated on the last morning with the ceremonial handing in of one's bedding at the blanket store, hiding, of course, the nasty hole that I had burned in Air Ministry property whilst using a blanket to press my best blues for one of the Swoman's parades. Great artists spent up to a week trailing around on their lap of honour but I could only manage two and a half days. Not bad, but unremarkable. I suppose that could be my epitaph.

I left RAF White Waltham with half a kit bag full of bits and pieces that the Air Ministry felt that I might need to help me maintain national security for the future since I was to be on reserve of one kind or another for many years to come. I also left with a surprisingly positive discharge certificate and a profound sense of relief. Most of the kit has been mislaid over the years so I hope that they won't want it back. However, I still have my housewife, complete with rusting Air Ministry thimble, two boot brushes and a clothes brush, each imprinted with my now venerable service number, and somewhere an RAF tie, useful for funerals. These and my preserved demob chart and a tattered chitty permitting me to attend early lunch are my last tenuous links with the Royal Air Force.

The NAAFI

The Navy Army and Air Force Institute was, I understand, established to provide comforts to the armed forces during the war but my own experience of it ran from only 1951 to 1953. That was quite long enough. Don't get me wrong, I was not unappreciative of the services the NAAFI offered, basic though they were; it was just that two years of doing my bit for the nation seemed like more than enough. After all, what did my nation ever do for me?

My first encounters with the NAAFI were whilst I was engaged in my recruit training, or square-bashing as it was called, at RAF Padgate. Each morning at about ten thirty we were marched to the NAAFI for tea and a wad. The problem was that so were the rest of the recruit training wing. Long columns of thirsty airmen converged on the NAAFI from all directions and all at the same time. Each column was marching at the rate of the Highland Light Infantry in a desperate bid to get to the NAAFI first. Despite all this effort the chance of getting served, let alone consuming said tea and a wad before our corporal shouted, 'Back on parade, Three Flight!' was remote in the extreme.

Evening visits to the NAAFI at Padgate were infrequent. We were so busy in the evening polishing brasses, blancoing, webbing and bulling boots to perfection that we were only allowed to send a single emissary to the NAAFI to purchase essential supplies for the billet. These consisted of Brasso, blanco, Cherry Blossom and Woodbines. These were the only necessities of life that the authorities recognised.

Once recruit training was completed and I was posted to RAF White Waltham I was able to develop a slightly less frenetic relationship with the NAAFI.

First of all there was the NAAFI wagon which toured the camp twice a day to provide life-sustaining quantities of stewed tea. The wagon, a small Bedford van in khaki livery, would arrive outside our workplace with a cheerful toot and we would all pour out with our pint mugs at the ready. The NAAFI girl would be behind her counter dispensing the tea from an urn that would have given a five-hundred pound unexploded bomb a sense of inadequacy. The NAAFI girl was worthy of note herself. She was a large, healthy-looking girl with magnificent bosoms and with a splendid tan that looked as though she had just returned from a tour of duty in Cyprus. It was some months before I saw the rest of her. She was always behind her counter. When one day she emerged from her van it was a grave disappointment. From the waist down she was built like a water buffalo.

The NAAFI building at White Waltham was well away from the main part of the camp as if the Royal Air Works wished to disown it. It was, nonetheless, well frequented by the national servicemen, most of whom were struggling to survive on pay ranging from twenty-eight to forty-two shillings a week. The great thing about the NAAFI was that one could stay in there all evening without spending more than the price of a cup of tea. Tuppence, I think it was. The other benefit was that during the winter months it was distinctly warmer than our billet where it was the custom to go to bed with your greatcoat and socks on.

The joys of social life in the NAAFI were an acquired taste. Apart from making a cup of tea last all evening there was spinning the large plastic ash trays like tops and listening to the radio. If it had been left tuned to the BBC this probably meant Primo Scalas Accordion Band or *Have a Go* from Chipping Campden. If, however, the staff were in a good mood and had tuned the wireless to Radio Luxembourg then with a bit of luck it might be Al Martino or Kay Starr with a dash of Guy Mitchell.

Geordie Smythe was often presiding over a discussion group at one of the tables. The discussion tended to follow the line that Newcastle United were the tops and Geordie would smash in the face of anyone who said differently. When Newcastle beat Arsenal in the 1952 Cup Final most of us stayed away from the NAAFI until Geordie had calmed down. You only had to say Jackie Milburn to set him off again.

There were other characters to be wary of. The Christian Fellowship had taken over the NAAFI reading room and an innocent going in there could easily be roped in for a Bible reading or a quick prayer or three. The leading light was Bunny Bartholomew a devout Baptist from Addiscombe who, once he caught you with his steely gaze, could effortlessly convince you that the world could easily come to an end before your next thirty-six hour pass and that the time had come to repent.

One pay night I discovered steak on the menu in the NAAFI. Now that may not sound very startling to you but in 1952 and in the RAF steak was rarer than a WAAF with her virtue intact. I should have been less trusting. There was something furtive about the way the NAAFI girl served me and about the way the steak flaked as I prodded it cautiously with my fork. The slightly sweet taste of the meat was also unfamiliar to my taste buds. I reckon that steak had been granted early retirement after losing the last race at Newbury. After that I reverted to my traditional pay night treat of egg and chips and a bottle of brown ale.

The counter staff in the NAAFI were unmemorable apart from one gargantuan girl who unkindly but rather poetically was known as the camp bicycle. Mind you, I don't know why I should feel sorry for her. She was never short of a consort even if she was seldom promenaded in public. Despite her lack of glamour she generally had a self-satisfied smirk on her face. After all, there were five hundred sex-starved airmen in the camp.

Once a month a camp dance was held in the NAAFI but having three left feet I tended to keep away from these. I regret it now but I was a shy, spotty and naive youth and I hadn't grasped that NAAFI dances were just lightly disguised orgies.

The NAAFI had a table tennis table but this was controlled by a group of table tennis fanatics led by LAC Roast who claimed to be the junior county champion of Shropshire. I never managed to get a game of table tennis. Apart from anything else you had to buy your own table tennis balls and the communal bats were in an advanced state of decomposition. LAC Roast had his own personal bat with some special surface that he was always boasting about.

Still, I used to get my own back by calling the game ping-pong which infuriated old Roastie.

The officers' mess and the sergeants' mess were located elsewhere but the corporals' club was an annexe to the main NAAFI. When I became a corporal I marched proudly into the corporals' club. I had secretly hoped that the corporals' club would have deep leather armchairs and waiters serving brandy and soda and copies of *The Times* scattered around. In reality it was much the same as the airmen's NAAFI but the queue was shorter. It did have a well worn billiards table but you had to book two days in advance to get a go on that and one of the cues was so bent that you could have used it as a back-scratcher.

When I was orderly corporal it was one of my duties to lock up the NAAFI last thing at night. Happily, I was not on duty the night that someone nicked the NAAFI safe. Mind you, I think that it must have been civilians who did the job. Any national serviceman could have told you that since it wasn't pay night there would be nothing in the safe worth having anyway.

Still, my abiding memory of the NAAFI is that last glimpse of the deserted building with its tea-stained Formica tables and the ashtrays overflowing with Woodbine dog-ends and then the sound of my key turning in the door lock for the last time in April 1953.

Warrington

It is strange, isn't it, the way that certain places leave indelible images in one's mind? I have seen the view from the top of the Empire State Building and I have sat drinking coffee in St Mark's Square and I have seen the Golden Gate Bridge glistening in the setting sun. Yet, strangely, it is Warrington that remains most vividly in my mind. Mind you, I only visited the place on a few occasions and it could scarcely be described as beautiful but it remains one of my more enduring memories.

I first arrived in Warrington in the late afternoon of a grey and gloomy day in early April 1951. I had just been called up to do my bit for the nation and I was feeling less than cheerful about the whole business. I had never been that far from my mum before and it had taken about five hours to chuff all the way up from Euston. Finally the train had arrived at Warrington (Bank Quay). The first thing that impinged on my consciousness as I emerged from the train was the soapworks. I had never seen a soapworks before. My home town of West Wickham was noted for a complete absence of soapworks. In fact, apart from the stables of the Amalgamated Dairies at the bottom of the High Street, it didn't have any industries at all.

The soapworks was by the side of the station and for some reason or other it had a series of pulleys and conveyor belts that emitted irregular, if disturbingly frequent, squeaking, groaning and grinding noises that immediately set my teeth on edge. The factory boilerhouse contributed to the harmony by squirting out sudden and unexpected jets of steam with a noise resembling a giant's suppressed fart. I don't know if it was meant to do it but somehow it seemed to set the tone for my arrival in Warrington.

The next attack on my senses was the aroma. The air was scented with a combination of sulphurous smoke, coal gas and soap. There was also another more complex pong that reminded me of our road when Jerry blew up the main sewer during the Blitz in 1941.

A small group of conscripts had emerged from the train and shambled like nervous sheep down the grimy stone-flagged steps and along an ill-lit passageway with walls of peeling whitewash enhanced with a faint smell of urine. It looked as though the whitewash dated from when the London and North Western Railway had last refurbished the station in about 1875.

As soon as we emerged blinking into the station forecourt we were herded into a Royal Air Works transport and driven off to RAF Padgate. As we whizzed through the town I only managed a few brief glimpses of bleak buildings, smoking chimneys and grimy brickwork. The local citizenry didn't look all that cheerful either. The women seemed to have a penchant for headscarves and wrinkled stockings and for the men it seemed to be de rigueur to wear a cloth cap and a collarless shirt and to have a Woodbine hanging from the lip. Anyway, this was how my brief introduction to Warrington came to an end.

It was two weeks before the authorities allowed me to resume my acquaintance with Warrington. By that time I had become so numbed by the inanities of the Royal Air Works that I felt that I was ready for almost anything. Nonetheless, Warrington was a stern test. Even with the mellowing effect of the best part of fifty years I have to admit that my memories of Warrington remain unique.

I don't think that the sun ever shone in Warrington. If it

did, I missed it. The town seemed to be shrouded in a smoky yellowy haze. When you took a deep breath it was like smoking a Capstan Full Strength.

On our first Saturday visit to Warrington we discovered the Young Women's Christian Association. The Warrington YWCA opened its doors to all the pink faced youths from RAF Padgate. Don't ask me why. I have no idea. I suspect that it may have been because the young men of Padgate presented less of a threat to the maidenhood of Warrington than the Americans based at Burtonwood. Mind you, most of the maidenhood of Warrington weren't in the YWCA. Most of them were down at the bus station waiting for the arrival of the buses from Burtonwood.

I cannot pretend that the YWCA was a particularly exciting venue. In fact, it made Stowmarket on a Sunday look like the Chelsea Arts Ball. Still, there wasn't anywhere much else to go; not on twenty-eight bob a week there wasn't. They did make a decent cup of tea however, and if you wanted to push the boat out you could have a sticky bun as well.

In addition to refreshments the YWCA also offered some indoor sporting facilities but we were unable to avail ourselves of these because someone had trodden on the ping-pong ball.

Then there was Bank Park. This was the only green space that I can recall in Warrington but, sadly, the municipal tulips drooped their pretty heads as if suffering from acute depression and Bank Park was the only place in the world where I have ever seen grey daffodils. The whole town seemed to be shrouded in a pall of smoke and even the Warrington sparrows seemed to have bronchitis.

There was also the River Mersey. When we got off the bus from RAF Padgate on our first Saturday afternoon visit the bus decanted us at the bus station. This was located right next to the River Mersey. The first thing we did after we got off the bus was to lean over the wall and look at the river. I had understood that the River Mersey was quite famous and I was looking forward to the view. It turned out to be like no river I had ever seen before. The buildings on the far bank were enveloped in a greyish haze which seemed to come from a cement works. Or it may have been the gas works. The river itself was slow-flowing and a rancid brown in colour. Great mounds of yellow-grey foam drifted with the flow like putrescent icebergs. The river had the now familiar pong of sewage and soap and, although it may have been my fanciful imagination, I think I saw a dead cat drifting slowly downriver to meet his maker.

The bus station itself was the hub of activity in Warrington. Buses came in from all sorts of faraway places with strange sounding names. Wigan and Eccles spring to mind. Young women arrived in hordes, keen to find a partner from amongst all the uniformed young males available. The young women, freed from the weekday tyranny of factories and mills and offices, were dressed in their best. They were deploying every possible beauty aid and accoutrement to add to their charms. Toni home perms were very popular. ('Can you tell which twin has the Toni?' the advert used to ask.) There were high heels and peep-toes and wired bras and tight girdles and best nylons with seams and mum's best imitation pearl earrings. As each bus disgorged its cargo of young women great wafts of Plaisir D'Amour, April in Paris and L'Amour de Nuit emerged with them. A busload had enough perfume, lipstick and face powder to stock the Warrington branch of Boots for the best part of a month.

In those early post-war days most young men were doing their national service and were in uniform. Warrington was surrounded by military establishments so the town was full of servicemen. There were soldiers, sailors and airmen and if that was not bad enough there were American servicemen as well. The Americans were not popular; well, they were with the girls and that was the trouble. I began to appreciate the wartime saying that the problem with the Americans was that they were oversexed, overpaid and over here.

Rumour had it that on the American airbase there were slot machines in the lavatories that sold French letters. Mind you, we thought that this was fanciful rubbish. This was just after the war when you couldn't even get a packet of Players out of an automatic machine and when any reference to birth control was considered an incitement to immorality amongst the lower orders. Still, it had to be faced that the Americans did seem a bit, well, forward. When they weren't seeing to the local girls they seemed to be laying into the local lads.

The town was patrolled by military policemen to keep the servicemen in order. The American military police were the worst. They had white belts and gaiters and four-foot-long riot sticks and looked as if they were on detached duty from Alcatraz. When a jeep full of these characters arrived on the scene the local police went and hid round the back of Woolworth's.

One of my problems in adapting to Warrington was that I had no understanding of Northern culture. In fact, I had never previously been farther up the Northern Line than Leicester Square. The first thing I had to appreciate was that Warrington Consolidated played Rugby League and that was a very different game from the rugby I had played at Ravensbeck Grammar School and bore absolutely no resemblance at all to Association Football. When Warrington Consolidated were playing on a Saturday afternoon there was no other topic of conversation, apart perhaps from whippet racing. I went into the hairdresser's one Saturday and someone asked me what the score was. I said that I didn't know but I was hoping that Crystal Palace would win. After that things began to look distinctly nasty.

Everything about Warrington was alien. It was like being in a foreign country. All the streets seemed to be surfaced with cobblestones and the houses had front doors right on the street and everywhere you looked you saw another factory chimney. All the buildings seemed to be gaunt and grim and the residents had appearances to match and spoke in extremely strange accents.

The High Street was different as well. Mind you, in those days shopping centres had individuality and weren't just filled with chain stores and building society offices. The most noticeable thing was the names over the shops, names like Entwhistle and Postlethwaite and the Wigan Co-operative Society. I tell you, Warrington in 1951 was more of a culture shock to me than Agadir in 1985.

Even the buses were weird. They had 'Ribble' written on the side. No, I don't know what it means either. I assumed that it was some sort of insult. The livery was a two-tone affair of off-white and dog-poop brown. The upper deck had a sort of sunken gangway along one side and a bench seat for four at a higher level so that you were all squashed up on one side of the bus. It is a wonder all their buses didn't topple over. When you got up out of your seat you hit your head on the ceiling, went dizzy and then fell down into the sunken gangway. Even the bloody conductor was alien. Instead of a proper rack of tickets and a bell punch these conductors had strange machines that with a twirl of a handle produced a ticket like a piece of mouse's lavatory paper with indecipherable script on it. Those weren't proper bus tickets. You couldn't tell where you had come from or where you were going. You felt cheated and, worse still, you couldn't even understand what the conductor was talking about.

On that first Saturday in Warrington, after we had exhausted the potential of the YWCA, which in practice meant that we had finished our cup of tea and sticky bun, we made our way to Bank Park. There was a broad path through the middle of the park lined with flower beds and park benches. Here the maidens of South Lancashire awaited their fate. At least those who had not already sealed it by a tryst with an American from Milwaukee or Albuquerque.

I had never acquired the skill of picking up girls. Although I tried to look as though I flew a Canberra during the week, my ill-fitting brand-new air force uniform fooled no one and I realised that my pulling power was not great. Fortunately, I was in the company of a shoe repairer from Market Harborough who claimed to be very experienced with women. His social skills turned out to be more limited than I had hoped but luckily we found that "Ullo, darlin', wanna come to the flicks?' seemed to suffice. My girl came from Runcorn. She was quite pretty in a thin, anaemic, sniffly, adenoidal sort of way. She was called Doreen. She kept saying things like, 'Right Monkey,' and, 'Eeh by gum,' and sounded just like Gracie Fields.

Then we headed for the Warrington Regal. We could only afford the one and nines. But on twenty-eight bob a week minus barrack room damages what could any girl expect? Mind you, the bloody Americans were all up in the two and nines surrounded by adoring blondes and smoking Camels and chomping off-the-ration candy. Doesn't privilege make you sick?

The four of us spent the rest of the evening in the company of John Wayne and the US cavalry. When we emerged from the Regal it was time to see the two girls back on the last bus to Runcorn. Intoxicated with the pleasures of neck nuzzling and kissing in the back row of the one and nines we made plans to meet at the bus station the next Saturday afternoon. Sadly, it was not to be. By next Saturday I was in the RAF hospital at Padgate. I had contracted some mysterious lurgy that had made me lose my voice and go bright red and the authorities, fearful that an attack of bubonic plague was about to rage through the camp, decided to put me in quarantine.

I never saw Doreen from Runcorn again. When I recovered from my mysterious lurgy I was packed off on sick leave. My illness was never given an official diagnosis but I must have been quite poorly because you didn't get sick leave in the Royal Air Works unless you were dead, dying, infectious or something was dropping off you. On my return from sick leave I did visit Warrington a few more times before I was finally posted away from Padgate but it was never the same. Somehow it had lost its magic. Still, I suppose that in a funny sort of way it could be said that I left my heart in Warrington.

The Command Drafting Office

Even I have to admit that my period of national service was a bit of an anticlimax. It was my own fault really. I suppose that I should have volunteered for the RAF Regiment or something equally bizarre. The trouble was that I had always been told that in the services one should never volunteer for anything, so I didn't. Perhaps this explains why, after my initial training, I was posted to RAF White Waltham in deepest Berkshire. My posting order showed that White Waltham was the headquarters of Home Command and that I was posted to the Command Drafting Office as an AC2 u/t Clerk Personnel. I quickly learned that u/t meant under training although what the training was I never really discovered.

Anyway, one day in August 1951 I arrived at RAF White Waltham complete with large pack, small pack and kitbag. Why they couldn't just give you a suitcase I could never understand. After all the preliminaries of finding billet and bedding I made myself known to the Home Command Headquarters Drafting Office. Here were kept all the personnel records for the Command and from hence all the posting orders were issued. Considering it was part of the RAF, it seemed to function quite well. It was headed by a flight lieutenant, an amiable man with a Yorkshire accent who had obtained a short service commission as an air gunner during the war and had clung on grimly to his privilege in the post-war years.

Command headquarters was littered with commissioned

officers. It had an air vice-marshall in charge, several air commodores, a positive clutter of wing commanders and a surfeit of squadron leaders. Saluting at White Waltham could have been a life's work. Like everything else in the RAF, it was best to keep one's end up with a little subtlety. I used to salute all the commissioned ranks with great respect, just like they had taught me. Hup-two-three-four-down. Long way up, short way down. They all got the full treatment. It forced them to salute back and after a while the buggers got fed up with it and scuttled out of the way to avoid all the rigmarole.

In all this hierarchy flight lieutenants were very small beer indeed. There was a kind of great divide between flight lieutenants and squadron leaders. The rapid promotion of the war years had seized up and whilst squadron leaders and above could still nurse hopes and aspirations, flight lieutenants were unlikely to be going places except reluctantly to collect their demob suits. Our flight lieutenant clung on grimly. He was not, I gathered, suitable post-war officer material. I suspect that he was probably a very good air gunner and he had some medals to show for it but, when the shooting stops commissioned air gunners are not in great demand, especially if they have Yorkshire accents.

Poor Flight Lieutenant Morley had the haunted look of a man whose days were numbered. Mind you, the whole drafting office was staffed with strange wraith-like characters, mostly national servicemen spinning out their time until demob but with a smattering of regulars. The second in command was Warrant Officer Crimm, a clerk (general duties), who was nearly at the end of thirty years of clerking for the RAF. We once overheard, with horror and disbelief, a conversation in which he expressed unhappiness that his time with the air force was coming to an end.

Warrant Officer Crimm sat at his desk in the corner of

the drafting office applying his strange circular signature to every posting order that was placed in front of him. He didn't often say a lot but occasionally he would emit an 'Eeh' and, even more occasionally, 'by gum.' I think he came from Accrington, so I suppose you have to make allowances.

Flight Sergeant Griffin, by contrast, was a perky, talkative and elfin little man, a bit like a scruffy garden ornament. He had served in the Middle East during the war and was always going on about the 'exhibishes' he had seen in Port Said. They were strange affairs, by his accounts, which involved ladies and donkeys in various permutations. There was nothing remotely like that at RAF White Waltham.

There was, however, Sergeant Heather. He tried everything he knew to entice uninitiated AC2s to join him in his quarters for a cup of Nescafé and various other unspecified social activities. Sergeant Heather used eyebrow pencil on his moustache, powdered his cheeks and kept a coloured handkerchief tucked in the sleeve of his tunic. No one took much notice; after all he was a sergeant. Actually he was quite good company and we shared one or two Sunday lunchtime pints down at the Bell at Waltham St Lawrence where, provided you were off duty and in civvies, you could pretend that you were equals. Mind you, you had to keep an eye on him. If women think that sexual harassment is their exclusive cross to bear, they haven't heard of the Sergeant Heathers of this world.

Then there was Sergeant Cranwell, who had come from Bombay via RAF Cardington. He was a delightful man but he had an antisocial passion for his national dishes. Remember, this was in an era when curry was still considered exotic and the nearest Indian restaurant was probably in New Delhi. He may have thought our stand-offishness was some deep-seated racial prejudice but I can assure you (and the Commission for Racial Equality) that it was self-preservation based on a dislike of second-hand biryani. When he leaned over my shoulder to check the number of cooks at RAF Lytham his breath used to make my eyes water.

Then there was Corporal Fox. Poor man. He was suffering from a terrible wasting disease and devoted all his fast-dwindling energies to concealing the fact so that when the inevitable medical discharge finally arrived he would qualify for the maximum pension. Anyone who fought the system with such resolution, even if he was a regular, had the support of all the national servicemen.

The more I think about the motley band that made up the staff of the drafting office the more I marvel that it functioned as well as it did. I think that it was because no matter what lunacies were going on elsewhere in the camp (the station warrant officer made us cut the grass around the billet with nail scissors one bull night), the office was a refuge where no one took the RAF too seriously (except Warrant Officer Crimm, of course, but as I have already explained, he came from Accrington).

My national service colleagues in the drafting office did their best to preserve their personal identities within the system. We did our jobs in the office fairly conscientiously partly out of loyalty to Flight Lieutenant Morley and partly as an assertion that we were not quite as moronic as the RAF liked to think us. Apart from our routine office duties we maintained our demob charts as an expression of our faith in future sanity and we pursued our individual interests and hobbies.

SAC Protheroe practised his part in *The Mikado*, due to be performed by the local operatic society; LAC Bartholomew continued his efforts to convert an ungrateful world to Christianity, and our telephonist, who was a silver service waiter at a Brighton hotel in real life, conducted a

338

long-range seduction of his WAAF counterpart on the switchboard of the central RAF records office in Gloucester. We listened to his perfidy with admiration because he was engaged in a much less distanced relationship with one of the WAAF teleprinter operators on our own camp. As we understood, it was mostly conducted on a groundsheet in the copse behind the WAAFery. There was also LAC Nobbs who played right half for Maidenhead Town every Saturday. They were an amateur club but they slipped old Nobby thirty bob each week which was nearly as much as he collected on pay parade.

The conscript erks constantly fought the system, not with any hope of total victory because it was well known that only death or demob could bring that, but every time the system was circumvented was a minor boost for the spirit. We managed to persuade Flight Lieutenant Morley that we could work more efficiently on a shift basis and then arranged the shifts so that we finished work late on a Friday evening and were thus eligible for a forty-eight hour pass most weekends instead of the thirty-six hours normally allowed. We coaxed Flight Sergeant Griffin to sign little chits that certified that we were shift workers and thus avoided morning reveille and gained access to the mess for early meals before the stew congealed or they ran out of custard. Chitties dominated our lives. Chitties were better than currency for improving the quality of life.

Although he was an officer I quite liked Flight Lieutenant Morley. Sometimes he even invited our views about how the work of the unit could be improved. This, of course, was close to Bolshevism in the RAF and most un-officer-like. Being asked to offer ideas and to think thoughts was a bit disconcerting because the post-war RAF didn't normally work like that. Sometimes we could actually see the point of the work that we were doing which threw us into confusion. Still, it was better than whitewashing the coal or polishing the fire hydrants.

Slowly I passed through the system as a clerk personnel: AC2, AC1, and LAC. Then, after an exhaustive trade test that included typing at a laboured ten words a minute, I was promoted to senior aircraftsman and wore a little three-bladed propeller on my arm to prove it. I was moved around the office, undertaking different tasks and sitting at different desks working at great banks of patent metal card index cabinets. Each working point had a little notice: '61 Group', '62 Group', 'A Fluctuation', 'B Fluctuation', 'POR Checking', 'Stats Returns', and so on. There was little purpose to all the signs. Those who worked there knew where everything was anyway, whilst strangers hadn't a clue what it all meant. Still, it was nice to see the look of pride on Warrant Officer Crimm's face as he showed some group of high-ranking officers round his little empire. After they had gone, suitably impressed, he would sometimes be moved to say, 'Eeh, by gum,' with a tremor of pride in his voice. I suppose those little notices served the same purpose as whitewashing the stones round the flagpole or polishing the guardroom lino when it was already shined to a dazzle. I always felt that whilst the official motto of the Royal Air Works was *per ardua ad astra*, parodied to *per ardua ad* asbestos (Blow you Jack, I'm fireproof), it should really have been whatever the Latin was for 'bullshit baffles brains'. Mind you, the RAF has never had exclusive rights over that particular principle.

Eventually I was promoted to the elevated status of senior aircraftsman/acting corporal (paid). I ended my service days as corporal i/c B Fluctuation earning two pounds ten shillings a week. (Well, I know it isn't the same as flying a Spitfire in the Battle of Britain but you wouldn't want me to lie about it, would you?) We also served who only sat and wrote, you know. Anyway, operational control of the intricacies of B Fluctuation had its moments. In a flash, or at least moderately quickly, I could tell Warrant Officer Crimm how many nursing attendants, cooks or gunner instructors were in post and what their ranks were at any unit in the Command. Or at least, how many we thought there were. I expect that they do it by computer today. No doubt they still get it wrong.

Periodically the Command Drafting Office fell into a panic when it discovered that its records bore even less resemblance than usual to the personnel in post at the stations for which we were responsible. On such occasions I was detached on temporary duty to check our personnel records against those of the chosen unit. Visiting a strange camp was fraught with perils. The station police and the guardroom sergeant were unknown quantities, and a weather eye had to be kept open for the station warrant officer (most of whom it transpired were, like ours, quite mad), and a fresh set of cookhouse staff had to be humoured if you wanted a decent piece of bacon at breakfast time. My corporal's stripes did me no good at all but I used to let it be known that I came from the Command Drafting Office and various erks would sidle up to me to acquaint me with their ambitions for a posting nearer home or to be regraded to a trade more to their liking. I never promised anything, mind you, but I listened attentively and perhaps made a note or two and never explained the principle of responsibility without power. Still, more often than not I got a decent piece of bacon at breakfast time.

I finally left the Command Drafting Office at RAF White Waltham in early April 1953 with a discharge certificate signed by Flight Lieutenant Morley which was surprisingly generous in its comments. It said, 'An excellent NCO. Will make a good executive with training.' No one had ever said anything as kind as that about me before. I hope the flight lieutenant managed to hang on to his commission. The RAF was a bit short of officers who behaved like human beings.

The Ground Combat Course

During the Korean War the Air Ministry was struck by panic because it realised that most of its non-flying personnel hadn't touched a firearm since their initial training. In my case, even at that stage I had been unable to score more than two outers and three ricochets off the side wall of the rifle range. Mind you, it scared the shit out of my beloved instructor, Corporal Bogley, who, although a high-grade psychopath, was wise enough not to demand that I fire a further five rounds. I suppose that I was deemed to have passed by default but I don't expect that the Air Ministry knew the details. Anyway, in 1952 a combined fear of the Koreans and the Russkies led to an outbreak of combat courses for erks who were packed off protesting, in droves, to be taught how to become ruthless fighting machines. They then returned to their units and resumed their normal duties as cooks, batmen, admin orderlies, clerks and storemen.

Inevitably my turn came and, clasping my temporary posting order and transit instructions, I was routed as indirectly as possible to RAF Weston-on-the-Green to take part in Number Thirty-two Ground Combat Course. The RTO always routed us the longest way round. I don't know if they got a percentage from British Railways or if they just enjoyed the intellectual challenge. On one memorable occasion they devised a route for me that involved taking all day to travel seventy miles and ended up with me dismounting from a bus at eight o'clock on a pitch black night in the middle of Salisbury Plain at the height of a snowstorm. You think I jest. You don't need to make up jokes about the air force.

But I digress. (I am, as you will observe, prone to err in this way.) Now where was I? Ah, the Ground Combat Course, Number Thirty-two. It was only a week, for that at least I was grateful, and my memories of ground combat are now a trifle hazy. Like most courses the bits that one remembers are not usually the bits that those in authority intended. For a week we guarded the airfield at Weston-on-the-Green as if it were under threat from an enemy and as if we would have cared much anyway. In fact, it was semi-derelict and hadn't seen an aeroplane since a false landing by a Harvard trainer in 1947. The airfield's state of dereliction reduced the atmosphere of drama somewhat but the Air Ministry would never have trusted our rabble to guard a real one. Guarding the real ones was a job reserved for the RAF Regiment, a fearsome lot with large boots, pugnacious expressions and a marked proclivity for punch-ups outside the NAAFI after it closed on pay nights.

On the combat course we were issued with rifles and instructed to keep them by our sides at all times, ready for instant action. Very wisely, they didn't trust us with the bullets to put up the spout. I learned that going to the lavatory with a rifle is fraught with difficulty, even when it doesn't have a bullet up the spout.

The best part of the course was the dawn patrol round the perimeter track. The airfield was renowned for its mushrooms. In addition, our instructors and persecutors, who acted as the enemy, were too bone idle to get out of their pits to launch a dawn attack so we had the dawn, and the mushrooms, to ourselves.

The rest of each day, however, was pretty excruciating. We spent the days crawling through drainpipes (did no good to my claustrophobia), swinging from ropes (played havoc with my vertigo) and leaping muddy ditches, or, in my case, more often falling into them, usually up to my vitals. I had never realised before just how muddy Oxfordshire was. I seem to recall that we also spent an inordinate amount of time sticking our bayonets into straw-filled sandbags whilst emitting wild warlike noises. As a variation we balanced on precarious rope bridges or sat in trees and all this whilst we were pelted with thunderflashes. If that is what war is like I should want considerably more than the promise of medals to take part.

The final event of the week was an exercise in total war when we rushed around firing blanks at each other. The only casualty was an unfortunate erk who was shot by a blank at close range and who leapt around with a piece of hot wadding up his trouser leg.

Happily, I was never called upon to guard real aeroplanes against a real foe although I suppose that in theory the Air Ministry assumed, rather naively, that I was suitably equipped to do so. I have to say that they had more faith in me than I had in their judgement. I was called upon on one occasion to guard the WAAFery at RAF White Waltham with a pickaxe handle after an overimaginative WAAF had complained of a lurking sex maniac in the shrubbery – wishful thinking, I suspect. Guarding the WAAFs was a marginal improvement on fire picket duty. I can't understand why women object to being desired for their bodies. I wish that someone desired me for mine, that is, someone other than the dissecting department of the St Ethelburg's Hospital Medical School.

Be that as it may, guarding the WAAFery was the only time my training on the ground combat course was put to any practical use. Still, if you know anyone who wants to employ a pensioner who, in 1952, was trained as a ruthless fighting machine you know where to send them.

Corporal Podger

Corporal Podger was in charge of my hut when I first arrived at RAF White Waltham in 1951. Hut Number Ten it was. I say 'in charge' but it was hard to envisage Corporal Podger taking charge of anything; even supervising a white elephant stall might have overextended his managerial capacities. His trade in the RAF was a personnel selection assessor. I never knew what he was doing at RAF White Waltham. No one there ever got selected for anything except for fatigues or the fire picket. Corporal Podger had a degree in psychology and a markedly eccentric manner. He had his own personal jar of marmalade and had a disturbing habit of eating his daily breakfast sausage with dabs of marmalade, rather as others used mustard; he argued that since RAF sausages were ninety per cent bread anyway, his approach was entirely logical. Besides, he added, he liked marmalade. I have been suspicious of psychologists ever since; too bloody clever by half.

Mind you, Corporal Podger's regime was benign but nutty, rather like being supervised by a mildly schizo-phrenic teddy bear. Being a national serviceman he had no more understanding of the RAF than we had. We all had our own ways of coping with the lunacies of RAF life and Corporal Podger's way was to serve his time in a semi-trancelike state. He always had a happy smile but gave the impression that half of him was somewhere else – probably on Mars, or the Isle of Wight.

We all tended to assume that the Air Ministry, like God,

operated in ways that were not just mysterious but downright unfathomable. This gave us a useful theoretical base to make sense of the nonsensical. For example, when the station warrant officer ordered us to cut the grass outside our hut with our nail scissors we just shrugged our shoulders and said, 'Oh well, that's the air force for you!' Mind you, I would rather have been one of the First of the Few up in the sky with my Spitfire than one of the Last of the Many down on my hands and knees cutting the grass with my nail scissors and feeling a bit of a twit. Still, that's life, isn't it? We weren't all destined to save the civilised world, even, that is, if we thought that it was worth the trouble.

Anyway, returning to Corporal Podger, his deficiencies became most apparent on bull nights. To explain to the uninitiated, this was a regular Tuesday evening phenomenon when all the erks were required to clean their billets. Well, not so much clean them as polish them to sparkling perfection. This required considerable organisation because each hut only had one broom, a single large splodge of polish drawn from the stores and one 'bumper' (a weighted polisher) to shine up the lino. Oh, I had forgotten, there was also some metal polish to shine up the tops of the fire extinguishers, the window brasses and anything else that could be given a high sheen.

With Corporal Podger in charge the whole bull night exercise was a cross between the sinking of the *Titanic* and the *Billy Cotton Bandshow*. After a while most of us gave up and crept off to the NAAFI. Mind you, when the orderly officer arrived the next morning to inspect the shambles that was Hut Number Ten he would be met by Corporal Podger with his RAF beret perched on his head like a chef's hat and then welcomed by a sloppy salute and a lopsided grin. However, it was common knowledge even among the commissioned classes that our corporal was both seriously clever and more than a little potty. The orderly officer usually decided not to tangle with our corporal who seemed completely oblivious to the dog-ends in the fire bucket, the cobwebs hanging from the lampshades or the generally shambolic state of Hut Number Ten and appeared to be waiting for some sort of official commendation.

The Festival of Britain

Crumbly though I am, I was not around for the Great Exhibition of 1851. Even if I had been it seems unlikely that Prince Albert would have extended a personal invitation. Sadly, even if there is one, I am not expecting to attend the 2051 Exhibition. The 1951 Exhibition however, entitled rather grandiosely the Festival of Britain, I can speak about with some authority.

1951 had not looked like being a good year from the outset. A few months before it started, the Prime Minister announced that in 1951 he wanted me to begin two years' national service instead of the eighteen months that I had been anticipating. The pay would be unaltered at twenty-eight bob a week although as a consolation prize he would pay me a regular's pay of forty-nine shillings a week for the last six months. However, it was not just me who was fairly cheesed off at the thought of 1951.

The Labour Government started the year by cutting the meat ration and then abandoned the Ground Nuts Scheme and wrote off the £36,500,000 it had cost. That, I thought, was a lot of twenty-eight bobs a week. Mr Gaitskell, the Chancellor of the Exchequer, also introduced prescription charges and increased income tax and purchase tax. Not anticipating much income and having therefore very little to purchase anything with, I had the dubious advantage of being unmoved by these later announcements.

I think that the original intention was for the Festival of Britain to cheer us all up after the trials and tribulations of the war. In retrospect, I'm not sure that I didn't prefer the war. At least you didn't have to pay to go in to that.

King George VI opened the Festival on 3rd May which was a bit inconsiderate because I was pounding a parade ground at RAF Padgate at the time. I didn't get to see the Festival until I had some leave later in the year. When I finally got to the South Bank site it seemed that everyone else had got there before me. It was packed. This heightened the excitement. It must be very special to attract so many people, I thought. Mind you, in those days you could find a queue half a mile long for off the ration stewing goat at 1s 6d. a pound.

Anyway, eventually I was admitted. I can't remember how much it cost but the souvenir programme alone was almost a day's pay so you will understand why I only visited the Festival once. It was a funny sort of place. There were very large sculptures littered about all over the place. They were all chunky and misshapen and one or two of them looked a bit rude to me. Well, how many women do you know with square bosoms? The buildings were all a bit funny too. They were supposed to demonstrate the achievements of modern architecture but they knocked most of them down afterwards.

The Dome of Discovery was, well, unusual. I remember going up an escalator to the top gallery and noting that the dome seemed as if they had forgotten to finish it. It was all bare concrete and steel girders. It was very big as everyone kept telling me. I can't remember what was in it except for a huge telescope and that didn't actually do anything. I think that it was all about stars and explorers and things like that. Certainly there was a totem pole and a wax model of Captain Cook. But mostly it was tramping round and round and up and down stairs and looking at drawings and photographs and models and things. Personally, my sense of discovery was reduced to a great yearning for a cup of tea. The cafeteria was the Aerated Bread Company with bunting and spindly little metal chairs that were very modern but hurt your bum. This was, I think, a clever device for ensuring that you didn't hang around too long although they said they were examples of contemporary design. There was also a posh restaurant with a view of the Thames from the terrace but you would have needed a wing commander's pay to have got in there. It had coloured umbrellas over the tables which was considered very avant-garde but the view wasn't all that good when the tide went out.

The whole South Bank site was split in two by a grimy brick viaduct leading to Hungerford Bridge and Charing Cross Station. From the trains on the viaduct you had a very good view of the Festival site; from the Festival you had a very good view of the railway viaduct. Mind you, they tried to pretty it up a bit with some white painted fencing, some brightly coloured hardboard and lots of bunting but it was still a railway viaduct.

The powers that be intended to demonstrate the country's contribution to civilisation, its traditions and heritage, its creative and commercial potential and its importance in the post-war world. Anyway, that's what the programme said. What it demonstrated to me was never to believe pretentious political claptrap and to remember that exhibitions always make your feet hurt.

There were lots of other buildings called pavilions that had themes like 'Sea and Ships' and 'Transport' but the buildings were a bit like aircraft hangars decorated with funny canopies and strange heraldic devices. Mostly you just looked at things; it was a bit like the Science Museum with decorations. There were murals as well and lots of bright paint and bunting but the overall effect was something between a circus and a building site.

There was a great big fountain thing made of stainless

steel that trickled water into a scoop which when full tipped the water into a bigger scoop and so on and so on… until when the bottom scoop was full it tipped all the water into a pool with a giant swoosh. This all took about twenty minutes and if you stood too close you got a bootful of water. There was also, of course, the Skylon. It didn't look very impressive up close and in daylight but at night it looked like a giant floodlit finger making a rude gesture of defiance. They used up a hell of a lot of electricity at night; everything was lit up in a way that we were not used to. Then in October the Government declared a fuel crisis and banned lights in shop windows and advertising signs. It seemed that we had run out of electricity. So much for our commercial potential.

There was also the Festival Pleasure Gardens at Battersea but I never got there.(No money left and where the hell was Battersea anyway?) I read in the papers about the Emmett Railway and the Guinness Clock but apart from these it sounded like Dreamland without the seaside.

It would be nice to record that all the hopes of those distant days and that optimistic Festival were fulfilled. God knows, in those grotty immediate post-war years we needed some hope. Still, it has to be admitted that all those bits of the South Bank site that were described as 'gay' would not be described like that today – for a number of reasons. By 1991 the eastern part of the site was occupied by cardboard city where London's homeless and dispossessed slept. At the other end of the site was St Thomas's Hospital which was under intermittent threat of closure and County Hall which had been flogged off to the Japanese. In the middle of the site was a large area of brown grass and an even larger National Car Park. The railway viaduct, however, was still there.

I recall that the Festival exhibition had displays about the rich promise of our modern mining industry, our

wonderful National Health Service and our splendid
architecture. The exhibits also highlighted our progressive
shipbuilding industry and the potential of our car,
locomotive and aircraft industries, not forgetting, of course,
our splendidly modernised steel industry.

So what did I make of the Festival? As I travelled home
on the Southern Region Electric train to West Wickham I
passed innumerable bomb sites and decaying air raid
shelters. I observed endless streets of grimy buildings pitted
with bomb splinters and with woodwork that had not seen
a lick of paint since 1939.

I was only eighteen and a half at the time and I still had
eighteen months of my national service to complete.
Everyone seemed to be telling me that the future was
bright. The Festival souvenir programme that I read on the
train home told me that Britain had a great past but that it
looked forward with confidence to its even greater future.

I wasn't entirely convinced, but then my leave finished
on Monday and eighteen months in the Royal Air Works is
a very long time. When I got off the train at West Wickham
it was piddling with rain. I did up my utility raincoat and
began to whistle. With any luck there might be a spam
sandwich when I got home.

A Venture Into Commerce

My career with the Meticulous Weighing Machine Company was precarious and brief. The precariousness was not because my employers viewed me with any personalised disfavour, but they had a curious attitude to office staff. Office workers did not make anything, repair anything or sell anything so they were regarded as a bit of a luxury. If one's services were no longer required it was a week's pay in lieu of notice and goodbye and good luck and, by the way, don't forget your P45. If you left under a cloud (groping the office manager's secretary, fiddling the stamp book or too often signing one's name under the red line drawn at one minute to nine), then it was goodbye without the good luck and by the way, don't expect a reference. This strict office discipline did tend to sharpen one's motivation (and one's anxiety). No one in the Meticulous hierarchy had, I suspect, read much on industrial psychology and they were much more into sticks than carrots for their office staff.

I had arrived in Gravesend in April 1958 with my new Revelation expanding suitcase containing my worldly goods. The suitcase was far from fully expanded which must say something about my material achievements to date. Never mind, I was wearing my new made-to-measure Hepworth's Harris tweed sports jacket and I was ready for anything. In the jacket pocket was a Post Office book with £30 in the account and a letter containing an offer of employment with the Meticulous Weighing Machine

Company at their Gravesend office. I was, the letter told me, to be employed as their assistant chief repairs clerk at a salary of £520 per annum, payable weekly. The contract was terminable by a week's notice on either side. I never dared ask what had happened to the previous assistant chief repairs clerk and he was never mentioned (instant dismissal or an attack of bubonic plague, I suppose).

The Meticulous empire originated in the industrial north where they had a large factory somewhere downwind of Rotherham but Gravesend was their key outpost in the south and controlled the activities of a motley collection of workshops and showrooms littered about anywhere nearer civilisation than Watford.

The assistant chief repairs clerk's duties were multi-farious, mainly because the repairs department consisted of the chief repairs clerk, me, and a young girl straight from school who passed her working day in a state of myopic torpor. She was plump but quite pretty in a blank sort of way but I think that she was in love with Cliff Richard at the time. (Or was it Tommy Steele?) Whoever it was her loyalties clearly lay elsewhere. One of her duties was to check my calculations of the mechanics' overtime payments and I had even less confidence in her checking than in my calculations. It was overpayments I worried about. There was no risk of underpayments going undetected since any mechanic worth his salt could calculate his wages, overtime and minuscule bonus to the last halfpenny and this was before the days of pocket calculators. Top whack for a branch foreman was, I recall, about £12. 15s. at the time so most of them had a slightly aggrieved air and were prone to engage in a little private enterprise when the opportunity arose.

I also used to prepare the quotations for all the repairs whether they were for the balance in the chemist's in the High Street or the weighbridge at the toffee factory. I calculated labour and parts costs from a time and materials estimate submitted by the branch foreman and my Meticulous parts catalogue was as well thumbed as a Jehovah's Witness's Bible.

Invoicing the completed jobs was fraught with difficulty. We had standard wordings for many of the jobs and if a standard wording was used a standard charge went with it. 'Adjusting, testing and balancing' a fan scale was about £3. 5s. whilst 'thoroughly overhauling and repairing' the same scale was charged at about £6. 10s. The difference between one and t'other was sometimes no more than the supply and fitting of a couple of penny halfpenny knife edges or a tuppenny bearing. I fought an unremitting war with the chief repairs clerk about these charges. I would draft the invoices on a strict time and materials basis (with an appropriate profit loading of course, since no respectable commercial organisation could ever conceive doing anything without an appropriate profit loading). The chief repairs clerk would change these invoices to a standard wording with a fixed charge. Thus, with a few strokes of his Waterman's broad-nibbed pen he could increase the company's profit by about fifty per cent. Anyone would have thought that he had shares in Meticulous but I expect that he was just worried about his job. He had farther to fall I suppose (about £300 per annum farther, I would guess).

In later years these experiences left me with a permanent sense of unease about how the charges for servicing my car or television or gas boiler were calculated. In the end I grasped the unwritten policy of the Meticulous Weighing Machine Company which was not so much 'charge what the market can bear', but more like 'anything short of armed robbery is all right by us'. Anyway, I now understand that no one pays for the work done, one pays for the words on the invoice. Of course, the legal profession has applied this principle for years so I suppose that it must be respectable.

Gradually I adopted the mores of the company but occasionally when I felt that the standard charge was particularly outrageous, or when I just felt like living dangerously, I would revert to a time and materials basis and watch to see if I could slip it past my chief. I could tell every time that I lost; my desk faced his and I could see him checking the invoices, fingering his small black moustache as he flicked through them. When he saw one that offended his business acumen he would glower in my direction and make a few deft strokes with his Waterman's.

The senior members of staff (I just qualified under this heading) had to take it in turns to man the office on Saturday mornings. On these occasions I acted for the repairs, accounts and sales departments and had to attend to the showroom. It was a bit boring really. Well, how often have you popped out on a Saturday morning to buy a weighing machine? However, there was one Saturday morning when I actually sold a greengrocer's scale and against my better instincts I felt quite proud of this until I learned to my chagrin that the company didn't pay commission on showroom sales.

The outside representatives were the elite of the Meticulous empire. They dashed about their assigned areas, selling an incredible variety of weighing machines. There were cylinder scales and fan scales, sweet scales and tobacco scales, vegetable scales and steelyards' scales with price charts and scales for coal, scales with scoops and scales with pans, coin-freed personal scales, platform scales, weighbridges and chemical balances and baby scales with wicker baskets and many, many more.

The successful representatives won holidays in Switzerland and had their photographs in the company magazine whilst the unsuccessful ones developed a hangdog air and avoided the sales manager's office like the plague. Finally, the day would come when they were asked to hand in the keys to their Hillman Huskies and their names would be expunged from the sales charts. There was, I learned, nothing more highly valued than a salesman who could sell and nothing more surplus to requirements than a salesman who couldn't. In fact, an unsuccessful Meticulous salesman had about the same status and future as a hen that couldn't lay. They disappeared as swiftly and completely as comrades on Stalin's purge list.

As time passed I began to get quite interested in the internal workings of scales and I took what opportunities I could to slip out to the workshops at the rear of the offices to consult with the foreman about some real or mythical query on a job card. I had learned the skill of carrying a piece of paper about whilst in the Royal Air Works. If asked where you were going you produced the piece of paper and explained that you were either taking it somewhere or bringing it back from somewhere else. Pieces of paper are magic; I have never known them to fail.

Anyway, I began my regular visits to consult the foreman. After he had put me in my place, since all office workers were, in his eyes, (a) twits, (b) toffee-nosed, (c) management spies, we got on moderately well. He discovered that I was really interested in the internal workings of his beloved weighing machines and he used to explain what was involved in repairing them. He also used to tell me some totally obscene jokes and then about his vendetta with the Borough Council's Weights and Measures man.

Unfortunately, learning about the mysteries of scale repairing induced a further crisis of conscience since I realised that even on a strict time and materials basis most repairs were as fair as a crow's feathers. Mainly because the mechanics often charged for materials that hadn't been used. This was either to cover those fiddly bits that had fallen down the back of the work benches or to cover the other bits they used on little private assignments with various small traders in the town. The time element on jobs tended to get a bit distorted as well, to compensate for the time spent on innumerable cups of tea and bacon sandwiches in the Cozy Café and the occasional extended lunchtime booze-ups in the Wagon and Horses.

On one memorable day the chief repairs clerk allowed me to accompany the foreman and his team of trusty mechanics on a big job. At first I thought that the company was launching an imaginative programme of in-service training for its office staff, but, silly me, I subsequently realised that they just needed some extra unskilled labour and I was cheaper than drafting in a mechanic from another branch.

We were scheduled to dismantle a large weighbridge at a factory on the outskirts of town. It was all rather exciting. Clad in our oldest and scruffiest gear we rendezvoused at an early hour, piled into the 15 cwt van and raced off into the unknown like a band of commandos on a secret mission. It was a raw winter morning and it was snowing. When we arrived at the factory we silently contemplated the disused heap of machinery we had come to dismantle. It was very large, very rusty and shrouded in snow. We retired to a nearby café to consider our strategy.

After tea and soggy doughnuts we returned to the site and set up a gantry to lift off the heavy main plates. Someone had forgotten one of the vital bits of the gantry so the foreman took the van to collect it whilst the rest of us went off for more tea. By lunchtime we had lifted the main plates off and we then returned to the café for sausage, egg and chips and two slices washed down with more tea. After lunch we reluctantly returned to the working site. Enthusiasm was waning by this time. The day had never progressed beyond the early morning murk and it was still snowing. The open weighbridge pit was full of snow, slush and twenty years of oily gunge. Someone had to get into the pit to unbolt the main levers. I was unanimously elected. I removed four rusty bolts and most of the skin off my knuckles before I was relieved. I took some comfort from the fact that none of the others did all that much better.

Then it was time for afternoon tea, but without the niceties of cucumber sandwiches, I recall. After that, as the afternoon gloom was merging into dusk, we began to plan our retreat. We loaded all the portable bits aboard the van and surveyed the scene of our endeavours. 'Tomorrow is another day,' the foreman announced sententiously and everyone nodded wisely. Then we piled into the van and returned to base.

The chief repairs clerk greeted me on my return. 'Had a good day?' he enquired. I stood, hair dripping with melting snow, shoes covered in oily gunge, knuckles still bleeding slightly, wet clothes steaming. I was too full of tea to do much more than burp gently. Oddly enough, when I discovered that I would not be needed the next day (the heavy labour having been completed), I was distinctly miffed.

At another stage I was sent round the branch workshops on a quest for new premises; not a moment too soon, I thought. The workshop at Redhill was a case in point. It was a converted stables up an alley at the back of the High Street. Heating was by a coke stove in the middle of the floor. On the stove was a galvanised bucket full of simmering greasy water which constituted the washing facilities; there was also an outside privy which didn't flush. (An alternative use for the galvanised bucket was to provide occasional flushing facilities). God alone knows what the Health and Safety Executive would have said about it all but this was 1958 when you could die, and probably even decompose, at work without officialdom taking much notice of it.

The mechanics spent most of their time between assignments huddled round the stove which emitted some heat and a great deal of sulphurous smoke. The workshop was full of the detritus of thirty years of scale-repairing. There were dismembered weighing machines everywhere, mostly 'trade-ins' that had been deemed to be beyond repair and not even capable of being flogged off on the side by the foreman. If you wonder where old weighing machines end their days (doesn't everyone?), I have the answer.

I never did find the Redhill branch a new workshop, nor the Hastings branch either. Still, no one seemed to care; the company was relieved to save the costs and the foreman and the mechanics were aware that the chaos in which they worked obscured one or two nice little earners. The foreman at Redhill used to book a regular hour's overtime every Friday marked on his time sheet as 'tidying up' which, having seen his establishment, always made me giggle a bit.

Back at the office I resumed my role at the heart of the technological revolution. (Yes, it started earlier than you thought.) The assistant chief repairs clerk acted as a sort of intermediary between the workshop foremen and the technical department experts at the main factory. A foreman would write in on a special form: 'With regard to the coin-operating mechanism on the R101 coin freed personal weighing machine, replacement part No. SHT/723/6A does not engage with the sprocket wheel activating the variable cam.' Without understanding a word of this I would dictate a memo to the technical department paraphrasing all that. When, several weeks later, a reply was received I would dictate a memo to the foreman paraphrasing the reply: 'Technical department advise us that the sprocket wheel should be replaced by part No. CRP/723/64C.' By this time the foreman had usually become bored with the whole problem and had resolved it with a bent screwdriver and a piece of chewing gum. Why, oh why, I used to wonder, can't the foreman just phone up the technical department and save us all a lot of bother? I never dared to suggest this however, for fear that I might be found surplus to requirements.

When I had mastered the technical knowledge of my high office I began to grasp some of the subtler aspects of office relationships. Like every office I have ever worked in they were, to say the least, complex. The chief contracts clerk, who seemed a bit poofy to me, spent hours in earnest discussion with his secretary, a married lady who, rumour had it, was experiencing fertility problems. She looked pretty fertile to me, but then nature is a cruel deceiver. But I digress. The assistant chief contracts clerk had something going with one of the accounts department typists who was betrothed to the sales manager. In fact one evening over an after-work pint in the Railway Tavern the assistant chief contracts clerk told me in some detail what he had going. What the accounts department typist did in the back of his 1950 Ford Popular was quite surprising. Well, it surprised me, and the sales manager might have been a bit surprised to discover what a gymnast his fiancée was proving to be.

Then there was the pretty dark-haired girl in the post room who disappeared for a few days for what she described as a 'minor operation'. There was much nodding and winking about this but no one claimed responsibility.

Personally, I had this passion for a married typist who worked in the new sales section. She had elegant legs and a dimpling smile, a combination that made me go trembly all over. I recall that a glimpse of her stocking tops (Pretty Polly fully fashioned) once made me seriously misquote for the repair of a baby scale at the chemist's in North Street. Apart from these occasional glimpses of her suspenders we did share one illicit Saturday morning at one of those newfangled espresso coffee bars in the town centre. Her husband thought that she was out shopping whilst my fevered imagination thought all sorts of things. It was a bit poignant, a bit like *Brief Encounter* without the railway station. Unfortunately, my lusting outstripped my resolve and my resources. Where could I take her to advance our relationship, I asked myself. No car, an extremely puritanical landlady and a municipal park that would have been far too soggy even if she had been an outdoor girl, which she clearly wasn't. Ah, well, another of those might-have-beens that linger in life's wake. If only I had owned my own flat or had a Ford Popular or the self-confidence and cash to rent a room at the Crown Hotel (two star, AA approved, special terms for weekly residents and don't forget to visit the dive bar). Heigh-ho. I console myself that she probably wasn't ready for infidelity anyway, but I have continued to think about it for well over thirty years. That isn't bad going for a relationship based on a bit of hand-holding and a lot of meaningful glances – not forgetting the stocking tops, of course.

My time as a cog in the mighty Meticulous machine was running out. A combination of disenchantment with commerce, a certain sense of failure concerning the new sales section typist and a general feeling of futility and malaise was beginning to overwhelm me. What was it all about, I asked myself. Where would it all end? It was all too much and besides my library tickets had expired and Gravesend Amalgamated had been knocked out of the Cup. Decisive action was called for so I packed my expanding suitcase (still not fully expanded) and shook the dust of Gravesend from my feet for the last time. I think that I had about £42 in my Post Office account by that time so no one could suggest that the year I spent in Gravesend was without profit.

A Key Man in a Key Job

This was the Prison Service's recruiting slogan in 1959. It demonstrated a certain triteness which I should have viewed with greater suspicion. Unfortunately, however, I was a naive young man: Nothing much changes – now I am a naive old man.

It all came about when I was suffering a particular trough in my fortunes. Not for the first time, I might add. I decided to relinquish worldly things to go off to do good works. Although to be honest, the only worldly goods I had to relinquish were £42 in the Post Office, a rather precarious office job paying ten pounds a week before deductions and some clothing and personal effects scattered around my small bedsitter which, when gathered together, would just about fill two medium-sized British Home Stores suitcases.

Unfortunately I discovered that I was ill-prepared to do good works and that those organisations that operated in the sphere of do-goodery were not prepared to let me loose on their unsuspecting clientele. I decided that I should have to do my good works in some unfashionable location and the local prison sprung to mind. You must appreciate that this was before the days when a vast industry had sprung up around prison reform and before the quickest way to acquire a liberal image and an OBE was to deplore the closing of the budgie aviary in Wormwood Scrubs as a fundamental attack on human rights.

Anyway, I decided to become a key man in a key job. It

was a mistake. Not to put too fine a point on it, it was an unmitigated shambles. First of all, my offer to do good works in the Prison Service was not met with the wholehearted enthusiasm that I would have liked. My own conviction that I would be the best thing to hit the Prison Service since Elizabeth Fry was regarded with a scepticism that I found downright hurtful. Apparently my sole qualification of a medium-good School Certificate placed me in a no man's land. I was too well educated to be a prison officer, they said, and inadequately prepared for the heavy responsibilities and intellectual demands of a position in the governor grade. Governors, it seemed, needed a degree, an education at a minor public school or twenty years in the armed services (commissioned rank, of course). Was there no other way, I enquired? It transpired that it was possible to start in the uniformed ranks and then, if found suitable, to be seconded to the governors' training course. There seemed to be a suggestion, however, that if I made a success of being a prison officer this might beg questions about my suitability to be a governor. It was all very confusing but I persevered in my efforts and eventually they agreed that they would accept me for training as a prison officer.

The Prison Service recruiting programme at that time was really a little too good. It sold the idea of manly good works, achieved by a combination of example and discipline, and resulting in the conversion of wicked criminals into law-abiding, family-loving, model citizens. I was at an impressionable age (come to think of it, I always have been) and I was sure that if the Prison Commissioners said this in their recruiting pamphlet, then it must be so.

The training began with several weeks at my local prison observing and keeping notes. Everything I did and everywhere I went and everything I learned was recorded in my best handwriting in an exercise book that had to be covered in brown paper. (The authorities were very hot on this for some reason or other.) It was all checked by the principal prison officer (Training) who annotated my work with red ticks or scrawled corrections. I still have the exercise book completed in tedious detail. Did you know, for example, that for tea in Gravesend Prison on 7th June, 1959, there was one pint of tea, bread, margarine, a rock bun and a slice of pressed beef?

Apparently my progress was satisfactory because I was then sent on the ten-week residential training course for prison officers in Wetherby.

The prison officers' training course in Wetherby seemed to be designed on the basis that original thought was a breach of the Official Secrets Act and probably treasonable as well.

The first thing the authorities did when we arrived was to take photos of us in our training groups. At first we thought this was a kindly gesture to give us a memento for our photo albums but later we found all the photos were pinned up in the chief officer's room with our names underneath so that he could identify any transgressors or malcontents.

The training establishment was run like an army camp and, having only completed my national service six years before, the inanities of service life seemed reassuringly familiar. The accommodation was in Nissen huts and the main assembly room was built of corrugated asbestos which would probably cause a twitter of excitement today. Our huts were named after prisons to create a homely touch and, of course, we each had a group and a number to make it really personal. I was B12, I remember. One other gesture of cosiness was to provide each bed with a bedspread. The bedspreads had the Royal Fleet Air Arm crest embossed on them. Don't ask me why. I suppose they were going cheap and the Prison Commissioners had an eye for a bargain.

Various situations and subterfuges were devised to test our temperament and suitability. At one stage the PT instructor flew into a rage and insulted me in front of the whole class. My time at grammar school and in the RAF had prepared me well for insults but even so I was hurt because twit I might have been, but stuck up I was not. Luckily I did not react. This was assumed to mean that I had a stable temperament and good self-control. What it really meant was (a) I was too surprised and (b) I was a bit frightened of the PT instructor.

At another stage we all had to be interviewed by a psychologist. He asked me to name a recent book I had read. His suspicions were obviously aroused by the fact that I had read a book at all and my opinion on the character of Joe Lampton reinforced his view that I was a smart-arse.

We discovered the reasons for all this testing at the halfway stage in the training course. We had been warned that those who were found wanting would be weeded out during the course but no one explained what the criteria were or how we would discover our fate. Then after five weeks of training and assessment a special parade was called. Names were read out and half the course members were marched away. The remainder of us were marched into the main assembly hall. We were still not sure what was going on. Then the chief officer offered congratulations. Apparently we still had a job. We never saw the other half of the course again. They had their bags packed and were transported to the station before we emerged from the assembly hall. There was never any explanation for this curious procedure.

After this we were measured for our uniforms so we knew we were safe. The Prison Commissioners would never have gone to the expense of paying for our uniforms unless they had decided to keep us on the payroll.

To equip me for my new job I continued to be subjected to an intensive training in judo, first aid, civil defence, basketball, the prison rules and procedures and some rather vague lectures about the causes of crime by a bespectacled criminologist from a provincial university. The criminologist would present some elaborate theory about the causes of crime and then, when I was totally convinced that he had identified the root cause of the crime wave if not the meaning of life, he would demolish the theory and introduce another one. He did it rather like a small boy building sandcastles and then petulantly flattening them with his wooden spade. I was forced to the conclusion that it was easier to recognise the consequences of crime than the causes and that this probably sums up the whole field of criminology. It seemed a bit like economics; it would be a precise science if only there were no human beings to muck up all the theories.

Criminology made my head hurt. Most of the lectures we received had to be copied out into our exercise books in our best handwriting. We were not allowed to take notes but instead had to write down the lectures word for word from a duplicated script. For some reason we did not have to write out the criminology lectures. I can't say that I was sorry; they did go on a bit.

Never mind, I learned to march a group of prisoners from here to there and then from there to here and how to referee a basketball game and I learned how to remove a protesting prisoner from the dock before he told the judge too much about his parentage. They also showed us the birch and the cat which were still in favour at the time. Thankfully, we didn't have to practice using them: the judo training was painful enough.

The Prison Commissioners seemed very keen that their prison officer trainees should suffer as much pain as possible. There were scuffs and grazes from the basketball, the strained ligaments from the judo, and the aches and pains from a surfeit of PT. There were also the bumps and bruises resulting from being lowered in a stretcher from the fourth floor of an abandoned woollen mill building somewhere on the Yorkshire moors which was the climax of the civil defence training.

The Prison Service at that time was obsessed with civil defence. It seemed that it was expecting the Russkies to blow up all its prisons at any minute. I was expected to do something about this, hence the civil defence training. Recovering bodies from ruined buildings and applying splints and a shoulder slings and humping people about on stretchers filled many happy hours. I also learned to speak with great authority about roentgens. Whatever happened to roentgens? One of the principal prison officers teaching on the course was deemed to be an expert on civil defence. He had his own personal Geiger counter. According to him it all came down to roentgens. Either you were radioactive or you weren't. If you were you were done for; if you weren't you jolly soon would be. Inevitably he was nicknamed Roentgens.

There was another principal prison officer on detachment from Canterbury nick who was far too amiable to be a prison officer. Sadly, nice man though he was, he was incredibly boring. PO Cromwell could have bored a prison full of rioters into submission; perhaps that was how he got promoted. He could go on about the emergency unlocking procedure until his class became catatonic. We tended to become extremely vicious with each other in the judo class after one of his sessions.

One of the other hurdles was the civil service exam we had to pass before we could be formally appointed. Many of the course members were coalminers or builders who were not used to doing a lot of reading and writing so a certain amount of panic ensued. In the event, filling in a football coupon would have been more of an intellectual challenge so it was a bit of an anticlimax.

There were lots of other funny activities and I remember having to lecture my class on a subject of my choosing in order to demonstrate that, if necessary, I could hold the attention of a group of prisoners. I gave a lecture on my experiences of gliding in the RAF which was about the most exotic thing I could think of. I avoided mentioning that my knowledge was based on just two flights in a dual-controlled glider. It would have spoiled the romance somehow. Anyway, my fellow trainees listened attentively – probably because they wanted me to reciprocate when their turn came.

There were only four women on the course and they were generally kept in purdah. In any event, one of them was well past her prime whilst another was mountainous in build and another was the daughter of the chief officer at Winston Green. The fourth was quite comely and had been a clarinettist in the WRACs. I never discovered the reason for the career change. I took her out on our Saturday off but this innocent activity was carefully noted by the chief officer whom I saw checking our names against his photographs when we returned.

I hardly know how to tell you this and to this day I don't know whether to boast about it or apologise. The truth is I was adjudged best recruit of the Forty-Third Prison Officer Training Course at Wetherby in 1959. Make what you will of that. It certainly confirmed the authorities' suspicions that I was a smart-arse.

When my training was completed I was invited to choose the type and location of the establishment in which I would like to serve. I chose a borstal or, failing this, a detention centre where my good works could be directed at young offenders. I helpfully suggested a number of institutions in rural locations where my reformative efforts could be conducted in a healthy fresh-air environment. I was immediately posted to a large central London prison jam-packed with adult prisoners and old lags. So that is how I became a key man in a key job.

HMP Penworth Heath

After completing my training at the Prison Officers' Training School my request to do good works with young offenders in a detention centre or borstal in some leafy location was duly considered by the Prison Commissioners. They promptly posted me to a central London prison bursting with recidivists. 'That will teach the silly bugger,' seemed to be their thinking. Later on I discovered that there was a shortage of married quarters at Penworth Heath and as I was single at the time I would not clutter up the waiting list for housing.

Thus it was that I arrived at HM Prison Penworth Heath late one wet and windy evening in 1959. Yes, they told me gravely, they did have a spare bedroom which I could use for a few nights until I found some digs but it was over the officers' mess and inside the prison walls so I would have to be in by 9 p.m. when the prison locked its gates to the outside world for the night. After that, I must appreciate, the only way in was over the wall and this was not a route to be recommended since it tended to throw the night security staff into a bit of a tizzy.

In due course after a period in digs I was provided with a room in the bachelor quarters just outside the prison. There seemed to be more women than men living in the bachelor quarters and none of them seemed to be on the payroll. Despite these increased opportunities for extending one's social life, bachelor quarters did have their snags. It was at that time the custom at Penworth Heath to solve the

problem of night patrol officers who went sick at the last
minute by the chief officer raiding the bachelor quarters
and enlisting the aid of any young unsuspecting off-duty
officer who was foolish enough to have his door unlocked
and his lights on. It was therefore unwise to spend one's
time lingering in the bachelor quarters in innocent pursuits
like darning one's socks or reading Freud.

The young officers recruited for emergency night duty
were most likely to find themselves patrolling the boundary
wall since this was the most unpopular duty and gave no
opportunity for a quiet noddy in some cosy tea room in one
of the cellblocks. At this stage I must say that I doubt that
these revelations about the security arrangements will
breach the Official Secrets Act since they are more in the
nature of ancient history than official secrets. The modern
prison service is, I am sure, throbbing with technology:
closed circuit television, walkie-talkie radios and doors that
wheeze shut pneumatically at the touch of a button.

The security system that I remember was somewhat
more basic. I recall being tested on security procedures by
an earnest assistant governor. 'What would you do,' he
enquired, 'if you found a prisoner climbing the boundary
wall?'

'Try to pull him down,' I said, doing my best to be
helpful.

'Wouldn't you blow your whistle to give the alarm?' he
asked.

'I haven't been issued with one yet,' I explained. 'The
stores have run out.' It was apparently not the right answer.

But back to boundary wall patrols. They did tend to
throw one back on one's own resources. There wasn't a lot
to do but think one's thoughts. I used to make up poetry,
whistle songs and indulge in fantasies, many of which
seemed to involve Doris Day in situations which both Miss
Day and the great movie-going public might have found a

bit surprising.

So there I was, plodding round the wall, fifteen minutes per revolution, pausing only to press the button that recorded my alertness on a time clock in the chief's office. Round and round, watching the cell lights extinguished one by one as the night patrol officers in the cell blocks checked their charges. Slowly, light by light, the vast blocks slipped into darkness like clones of the *Titanic* slipping into the black sea. As the night progressed it got lonelier and colder. The only sounds were the hiss of escaping steam from the boiler house. It was my fervent hope that nothing else would be escaping on that night.

Occasionally there would be the distant rattle of a District Line train on a late night journey to Upminster. It got steadily frostier and lonelier and one began to imagine shadows and shapes moving and lurking just outside the range of the floodlights. I couldn't help thinking about Slasher Perkins (ten years for armed robbery), who had neatly felled the principal officer in A Wing with a smooth overarm swing from his chamber potty and was now said to be hell-bent on escape to avoid the consequences of his foul deed which might involve exclusion from the inter-wing table tennis tournament.

I decided to carry my truncheon up my sleeve for comfort. Not that I was in any way afraid, you understand, because everyone knows that criminals are just victims of society and only need a little understanding. It was just that when I was on boundary wall patrol I found little comfort in sociological research. Suppose Slasher Perkins was unfamiliar with that particular theory?

Liberal-minded friends who knew of my job used to ask me how a sensitive soul like me could bring myself to lock people up. I used to explain that it was because I felt a great deal safer when my charges were behind their cell doors but I think that they believed that this was just my strange sense of humour. Perhaps everyone should do a boundary wall patrol at least once in a lifetime, particularly leader writers in the *Guardian*.

Round and round I went, four revolutions to the hour from 9 p.m. to 7 a.m. with a half-hour break for supper, or was it lunch? Night duty does tend to get one somewhat confused. That seemed to make about thirty-eight circuits before I could demand my bacon and egg breakfast in the officers' mess. It was, I suppose, my small contribution to the security of the nation. However, the only public recognition I ever received was as I was coming off duty one morning when a passing lorry driver whom I had never met before leaned out of his cab and screamed, 'You bleedin' bastard!' He was, I assume, what is known in the legal fraternity as an interested party. It is surprising what you will put up with for fourteen quid a week.

What else did I think of on my rounds? I can't really remember but perhaps I dreamed of the day when I would become a governor. Before the rise in power of the branch secretary of the Prison Officers' Guild, the governor was the most important man in a prison. I only met the governor of Penworth Heath on a few memorable occasions. Once was on the day after my arrival. He was so important that he only spoke to me through an inter-mediary: 'Does this man want married quarters, Chief?'

'Do you want married quarters, Edom?'

'I'm not married, Chief.'

'He's not married, sir' This tripartite interview was quickly over. It's not surprising really. It is a very time-consuming and tiring method of communication.

As a very junior member of what the prison department charmingly described as 'the subordinate staff', I was never invited to join the select band of senior officers and hangers-on who vied to buy the governor double whiskies at the bar in the officers' club so our relationship remained somewhat distant. It was said that he once demolished a lamp-post with his car after a particularly convivial evening at his acolyte's expense but I have no evidence of that. Still, he did tend to favour the lawbreaker rather, to the extent that in one year of his reign at Penworth Heath fourteen of his charges obtained early release: thirteen of them over the wall and one of them by hanging on to the underside of a corporation dustcart as it drove out of the gates.

I once put a prisoner on report for threatening me with a severe duffing up and for a public expression of his views about my sexual proclivities and ancestry which were a trifle unjust. The governor heard the case and listened sympathetically whilst the prisoner explained with tears in his eyes that I had provoked him. I didn't think that it would help my case to explain to the governor that the thought of provoking 737 Shanks set my teeth on edge, knowing as I did that the last person to do so, in a pub in Forest Gate I believe, had ended up with a broken bottle in his face. The governor was clearly uncertain about who to believe but played safe by merely admonishing the prisoner who, whenever he saw me thereafter, leered threateningly but otherwise refrained from comment. He wasn't with us much longer anyway. A few weeks later the mildest screw in the nick picked on him. Poor Lennie Shanks, he had no alternative but to crown the screw with a cell chair. The screw was in intensive care for three weeks with a suspected skull fracture and in due course the medical authorities decided that poor Lennie was as nutty as an almond slice and sent him to Broadmoor. For all I know he may still be there, complaining, no doubt, that everyone is picking on him. By the way, our governor was promoted shortly after this but I expect that this was just a coincidence.

It was at about this time that I was having a little trouble with the chapel working party. Every Tuesday morning I was saddled with the job of taking ten prisoners to the C of

E chapel to clean it. It was impossible to keep an eye on them all in the vast, echoing, rambling building and I knew that one of them was systematically poking out the small pieces of coloured glass from the stained glass windows when I wasn't looking. I was desperate to get off that particular working party before someone in authority discovered what was going on (God, the C of E chaplain or the chief officer). I suspected one particular small, belligerent, educationally sub-normal Irish prisoner. He was a Catholic, and at one stage when my anxieties were at their worst I feared that I might become embroiled in some deep-seated religious controversy. If only I could have caught the little sod in the act, but he was ex-approved school and ex-borstal and had learned to run rings round far more vigilant supervisors than I was proving to be.

Supervising in the workshops was a task I detested. The mailbag shop was the worst because there is probably only one thing worse than sewing mailbags and that is watching other people sewing mailbags. Occasionally the prisoners had a little riot just to relieve the monotony and if they didn't the officer in charge sometimes pressed the alarm bell anyway just to get some company. There was also a wood shop where prisoners reduced railway sleepers to bundles of firewood with the help of hatchets. The expressions on their faces used to make me want to wet myself. As for the mattress shop, this was where the long-termers from D Wing used to amuse themselves. They made the mattresses with the help of long steel bodkins that they deployed like disembowelling instruments.

Morning unlocking was another trial. If I was slow the wing principal officer was not pleased. If I rushed and got the count wrong the whole prison was displeased because no one got breakfast until the morning count was correct. I usually ended up on the fours for this job, The older officers got the lower landings and the younger ones got all the stairs and were last down for breakfast. There was a rhythm to doing the count: flip the spyhole cover, rattle the bolt, check that the shape in the bed was moving; that's one, and so on until you got to the end of your side of the landing. You added your tally to that of your colleague on the other side and then shouted down the total to the principal officer: 'Eighty-one on the fours, sir.' Then you waited anxiously whilst he checked with his numbers board to see if we had got it right.

If all was well he would bellow, 'All correct. Unlock!' Perhaps they do it all by computer now, although I expect that there is still some poor sod up on the fours counting the bodies.

I recall that after one particularly boozy night in the officers' club we lost count halfway through the tally on the fours in A Wing and had to start the count again. Doing a count with a colleague half-slewed is a nerve-racking experience. In the end I locked him in an empty cell and did the count myself.

The principal officer allowed the wing redband to help him with the figures. The man was well qualified, being an accountant by profession, but since he was doing six years for embezzlement his participation did not inspire confidence in the system.

Then there was the task of supervising the recesses whilst slopping out took place. The prison reform journals often refer to the degrading experience that this presents for prisoners but you have my word, it's not much fun for the officers either. One morning I got a full potty spilled all down me, whether by design or accident, I do not know. It wouldn't have been much consolation either way. Fortunately, I was wearing my raincoat at the time.

One of the key personnel in Penworth Heath was the recess redband. He had a roving commission and was the sort of Batman of the place. He was called in whenever a sluice blocked up and threatened to turn nasty. He could unbung a blocked sluice in a trice. Sluices were always getting blocked up. Throwing a scrubbing brush down one tended to relieve the tedium for a prisoner. Bread rolls went down there too. If the cook and baker officer had an off day and the rolls were too hard at teatime the whole prison suffered from overflowing recesses the next morning.

Thank God for the redband. Mind you, it was not a sight for the squeamish. He just rolled up his sleeve and reached in up to his armpit. Very effective but not very beautiful. That went for the redband too. He tended to pong a bit by the end of the day. He used to be allowed to stay up late to watch *Perry Mason*. This was a perk that went with the job. A new officer who didn't appreciate the significance of *Perry Mason* switched it off one night and the redband worked to rule the next day and A Hall was awash with sludge. After that all the staff accepted that *Perry Mason* was inviolate. I expect that when the *Perry Mason* series finally finished urgent industrial relations negotiations took place in Penworth Heath. Happily, the redband's services were likely to be available to the prison for some time to come. The Home Secretary was probably not all that well disposed to men who separated from their wives with the help of a meat axe. Consequently an early release on licence was not anticipated.

Recesses were also the place where, by tradition, differences tended to be settled. It was always wise to walk cautiously into a recess. One morning I came upon a recess in which one prisoner was breaking a broom handle over another inmate's head. I was highly relieved that when they saw me all aggression ceased and sweeping and cleaning resumed. Prison was like that, lots of tedium and routine interspersed with sudden, violent bursts of activity that were extremely disconcerting. It did my nerves no good at all.

Prison was a mysterious world with so much for a young screw to learn. How the older screws always managed to avoid being placed on the draughty corner of C Wing exercise yard during the months of January and February, for example. Then there was the alarm bell. When it sounded the staff immediately divided into two groups: those who didn't seem to hear it and those that were already halfway to the trouble as if by sixth sense.

I have always had a special sympathy for prison officers. Being a screw is no joke, believe me. It is mostly boring, occasionally frightening and there is always some patronising sod to put you down. Mind you, the job does tend to make you a bit strange. During my probationary year the principal officer took me aside and told me that I was not asserting myself enough. Further elucidation revealed that I had to shout louder. Apparently, when I called out for a prisoner on the fours to come down for a bath, a visit or to change library books the said prisoner sometimes claimed not to have heard me. A screw who could not be assertive was no use to the Prison Service apparently. Having no other job to go to I took the hint. I developed a bellow that could be heard from one end of A Wing to the other and even made the principal officer flinch. Even to this day if I forget myself and become a bit irritable I can muster enough bellow to lift the dust in the carpets and make our cat leave home.

Several of my colleagues remain in my memory even after all these years. There was 'Boots' Mullaney always first when the alarm bell sounded and always spoiling for a punch-up. Very reprehensible no doubt but a welcome sight if you were the one who had pressed the alarm bell. Then there was Mr Reagan who every time I saw him told me how he had quelled a riot single-handed in Parkhurst in 1956. Then there was Mr Pretty. I only ever saw him up in the turret room at the top of the fourth landing in A Wing. I never saw him anywhere else. Either he lived up there or he was just an apparition. There was certainly something ghost-like about Mr Pretty. His sole subject of conversation was his retirement plans.

Then there was the specialist staff, all a bit of a mystery. There was, for example, the young lady social worker who persisted in wearing incredibly short skirts. Every time she climbed up the steep iron stairs on to the landings the whole hall was hushed as both inmates and staff tried to catch a glimpse of her knickers. I still don't know how it was that she avoided a fate that is said to be worse than death. Mind you, not having been on the receiving end of either I am not in a real position to judge.

Then there was the senior psychologist. He used to wander round the prison singing bits from Wagnerian opera. At least I think that it was Wagner but I didn't like to ask in case he didn't know that he was doing it. It was certainly a little strange and German is such an unmelodic language, isn't it?

I used to have to unlock the prisoners for evening classes. I could never understand the remarkable enthusiasm for the art appreciation class. That is until one evening when I saw the art appreciation teacher. She used to sit up on her desk displaying her elegant legs and giving her discourse on the French Impressionists. That lady did more to lift prison morale that the entire welfare department.

Then we got a new governor, an intellectual and a rising star. He had been a deputy at a borstal with a very progressive reputation and an eccentric governor who had obtained his OBE and then retired with a nervous breakdown. Our new governor had then had a spell at the staff college, undertaken some special duties at Prison Service Headquarters and had then had a spell on secondment to the prison authorities in Ngumbia. He was also well known for a highly thought-provoking article in the *Prison Times* on therapeutic communities in detention centres. The biographical note in the *Prison Times* referred to his leisure interest as a pressed flower collection. All in all, he seemed the obvious choice to be number one governor at Penworth Heath.

The fabric at Penworth Heath was causing anxiety even in those days so I shudder to think how it is faring today. Security was a nightmare. When they were repairing the dry rot in the chapel the altar ropes went missing and to my best knowledge were never found again. Everyone expected them to turn up dangling over the boundary wall but they never did. Perhaps the culprit, like some overzealous squirrel, hid them away so well that he could never find them again.

The main sewer was causing trouble as well and the works staff had to do all the work themselves for fear that if they sent a prisoner down there they would have to guard every manhole cover in London until he came up again. Then there was the boundary wall; three feet fell off a section on the west side. Repairing it was hell because the prisoners stood around looking at the ladders like greedy children looking at the sweet jar.

Then there was the problem of the still in C Wing. They brought in a police dog to sniff it out but all he found was a plate of putrefying braised steak in an empty cell on three landing. The still wasn't a serious problem but the atmosphere in C Wing did get a trifle euphoric by locking up time every night.

The calibre of prisoners in Penworth Heath was rather poor but it had its celebrities. There was the odd (and I use the term with precision) unfrocked priest, a smattering of lawyers, a doctor who had anticipated the Abortion Act by about twenty years, a couple of senior detectives and a motley band of rapists, murderers and bash and grab merchants. It gave me a rather jaundiced view of human fallibility that I have never quite been able to shake off. It certainly broadened my knowledge of the extent of sexual naughtiness to an astonishing degree. Whilst I was there a man was admitted to serve four years for, amongst other things, unlawful sexual intercourse with a Rhode Island Red. What the poor old Rhode Island Red thought about it I don't know but the prisoner had to go into the segregation block until the attitude of any animal lovers in B Wing could be assessed.

Well, that was Penworth Heath. I left the establishment and the Prison Service in 1960 having come to the conclusion that my good works were not greatly appreciated. It is not the sort of place you can drop back to visit to see how things are going and anyway I still feel a bit guilty about the stained glass windows in the chapel. Anyway, as I said, I expect that the Prison Service today is very different from how I remember it.

Courts of Justice

In 1995 I gave up the criminal justice business. I had been in the trade for something over thirty-six years so it was time enough. A major part of those years had been spent in and around the criminal courts. Whenever I went into a court I was always reminded of *Alice in Wonderland*. I suppose that it must have been the first observations about a court that I ever read: 'Alice had never been in a court of justice before, but she had read about them in books and she was quite pleased to find that she knew the name of nearly everything there...' Mind you, I have to say that nothing I read in *Alice in Wonderland* seems in any way remarkable after the last thirty-six years.

My first experience of court was to be assistant dock officer at Gravesend Quarter Sessions in about 1959. The assistant dock officer escorted the prisoner up into the dock from the cells below and then down again afterwards but I only gained the briefest glimpses of the goings-on in court. It all seemed to be oak panelling and a sea of curly wigs. Personally I was a bit nervous about lingering in the dock in case the judge got confused and sentenced me to four years' corrective training. At this stage in my criminal justice career there were still all sorts of now long-forgotten sentences. You could get sentenced to preventive detention if your record was bad enough. Some old lags had been known to get twelve years for nicking a pound of sausages. Even worse, they still dispensed the cat and the birch and if you were really naughty you could still get seriously hanged as well.

Sometimes I had to escort young prisoners from Penworth Heath to the Kensington Quarter Sessions. There was a judge there who sent all young offenders to borstal. Rumour had it that he didn't know there were any other sentences. When the young men knew they were appearing before Judge Reginald Certain they wrote to tell their relatives of their sentence the day before they appeared in court. Judge Certain distributed borstal sentences like pamphlets for double glazing.

During the year and a bit that I worked for the Prison Service I used to do quite a few court escorts but it wasn't until I joined the probation service that I became heavily embroiled with the court processes.

My earliest experiences as a probation officer were at the Walworth Juvenile Court. It was an era when nearly every young man had a motor scooter. In Walworth it was usually someone else's. The lay justices at Walworth Juvenile Court were carefully selected for their special knowledge and understanding of young people. The senior lady magistrate whose husband was big in gin distilling automatically remanded all the scooter pinchers in custody for three weeks and then put them on probation for two years. She scarcely listened to the evidence and just wanted to get on with the sentencing.

Mr Longport was headmaster of the local grammar school. He was prone to lecture – at great length. He didn't mind who he lectured but the defendants were usually the most convenient. The defendants bore him no ill will. His sentences were lenient even if his lectures were long. Mr Longport never used one syllable when he could find a word with three or four. Most of the lads didn't even know what he was going on about. Quite a lot of them seldom went to school at all, let alone a grammar school – not unless the school board man was having one of his purges.

They just stood there looking baffled whilst he went on: 'reprehensible behaviour, incomprehensible that you should subject your parents to this ignominy and distress... deserving of condign punishment... I trust that you are contrite... never let there be any repetition...' and so on until he let them go home.

When they got outside the court they would invariably turn to whoever was nearest and enquire with a bewildered expression, 'Wot wos the old geezer going on abaht, mister?'

I also worked at another juvenile court for quite a while. This was the Tooting Juvenile Court which sat every Thursday in the Lighthouse Mission Hall near Tooting Bec. The Mission Hall was a strange rambling building. The main hall which served as a waiting area was divided by a whole row of cubicles each with just a curtain across it. Here, apparently, the various Bible classes met on a Sunday. On Thursdays, however, the cubicles were assigned to the various departments that served the court. The largest curtained area acted as the custody room. It was a miracle that youngsters seldom escaped from this area. A miracle, that is, until you saw the police custody officer. Tiny was six foot six if he was an inch and that was without his size twelve regulation boots on. The most recalcitrant youth took one look at Tiny and decided that he would delay his bid for freedom until another more propitious occasion.

The Tooting Juvenile Court was staffed by a strange band of delightful people. The clerk who drafted the probation orders and produced all the other documentation was an all-in wrestler in his spare time. He was short and squat and had muscles where no one had a right to have muscles. When he pounded his Remington typewriter with his hamlike hands he made it sound like the anti-aircraft guns on Hayes Common in 1941.

The representative from the London County Council

children's department was a ballroom dancer in his leisure hours. He dressed immaculately and wore patent leather shoes and had his hair slicked down and with a parting as straight as a ruler. When he stepped forward to present a school report to the magistrates he sort of glided and I was always waiting for him to do a double reverse turn or something.

Two of the older lady probation officers wore hats to come to court. There was an intense rivalry between them and they hadn't spoken to each other directly for years. Sometimes I was caught to act as an intermediary. 'Mr Edom, will you tell Mrs Blythe that her case was called into court five minutes ago and the magistrates are waiting for her report.' Several of the lady probation officers who worked in the juvenile courts were ladies of distinction and means and did their good works without thought of reward. Chance would have been a fine thing. There was the Honourable Vera Framlingham-Woods and there was Lady Vanessa Pucey. The line up at the probation officers' table often sounded more distinguished than that on the bench, which miffed the magistrates no end.

Although the magistrates were supposed to have a special knowledge of children and their problems most of the chairmen were old and middle-class. There was Mr Weaver, for instance, who had written a book about juvenile delinquency and was hoping for an OBE. He was quite severe with the young male delinquents but if a defendant was young, female and pretty that was a very different matter. He liked to make grants from the poor box for such cases and sometimes almost forgot to sentence them. 'I am sure that if you had a pretty new dress you wouldn't steal again, would you, my dear?'

Then there was Mr Morton who was distinctly aged and tended to get very erratic in the afternoons, especially if the magistrates had shared a bottle of wine at lunchtime. He once gave a little delinquent a severe wigging for having an IQ of eighty-three. 'You'll have to try harder than that,' he chided.

Perhaps the most startling of all the characters who attended the Tooting Juvenile Court was the lady police surgeon. In those days there was a procedure for dealing with naughty girls who ran away from home. Most of their misdemeanours seemed to be conducted in a recumbent position and when apprehended they were then deemed to be in need of care and protection. The lady police surgeon, who would have given Himmler a bit of a scare, was built like a water buffalo and was about as feminine as Rod Steiger. She was very happy in her work. She would describe in great detail and with lip-smacking relish how she had examined some blushing fifteen year old girl. The magistrates would listen spellbound with only an occasional tut-tut to break the silence.

Arnold Granville-Creak was the senior stipendiary magistrate at Streatham Magistrate's Court in 1963. Or was it 1965? Time passes so quickly when you are having fun. Granville-Creak was a terror. One had to acknowledge that he was consistent in his sentencing but that was his only virtue. His favourite target was any young pink-faced constable presenting his first case. Granville-Creak delighted in picking the prosecution to pieces, throwing the case out, ordering costs against the police or complaining to the police inspector in charge of the court.

The police had their own way of coping as the police are prone to do. They introduced a special tie which was awarded to every police officer thrown out of Granville-Creak's court. After three months they ran out of ties. They are probably collector's items today. The police also appointed a near brain-dead police inspector to represent them in Granville-Creak's court. This inspector suffered all the insults dished out without a flicker of an eyelash. That man was so thick that he wouldn't have noticed if a Black Maria had hit him up the bum. The fact that he didn't seem to notice when he was being insulted used to drive Granville-Creak into paroxysms of rage.

Granville-Creak was even-handed with his abuse. He quite liked picking on young barristers and was always complaining if the usher was slow in administering the oath. Things got very tricky when there was a Chinaman in court, and no one dared to be an atheist. He also had an ongoing feud with the gaoler who was expected to control the lighting in the court. This was never to Granville-Creak's liking. It was either too dark or too light. Usually he only allowed the light over his bench to be switched on. The rest of us had to sit in the gloom. If the gaoler switched the wrong light on or off Granville-Creak flew into a rage. The gaoler became so neurotic that he had every light switch labelled in large block capitals so that he could read them in the gloom.

When lost for anyone else to be nasty to, Granville-Creak would turn on the duty probation officer. On Wednesdays that was me. With ominous courtesy he would put a case back and ask the probation officer to enquire into the defendant's circumstances. Half an hour later the probation officer was expected to return and give a verbal report on his findings. Having heard the verbal report Granville-Creak would ask supplementary questions. The unspoken object of this game was for him to succeed in asking a question that the probation officer didn't know the answer to. 'And how much is his electricity bill, Mr Edom?' If the answer was not forthcoming he would throw his pencil across the court and stand the case down again. 'Until you do your job properly.' If he was in a particularly nasty mood he would call for the senior probation officer. She would scuttle into court and start apologising even before she knew what the problem was.

Another technique of Granville-Creak's was to mumble. If you tried to guess what he had said he was furious when it eventually became apparent that you were answering the wrong question. If, on the other hand, you asked him to repeat himself he threw a tantrum.

Some of my colleagues were even more intimidated by Granville-Creak than I was. During one particularly traumatic court duty Ron Birmingham went and hid in the broom cupboard and refused to come out until it was all over.

There was only one probation officer who could really cope with Granville-Creak and that was Harry McNurdle. I shared Wednesday court duties with him. Harry had a beer belly so big that he could scarcely squeeze in and out of the little pew assigned to the probation officers. But when he finally managed to stand up Granville-Creak actually stopped ranting and listened. This was magic. The more so because Harry had such a broad Scottish accent that no one really understood much of what he said. A few words from Harry and Granville-Creak would make a probation order and thank Harry for his excellent report. Since the report usually began, 'Och, well your worship,' and then lapsed into unintelligible Scottish interspersed with a few recognisable phrases: 'in need of a wee bit of guidance... the laddie regrets breaking open the gas meter... if your worship was minded to take a certain course...' It was magic. I just wished I could learn how to do it.

Mind you, Harry had his limitations. At one o'clock he went over the road to the Wig and Crown and stayed there until closing time. Then he returned to his office, locked himself in and went to sleep. Harry was a kind and generous colleague who protected me from much of Granville-Creak's nonsense but after one o'clock that was different. I was on my own.

The other stipendiary magistrate at Streatham

Magistrates' Court was Sir Geoffrey Hammersmith. He was somewhat pallid in comparison with Granville-Creak although he too had his funny little ways. For starters he had a great sympathy with the mentally disordered. Not that the sympathy was always appreciated. Crafty barristers used to play on his sympathy on behalf of their clients by emphasising their clients' little peccadilloes. Sometimes this could go horribly wrong as Sir Geoffrey, rising to the bait, would remand the luckless defendant to Wormwood Scrubs for medical and mental reports. There were occasions when it might have been better to have been represented as a bit naughty rather than seriously nutty.

Sir Geoffrey could get very impatient. Those who sat in his court frequently could tell the signs. First there was the drumming of his fingers on his desk and then a champing noise rather like the noise my pussy cat makes when being provoked by a blackbird.

Then I worked at Peckham Magistrates' Court for a while. By contrast with Streatham which was modern and impersonal, Peckham Magistrates' Court was quite intimate. It was early Victorian and was designed like a church. The floor of the courtroom was covered with lead which, it was said, was to muffle the sounds of the hobnailed boots. Well, I suppose that it was as good a reason as any for having lead instead of lino as a floor covering. One of the magistrates at Peckham was Mr Easy. He was an old Etonian. He used to keep his *Times* on his lap concealed by the bench and if a case got boring he would start to do the crossword puzzle. I suppose that is the advantage of a good education.

Then there was the Detention Centre King. Mr Blunt was a stipendiary who normally worked at Waterloo Bridge Magistrates' Court. However, he sometimes lent a hand at Peckham when Mr Easy was on his holidays or was having one of his frequent attacks of the vapours. Mr Blunt had an unflinching belief in the efficacy of detention centres for young men. When he came to do relief duties at Peckham chaos ensued. Unlike Mr Easy who never did anything controversial except wear his old Etonian tie, Mr Blunt made waves. Any young man who got in the dock was on his way to a detention centre before you could say, '1948 Criminal Justice Act'. If you so much as just looked a bit naughty you could get three months. Panic always set in when it was known that Mr Blunt was sitting. Solicitors made last minute requests for adjournments and medical certificates were littered about like confetti. Even the gaoler looked distinctly uneasy and he was a firm believer in the efficacy of castration for sex offenders.

The other regular stipendiary at Peckham was Mr Ready. He was at his best in dealing with fine defaulters. He would listen patiently to how impossible it was for some unfortunate to pay his fine. There were sick children and a heavily pregnant wife and threats of eviction and urgent bills for medicines and not a bite of food in the house and it was clearly impossible to pay off the fine at more than half a crown a week. When the tale of woe finally ended Mr Ready would put his head in his hands and say sadly and wearily, 'Oh, dear. I suppose the only way to help you will be to send you to prison in default. That will clear the fines for you.' It was miraculous how often the defendant remembered a sudden windfall – an unexpected legacy or a win on the one thirty at Sandown Park or something equally providential.

In addition to the stipendiary magistrates in the London Magistrates' Courts there were also lay justices who received no pay and did the job for fun. Always, I suggest, view with circumspection anyone who offers to exercise authority for nothing. The lay justices in London tended to be famous people, mostly rich, with time on their hands who wanted even more fame and distinction. I was astounded at how many important people I met who were lay justices. Wives of politicians, university lecturers, people who had sat on governmental committees or who had written erudite papers or rich business men in the market for OBEs. Why they wanted to sit in judgement on their fellow beings heaven alone knows. What really impressed me, however, was how such clever, famous people could make such crappy decisions. It does make you think a bit about the ruling classes. If it doesn't then perhaps it should.

Saturday afternoon court duties at Peckham Magistrates' Court were the worst of all. Saturday afternoons were reserved for the hearing of neighbours' disputes. Usually each summons had been met with a cross-summons and the neighbours would arrive at court with family and friends and often with solicitors as well. By four o'clock the magistrate was usually getting pretty bored. His favourite device was to try to get the case adjourned for the probation officer to mediate. If he could persuade the warring parties to accept such a proposal he could shove off home to tea and crumpets and leave me surrounded by the warring parties.

When I was the senior probation officer at Plumstead Magistrates' Court I used to deal with the domestic court. When both parties to a domestic dispute were represented this could be rather tedious. Sometimes, however, if the parties were represented by Mr Twiddle and Mr Dudley things could be entertaining. Poor Mr Twiddle had a stammer and a bad facial twitch. Why he chose to earn his living as an advocate I really cannot understand. Mr Dudley evoked less sympathy. His general manner was syrupy but he never prepared his cases very well. He tended to make things up as he went along and if this didn't work he would bluster and shout. If his client dared to point out that Mr Dudley had got something wrong he could get very nasty indeed. Sometimes it was hard to tell whose side he was on.

The combination of Twiddle and Dudley was as near Abbot and Costello as you could reasonably expect.

The deputy chief clerk at Plumstead Magistrates' Court was positively feudal in his approach to those who appeared in the court. He had a pompous, lordly manner, used words of inordinate length and legal phrases that made even the stipendiary magistrate blink. If anyone was foolhardy enough to say they didn't understand he would cup his hands to form a megaphone and repeat the words several decibels higher and very, very slowly as if speaking to a deaf and imbecilic foreigner at four hundred paces. If he was speaking to the defendant then he got even nastier. I think that he had been to public school as well. He obviously felt confident that he knew how to deal with the lower orders.

Of course, I had to visit lots of other courts. I attended Cheam Court on one occasion. I was due to present a report in the adult court. On one side of the waiting area was a door marked 'Magistrates' Court'. In there were all the usual accoutrements: oak panelling, magistrates' dais, little pews for counsel, dock with a rail round it and so on. On the other side of the waiting area was a door marked 'Juvenile Court'. I couldn't resist looking in there. Everything was exactly the same as the adult court except that it was in two-thirds scale. That really was like *Alice in Wonderland*. I kept having peeks back in there in case it had grown larger or smaller when I wasn't looking.

Whilst courts are prone to look intimidating and the majesty of the law is presumed to be totally objective I wouldn't believe it if I were you. Some defendants certainly learned how to play the system. Stanley Gore was one of them. He was what used to be described as an old lag. Today I suppose he might be called morally disadvantaged. Anyway, after about his tenth prison sentence he had cracked the system. For a while, for what seemed a very, very long while, Stanley was on probation to me. Not that he stopped offending. It was just that courts kept putting him back on probation. Then one time I went to court with him and saw him perform. After that I understood the secret of his success. He could do a better plea in mitigation than any barrister I ever saw. The judge began in threatening tones, 'Is there *anything* you wish to say before I sentence you, Gore?'

Then Stanley started. 'My lord, I want to apologise, not so much for what I have done as for what I am. Life has shaped me in ways not of my choosing but I realise that I have to accept responsibility for my misdeeds and that I deserve severe punishment.' He then launched into a long story of how he never knew his father and how he was taken into care at the age of five because his mother was on the streets and how he had lived in an orphanage where he was beaten weekly and had only porridge for breakfast. He had, he said, lived in institutions all his life. 'I have never known the comfort and security of a real 'ome, My lord,' he explained. His presentation went on for quite a long time. Some of it was true. By the time he was finished there was not a dry eye in the house. Except mine. The judge positively begged me to take him back on probation.

Judges were like that sometimes. Judge Henry Elders was like that all the time. He was a very nice man, no doubt about it – far too nice to be a judge. He could have given Saint Peter lessons or been an adviser for Mothercare. One of my clients who had just broken his fourth probation order was lucky enough to appear before our Henry. I was called to the South London Quarter Sessions to report on my probationer. Henry was quite cross with me. It was, it seemed, all my fault that Fred had been shopbreaking again. Mind you, Fred said that it was all a misunderstanding and that he had only been in the back yard of Woolworth's at one thirty in the morning to have a slash. I noted, however, that he was a bit vague about why the police had found him halfway down the drainpipe with twelve boxes of Black Magic stuffed up his donkey jacket. Still, enough of the detail. The judge wanted me to try again. He felt sure I could do better. It became clear that he expected me to make an impassioned plea for more probation for Fred. My performance was not convincing. Still, it was enough for the judge. Fred was on probation again before I could finish speaking. I don't think that Judge Henry ever sent anyone to prison. With Henry in charge Guy Fawkes would have got a conditional discharge.

I never liked appearing at the South London Quarter Sessions. The courtroom was designed to intimidate and it certainly intimidated me. The witness box was like the pulpit in St Paul's Cathedral. You climbed up so many stairs to get into it that it made the muscles in the back of your legs ache. Once up there you looked across a chasm to speak to the judge who sat on a high-backed seat beneath a canopy big enough to shelter most of the Chelsea Supporters' Club on a cup tie day. I used to get stage fright in that witness box – that and vertigo.

Of course, everyone has their favourite court story. The Central London court of Bleak Street was well known for its eccentrics so it had more than its share of such stories. At one stage in my career I was offered the senior probation officer's post at Bleak Street. I knew then that my career was past its best. In those days you only received an offer like that when the authorities had deduced that you were a bit of an oddity. Anyway, one of the probation officers at Bleak Street was a great pipe smoker. Called into court unexpectedly one day, he hurriedly thrust his pipe into his pocket. In the witness box he became aware that he was smouldering. 'Sir,' he reported to the magistrate, 'I fear that I am on fire.'

'In that case we will adjourn whilst you go and put yourself out,' was the considerate response.

I try to have as little to do with courts as possible these days. After thirty-six years I feel in need of a rest. It is not that I think that courts are any sillier than any of our other institutions. In fact, my theory is that the courts just reflect what is wrong with most human endeavours. That is, they tend to take themselves rather too seriously and to look rather more impressive than they really are. If you don't believe me take a closer look at your own chosen sphere of activity. I doubt if it will stand up to close scrutiny.

Stonepark Hostel

I once worked as an assistant warden in a probation hostel
in Rugby. That was in 1963. It was only for a very short
period, thank goodness. I don't think that staff, residents or
I could have coped with a longer tenure of office.

I was in one of my earnest doing good works phases at
the time so my efforts were on a voluntary unpaid basis. I
did receive free bed and board although this was a mixed
blessing since the eating habits of the residents meant that
meal times had the ambience of feeding time in a vulture
aviary.

The hostel office had one of those funny notices: 'You
don't have to be mad to work here but it certainly helps.' At
first I thought that it was a joke.

Working for a living was so unusual for our residents
that when they had completed a day's work they all
expected a full debriefing. Air crew returning from a raid
on Düsseldorf probably got less attention than one of our
lot returning from a full day's work in the local scrapyard. I
have heard more stories about unkind foremen and
uncaring employers than anyone I know.

Then there was first aid. We had a first aid kit in the
office. One of the lads returned from work with a small cut
on his finger. Anxious to establish my helping role I
carefully washed the tiny wound and put a plaster on it.
After that there was a queue for first aid. Everyone needed
their share of attention and sticking plaster.

Some of the residents never got the hang of working at

all. Even if we found them a job they tended to wander off absent-mindedly and spend the day in the park. Often it was not until pay day when they were called upon to pay for their bed and board that the truth emerged, although even then the long involved stories about lost pay packets or working a week in hand had to be admired for their sheer inventiveness.

Convincing excuses for not going to work at all were also highly imaginative: lack of bus fare money, loss of memory, severe back pain that came and went according to the day of the week, raging toothache on wet Monday mornings that was in remission by the time a dentist's appointment had been arranged, to name but a few.

One of the worst bits about working in a hostel was the early rising. We had a rota for staff to get up early to get the residents breakfasted and off to work. On one occasion when it was my turn to do the early turn I overslept. Of course, the residents were delighted. There was nothing they liked better than an excuse to avoid going to work, especially if they could blame someone in authority. When I awoke and saw the time I went into panic mode. I hurled sleepy residents out of bed, shovelled cornflakes down them and then drove them all to their places of work. Fortunately, most of them who had jobs either worked in the scrapyard or the pickle factory so I was able to deliver them in job lots.

The cook did not come on duty until a civilised hour so the staff member on early turn had to prepare breakfast. Fortunately, it all came out of a cornflakes packet and a frying pan so the culinary skills required were not great. So long as I didn't let the baked beans boil dry, preparing breakfast was the least of my troubles.

One of the infuriating things about residential work is that living with about twenty fractious teenagers is nerve scraping and exhausting. It starts at about 6 a.m. and by the time everyone is coaxed out of bed, fed and watered and despatched to work, or at least to look for work, the day already seems to have gone on for far too long. Somewhere about eleven o'clock whilst drinking a cup of recuperative coffee and contemplating a career change, a visiting probation officer would inevitably arrive and quip about what an easy life residential workers had. 'Nothing to do all day but sit about drinking coffee.'

I was not entrusted to undertake anything other than the most menial tasks within the hostel office. The most frightening bit of the office routine was the accounts. The hostel received Home Office funding and was therefore required to apply a strict formula for recording the residents' earnings and how much they had to pay for their keep. It was worse than filling in a tax return. The combination of Home Office bureaucracy and our residents' deviousness meant that keeping the books was a nightmare, one that happily I was able to avoid.

I was allowed to contribute to the hostel log which recorded the crucial events of the day: 'RE spoke to MH about excessive use of milk on cereal' or 'RE found BK playing his Beatles records at full volume when he should have been vacuuming the hall.'

I quickly discovered that an assistant hostel warden has to be a jack of all trades. I mended broken beds, played table tennis or draughts as required, supervised the potato-peeling machine, listened to the residents' highly embroidered accounts of their plans for the future and the deficiencies of the criminal justice system and sought recruits to tidy the garden. Sometimes we took the residents on outings, an exercise fraught with difficulty as we tried to ensure that the local populace was not raped, pillaged or generally mucked about. On one occasion I was deputed to assist in a canoeing exercise for the residents. The outing was not a success but luckily the river was not all that deep. But have you ever tried to dry out a dozen wet and sulky teenagers?

The evenings tended to be the worst time for crises at the hostel. The residents were allowed to go down to the town for the evening, although theoretically at least, they were supposed to be back by 10 p.m. In reality if they returned by that time it was usually because they were being pursued by some of the locals who had taken exception to having their bikes, drinks or girls pinched and were set on exacting revenge and/or seeking compensation.

Sometimes the police had to be called and they always extracted the maximum satisfaction from the fact that those probation people had their knickers in a twist yet again. Sometimes the police came uninvited, usually with a search warrant. The ingenuity of our residents in acquiring things and hiding them never ceased to astonish me. The only blessing was that all this was taking place in 1963 before our customers had become familiar with the benefits of amphetamines, let alone the pleasures of crack cocaine and ecstasy. Nonetheless, you would have been surprised what our lot could do on ten pints of Rugby Breweries high octane best bitter.

Once the residents were finally packed away in their dormitories the staff on duty would try to calm shattered nerves with a large whisky and all four movements of Beethoven's *Pastoral Symphony*. My own preference would have been to reverse the formula.

After my time at the hostel I wrote a eulogistic article about the regime. I suspect it was probably as a penance for the disorder I left behind me. Mind you, I felt rather pleased with my article which was full of impressive-sounding phrases. I wittered on about the benefits of permissive environments, the importance of countering the effects of institutionalisation and the importance of socialising influences. The organisation which ran the hostel featured the article in their annual report. I felt very proud that my views were given such prominence and was too naive to appreciate the fact that articles will always get published if they say the right things and are sufficiently adulatory. It must have gone right over the top because they put it in the following year's annual report as well.

Escorts

I have undertaken more than a few escorts in my time. Well, far too many actually. It started in the Prison Service where many of its customers were deemed unlikely to reach their correct destination without a little guidance, preferably using handcuffs. The first escort I undertook was to assist in the transport of twenty reluctant prisoners from Gravesend Prison to Wandsworth in about 1959. Now Wandsworth wasn't a popular prison at the time (thinks… has it ever been?), so the prisoners were not a happy band and looked as if they might wish to rearrange the itinerary. It was a relief when the gates of Wandsworth slammed shut behind us. Well, it was a relief to me anyway.

At a later date I was assigned to HM Prison Penworth Heath where escorts were an everyday occurrence. Unfortunately, the junior screws like me were assigned the local escorts whilst the older screws undertook the longer-distance ones in the hope of knocking up a bit of overtime. As a junior screw I usually ended up travelling to exciting places like the Lewisham eye-fitting centre or the local clinic for infectious diseases whilst my prisoners entertained me with details of their disorders.

The only time I was assigned a long-distance escort I had a bit of a shock. Whilst our prisoner was locked safely in the court cells my colleague and I adjourned to a pub for refreshment. We sat at the bar drinking our pints and then to my surprise my large butch colleague place his hand on my knee and told me he was in love with me. It quite put me off my pork pie.

I often escorted prisoners to the local hospital for X-rays or treatment and one occasion I escorted one of the great train robbers. He was a formidable man, too formidable for me to mention his name. Mind you, at the time he hadn't actually got around to doing the great train robbery and was doing time for some other little indiscretion.

On another occasion I escorted a prisoner to the Royal Courts of Justice. The prisoner wanted a pee and a uniformed attendant showed me where the toilet was. When the prisoner emerged from the toilet after a long and anxiety-provoking delay the attendant cheerfully told me that Alfie Hinds had once escaped through the window of that very loo. I thought that it would have been more helpful if he had told me this before I let my prisoner go in there but I think he had been hoping for a bit of excitement to brighten his day.

I once escorted a young man to a probation hostel in Manchester. At Manchester Central Station we paused for lunch. My client was so agitated that he used the sugar shaker on his cod and chips and then to cover his confusion insisted on eating it. He assured me that it tasted quite nice but he didn't half pull a funny face.

I have escorted a large number of young men to probation hostels. The experiences were usually surprisingly similar. I would travel for hours to some distant region, very conscious of the saying that it is better to travel hopefully than to arrive. I would gently humour my probationer by explaining what delightful places hostels were. I was always afraid that one of my charges would panic and leg it en route. Turning up at a hostel minus the customer was generally regarded as a breach of etiquette. Anyway, invariably when we arrived at a hostel the warden would leave me and my client standing in front of his desk whilst he launched into a long homily and a recitation of the hostel rules and the dire consequences of breaking them. The warden always seemed unaware that what we really needed was a recuperative cup of tea and a Wills Woodbine. The warden used to frighten me nearly as much as he did my client but at least I could go home afterwards.

One of my lady colleagues who seemed to have taken a fancy to me once asked me to accompany her when she escorted a small boy from one children's home to another. The little boy's sole possessions appeared to be a Dinky Toy and a comic. He placed his hand in mine as if one adult was as good as any other and let me lead him to the car. The poignancy of this was overshadowed by my anxiety about my lady colleague who I suspected had designs on me. She was distinctly overdressed for an escort duty and wore a red hat. I felt a bit uneasy in the car. Well, you know what they say about red hats.

Another lady probation officer invited me to assist in an escort to a hostel in Margate. This was another anxiety-provoking event since my lady colleague drove like Mike Hawthorn. Older readers will be aware that Mike Hawthorn went to that great racetrack in the sky after trying to drive up a tree on the Guildford bypass.

My regular readers will know about the time I escorted William Harmful to a psychiatric hospital in Hemel Hempstead. William had what is nowadays described as a personality disorder. Since I didn't have a car at the time we had to travel on a Green Line bus. My client was in a particularly boastful and boisterous mood. Well, downright potty actually. The other passengers sat as far away from us as possible and the bus driver's steering became very erratic. It seemed a very long way to Hemel Hempstead.

My regular readers will also know of the client I took to hospital because he was suffering from DT's. His voices came with us but happily the large green creatures did not arrive until he was safely tucked up in bed.

Then there was a young man who truanted from school. I counselled him earnestly about his school phobia and eventually he agreed to attend if I took him for his first day. All the way on the bus he nervously picked at the quick of his fingers until they bled. He made me feel as if I was taking him to the vet to be seen to. We met the headmistress, a well intentioned lady, who talked to him in a kindly manner – well, in as kindly a manner as any schoolteacher can manage. Then my client was escorted to his class. I returned to my office with the warm feeling of a job well done. When I reached my office a message was waiting for me. My client had asked to be excused and had gone walkabout.

I also escorted an old lag to a hostel in Swindon. The old lag who, on the few occasions when he was not in prison, drove a lorry for a living, gave me unsolicited advice on how to improve my driving all the way down the A4. Since the lorries he drove were invariably of the kind that things fell off the back of I did not take kindly to his advice. I had only found him a hostel place on the firm instructions of a magistrate who was heavily into good works and like all magistrates was convinced that he knew best. I tried to tell him that the old lag wouldn't last two days at the hostel but my views were disregarded. In the event I was wrong. He absconded after one day.

Of course, there were other escorts, to and from hospitals, hostels, children's homes, courts and miscellaneous other places but at the end of all my escorting experiences I was driven to the conclusion that if someone couldn't get somewhere without my assistance they were probably best left where they were.

Home Visiting

During the course of a long and traumatic career as a probation officer I have done my share of home visiting. From high rises in Camberwell Green to low rises in Plumstead, I have done my bit. I used to feel that there was a deep-seated conspiracy to test my home visiting stamina since all the problem and/or delinquent families I had to visit always seemed to be located in the most inaccessible places. I would arrive at Victoria and Albert Buildings and know instinctively that number sixty just had to be on the top floor and at the end of the balcony; it always was. Whether this was deliberate housing policy or merely a manifestation of my acute paranoia I have never been able to tell but whenever a client was assigned to me it was always a no lift, top floor, end of the balcony job. Even when my clients were rehoused in modern blocks, they were still the sort of blocks where the lift was permanently out of order or, at best, where the lift served as a supplementary public urinal and the lights didn't work.

From bitter experience I slowly learned the conventions of home visiting. Never, for example, visit on a Friday night, pay night; everyone was out or drunk or both. Never visit during *Coronation Street*, *What's My Line*, *Double Your Money* or *Opportunity Knocks*. (What chance had I of competing with a precocious twelve year old playing 'Oh, Mine Papa' on a slightly flat trumpet?) Never visit before noon. This was considered to be hitting below the belt by my clients and could easily disclose hangovers, ill-concealed absconders from approved schools and lodgers in the wrong bedrooms. Monday mornings, I discovered, were especially difficult, with wet washing dripping from every balcony which played havoc with my trubenised collar.

Finally, never, ever visit on Guy Fawkes night. I remember in my early earnest social work days, determined to do good works at all costs, I visited a square of local authority tenements off the Wandsworth Road on 5th November. It was like a scene from Dante's Inferno. They were firing sixpenny rockets horizontally across the first-floor balconies at each other. When one of those dipped slightly it had the potential to scalp and incinerate any unwary probation officer who ventured into the square. In addition, I discovered, there was also the particularly malevolent little sod who would try to see you off with a carefully lobbed tuppenny thunderflash up your duffel coat.

On that memorable night I did my duty and completed my calls but after that my nerves were completely gone – positively shattered in fact. I never visited on 5th November again. If I had been in the army my nervous twitch would have marked me down as someone who was clearly lacking in moral fibre. Still, I doubt if Dunkirk was all that much worse.

I have drunk my share of tea sweetened with condensed milk out of a congealing tin and proffered in cracked, saucerless cups that set your teeth on edge. I have also sat on innumerable greasy sofas desperately resisting an almost overwhelming urge to scratch. I have hammered on innumerable doors that remained defiantly closed despite the whispered conversations going on behind them ('It's that silly sod from the court again') and I have been kept waiting in the cold whilst seemingly rabid Alsatians were chained up in broom cupboards. 'Just a precaution, Mr Edom, he only bites people he doesn't like.'

Dogs are a particular cross for visiting probation officers to bear. My heart would always sink when I rang, buzzed, hammered or kicked on some unfamiliar door and was answered by bark, growl, whine or howl or, more ominously, by the thump of an enraged canine hurling itself against the door like something out of *The Hound of the Baskervilles*.

Strangely enough, my worst encounter was with a chihuahua. He focused his eyes on me from the moment I entered the room. There I was, holding court before the whole family, explaining why little Freddy really must stop nicking stuff from Woolworth's, when this personality-disordered chihuahua strolled across the room, drew itself up to its full height and sank its needle-sharp teeth into my ankle. I would have kicked it but for the fact that the whole family was falling about in merriment and I felt that it would have been churlish to spoil their fun. More to the point, I felt it best not to provoke the little Mexican monstrosity. It was a case of turning the other cheek, or ankle, as it were.

I remember visiting a shabby house in a black ghetto in Balham back in about 1965. (We didn't actually say 'black' in those days. It was considered impolite; we used the word 'coloured' instead. These days using a word like that could get you seriously fired. Such is the changing fashion in the race relations industry. Race relations always makes my head hurt.) Anyway, my knock on this particular door was answered by a little black girl in pigtails. Her eyes widened in horror at my appearance and she fled into the back of the house shouting, 'Mummy, Mummy, there's a white man at the door!' So much for integration.

I also remember visiting a block of flats in Clapham where a goodly part of the juvenile population were under my supervision. This was about 1961 when I was new at the business and deeply committed to the social worker's sacred code of confidentiality. How did I make six assorted home visits without everyone in the square knowing exactly who was under probation service scrutiny? It was a summer evening and the residents leaned on their balconies and conversed and observed. I needn't have worried; it was clearly a status symbol to be under official supervision in Herbert Morrison Square and all my young clients, and a few who weren't, turned out into the square to greet me and to claim their share of my attention. I felt like the Pied Piper of Hamlyn.

Then there was that squat in Plumstead where despite the Stygian gloom I realised that some of the bedding in the corner was remarkably familiar; it turned out to be the curtains out of my office waiting room. (Never have curtains in the waiting room. If they don't nick them, they set fire to them or shred them with razor blades. In fact, never have anything in the waiting room that is inflammable, portable or destructible.)

When I was younger, I used to get quite a good reception from some of the mums. I suppose that I was a slightly better option than scrubbing the kitchen floor or doing the family wash. Mind you, some of these contacts with parents required diplomatic skills of a high order. One mum, whilst deploring her son's passion for Cliff Richard and Adam Faith, assumed that since we were of an age I shared her own devotion to The Bachelors. I felt unable to disabuse her but containing my true feelings about The Bachelors was, I felt, one of the larger sacrifices I made during my social work career.

Talking of sacrifices, I recall one mum holding her ninth and smallest in her arms and standing over me as I sat drinking my tea (sterilised milk on this occasion and three spoonfuls of sugar). She was regaling me with the misdemeanours of her first and largest. 'He's been at the gas meter again, Mr Edom.' I watched with awed apprehension as she stood above me, her baby's bare botty over her arm. I had this feeling of inevitability, of fate running its relentless course… and then, like a torrent, nature had its way, all over the lino and my Hush Puppies. Mother continued as if nothing had happened. '…and he doesn't get up in the mornings, you know, hasn't signed on for weeks.'

I have attended endless family conferences about delinquent or workshy or truanting sons. I have formulated innumerable plans and strategies for making it all better. I have consoled weeping mums, placated enraged dads, humoured scores of siblings, written hundreds of reports. I have shared an infinitude of family crises. 'He's a good boy at home, Mr Edom, just easily led. Besides if he's sent away, who's going to feed his rabbits?' I have attended family conferences where they didn't want to let me in and quite a few where they didn't want to let me go. There was a phase when I used to doze off on the last bus home each night after a round of visits only to stagger into my bedsitter to switch on the radio just in time to hear the BBC playing 'God Save the Queen'.

However, my days of relentless good works were probably most severely tested by my occasional contacts with the middle classes. Middle-class delinquents are the very hell. Not only do their parents expect explanations for the odd behaviour of their offspring, but they expect solutions as well. What do you say to the parents of a clothes' line bandit who has been found to have forty pairs of ladies' knickers and sixteen suspender belts shoved up his bedroom chimney?

Then there was the son of a general practitioner in… I'd better not say where or the Medical Defence Union will be after me, since everyone knows that doctors are infallible, don't they? Anyway, this doctor was unimpressed by my qualifications (a one-year crash course in probation social work) and felt that nothing short of the combined efforts of Freud, Jung and Adler were sufficient to engage with the problems of his son who had pinched someone's split cane fishing rod whilst on a camping holiday in Bodmin. I didn't like to point out that his own MD, FRCP, FRCOG didn't seem to have been a lot of help since his relationship with his son was remote to the point of non-existence. That's the trouble with infallibility, isn't it? It tends to distance you from the rest of the human race.

I once moved very upmarket indeed to visit a family in a mansion block just off Knightsbridge. (It was a much better class of delinquent – a cheque book fraud I think it was.) However, middle-class delinquents were not to my taste; they were far too heavily into sophisticated defence mechanisms, intellectual rationalisations and Costa Rican coffee.

There was a very nice lady in Streatham who used to give me a glass of Madeira whenever I called. I felt bad about not being able to do much to help her with her psychopathic stepson and for the life of me I couldn't sort out what made him such a pain. He threatened to have me duffed up at one stage in our casework relationship and at another stage threatened to accuse me of making homosexual advances to him. As it happened, I had something rather good going with one of the lady probation officers in the magistrates' court at the time. Unfortunately, I couldn't have used that as evidence of my heterosexuality since in those days single probation officers weren't expected to have sex lives and I could have got us both fired. Anyway, eventually his parents threw him out and I ended up taking him to a psychiatric hospital in Hemel Hempstead. After that my home visits came to an end and I had to relinquish my acquired taste for Madeira.

One very snowy winter's night a grateful parent in Streatham gave me a very large Scotch. I think that it was an expression of gratitude. I didn't like to tell him that the reason that his son hadn't gone to approved school was less because of my impassioned pleas on his behalf than the fact that the magistrate who gave him a conditional discharge instead had just been awarded an OBE for his enlightened work in the juvenile justice system and was anxious not to spoil his image. Either that or he had been asleep when the evidence was given. Anyway, the Scotch was appreciated.

On another snowy occasion I trudged up and down the back streets of Wandsworth up to my kneecaps in snow looking for some well disguised address and longing for a St Bernard to bring relief. However, St Bernards are a bit of a rarity in Wandsworth, particularly the sort with little barrels around their necks. When I finally found the address the parents were miffed because I had upset their viewing schedule and when it was a choice between discussing William's coming court appearance or watching *Dragnet* there was really no contest.

Finding one's clients was one of the problems of home visiting. Often the doors didn't have numbers; even more often they didn't have knockers or doorbells. (My sort of clients didn't normally welcome visitors.) Town planners didn't help. Who would have thought that number sixty-three Uppingham Cottages would be on the fifteenth floor of a tower block? Apparently they called the flats 'cottages' to give the tenants a sense of rural togetherness. The tragedy is that you think that I am joking but urban planning is no joking matter.

I visited a family one night on the eighteenth floor of a block of flats in Camberwell Green and fatuously asked them how they liked living so high up. Without a word the lady of the house took me over to the curtained window and swept back the drapes to reveal plate glass almost from floor to ceiling. I had an acute attack of vertigo and backed away to the farthest solid wall.

I have done my share of hospital visits too. Visiting heavily pregnant mums in maternity hospitals became a forte of mine. I remember visiting Mrs Potts when she was in an advanced stage of ripeness. The nursing staff were sympathetic. If Mrs Potts wanted to talk about the welfare of her son Richard, who was currently dossing in the boiler room of the flats, having fallen out with his stepfather, a volatile Lithuanian who tended to get a bit nasty with the larger kitchen utensils and was concerned that the Russians were coming, then in the interests of a trouble-free birth they were in favour.

I must reassure Mrs Potts, who might go into labour at any moment, they told me. They ushered me into a side ward whose only furniture was a high padded table with leg stirrups that looked like something out of a medieval torture chamber. I felt somewhat out of my depth in this all-female environment of brisk nurses and pod-shaped patients.

Mrs Potts was a plump little body with doelike eyes. She was clad in a nightie and dressing gown and I couldn't keep my eyes off her large protuberance. I leaned nonchalantly against the leg stirrups and tried to reassure her. I prayed fervently that my latest news of Richard's little eccentricities would not induce the birth of the next little Richard and I left as soon as I decently could.

One never knew what to expect when making a first home visit and it was necessary to steel oneself for a wide variety of lifestyles. Albie Finch, for example, used to keep a 500 cc motorcycle engine in its component parts on an old blanket in his living room. He used to assemble and dismantle it lovingly like a jigsaw puzzle as a way of whiling away the endless months of his driving disqualification.

Then there was Mr and Mrs Dodgy. On my first visit I discovered that Mr Dodgy was unemployed. 'It's his back, Mr Edom; he's a martyr to his back.' Both the Dodgy boys were also unavailable for work, Michael Dodgy because he was pathologically workshy and Derek Dodgy because he was in borstal where no one ever worked. This left Mrs Dodgy who had a part-time cleaning job which, I observed, must have paid exceedingly well in view of the new and gargantuan TV set in the corner of the room (showing *Opportunity Knocks* with a man twitching his biceps in time to Elgar, I think it was). I also noted the well stocked bar in another corner (I was not offered a drink) and the lounge carpet, so thick that walking across it made your calf muscles ache. I didn't like to ask too many pointed questions but even with my trusting nature it seemed to me that this level of affluence could only be attributable to a win on Vernons or a great many items falling off the backs of innumerable lorries.

By contrast I remember my visits to a family in a small square just south of the river. It was a Regency house that had seen better days and was in multi-occupation. (It has since been gentrified and now houses a junior minister.) Anyway, my clients lived in the basement. They were what was described as a 'problem family' (a gross understatement in my estimation). When I arrived unheralded, I was immediately given a cup of tea. Apparently my appearance, i.e. a clean shirt and tie and corduroy jacket, indicated that I was official and thus best placated with tea.

The basement was heavily curtained despite the fact that it was early afternoon and in the gloom small creatures tottered and crawled about and lurked in corners like something out of a Spielberg movie. There were puppies and kittens and babies and toddlers in rich profusion. Mrs Quigley was pregnant; judging by the population in the basement I suspected that she nearly always was. Mr Quigley was there too, a small, unassuming man. His sole function, so far as I could gather, was to service Mrs Quigley who seemed to fall pregnant at even a friendly smile and Mr Quigley was self-evidently effective in this role at least. He had no other interests and no job. 'I used to go fishing, Mr Edom, but I don't have no time for hobbies now.'

After I had been given tea, the Quigleys expressed some vague interest in who I was. School care committee about new shoes for Willy? No. School board man about Willy's truanting? ('He can't go, you know, he ain't got no shoes.') No. Electricity board man about reconnecting the supply? No. Family welfare association about new blankets? No. National assistance board man? No.

I explained that I had come about big Fred's home leave from approved school. They were unimpressed. I explained that there might be a grant to cover his meals and they perked up no end.

The Quigleys made a career out of being poor and underprivileged and every welfare agency in South London beat a pathway to their basement door. Every visitor was made to feel extremely guilty and immediately made rash offers to get the electricity reconnected, provide boot vouchers (Freeman, Hardy and Willis), food vouchers (Home and Colonial Stores), second-hand clothes (WRVS), cots, nappies or blankets, or occasionally, if the Quigleys got lucky, hard cash.

I had difficulties with the Quigleys because I dealt with teenage delinquents and in the Quigleys ménage once anything started to grow up it became maladjusted or ran away or was thrown out. (This went for the cats, the dogs, and the children.) Mr and Mrs Quigley were patient and loving with anything small and helpless and were completely immune to dog poop, cat pee and nappies or potties but they really couldn't cope with anything much over three feet in height, particularly if it developed a penchant for housebreaking (like big Fred). It wasn't that they objected on moral grounds; it was just all the fuss it caused that they objected to.

The Wilkins were another family with a housebreaking son. After my first home visit in which I discovered that their council flat provided an uninterrupted view of Kennington Oval, I planned a series of afternoon home visits to discuss their parental responsibilities and difficulties. (Surrey weren't having a particularly good season that year but the location was superb and I would have been able to get an excellent view from just behind the bowler's arm.) Anyway, Alfie Wilkins let me down badly by a further spate of housebreaking quite early in the season and despite my eloquent plea on his behalf at the South London Quarter Sessions ('He has a good home and a job as a van boy to go to, my lord.'), Alfie was despatched to borstal and I had to give up all my fond hopes of pleasant summer afternoons watching Surrey lose the county championship.

Many of the families I visited had problems with the public utilities. Some used the slot meters like moneyboxes, whilst others ignored all bills, particularly those printed in red, and were eventually disconnected. Official disconnections tended to lead to unofficial reconnections. Somewhere in Stockwell lurked a shadowy specialist who, for a small fee, would reconnect the supply and neatly bypass the meter at the same time. I developed a Nelsonian eye since in some households it would have been naive in the extreme to assume that because the lights were on the electricity board had, in a sudden generous impulse, forgiven all previous transgressions and reconnected the supply.

The Warrens were one family locked in an ongoing conflict with the electricity board. One night I visited to find the flat lit by flickering candlelight. (I noted that the Warrens looked distinctly better by candlelight but on reflection they would probably have looked better still in total darkness.) As I sat talking to them about Terry Warren's impending court appearance for using a beer bottle label as a tax disc on his uninsured Lambretta, I became aware that something was not right. It was the television set. Against all logic it was on. My eyes roamed from the set and followed the power cable... round the wainscoting, up the wall, and out of the window. Another source of electricity had been found. The Warrens could go without light, deny themselves heat, care little about untaxed or uninsured Lambrettas, but a life without *Emergency Ward Ten* was clearly unthinkable. It was, I concluded, all a question of priorities.

Waifs and Strays

As one of life's inadequates (well, who else do you know who failed his School Certificate in woodwork?), I have always had an empathy with life's flotsam. Happily, I found a way of utilising this natural warmth for the bedraggled and downtrodden, and society elected to pay me a modest stipend to keep the aforementioned bedraggled and downtrodden from making a nuisance of themselves. As a probation officer I had ample opportunity to engage with the motley crew of misfits and incompetents who came the way of the courts of summary jurisdiction.

I have to confess that the more incompetent or smelly or downright potty they proved to be the more I seemed to warm to them. No doubt this was because they made my own little eccentricities or aberrations seem mild by comparison. I always felt that, but for the grace of that Great Potter in the sky, my own little pot might easily have been even more cracked or half-baked than it was.

I encountered my first waif whilst in my very first year in the probation service in 1960. Richard Potts was only seventeen when I met him. In theory he lived with his mum and stepfather in a high-rise in Streatham. I never met his real father and neither, I think, did Richard. His stepfather was a volatile Lithuanian who did not take kindly to Richard's easy familiarity with the family savings which for some reason were kept in a tea caddy on the mantelpiece. Every time there was a family crisis Mr Potts went potty and armed himself with the family carving knife. Whereupon Richard was turned out and then dossed in the stairwell of the flats or huddled in a convenient shop doorway. Poor Richard was the most inadequate young man I ever encountered. The only positive thing he ever did was to nick things but even then he never knew how to avoid being caught. He had never worked and regarded the Youth Employment Bureau as if it was a branch of the KGB.

Sadly, he was too old for the ministrations of the children's department and too young to be placed in an adult hostel or to claim benefits. Everyone seemed concerned about Richard but this was expressed by phoning me up and telling me that I should 'do something'. Richard was not easy to help. If I found him private lodgings his first action was to raid the gas meter. If I found him a hostel for adolescents he would just abscond, usually taking some souvenir with him. He always returned to the block of flats where his mum lived, whereupon Mrs Potts would phone me up once again to demand that I do something. I was never sure whether Mrs Potts was genuinely concerned about Richard or just found him an embarrassment. A bit of each, I suspect. In any event, she was invariably preoccupied with the brood of small children that Mr Potts had bestowed upon her. My memory of Mrs Potts was of a lady in a permanent state of advanced pregnancy.

I spent endless hours trying to persuade Richard to accept my various plans for his rehabilitation but he just grew sadder and scruffier. He had no friends and no ambitions. He would sit in my office for hours in hopeless silence until we were both deeply depressed. I know you are waiting for the happy ending but there was no happy ending. I think that all Richard really wanted was to be loved and cosseted by his mum and for Mr Potts to shove off back to Lithuania. All he eventually achieved, however, was to get himself to borstal.

Then there was my friend Den. I was very fond of Den. He treated me with a healthy disrespect that I found rather endearing. By the time I met Den I had reached the lofty rank of senior probation officer in charge of Plumstead Magistrates' Court. Den was not impressed. He refused to acknowledge that I had a name, let alone a position of seniority. He would arrive at the reception desk and with a jerk of his head enquire, 'Is 'e in?' Den was a tall, lank-haired man with heavy brows and eyes that looked in different directions. He drank a good deal but that was not really his problem.

Once he had gained entry to my office he would slouch down in the Parker Knoll chair provided for visitors and announce, 'They're at it again.' It was the voices, you see. Den had voices. Once I had gained his trust he had explained about the voices. They were not in his head you understand. That, in Den's view, would have meant that he was mad. No, these voices were from little creatures who lived in his ears. They told him things. When I asked him what they told him, a crafty look would pass over Den's face. 'Oh, just things,' he would say. Sometimes we would be in mundane conversation about the iniquities of the police or the social security office and that cunning expression would pass across Den's face. 'They have started up again,' he would say and we would have to stop and listen until they had finished talking to him.

Mr McClusky was a drinking man. He was a Glaswegian and a drinker. When he was being both at once he was almost unintelligible. I shared a good many crises with Mr McClusky. The worst was at Peckham Magistrates' Court in about 1966. He burst into my office one afternoon whilst I was still recovering from the effects of lunch in the police section house canteen. He rushed into the office clasping a milk bottle and hurled himself to the ground behind my desk. 'Get down, get down,' he hissed, pulling me down to the floor as well. I was expecting a mob of drunken and enraged drinking partners to pursue him into the room but nothing happened. He carefully eased himself up until he could see out of my window to the street outside.

'There they are, there they are!' he shouted, pointing at the sky. 'They' were soldiers coming down in parachutes with fixed bayonets. If this was not bad enough, they were wearing kilts as well. Once I had convinced Mr McClusky that they weren't coming for him he settled down to converse with someone who was hiding behind my noticeboard. It turned out to be his old mum who had been dead for ten years. She seemed to have a lot she wanted to say to him and he was very attentive. When the duly authorised officer had been called it turned out to be the DT's. It was arranged that Mr McClusky could be admitted to the local psychiatric hospital if I could manage to get him there. My Austin Mini seemed very small with me and Mr McClusky and all his friends and relatives in it. Somewhere halfway up Camberwell Hill he ordered the car to a halt. He said that there was a smell of burning. Someone had set the car on fire. Mr McClusky hurled himself down in the middle of the road and began to listen attentively to a drain cover.

We got to the hospital eventually. Just as well. The things had arrived by then. Fiendish things, mostly green and slimy and very large. There were also some smaller fluttery things that he kept beating down as they flew round his hospital bed.

I visited him a few days later. He was much better. When I mentioned the kilted paratroopers with fixed bayonets he looked at me as if I was mad. He wanted to know when he could be discharged. 'I could do with a drink,' he said.

Percy was a large, hairy, lethargic, shambling sort of

man, a bit like a yak. Percy's speciality was flashing. He didn't do a lot with his life; he had no job, no wife, no kids, no prospects and no money. However, he did have a substantial police record which showed that he had displayed his fundamentals to a significant proportion of the female population of southern England. No one seemed to be much the worse, or for that matter, much the better, for all the activity. I remember driving him back from one court appearance out of town after he had once again been warned or fined or something. Percy was always suitably apologetic to all concerned. 'It just came over me,' was one of his favourite explanations. As we crossed Chislehurst Common he pointed out no less than three locations where it had just come over him. He recalled the incidents much as one might identify the venues of some past sporting achievements. I chided him and told him he should be ashamed. 'Oh, I am, I am,' he said, beaming happily.

Mr Stamford didn't do a lot either. He had a blank moon face that neither time nor experience seemed to have touched. He was about forty and lived with his mum. He had been married but hadn't liked it much. If Mr Stamford didn't like something he didn't do it. He didn't like working and he didn't like going out. He didn't like collecting the dole either, but he forced himself. He certainly didn't like being on probation but he liked prison even less so he put up with me. Whatever I suggested he agreed with. He was very agreeable. He never actually did anything I asked him to do but he always had a good reason. 'I really meant to, Mr Edom. I just forgot.' He would sit and listen to my little lectures and homilies and smile and nod happily and then hurry back to mum as soon as possible.

Mr Tickler had an even more effective way of dealing with me. If I became too tiresome he turned his hearing aid off and just said, 'Eh?' for the rest of the interview. Sometimes he would come without any batteries in his hearing aid. Once we spent the whole interview trying to mend it. Another time he came without any hearing aid at all and I just bellowed at him whilst he sat looking at me with a blank puzzled expression on his face.

Alfie was a thirty-year old schizophrenic. His relatives had all abandoned him because of his funny little ways. The trouble was that Alfie had not abandoned his relatives. The relatives would call on me to keep the peace or persuade poor Alfie to go and be nutty somewhere else. When poor Alfie became very nutty the police would arrest him in desperation. The magistrate would remand him to prison for a medical and mental report and the prison doctor with a fine sense of self-preservation would declare that 'Alfred Bowler is a social problem not a medical one'. Then the magistrate would release Alfie again and Alfie would go back to pestering his relatives. I remember levering him away from an anxious relative at about eleven thirty one night and leading him down Plumstead Broadway in the direction of the nearest lodging house. Alfie decided to make a personal statement to the world. Well, all of sleeping Plumstead Broadway anyway. 'Look at them,' he roared. 'They are all mad, all mad!' Lights went on all down the Broadway and I dragged Alfie for cover.

Finally, one day Alfie went too far and hit a policeman. I visited him in Wandsworth Prison. He had a black eye and looked rather pathetic. 'How are you getting on, Alfie?' I enquired.

'Oh, I like it here,' he said. 'You get three meals a day and no one bothers you.'

I could see what he meant.

James Worth was a burglar. He had a bad record, had been to prison and was rather proud that a psychiatrist had once diagnosed him as a psychopath. He worked in the rag

424

trade and was a skilled packer. The trouble was he didn't like foremen. He lost jobs like other people lost stray thoughts. I persuaded him to give up burglary for a while but falling out with foremen and losing jobs was another matter. He would amble in to my office. "Fraid I lost that job, Mr E,' he would announce. 'The foreman was a pig.' Then as I began to remonstrate he would interrupt, 'But I got another one. The money's better but the hours are longer.' I swear that James had worked for every clothing manufacturer in East London and quite a few in West London too. He must have been a good packer. He certainly had endearing ways. Whenever he brought me some fresh tale of woe and disaster he would hold his hands palm upwards, look at the ceiling and say plaintively, 'What do you expect, Mr E, I'm a psychopaf, ain't I?'

Charlie had been diagnosed as an inadequate psychopath. He had a fine sense of the dramatic. He had the idea that my life was dull and that he needed to introduce some drama for me. He used to phone me up most days to tell me about his latest crisis. At one stage he decided that I didn't care enough. About seven one evening he phoned my office and announced, 'I have decided to end it all. I have just taken an overdose.' Colluding with the sense of crisis as I was prone to do, I demanded to know where he was. He went all coy but eventually told me. I rushed to the rescue and then began an interesting evening of hawking Charlie round to doctors' surgeries ('You had better take him straight to hospital'), hospitals ('We don't have an accident and emergency department here, you know') and eventually a real accident and emergency department ('Just take a seat and we will see him as soon as we can.'). The combination of Charlie's need to be coaxed at every stage coupled with the lack of interest of the medical profession meant that by eleven o'clock little had been achieved. By this time, however, Charlie had become bored with the game. Whatever he had taken (he was very vague about what it was) had evidently worn off and he wanted to go home to supper. When he presented his next crisis he was quite hurt at my reaction.

William Harmful was a psychopath as well but he was a bit nastier with it. The trouble was that I was never sure what to expect next. I was uncertain whether William was stark-staring potty pretending to be sane or sane pretending to be potty. Either way he was a bit unnerving and one thing was sure: he was a real pain. William was a large adolescent, only noisier and more horrible than most adolescents. He had some fairly peculiar habits and a very uncertain temperament. He used to fall out with his father and stepmother with depressing frequency and he was prone to using the gas meter as a money box and to flog the family possessions when he was hard up for a bob or two. If his stepmother took exception to his funny little ways he used to smash things up, whereupon his father would throw him out and then I would be called upon to arbitrate. Then the sequence would start all over again.

William was quite impartial; he was frequently horrible to me as well. At one stage he was threatening to have me duffed up and at another stage to accuse me of making homosexual advances to him. When all else failed, he used to vandalise my waiting room.

Finally, after some bit of naughtiness he was remanded to Wormwood Scrubs for a psychiatric report. Tooting Juvenile Court decided that he should be sent to a special adolescent unit at a psychiatric hospital in Hemel Hempstead. I was nominated to take him. Like all those in authority the magistrates did not wish to be bothered with the trivial practicalities like how do you got a loony like William to a hospital in Hemel Hempstead without a car. Eventually I found a Green Line bus that went to Hemel Hempstead.

It was not a fun journey. William's euphoria at being free from Wormwood Scrubs coupled with a natural tendency to show off was a bit tiresome. I herded him to the back of the bus where he regaled all the other passengers with colourful accounts of his three weeks in Wormwood Scrubs. He then explained that he was on his way to the 'Loony Bin' and then introduced me as his probation officer and gave a detailed account of his views about my personal qualities. By the time we reached Victoria all the other passengers were huddled up by the front entrance and the driver's steering was becoming distinctly erratic. It took a very long time to get to Hemel Hempstead.

There was also Mr Lurch and his canary. Mr Lurch had been a physical training instructor in the Navy for thirty years. He showed me photographs of himself in his prime: all tattoos and singlet and muscles. He looked terrifying. Then he completed his service and returned to civvy street. It was a disaster. His wife, unable to take undiluted Lurch, left him, he lost his civvy job and began to pine away. By the time I came to know him he was a gaunt, stooping and pathetic figure. For comfort he had only his canary and his hobby – shoplifting. The magistrates tried to be lenient with him ('He has an exemplary service record, your worship') but the shoplifting became more and more outrageous. Eventually he went to prison. Guess who had to look after his bloody canary? When he came out his shoplifting just got worse and worse. After that every time Mr Lurch went to prison there was not only prison visiting to do but canary sitting as well. It all became too much. I transferred to another court.

Henry was a bit of an enigma and I never got to know him very well. His only claim to fame was to be apprehended by the police one evening running across Plumstead Common in the pouring rain clad only in a pair of hiking boots. When asked what he was doing he said that he was a student of yoga. Keen as I was to solve everyone's problems, I felt I had little to offer Henry – except perhaps a pair of shorts.

Albie was obsessed with motor vehicles. He would have preferred to drive a motor mower rather than to have driven nothing. He kept getting disqualified. He was on probation for stealing tyres for a car he didn't even have. Albie was so obsessed with the pleasures of the open road that he forgot all else – motor insurance, car tax, test certificates, L plates, traffic lights, who owned the car. He was the only person I knew who kept a complete Norton 500 cc motorcycle engine stripped down on an old blanket on the lounge carpet in his flat. When I visited him he would sit on the floor fondling these bits and assembling and dismantling them like a well loved jigsaw. He had a moony expression on his face as if he was already at full throttle somewhere south of Godalming on the A3.

Mr Flanagan was another drinking man. He was a voluntary client. This meant I usually only saw him when he was desperate for money. Mr Flanagan resented spending money on anything except on drink. He slept rough and ponged more than a little bit. If I kept him waiting he would take his shoes off in the waiting room and begin to examine his feet. It was surprising how quickly he reached the front of the queue.

Alan Portsmouth was a peeping tom. His need to see ladies in the noddy was quite obsessive. My suggestion that a copy of a *Randy Days* or some such magazine might be simpler and safer was rejected out of hand. He was dedicated to his art. Ladders, drainpipes, flat roofs, scaffolding; he had been found in some fairly improbable locations in his time, all in pursuit of his specialised interest. The penalty for peeping toms was not severe, normally a bind over. Once the police found him up a

428

twenty-foot ladder at the rear of a block of flats in South Kensington. They charged him with attempted burglary. Alan was outraged. He wasn't that sort of a person. He called me to give evidence as a defence witness at his trial to prove that he was a habitual voyeur. Every man to his trade.

Then there was little Mrs Percival: grey-haired, neat and respectable. She seated herself demurely in my office and carefully removed her black lace gloves before she began to speak. It was her neighbours. I steeled myself for a long story about noisy televisions or a dispute about the height of the garden fence. It was the rays; they were transmitting invisible rays through the party wall. As if that was not enough, they were calling up Martians and sending them to pester her. It was not right, Mr Edom, and something had to be done. The tale of persecution continued with assorted little men and mysterious messages whilst I felt more and more at a loss. I need not have worried. After about an hour of patient if rather helpless listening, Mrs Percival carefully pulled on her lace gloves and got up to go. 'Thank you very much, Mr Edom. I'm sure that it will be much better now.'

Mr Dunwoody lived in one of the local authority old people's homes. The trouble with institutions like that is that you had to be the sort of old person the Peckham Council thought that you ought to be, that is sensible, staid, sober and old. Mr Dunwoody could only fulfil this role for about two months at a time. When he had saved about two months' pocket money he would go down to the Nag's Head and spend the lot on Old Peculiar. The effects on him were distinctly peculiar. He would then be refused admission to the home and be arrested by the police for drunk and disorderly behaviour. In the morning, sober, chastened and dishevelled he would appear before the stipendiary magistrate who would look to me to sort things out. Earnest telephone conversations with the matron of the old people's home would then follow in which apologies and promises of future good behaviour were made.

'Do you know what he called me, Mr Edom?'

'I'm sure he didn't mean it, matron.'

Finally all would be resolved – until two months' time. Thank God, Mr Dunwoody didn't get much pocket money.

Mr Bodily only troubled the probation service once a year. He prided himself on being a gentleman of the road, an honourable calling in his view. He spent the winter months in quiet hibernation in a lodging house in the Waterloo Road but when the spring arrived the open road called to him. On his way down the Peckham Road en route for Kent he would drop off to collect his new boots. The probation service records showed that every spring since the end of the war Mr Bodily had been supplied with a boots voucher. There was no question about it; Mr Bodily had called for his annual boot supply and that was that. Who was I to interrupt such a tradition?

We had vouchers for all our waifs and strays. There were coal vouchers, lodging house vouchers, grocery vouchers and boot vouchers. If all else failed it was usually possible to find a ten bob out of the poor box or a voucher for a meal down at the local pie and mash shop. Mind you, one had to be careful about dispensing cash. It was often spent on what was called one and one. This was a concoction sold in a dubious little shop under the railway arches and comprised equal parts of surgical spirit and lemonade.

There was a small core of hardened surgical spirit drinkers who used to inhabit the bomb site just to the south of the Elephant and Castle. They used to sit round a campfire passing round their bottle of one and one with wild-eyed enthusiasm, each swig taking them closer to oblivion, temporary or permanent. Every winter we would hear that one or two more had dropped off their perches for the last time, usually dying of hypothermia in an alcoholic haze without even knowing that they were freezing to death. Charlie Crow was one of these. Mind you, Charlie used to cause a bit of a stir when he called in at the office. He was always drunk, always wanted money, was extremely dismissive when offered a lodging house voucher and was inclined to throw chairs around when displeased which was every time that he called in. Mind you, when he finally pegged it there were quite a few of us who shed a tear or two for Charlie. He was a fighter, was Charlie. Pity he never fought the right enemy.

Of course, after the best part of forty years in the probation service there were some success stories but they seldom want to be reminded of their murky histories. In any event, it is the poor old no-hopers who linger in my memory. There but for the grace of God and all that.

Matrimonials

Marriage counselling seems to have become a very sophisticated occupation these days, peopled by those with mysterious talents and great knowledge. You will understand, therefore, that I no longer practice the art. Nowadays all sorts of clever people seem to be in on the act: solicitors, doctors, psychiatrists and a whole range of advice centres and counselling services. Mind you, there seems to be more marriage breakdown than ever but it might be a bit impolite to mention that, I suppose.

I did counsel people about their marital misfortunes for quite a few years but this was back in the dark ages, mostly in the 1960s. It left me more or less unshockable about people's funny little ways and remarkably relaxed about my own minor peccadilloes.

I first ventured forth into good works after a one-year crash course to equip me to be a probation officer. During the progress of this training which included such diverse subjects as the psychiatric aspects of delinquency, criminal law, child development, casework, social influences on behaviour and the National Assistance Act, I was provided with a series of three lectures on what was called matrimonial work. These lectures were provided by a rather intense, chain-smoking lady who viewed the vagaries of humankind through a haze of tobacco smoke and a very philosophic attitude.

I know that I carefully took notes at the time and wrote in my exercise book in my best handwriting careful headings like 'Reasons for increased marital breakdown' and 'Areas of marital tension'. I don't expect that anyone wants to know but human behaviour doesn't seem to change all that much; we just seem to find rather more obscure words to describe it.

Anyway, fully equipped with my new-found knowledge I ventured forth with my carefully written notes from my three lectures and a sixteen-page booklet entitled *The Basics of Domestic Law in the Magistrates' Courts*.

My little law book only recognised four categories of marital naughtiness that could lead to a separation order in the magistrates' court. They were desertion, wilful neglect to maintain, persistent cruelty and adultery. All my clients had to be squeezed into one of these compartments. If it wasn't in my book you couldn't have it.

Every morning at Plumstead Magistrates' Court the ladies of the neighbourhood would arrive to have their wrongs righted and I was the means by which they expected this to be achieved. As a rule of thumb I worked on the basis that ladies who were seeking resolution of their marital discontents were usually complaining of too little or too much. Too little money, too little (or too much) attention and so on. Sometimes the too much was of the thump and bash variety. Monday mornings were the worst – those and the day after the Christmas holidays.

There was a ritual in the London magistrates' courts in those distant days of the early sixties. The aforesaid aggrieved ladies of the neighbourhood could appear before the magistrate to apply for summonses against their husbands or the putative fathers of their little accidents. However they had to see the probation officer first to ensure that (a) they had a prima facie case and (b) that they really wanted to do something about it. The magistrate was always worried that the court's time might be wasted by abortive proceedings. Wasting the probation officer's time was an acceptable expenditure. Not surprising really considering they were only paying me about fourteen quid a week at the time.

If I thought they had a case I had to put them before the magistrate. It was a sort of cheap legal aid. Very cheap. Thus on a Monday morning I would find myself ushering into court a small gaggle of aggrieved ladies.

'Your worship, this is Mrs Myrtle Sidbury who is seeking a summons for desertion. She alleges that her husband left the marital home last Tuesday fortnight taking with him his new overcoat with the velvet collar and his entire collection of Beatles records. On departure he is alleged to have said, "You had better get your mum to live with you; she is round here most of the time anyway…"'

Summons granted.

'Your worship, this is Mrs Sheila Tremble who is seeking a summons for persistent cruelty. She alleges that on Saturday last her husband came home drunk, threw his dinner on the fire, punched her in the chest and locked her in the airing cupboard. She alleges three similar incidents on dates when Charlton have lost their home games this season…'

Summons granted.

At the end of application time I would shepherd my little group of ladies to the warrant office to arrange the service of the summonses and to fix dates for their grievances to be heard.

Many of the ladies I saw did not want summonses; they just wanted 'something done'. Sometimes I would write to the husband in suitably coaxing terms suggesting that he called in to see me to discuss his habit of peeing in the wash basin or whatever it was that had persuaded his wife to invoke the majesty of the law. Such letters seldom evoked a reply. Strangely enough, many of the ladies drew satisfaction from the mere despatch of such letters, even if I didn't include the lurid threats that they advocated (imprisonment, castration or worse). I suspect that the arrival of a letter in an official brown envelope and with the court letterhead may sometimes have reduced the extent of bashing or boozing or extramarital mucking about to a level that the wife concerned found acceptable.

It was fascinating to observe the various stages in a marital battle. My lectures told me that a lot of it was about dominance and submission. Sometimes a lady would decide that because the probation officer seemed unshocked at the news that her husband wanted to try the 69 position this amounted to official approval. I always adopted a stance of total unshockability and never gave any indication of my own personal preferences but I did learn quite a lot about the breadth of the marital spectrum. My lectures told me that I must be non-judgemental and ensure that my clients were free to make their own choices. I had to help them consider the options just like my course told me. Was twice a night excessive? Well, how do you feel about this, Mrs Spreadbury?

Often when ladies were given time and attention to describe their disappointments and dissatisfactions they would perk up no end. It was nice to see some of those transformations. Mind you, one had to be a bit wary. Many a do-gooder has come to grief doing a little too much good. Often ladies would appear as tear-stained, bedraggled and snuffly bundles but given time, patience and a listening ear they would begin to think and take decisions for themselves. On succeeding visits it was possible to see a transformation. They would dress more smartly, take some trouble over their hair and make-up and recover some of their sparkle and femininity.

On reflection, I am really rather proud that despite the quite powerful relationships that developed I stuck manfully to my role as impartial and objective counsellor, even when Mrs Trellis became transformed from a weeping drab into an extremely fanciable woman. Still, too much exposure to the devoted gaze from her soft brown eyes and too much attention to the way she crossed and recrossed her long and self-evidently elegant legs was extremely distracting. Fortunately, I was not subjected to many tests as severe as Mrs Trellis's thighs so I managed to preserve my professional reputation.

My senior colleague, Mr Keel, a battle-scarred probation officer of much marital work experience would occasionally regale me with some new dimension to the marriage guidance quagmire. I recall that at one stage he was engaged in counselling a lady whose husband's main desire was to strip her nude and then to affix clothes pegs to all her droopy bits. By this stage I had become so blasé about people's funny little ways that I was merely curious to know what she used for hanging the washing out.

I ceased to be surprised at anything. I would listen at a series of consultations to the depraved and brutal behaviour of some monster of a husband until finally the innocent, maltreated wife would decide to leave home. Then the monster would come in to see me to try to get his wife back. He would turn out to be all of five foot three and no more than ten and a half stone of weeping manhood. 'Can't you get her back, Mr Edom? I still love her despite that bloke at work who has been seeing to her.'

I found that most of my female clients were somewhat diffident about talking about their sexual relationships although in my experience there were precious few marital problems that could be resolved without talking about them. They would try though, and I would spend endless hours listening to money problems, disagreements over child rearing, catering arrangements, domestic chores and television programmes. Sometimes joint interviews would deteriorate into wrangles about personal hygiene. 'And do you know where she puts her dirty knickers, Mr Edom?'

The sexual problems usually unravelled slowly and reluctantly like clothing out of an automatic washing machine. I remember an elfin-faced, anxious-looking newly-wed who obviously had a specific problem on her mind. It took the best part of an hour to move from the fact that marriage was not exactly what she had been led to believe from her reading of *Woman's Weekly* to the fact that something was causing her unease in the marital bed. 'He keeps wanting to turn me over, Mr Edom.' I was slow to grasp her problem, especially since half my clientele were complaining that they weren't being turned over enough. At last she managed to be more specific. 'He keeps wanting to do to me what men do to little boys.' Anal intercourse was not in vogue at the time. *Last Tango in Paris* and innovative uses for margarine had not yet been heard of and it was another thirty years before they said 'anal intercourse' on the BBC. I adopted my usual non-committal air. At the time I didn't even know it was illegal. They had, I think, just made it legal for consenting male adults but not for consenting husbands and wives. Well, don't tell me the law is daft. You don't work long in the courts before you conclude that the law is not only an ass but a very silly ass. The young Mrs Potter never did let me know whether she decided to turn over or not.

The magistrates were not overly impressed with mental cruelty in the 1960s. They had a marked preference for the sort of cruelty where the bruises could be shown. I was always a bit uneasy about ladies showing me their marital war wounds for fear that someone would come in and misunderstand what was going on. Anyway, the pretty ones seldom volunteered. The trouble was that the law required some sort of evidence of cruelty and bruises tended to fade fairly quickly. 'Do you think this one is good enough, Mr Edom?'

'Do please pull your skirt down, Mrs Perkins. You will have to go and get a letter from your doctor.'

I never ceased to marvel at people's funny little ways. One morning a mountainous middle-aged lady marched into my office and wordlessly spread out on my desk a sheaf of glossy half-plate photographs of herself. There was a pause. 'What', she said, 'do you think of those?'

The photographs showed my visitor in her pants and bra, in her pants and no bra and in nothing at all. She looked even more mountainous in the nude I noted, and pale flesh overflowed in all directions. I wasn't sure what was expected of me, admiration or outrage. Either could have been seriously wrong. Her husband, it transpired, was an enthusiastic amateur photographer who insisted in photographing her in her underwear, or less. I gathered that she was not happy about this although I have to say that the photographs conveyed an impression of enthusiastic co-operation.

Then there was Mrs Turpin, a wizened and bulging lady in her later years whose wayward husband had returned home after an extended absence, either in the colonies or Parkhurst, I am not sure which. He had apparently picked up some funny ideas whilst he had been away. 'He wants me to wear short skirts and ankle socks,' she confided. 'He keeps calling me his naughty little girl and wanting to spank me.' Mrs Turpin, in her fifties and bulging in places and drooping rather a lot in others, was hard to visualise in ankle socks and short skirt. She seemed worried in case there was something wrong with her husband, or maybe she was wondering if she had been missing out on something all her life.

Mrs Venables brought her daughter. Mrs Venables told me what was wrong with her daughter's marriage and her daughter's husband. 'He's about your age,' she declared accusingly. 'He wants to be out on his motorbike or out drinking with his cronies all the time.' Mrs Venables then began to express doubts about me. 'Are you sure that you are a probation officer? You seem too young to help. Isn't there someone older? An older lady perhaps?' (All this of course was in the years when wisdom was thought to come with age. Now that age has taken its toll of me someone has changed the rules which has always seemed a bit unjust to me.)

I was rather worried that Mrs Venables's daughter hadn't had a word to say about her marriage so far. I suggested that her daughter should have a further appointment on her own so that I could discuss with her what she wanted to do about her problem. This was obviously a startling proposal. Nay, an indecent one. Mrs Venables was shocked and outraged. I don't know what her daughter's view was; she maintained her moon-faced passive position, sitting slightly behind her mother, knees clamped together and with an expression that conveyed that none of this was anything to do with her.

Mind you, interfering mums were fairly common. They nearly always brought their daughters rather than the other way round. Even if they allowed their daughters to do the talking they couldn't avoid offering helpful advice. 'Now tell the man what he did with the bath brush.'

Then they would give me advice as well. 'What you ought to do is write to her husband and tell him that if he does it again we'll divorce him.'

Interfering mums weren't averse to putting the law right too. 'Well, if spending all his time with his pigeons isn't mental cruelty, it ought to be.'

Mrs Bryan, a weeping middle-aged lady, announced that she couldn't go on. It was all too much. Her husband was beastly and violent and horrible. She began to list details of some really outrageous bashings and thumpings and similar goings-on. I tried to remain dispassionate whilst I listened to this long story of clonking and tyranny. When I could get a word in edgeways I asked one of my standard questions: How long had this been going on? Nearly twenty years, it transpired. So what had made her decide to do something about it now? The answer was hard to elicit. Probably because it was hard to admit. She loved the man. The thumpings and bashings that sounded so appalling to me were tolerable to her. What was intolerable to her was that her husband was now shaming her by taking out a young woman from the factory where he worked and was no longer asserting his conjugal rights. It's all a question of loyalties, I suppose.

I'm so very grateful to my matrimonials. They taught me a great deal. The diversity of human behaviour for starters. The wisdom of not imposing one's own prejudices on others for another. Finally, an awareness that if we were ever open and honest about the nation's bedroom secrets life would never be the same again. But I shouldn't hold your breath.

Up the Gross Glockner

'Now mit der schnoballs ve vill play,' announced our Austrian courier in a tone that indicated that instant obedience was the only option. Although he wore a woolly ski hat with a bobble on the top one was left with the impression that he was really on temporary secondment from the Waffen SS.

Our coach had wound its way up the thirty-two (or was it thirty-three?) hairpin bends of the Gross Glockner and we had arrived at the highest point where even in July there was thick snow. Determined that we should experience life to the full our courier now insisted that we dismount from our coach to play with the snow. Sheepishly we toyed with handfuls of snow but this was not enough for our courier. He formed a bullet-hard globule of snow and hurled it at my head. He was going to ensure that we enjoyed ourselves even if it killed us. As a matter of fact, so far as I was concerned he bloody nearly succeeded. I turned and twisted to dodge the snowball, my foot went through the crisp surface of snow and sunk into the soft snow that lay beneath. My leg was held firmly vertical whilst the rest of me fell horizontally. Something had to give, and it did. It was, they later explained, a Potts' fracture. I don't know who this chap Potts was but he gave his name to a particularly painful experience. To give your name to a condition like that you would need to be closely related to the Marquis de Sade or to be a major shareholder in a plaster of Paris mine.

Anyway, after a few exquisite moments that would have brought tears of joy to a masochist, I realised that I was lying face down in a slushy mixture of snow and Alpine mud. A geologically interesting mixture no doubt, but messy. I tried to get up but as soon as I put any weight on my left leg it gave way in a spectacular fashion and I collapsed with a yelp. Being a slow learner I tried this several times and floundered around rather like a stranded whale. My fellow tourists took this to be all part of the snowy fun and roared with laughter. (Thinks... why is it that whenever disaster strikes in Edom's life there are always some prize twits standing around laughing?)

At last I struggled up on to one foot and hopped inelegantly back to the coach. I had the presence of mind to abandon some edelweiss that I had picked for good luck since it was evidently defective stock. Back on the coach one of the ladies in the party announced with great authority that she was a state certified midwife and took charge. I almost expected her to call for large quantities of boiling water or make enquiries about my contractions but instead she confined herself to a close scrutiny of my ankle. Even I could see that the ankle was swelling at an alarming rate and had assumed a most curious shape. I was still thinking in terms of a bad sprain although it hurt and looked like no sprain that I had ever encountered before. 'I think that it is broken,' the midwife announced to the entire coach party with all the authority that her new found role gave her. She made the announcement in much the same way that she might have announced, 'I think it's twins.' Anyway, my wife promptly fainted and all attention was promptly diverted to her. I remember feeling slightly miffed that she had stolen my thunder.

The coach party was certainly getting its share of drama. Perhaps they made it a regular feature of the excursion thereafter. They were certainly an enterprising lot those

Austrians. I could imagine the poster outside the tours office: 'Grand tour of the Gross Glockner, with snowballs, mountain rescue and first aid practice. Inclusive tour price – one hundred Austrian schillings.'

The tour members began to join in the spirit of the thing. They began to exercise their ingenuity in devising a splint for my leg. It was a bit like one of those initiative exercises that they liked to set you in the services. You know, how to cross a ten-foot raging torrent without getting your feet wet using two bamboo canes, an old motorcar tyre and a three-foot piece of rope. Anyway, the coach party eventually managed to splint my leg with a tie, a belt and a camera tripod and some pessimist's umbrella. I had hoped that some comely young woman would strip off her stockings for the strapping but sadly this new dimension to all the excitement was not to be.

Someone gave me a cigarette and although I hadn't smoked for six years I sucked on it with great enthusiasm and six years of good intentions went up in smoke. Then we began the descent of the mountain (thirty-two hairpin bends, or was it thirty-three?). When we reached the little lakeside town at the bottom of the pass our coach wouldn't fit into the local hospital car park. (They are a very law-abiding lot the Austrians – stupid but law-abiding.) They conjured up a hospital trolley to trundle me through the street to the hospital with members of the coach party trailing along uncertainly behind like followers in some religious procession.

At the hospital (or should I say Krankenhaus?) life started to get difficult again. I lay unnoticed on my trolley whilst the courier conversed lengthily and gutturally with the hospital staff. I assumed that they were having an earnest and concerned discussion about my unfortunate accident. No doubt they were considering the extent of my injury and the best treatment and the prognosis. I felt vaguely reassured at all the careful thought that was being devoted to my welfare.

Eventually the courier turned to me. Was I insured? Yes, I was. Where was my insurance policy? At my hotel, forty miles away. Ah, that apparently was unfortunate. The hospital was not keen to give me any treatment until they were convinced that I could pay. I never did find out what would have happened if I had declared myself penniless and uninsured. I assume that they would have thrown me out. Anyway, eventually they agreed to accept my word that I had a holiday accident insurance that would cover their fees but now a further problem developed. How much would my insurance company pay? Could they afford the first-class ward, the second-class ward or perhaps only the third class? I hadn't a clue. I didn't even know that they sold medical treatment in Austria like railway tickets.

At last it was all arranged – a nice compromise. They would give me the second-class treatment. The important matters having been dealt with they turned to my leg. The leg, now encased in dried Alpine mud, was examined. It was a bad break and I could not travel. I must stay at the hospital. The coach party, who were now getting bored and wanted their dinner, departed together with my wife and the courier. The party was returning to England in two days and I had no idea how I was to get home when I was eventually allowed to travel. I had visions of hitch-hiking across Europe on a pair of crutches.

Anyway, I was left in the Teutonic hands of the Zell am See Krankenhaus. It was not a reassuring prospect. The staff only knew a few words of English and I only had my German phrase book. It was one of those little books for holidaymakers, helpfully divided into sections: 'Customs', 'In the hotel', 'Shopping', etc. There was not a section headed 'Breaking your ankle up a bloody mountain'. I turned to the section headed 'At the chemist' which seemed the most relevant bit that I could find. Unfortunately, 'Can you give me something to rub on it?' seemed to fall somewhat short of what was needed for the occasion. I wished that they had let me learn German at school, or better still, in view of my linguistic limitations, that I had taken my holiday in Scotland. At least in Scotland they had a National Health Service and at least some of the language was intelligible.

I was wheeled into the theatre and my very bent leg was examined with some detached interest, although the rest of me was left to fend for itself. An orderly produced rolls of bandages and vats of plaster of Paris. I wondered if I was to get an anaesthetic but my phrasebook was out of reach and anyway I doubted if the section 'At the chemist' would cover this eventuality either. In the event I soon discovered. Not a bit of it. Not an aspirin. Nothing. I couldn't work out if it was normal Austrian medical practice, a special feature of the second-class treatment or some local vendetta against the English.

The unsmiling head doctor disclosed that he knew a little English. 'I vas at East Gruinschtead during the var.' He had scars across his face that looked like duelling scars. All he needed was a monocle and I would have expected him to announce, 'Ve haf vays of making you valk.' I fervently hoped that they had treated him well at East Gruinschtead during the war. I did wonder if that was where he had got his scars.

'Ve must relax,' he pronounced. (Strange how medics the world over say 'we' (or 've') when they mean 'you'). One of his white-coated minions hauled on my leg whilst the head doctor pushed the broken bones back into position. It was a unique sensation which they accompanied with a chorus of 'Relax, relax'. (This was evidently the Austrian version of anaesthesia – not so effective as pethidine but extremely economical.) By this time I was forced to the conclusion that Herr Doctor must have had a very bad time indeed at East Gruinschtead during the war.

Eventually the setting and plastering was over. (What a very messy business it is, rather like playing with chalky mud pies.) Then I was installed in the second-class ward. All I will say about this is God help Austrian third-class patients. I recalled at about this stage that Hitler had been an Austrian. It seemed to make sense of my situation and from then on I regarded myself as a prisoner of war.

The second-class ward didn't go in for a great deal of nursing care. They did, however, bring food. I learned that hospital meals don't vary much from one side of Europe to the other. Perhaps there is a United Nations convention to ensure equality of gastronomic mediocrity in hospitals. Anyway Krankenhaus Apfelstrudel is about on par with National Health Service rice pudding. I speak with some authority. A certain series of thought processes leads me to refer to the toilet arrangements. The toilet was out of the small ward and down the corridor. The nursing staff watched with interest whilst I hopped on one leg down the corridor. I don't know how the totally disabled fared but I never saw a bedpan so I assume that they had to use will-power and try to abstain from food and drink and sudden movements.

At one stage they gave me a walking frame but this was soon whisked away to help a senile patient in the next ward. I think that it must have been the only one they had. I never saw any crutches. Perhaps such advances in medical science had not reached Austria at that time. Surprising really; you would have thought with all that mountain climbing and skiing and ice-skating a good few bones would have been broken and with all that timber on the mountain slopes some entrepreneur would have knocked up a few crutches or at least a walking stick or two.

In the next bed to me was a Dutchman. He had dived

into the local swimming pool at the wrong angle and had bounced off the bottom. Fortunately, he had not broken anything although he had a large bandage round his head and a slightly manic air about him. He practised his English on me all day and most of the night with great persistence. I understood about one word in five. After two days he was discharged. It was a comment on my situation that I felt a sense of loss at the departure of a pedantic Dutchman with a dented head, a permanently puzzled expression, a knowledge of England that was confined to the exploits of Manchester United and a transistor radio permanently tuned to a programme playing Austrian oom-pa-pa music.

The only other patient in the small ward was an elderly Austrian with a heart condition. He groaned a lot and the highlight of his day was when his wife and daughter came in to give him a bed bath. In the second-class ward they had a very marked do-it-yourself philosophy. Thinks… perhaps in the third class you had to go outside and stand in the rain.

My days seemed to be spent hopping down the corridor to the loo or looking at the fine view of Zell am See. The hospital looked out over the lake where Austrian holidaymakers disported themselves water-skiing and swimming and diving and sailing with all the lunatic fervour that the Germanic races are capable of. Unjustly, in my jaundiced view, not a single one of them seemed to break a single bone. The weather was idyllic and day after day the sun shone on the glittering blue lake whilst the holidaymakers splashed about with Teutonic commitment. I couldn't imagine how they lost the war. I couldn't imagine how they lost anything. Unless it was because they were all mad, like Hitler. There was a band playing by the lakeside. Oom-pa-pa music, of course. Interminably. Perhaps that was why they were all mad. It didn't do me much good either.

After a week they reset my leg. They used the same anaesthetic as before. Ten weeks later in England when the plaster finally came off it was found that they had set it crooked. I can't tell if this was the standard second-class treatment or just general incompetence. Perhaps I can begin to understand how they lost the war after all.

One further week of Apfelstrudel and oom-pa-pa and hopping about and then after a series of phone calls, arrangements were made for my repatriation. Ambulances in Austria seemed to be part of the free enterprise system as well. They also seemed to be built for midgets with all their limbs intact. I was surprised that the ambulance wasn't fitted with a taximeter.

I left the Krankenhaus at Zell am See without a single regret. It's the only hospital that I have ever been in where I didn't fancy a single one of the nurses. I suppose that it is the prospect of all those men in lederhosen that gives the girls such grim expressions and pessimistic natures.

Before I departed they thrust an envelope in my hand. My heart softened. I thought that it was a farewell card. Perhaps I had misjudged them. Behind those grim expressions perhaps there lay warm, caring human beings. I began to feel guilty about all my uncharitable thoughts. I needn't have worried. It was the bill. It detailed everything that could possibly have a price placed on it. My only consolation was that not even they had the gall to charge a fee for the anaesthetist. However, I was surprised that they had omitted the ten per cent service charge from the bottom of the bill.

The drive from Zell am See to Munich seemed to be interminable with mile upon mile of hills and mountains with Christmas trees all over them. It was like a never-ending chocolate box. For a long time we seemed to be following the signs to Salzburg and I feared that my ambulance driver would take me to the wrong airport. I lay prone in my hermetically sealed compartment and the driver sat in his cab hunched over the wheel and hurled the ambulance into improbable bends and up and down impossible hills. I made a silent vow to whoever is in charge of things that if I ever got out of Austria alive I would most certainly never return. Not even in the next life.

I was taken to the tradesmen's entrance at Munich Airport. I was driven straight out on to the tarmac where the British European Airways flight was waiting. The ambulance driver helped me scramble out of the ambulance, gave me his bill with a flourish and a click of his heels and, with an exquisite sense of demarcation, drove off rapidly leaving me standing on one foot on the tarmac. I was in a sort of no man's land. It was a bit like one of those dramatic films where our wounded hero struggles to cross the border to freedom.

A BEA steward stood at the top of the aircraft steps. He had seen the same film. He was obviously unwilling to spoil the dramatic moment. He watched benevolently whilst I hopped up the steps. When I reached the top he gave me a welcoming smile and said, 'Good morning, sir, welcome aboard.' I was too breathless to make any reply. I do recall that they were playing their current jingle: 'BEA, number one in Europe,' over the aircraft public address system at the time.

I felt quite emotional at being back in British hands. I must have been quite distraught. The in-flight coffee tasted like nectar and the little bits and pieces of food eaten out of a plastic box with bendy plastic utensils delighted me. I sniffed back a tear. It must have been the relief at realising that I would never have to eat Krankenhaus Apfelstrudel again. That, and being served my coffee by a lady who didn't have legs like tree trunks.

A wheelchair had been ordered for me at Heathrow. They couldn't find it. There was something immensely reassuring about being surrounded by British inefficiency. It seemed so much more comfortable than Austrian indifference. Anyway, I knew that they would get it right in the end. Eventually a creaking wheelchair arrived with an attendant to match. I quite enjoyed being wheeled through the concourse of Queen's Building. Passengers parted on either side as my rheumatic driver rattled through passport control and the customs hall. Thinks... has anyone smuggled contraband through the customs in a plaster cast? I huddled in my wheelchair with my small holdall clasped on my lap and tried to look as if my injury had resulted from a death-defying leap from the ski-jump at Kitzbühel. I suspected, however, that I looked rather more like a refugee from Eastern Europe who had been in the hands of the KGB.

Friends drove me home and back into the hands of the National Health Service. My metabolism patriotically awaited this moment before permitting me to become very ill indeed. A pulmonary embolism no less. My system must have known that I couldn't have afforded to be that ill in Austria. Not even in the third class.

All this happened in 1969. Since then, of course, thanks to Mrs Thatcher and friends, our own Health Service has become much more like Austrian health care. Anyway, I have never been back to Austria. I can't even bear to look at it on the map and as soon as it begins to snow I hide in a darkened room. I suppose that by now that oft-remembered Austrian courier must be distinctly middle-aged. I hope that his rheumatism is giving him gyp.

The Neurotics Association

I am one of those people who firmly believe that every silver lining has a dark cloud. Probably two.

I was never a very gregarious child. My brother and sister were much older than I was and although they were kind to me they tended to treat me a bit like a pet rabbit. In consequence I had to look elsewhere for playmates and when the war came and many of my little chums were evacuated I was often left to my own devices and my shrapnel collection.

I started going gloomy and sulky in 1941 during the Blitz but worse was to come. Ravensbeck Grammar School left me with permanent feelings of incompetence and inadequacy. After that, in rapid succession I went shy, spotty, self-conscious and jumpy. Have you ever felt that everyone is looking at you? Well, by 1949 I was convinced of it. I was never quite sure how to describe my funny little ways so by and large I kept quiet about them and lived with the fact that most people just assumed that I was a miserable sod. Then I came across the word neurotic. It sounded nicely scientific and steered a safe middle course between downright potty and psychopathically jolly.

When my dear old mum died in 1951 I thought that the end of the world had come. I even grasped at religion for a while so you will know that it was dire. Mind you, if you are feeling sad, sorry and wishing you were dead, there is nothing like a Church of England congregation to make you feel worse. There wasn't any bereavement counselling in those days. You wore a mourning band on your sleeve for a couple of weeks, put an advertisement in the 'Deaths' section of the *Beckenham and Penge Advertiser*, people sent you polite little notes of condolence and you sent them back little black-edged cards saying thank you. After that you just got on with it. In my case 'it' was the remaining eighteen months of my national service. But the dark days kept coming back. At one stage I thought I might end it all. I thought that a hundred aspirins would probably do the trick but since I had trouble in swallowing even two for a headache the practicalities defeated me. More to the point, I had an uneasy feeling that death might hurt.

My self-confidence was not helped by the fact that most girls treated me with the distaste normally reserved for something that the cat had puked up on the front room carpet. An ill-considered marriage didn't seem to improve things, not with a wife who obviously felt she had made great sacrifices by marrying me and clearly wanted her money back. Our acrimonious separation brought more dark days and by now I realised that there was nothing so bad that it couldn't get considerably worse.

By about 1959 I had reached the stage of feeling that not only was half the world against me but that the other half were just as bad. I tended to be anxious about everything including the fear that if the Russkies dropped the bomb then, knowing my luck, they would probably miss me. I was foolish enough to confide some of these thoughts to my doctor only to discover that he was an amateur psychologist. I think that he must have stayed awake during a series of lectures on psychiatry during his time at medical school in about 1931 and had never recovered. Always beware of anyone who claims to know just how you feel. Anyway, he said he had a colleague who was a psychiatrist who would make me feel that life was just a bowl of cherries in a trice, if not sooner. Well, one of my other weaknesses is an extreme naivety and no one has ever cured me of that either. So there I was despatched to see this psychiatrist clasping my appointment card. And all on the National Health Service too.

I didn't have much of a clue about what psychiatrists actually did but I rather assumed that he would listen sympathetically and take notes whilst I reclined on a comfortable couch and told him all my troubles. I assumed that after that he would explain why I was such a sad old lump and from thereon I would live happily ever after like the closing scenes of a Hollywood musical. I also took it for granted that the cure would lead to fame, fortune and the success with women that had so far eluded me.

My first shock was that the psychiatrist was located in a mental hospital. To make it more intimidating the hospital was in the middle of Gravesend Heath which was a good shilling bus ride away from civilisation. Even assuming you recognised Gravesend as civilised. The hospital buildings looked like a backdrop for one of Charles Dickens's more depressing little dramas and the possibility of anyone getting better from anything in a place like that seemed remote in the extreme.

The place was constructed like a prison and was one of those Victorian establishments built in red brick with high ceilings, stone floors and painted throughout in institutional bottle green. I was interviewed first by a male mental nurse who looked as if he had trained at Buchenwald and gave the impression that he was just waiting for the opportunity to throw me into a straitjacket. He created a large new file with my name on the front and laboriously wrote down every answer to his questions in large block capitals as if it was likely to be produced as evidence against me in court.

Then I saw the psychiatrist. He wasn't my idea of a psychiatrist. He had all the subtlety of my RAF drill instructor. He seemed obsessed by my sex life. I wouldn't have minded but I didn't have any sex life at the time and felt under great pressure to make some up. At the end of the interview the psychiatrist seemed to have come to the conclusion that I was a suitable case for treatment. By the expression on his face he seemed to have a lobotomy in mind. Personally, I had come to the conclusion that I would rather drain an alligator swamp than visit his establishment again. I didn't have the courage to tell him my views so I left carrying another appointment card and with a suitably grateful expression on my face. Privately, however, I had resolved that there was no way I would return to that establishment and that in future I would just have to learn to live with my funny little ways.

I understand that manic depressives have periods of misery interspersed with periods of great pleasure and excitement. Since my life was not noteworthy for its periods of great pleasure and excitement it seemed unlikely that I fell into this category. During one of my lonelier and more morose phases I saw an advertisement, in the *Sunday Observer* I think it was, for a group called The Association of Neurotics. It offered club meetings for sensitive souls who were lonely or otherwise distressed and in need of companionship.

I decided to join and sent off my subscription. I felt quite proud at being so positive and decisive. The meetings were held in the large basement room of a hotel somewhere in Marylebone. My first meeting turned out also to be my last. The room had all the comforts of a missionary hall. The advertisement had led me to expect a pleasant crowd of thoughtful, sensitive souls all wanting to make friends. What I discovered was a roomful of stone-raving nutters. The only thing missing was someone in a Napoleon uniform. The only therapeutic affect was that after half an hour I left hurriedly with the smug feeling that I was much more normal than I had thought I was.

In later life I came to deal with a great many unhappy and disturbed people ranging from the mildly odd to the stone-raving head-banging bonkers. In a way this gave me some comfort and led me to the conclusion that sad old sod I might be but nutters I was not. Well, only during the full moon or at Christmas anyway.

Tour of Britain

I hadn't had a proper holiday since my fortnight at Herne
Bay with the family in 1950. Now, in 1961 I was at last
earning enough money to contemplate a proper summer
holiday once again. Just about.

A colleague at work was thinking along similar lines and
we decided to take a holiday together. Neither of us had
seen much of the British Isles and a touring holiday came
to mind. The first difficulty to overcome was that neither of
us owned a car. Although bicycling around the United
Kingdom might have seemed an economical option it
might also, it seemed to me, easily have lead to a grievously
sore bum. As for clumping about in hiking boots and hairy
socks with a knapsack on my back this was just about as
attractive as a fortnight in an alligator swamp. After much
debate the problem was eventually solved by Glowerings
Luxury Coach Tours.

Of course, these days when people drive across the Gobi
Dessert in a second-hand Land-Rover or climb the
Himalayas without benefit of a Sherpa guide, a coach tour
of Britain may sound a bit tame but between 1951 and 1961
my only holiday was a day trip to Hastings with a morning
coffee stop at East Grinstead so you will understand that it
sounded a bit exciting to me.

Glowerings Luxury Coach Tours offered a grand
thirteen-day tour of Britain for a sum that would neatly
reduce my Post Office Savings account to a small pile of
peanuts. It wasn't strictly a tour of Britain because it left out

Northern Ireland but I have no intention of getting into a debate about that for fear that I might end up on an IRA hit list.

My friend and I joined the coach at the lower end of the Old Kent Road which didn't seem the most exciting gateway to a tour that was promised to be scenic, romantic and historic. The remainder of the party joined the coach at Victoria Coach Station. They appeared to be mostly American widows with blue rinses augmented by a mix of colonials doing Europe and a few elderly spinsters whose origins and motives were unclear.

We left London by way of the Finchley Road and the Barnet bypass. Barnet seemed pretty far north to me and I wondered where the coal mines started since I knew that they had a lot of coal mines in the north. Well, they did in those days anyway.

Our driver and guide was young and personable and prided himself on his knowledge of history. On our way up the A1 he introduced himself with the benefit of his microphone which he used with the technique of someone on *Opportunity Knocks*. He liked to be called Ronnie, he announced. The gist of his introductory remarks was that he was going to care for us with total devotion for the next thirteen days. Although he was far too subtle to say so it was clear that he hoped that such virtue would have its own reward on day thirteen. Ronnie, it seemed, could and would solve anything from poor service at dinner to a nasty outbreak of World War Three. We were to worry about nothing. Ronnie was there to see to it all on behalf of Glowerings Luxury Coach Tours. He was both our courier and our driver and he was totally up to the job. The blue rinse brigade were delighted with Ronnie. By the time we reached our lunch stop at Stamford they were all vying for his attention.

During the afternoon journey Ronnie treated us to

excerpts from his historical repertoire. Did you know, for example, that King John died in Newark-on-Trent in 1216 and that the twelfth-century castle withstood three sieges in the Civil War? Ronnie hastily added that the castle was now dismantled. He was anxious not to be talked into a detour by the American ladies who went into paroxysms of delight whenever the word 'castle' was mentioned.

Shortly after this Ronnie nearly fell out of his driving seat. To the right, he said, about twelve miles away, you could sometimes see Lincoln Cathedral if the weather was clear. As it happened, it wasn't.

We stopped the first night at Harrogate. The town was very crowded and all the hotels seemed to be full. We were scheduled to stay at the Great Bear but it turned out to be overbooked. We stayed instead at the Superior or was it the Remarkable? Or maybe it was the Impressive. Or the Outstanding or the Distinguished. I really cannot remember. There are some traumas that the mind mercifully blocks out. Externally the hotel was impressive. It was Victorian Gothic, a bit like St Pancras station. Or Dracula's castle. It had four floors and another one in the roof and there were wrought iron balconies and lots of cornices and finials and architectural bits and pieces.

The bedroom was extremely spacious. It was so large that the single light didn't reach into the corners. The ceiling was so high that you would have needed oxygen to whitewash it and you had to go into training before you set out for the en-suite bathroom. The bath itself was all marble and brass taps. It was a pity about the water which was brownish and coldish. Well, bloody freezing actually. To cap it all the lavatory smelled as if a rat had died down it in a fit of excitement on hearing about the relief of Mafeking.

It was certainly a very large hotel. I gained the impression that it had been closed since Queen Victoria died and had been especially opened up to accommodate Glowerings Luxury Tours.

The restaurant was what one might have expected. The carpets were magnificent and frayed and the windows high and semi-opaque. As for the curtains, these were velvet plush and had a moth kibbutz established in the folds. The chandeliers rattled in the draught and our waiter was geriatric and had bad feet. He was a youngster compared with the head waiter who started wheezing with the exertion of taking the order. Not that it was a very complex task. There was hot or cold and the hot turned out to be cold by the time we got it. The blue rinse Americans started the meal in good humour thinking that it was all part of the quaint English heritage but by the time they had got to the soggy apple pie and the furry cheddar they were getting distinctly tetchy. It was a relief to all concerned when the meal was over and the head waiter could get back to the old people's home.

Ronnie was nowhere to be seen that night. He was no fool. I expect that he had gone down to the pub for a pint and a pork pie. I can remember nothing of breakfast the next morning; I expect that it was gruel.

During the next day we progressed steadily towards Scotland. Ronnie told us that at Otterburn in 1388 the English led by Hotspur had been defeated by the Scots under Douglas. I was beginning to resent old Ronnie clever clogs. The only *Hotspur* I had ever heard of cost tuppence every Friday.

We crossed into Scotland at Carter Bar. I had never been to a foreign country before and felt quite excited. I wasn't quite sure what to expect but the locals didn't seem to be wearing kilts or using nobbly sticks or saying 'Och-aye' or 'Hoots mon' so it was a bit of an anticlimax. In fact, all I saw for the next ten miles was a Scottish sheep and all he said was baa.

Ronnie invariably arranged morning coffee stops and afternoon tea stops. In theory these were for sightseeing opportunities but in reality they were to ensure that elderly bladders did not become too distended and delay the tour en route. The trouble with these brief stops was that you had to make instant choices. Was it to be a cup of tea and a pee or a quick whip round Jedburgh Abbey? Ronnie's schedule didn't allow for both, that was for sure.

I still have a black and white postcard of Jedburgh Abbey. I have no idea why I bought it, or why I kept it. It looks a bit boring to me. It says, 'Greetings and Good Luck' on the back. It also says 'Real Photograph (Copyright)', and there is a thistle emblem with 'The Best of Scotland' printed underneath. The lady in the foreground of the photo looks as if she is wearing a bustle.

By the second night we had reached Edinburgh. This was a sort of crossroads for all the Glowerings Luxury Coach Tours. Glowerings had their own hotel in Edinburgh. It was small but comfortable. Just to make sure that you realised that you were in Scotland they had a piper who turned out to greet each coach and to pipe it away again in the morning. By the time we left Edinburgh the next morning my head was throbbing with 'Scotland the Brave'. I quite like the Scots but bagpipes for breakfast is a stern test. Ronnie took us for a little extra tour in Edinburgh. I think that it was one of his private little earners. We did the castle and Holyrood House and he kept going on about Greyfriars Bobby and Sir Walter Scott and all.

It didn't take long to come to the conclusion that Ronnie was a real pain in the arse. A proper show-off. When we joined the coach each morning there was Ronnie doing his favourite gymnastic trick of a slow somersault between the luggage rails in the aisle of the coach. This used to inflame the elderly American tourists who used to chorus, 'Gee, Ronnie!' as they eyed him in his tight trousers doing his neat somersaults.

Ronnie, in an informal moment, let slip that in the winter months, when tours of Britain were not in great demand, he drove a petrol tanker instead. He was certainly a very good driver and he manoeuvred our forty-seater coach down country lanes as if it were a Morris Minor. Still, ever after I couldn't help thinking that he drove us around much as if we were a 5,000 gallon load of Esso Extra high octane.

After Edinburgh we headed for the Trossachs. I had no idea what or who the Trossachs were. They sounded like something a Scotsman kept under his kilt. Our hotel was on the side of Loch Lomond. For some reason or other we had to approach the hotel by way of a small motorboat. It was very romantic. Well, Ronnie said it was and he sang 'Annie Laurie' twice to prove it. Ronnie was in full spate by now. Names like Robert Burns and Rob thingy tripped off his tongue as if they were old mates of his. He tried to get us to sing 'My love is like a red, red rose' as we floated across the loch but it was not an unqualified success.

After dinner which was a distinct improvement on the Superior or whatever, we all strolled on the terrace and watched the moonlight glistening on the loch. My mood had been much improved by two glasses of Auld Highland Moose which I had concluded was the best way to form an optimistic view of a Glowerings Luxury Tour. Ronnie was at it again telling romantic stories about Rob thingy and Flora McDonald.

It was at this stage that I first became conscious that there were two young women in our coach party. They had been sitting at the back of the coach and had adopted an extremely low profile. Well, totally flat actually. No, I don't mean physically flat; in fact they had bosoms and other bits that were quite noteworthy. I can't think why I hadn't noticed them before. Not that they showed the least interest in me or my mate. In fact, they were usually under the shadow of an elderly Australian couple who kept saying things like 'fair dinkum'. I never believed that people actually said things like that but if you disbelieve me then go on a Glowerings Luxury Tour.

The tour started to go downhill after Loch Lomond. Well, actually the coach went up to Crianlarich to give us a long distance view of the Highlands (you will remember that it was a tour of Britain). After that we headed for the Lake District. We stopped off in Gretna Green for a bit of tourist nonsense. They wanted to re-enact a marriage at the blacksmith's forge for us. I was under pressure to role play a marriage with the prettier of the two young women but I was too bashful. Still, by the time we got to Windermere I was having elaborate fantasies about what it might have been like if I had eloped with her.

During that day we passed through Glasgow at a fair rate of knots. Ronnie seemed lost for words and for once concentrated on his driving. Nothing I saw as we passed through made me think that he should have driven any slower.

Personally, I found the Lake District a bit boring. It was pretty enough but after you have said ooh and aah a few times what are you left with? In the Lake District Ronnie excelled himself. Not that we saw all that much of it. We saw Skiddaw from a distance, shot through Keswick, caught a glimpse of Thirlmere and Grasmere and rocketed through Ambleside. All the while Ronnie was going on about Wordsworth and Coleridge and Southey and Shelley. He made them all sound as if they were all old school chums of his. The colonials were enthralled. I think they were expecting Ronnie to invite them all round for tea.

We stayed at a hotel on the side of Lake Windermere. It was one of those hotels that let you know that they didn't really approve of coach parties. They were clearly a bit desperate for Glowerings fortnightly cheque but the staff were distinctly pissed off because all gratuities were supposed to be included in Glowerings tour price.

I hadn't really got used to staying in hotels. In fact they made me distinctly jumpy. Two years in the Royal Air Works on full board terms was the nearest comparable experience I had and the airmen's mess at RAF White Waltham did nothing to help me cope with the intricacies of an à la carte menu. Or any other kind of menu come to that. There were real mysteries about staying in hotels. Could you really put your shoes out to be cleaned? And did they put it on the bill? And what if someone nicked your shoes?

I didn't know how to deal with waiters and I was terrified of the wine list. From the moment you arrived at the hotel there were problems. For starters, I was never sure if you were expected to wait for someone to carry your case up to your room or whether you humped it yourself. I never had problems like that with my kitbag in the Royal Air Works. And when did you tip people? I spent most of my time hiding from the hotel staff in case they expected a tip. This was partly because I didn't know how much to give them and partly because I couldn't afford it anyway.

The next day we shot through Liverpool at high speed. Liverpool in those days had docks, miles of them. I don't know what it has these days. Apart from unemployment. Of course, there was also the Mersey Tunnel. Did you know that 1,000,000 bolts were used in the cast-iron lining? Ronnie did.

It got nastier after that. Llannberris. All slate quarries and Welshness. Indeed to goodness. We went in a pub and they all started gabbling in this foreign language. Yes, yes, I know, I'm culturally insensitive and thoroughly racist to boot. So would you be if you went in a pub and couldn't get a pint of Watneys Red Barrel when you were parched.

It was a great relief to get out of Wales even if we did have to go up Snowdon before we could do it. Snowdon was extremely boring. There was fog halfway up and cloud at the top and I got snow in my Hush Puppies. On the way down it started to pour with rain. Culturally insensitive indeed. No wonder they are such a bloody miserable lot.

Then we headed for Ross-on-Wye. Even I had to admit that Ross-on-Wye was pretty. Pity about the hotel. There wasn't room to park the coach so it had to be left at the bottom of the hill whilst we trudged up to the top with Ronnie extolling the virtues of the view and insisting that the walk would give us a good appetite for dinner.

I had begun to notice by this time that Ronnie was paying a good deal of attention to the two young women. Even I realised that his interest went beyond a healthy interest in their tip potential and I am pathologically naive. I started to get a bit jealous. Well, they hadn't even spoken to me since I had chickened out of the mock marriage ceremony at Gretna Green. Well, apart from saying good morning in Llanberris, and that didn't count because there wasn't much else to do in Llanberris.

I am pleased to report that they seemed to go off Ronnie after Ross-on-Wye. Something must have happened. They started chatting to me and my chum. It turned out that they were South Africans. They kept talking about the black servant problem but otherwise they seemed quite normal. I took a fancy to Rose. Rose had come to England to find herself. I noted that she also had extremely nice bosoms. Her legs weren't at all bad either. She was destined to marry a rich farmer but wasn't quite sure about it. Apparently he was quite a lot older than Rose and a Roman Catholic to boot. Personally I couldn't see the problem. I mean we were talking seriously rich. Like ten thousand acres. Still, Rose was enjoying her dilemma and I was too polite to bet on the outcome, even though it was worth a tenner of anyone's money.

To Rose and her chum Melanie the tour of Britain was a small sideshow. They were doing the whole of Europe and the British Isles was just the hors d'oeuvres. Just a titbit on toast. I tell you, those girls made a royal tour look like a tuppenny bus ride.

I still have a photograph of me and Rose standing in front of Glowerings Luxury Coach whilst it was parked beside a no parking sign in Dunster (afternoon tea stop). Rose is captured for all time looking up at me adoringly as a perpetual reminder of yet another Edom missed opportunity. I was beginning to quite fancy Rose but time was running out and I was never noted for much initiative. By the time we got to Lynmouth Rose and I were on quite friendly terms. It was here that I discovered what had happened in Ross-on-Wye. Ronnie had disgraced himself by persuading Rose to join him in the back of the coach after lights out. She seemed to be under the impression that they were searching for her mislaid tour guide but Ronnie had tried to conduct a much more personal search. Rose was outraged. She was not that sort of a girl, she explained to me. Just my luck. Besides, she was promised to another. This all had an extremely inhibiting effect on me. We did manage a little kissing and hugging but apart from that it was like an scene from *Brief Encounter* without the steam engines.

Just after Clovelly (coffee and postcards but no time for the donkey ride) we passed into Cornwall. We had told the two girls, with whom we were now distinctly chummy, that they would need their passports to enter the Duchy and that they would need a phrase book to communicate with the natives. When Melanie found out that this was just our strange English sense of humour she got quite nasty.

Rose and I did a bit more canoodling and neck nuzzling

in Falmouth which was our next overnight stop. It was quite romantic looking out over the harbour at Falmouth with great ships anchored in the bay. Sadly, however, Rose was determined that she should stay inviolate until she made up her mind about old ten thousand acres. My only consolation was that my mate was making even less progress with Rose's chum, Melanie, who although quite pretty was extremely moody. Some days she behaved as if the Boer War was still on. When she behaved like that I wished that it still was.

Falmouth was our turning point. After this we were heading back for the smoke although we still had a couple of overnight stops. At the end of the eleventh day we arrived in Taunton.

There isn't much to say about Taunton. Mind you, Ronnie did his best and kept going on about Judge Jeffreys and the Bloody Assizes. To tell you the truth, I can't remember much about the place. Perhaps the only thing in its favour is that it has to be better than Okehampton.

The next day we headed for Bath. On the way we visited Cheddar Gorge but that was extremely boring. It was all cliffs and caves and souvenir stalls. Besides, I could never tell my stalactites from my stalagmites so much of it went over my head. Sorry, I couldn't resist the joke.

We also did some sightseeing in Wells which, Ronnie told us, had the finest collection of mediaeval sculpture in England. For the life of me I can't remember anything else about Wells and Ronnie probably made up the bit about the medieval sculpture anyway.

Bath was boring. It may have been that no place could live up to the advance publicity that Ronnie gave it but I think that it was also that the tour was running out of steam. Ronnie was by now claiming to be a great authority on architecture but even the blue rinse brigade were beginning to lose interest. Everyone was looking distinctly crumpled and getting a bit tetchy. Even Ronnie was looking jaded and was having to look things up in his tour guide and his anecdote rate had dropped to about ten an hour.

In the evening we walked around Bath and looked at the architecture. I was unable to detach Rose from the rest of our party and I have never forgiven Bath for being the scene of my final lost opportunity.

Personally, I was distinctly hurt that my relationship with Rose, far from flourishing into a passionate affair was withering on the vine. Although she didn't say so, I think that at about this stage she had decided that Roman Catholicism and ten thousand acres wasn't a bad deal and was keen to do the rest of Europe as quickly as possible so that she could return home and get on with it.

Anyway, Bath was distinctly boring. Mind you, the Romans have always had that sort of effect on me. All straight roads and bath nights and mosaics and things. Although the orgies were probably all right. Not that I saw anything remotely like an orgy whilst I was in Bath.

The final day included a guided tour of the colleges in Oxford. It only lasted two hours and we had to skip lunch to fit that in. Still, it was the nearest I ever got to an Oxbridge education.

Then we headed for London, passing Maidenhead on the way. The tour guide described Maidenhead as 'a gay upriver resort'. Try getting away with that today.

The rest of the coach party disembarked at Victoria Coach Station. Farewells were hurried and perfunctory. Already the group spirit was dissipating and the tourists' minds were on other things.

Rose and I exchanged a poignant and meaningful glance, still very much in the *Brief Encounter* mode, but I had the impression that I was already consigned to a small segment of her numerous holiday memories along with the thatched cottages and ruined castles. I know that she kept a diary of her travels. I suspect that I probably merited a small paragraph somewhere around day ten or eleven.

Ronnie stood at the door of his coach exuding bonhomie and gathering in a rich harvest of tips. Eventually my mate and I were the last survivors on the coach.

Ronnie dropped us off at the lower end of the Old Kent Road. He accepted his gratuities from us as if they were no more than his due and then drove off in a cloud of diesel fumes and with a farewell toot on his hooter in the direction of his depot in Deptford. The Grand Tour of Britain 1961 was finally and irrefutably over.

Lonely Hearts

It was during a particularly lonely period in my life when I was living in central London that I came across a newspaper called *The London Weekly Advertiser*. I discovered that it had pages of advertisements for people seeking friends of the opposing gender. Dating agencies as such were not known in the early 1960s but there were matrimonial agencies that offered introductions for those seeking 'friendship and marriage'. In addition, some brave spirits also advertised for partners independently. In those days you could advertise for a marriage partner or a chum but you certainly couldn't even hint that you had nooky in mind. Even so, seeking a soulmate by advertising was generally viewed with great suspicion and there was a view that it was either for the wimpish and odd or was a device for locating professional services of the horizontal kind.

There were a number of marriage bureaux advertising in the personal columns of *The London Weekly Advertiser* which also included advertisements offering 'Bust Beauty Yours' and 'Stop Smoking in Three Days or Your Money Back'. The marriage bureaux made tempting promises. 'Lonely, bored and fed up? You can be introduced to new and exciting friends'; 'Happy friendships and life partners'; 'Find Romance!' The temptations were too great. Thus it was that I signed up with the Marjorie Gibson Marriage and Introductions Bureau which promised 'You Need not be Lonely in the Evenings and at Weekends'. Even at a fee of fifteen guineas that seemed a pretty good offer. The arrangement offered unlimited introductions until a suitable soulmate was found. 'All communications sent in confidence in plain sealed envelope.'

I indicated to the Marjorie Gibson Bureau that I wished to confine my forays to London and the south-east. The farthest I was despatched was to Southend. That particular journey tended to prove the law of diminishing returns. The lady in question was pleasant enough, if a bit podgy, but the introduction slip from the agency had omitted to mention her mother. Mother took charge of the whole event. First mumsy gave me a lecture about the last caller for her daughter's favours who had arrived bringing his pyjamas in a paper carrier bag. This had displeased mumsy. Daughter did not express an opinion. I decided not to mention that I slept in the noddy. Somehow I suspected that it would not be a helpful contribution to the debate. Anyway, I was allowed to take daughter for a walk along the prom and I was given a nice tea with scones and raspberry jam but on balance I decided not to pursue the relationship. I had enough trouble coping with women without contending with their mothers as well.

Next I visited a lady who had her own council house in Addiscombe. This was not a success. She had two small children asleep upstairs and kept telling me about her wicked ex-husband and her bad back. I assumed that this was her coded message for telling me she did not fancy me and would not take kindly to being jumped upon. I wasn't all that upset; she had an ominous collection of Elvis Presley records.

At Easter 1961 I had an assignation with a young woman in west London. When I called at her flat I discovered that she had omitted to mention that she had four children, all of whom seemed to be hyperactive or maladjusted or both. She was a very nice but rather sad lady living in a level of chaos that I found distinctly intimidating. The kids accepted me with such ease that I suspected that I was not the first honorary uncle who had come to call. They were keen to involve me in the riots and civil commotion that passed for playtime in their scheme of things and I feared that I might suffer some grave and permanent injury. I was overcome with guilt that I did not feel up to getting involved in a relationship that included four disorderly little blessings whose dad I understood was an absentee Turkish Cypriot. I missed my last bus home and had to stay the night but I slept in nervous and chaste isolation on the sofa. In the morning I went out and bought Easter eggs all round and then left rapidly to keep an urgent appointment with my sick grandmother.

Then there was a very prim and demure young woman whose name I forget. I used to meet her in my favourite espresso coffee bar in the Strand. For several evenings we drank espresso coffee and then sat and held hands in the dark in St James's Park. She was petite, pretty and always very neatly dressed and had the appearance of a china doll. She invariably sat on the park bench with an umbrella clasped firmly between her rather pretty little knees. The umbrella handle was I recall in the shape of a duck's head with a sardonic expression on its face. I eventually came to the conclusion that the umbrella handle was the only thing that was ever going to get between those pretty little legs.

Ellen was a really nice woman and was the most successful of my lonely hearts assignations. Her husband had run off with another woman and Ellen was desperate to discover what extras the other woman had offered. Ellen was very curious about the mysteries of advanced sex but was wary about putting theory into practice. She was always going on about a married friend whose lovemaking incorporated an ironing board. No, I don't know how either. Anyway, anything that happened to Ellen had to happen in the dark and preferably under several blankets.

For some reason she was also always incredibly reluctant to abandon her Playtex living girdle. Making love to her was a bit of a struggle. She kept pushing me away and saying, 'No, no,' but whenever I stopped she would ask me what was the matter in a very hurt tone. I think that she had seen too many Fred Astaire and Ginger Rogers films. Ellen was a ballroom dancer and loved fluffy dresses with sequins and wanted her love life to be romantic. It was hard to tell why she put up with me since I had three left feet and was as romantic as Lou Costello. I really liked Ellen who would even come and watch Fulham with me so I knew my feelings were reciprocated. Although our love life was always a struggle she was a good friend.

Doris was married to a regular soldier but she was separated and said she was seeking a divorce. She had a photo of her spouse sitting on a horse and wearing a tin waistcoat and a funny hat. I suppose he must have been in the Life Guards. Either that or he liked dressing up. Although Doris was a very nice lady and appeared quite fond of me she seemed to live a strange, mysterious and unsettled life. She had a baby who lived with her relatives in Devon and she used to disappear to Totnes periodically. She had a number of friends and acquaintances all of whom seemed to have even more eccentric lifestyles than she did. Doris worked in the restaurant business and always fed me well. She also allowed me to drive her car which in view of my driving skills was incredibly trusting, or foolhardy. Doris was always changing jobs and digs and I used to visit her at her various flats and bedsitters. She always seemed to live in houses with the most odd collections of tenants. On one occasion when I met her she was nursing a black eye which she said she had got through walking into a door. There was much that was unexplained about Doris. I suspect that she was in the Mafia or something.

Frankie lived in a semi-derelict flat just off the Portobello Road. She gave the impression of only just suppressed sensuality but she tended to blow a bit hot and cold and I suspect that she had other irons in the fire, if you will forgive the expression. I was always hoping that our relationship might develop into something torrid and unrestrained but it never did. Although we met on a number of occasions she was more of a mystery than Doris and I couldn't cope with the suspense.

I also visited a lady who lived in furnished rooms in the Walworth Road. I never felt very comfortable that close to the Elephant and Castle which in those days was a bit naughty, especially when the pubs turned out. This lady announced that she had dropped her previous boyfriend when he went to prison for GBH. She was unhelpfully vague about his release date and I spent the entire evening in acute anxiety wondering if he would burst into the flat wielding a cut-throat razor or a sawn-off shotgun. I don't know if it was my nerves but I can't remember anything else about that particular assignation and it was never repeated.

Beatrice was a rather superior but very attractive lady with memorably long and well shaped legs. Curiously, she came originally from Grimsby and could get quite nasty if you mentioned it. Her first husband had turned schizophrenic and Beatrice always seemed to be watching me rather quizzically as if she was searching for the first signs. She lived in an elegant flat in South Kensington which was all white paint and Heals furniture. She used to take me off to concerts at the Festival Hall and gently patronise me because I preferred Tchaikovsky to Mahler. I remember that we spent a very nice Christmas together in her flat in 1964. She was a radiographer and it was evident that she had a very good grounding in anatomy. She had lots of medical friends and moved in rather cultured circles. Although the phrase was not in common parlance at the time I think that I was probably her 'bit of rough'. She was also very authoritative. 'Get on with it if you are going to,' she would say, 'I don't like any messing about.' She eventually abandoned me for someone who was heavily into Shostakovich.

I must say that the Marjorie Gibson Bureau gave me good value. They never succeeded in finding me a permanent soulmate but they certainly broadened my experience of the opposite gender who until that time had been a bit of a mystery to me. Come to think of it, I suppose that they still are.

Interviews

I have had rather more than my share of unsuccessful interviews in the course of a somewhat chequered career. I refer to chequered as in chess. I see myself rather like the knight that moves across the board in a series of confusing zigzags and doesn't make as much progress as some of the more influential pieces on the board. I have always envied the bishops and castles of this world with their more incisive approach to life's little challenges. Still, we are all, I suppose, how the great chess set maker in the sky designed us. Do you detect a touch of Omar Khayyam in all this? Well, what do you expect for this price, Rabindranath Tagore?

But I digress. I was going on about unsuccessful interviews. I suppose that the very first experience that loosely falls under this description was my interview for a scholarship place at Ravensbeck Grammar School. For some reason that I have never understood my parents felt that a place at Ravensbeck Grammar School was highly desirable. Not in my view it wasn't. Anyway, having spent an excruciating morning doing what passed for the eleven plus in 1944 I was called back for an interview by the headmaster. Mr Oxo Brown, MA (Oxon), was a large, fat and loud man to whom I took an instinctive dislike. He was, however, the sort of man who encouraged you to keep your opinions to yourself. He asked me all sorts of questions and then I had to read out loud to him. I can't remember what it was I had to read but it was sure to have been something suitable. Adults had very clear ideas about suitable reading material for children in those days and the adventures of Deed-a-Day Danny in my *Knockout* were clearly not on the approved list. It was a funny sort of interview altogether and I wasn't awarded a scholarship although they did agree to admit me. Unfortunately.

The next interview that I remember was an interview arranged by the school careers master in about 1949. I had decided that I wanted to be a press photographer. The decision was based on that famous photograph I had taken of the West Wickham Sea Cadets drum and bugle band leading the Fair and Flitch procession in 1948. If I say so myself, this was a masterpiece of topicality and action. The leading sea cadet's drumsticks were caught in mid thump at one five-hundredth of a second for posterity.

The careers master arranged for this man he knew who worked for Reynolds News to come to interview me. The interview itself was a bit of an anticlimax. The man was not impressed with my photograph of the West Wickham Sea Cadets drum and bugle band. Neither was he impressed by my willingness to work for Reynolds News at a reduced rate. Apparently Reynolds News wasn't all that interested in Fair and Flitch processions. Not even at one five-hundredth of a second. He was prepared to offer advice but certainly not employment. The essence of his advice was that press photography was highly competitive and best forgotten. He suggested that I should find a nice steady secure job in a bank, or an insurance company.

During my time in the Royal Air Works I was assessed to see what work I was best suited for. I indicated that I would be quite willing to fly one of their Canberras for them but the personnel selection assessor indicated, rather unkindly I thought, that since I couldn't tell my reddy browns from my browny greens I was deemed colour blind and wouldn't therefore be considered suitable to fly a

476

bloody kite, let alone a Canberra.

Amongst some of the firms I never worked for was Pricketts the Grocers. They were advertising for an assistant buyer. Pricketts sold cheap groceries through a chain of small stores around South London. I say a chain but actually it was three. Or was it four? Anyway it was before the era of the great supermarkets and Pricketts were beginning to put some of the smaller grocery shops out of business by discounting. Eggs were their speciality. Pricketts' eggs were as fresh as the country air, or so they said.

Their headquarters was located in a series of railway arches somewhere near Camberwell Green. The two partners who interviewed me had an interviewing technique worthy of the serious crimes squad. The tall one was suave, friendly and civilised. He took my coat, found me a chair and offered me a cigarette. (This was before the days when the offer of a cigarette was a test to see if you had any filthy antisocial and life-threatening habits.)

The other partner was small, squat and thuggish. His interviewing technique was aggressive, inquisitive and persistent. In the course of fifteen minutes he had written off my education, assassinated my character, exposed my lack of ambition and ridiculed my career to date. He made it entirely clear that my prospects for the future were extremely unpromising and he seemed to think that I wouldn't recognise a lorry-load of general groceries if it ran over my big toe. Long before the interview was over we were both moving to the conclusion that our employer–employee relationship would not be a rewarding one. I was not offered the job. The only consolation is that Pricketts and their country fresh eggs went out of business a couple of years later. Serves the buggers right.

At one stage I decided that I would protect the community from the rising crime wave. I applied to join the police and was invited to their recruitment centre. I remember that there were all sorts of little intelligence tests and interviews. 'And why do you want to be a policeman, Edom?' I was scarcely likely to say that it was because I fancied the opportunity to whack people over the head with my regulation truncheon, was I?

There was a medical as well which involved trailing around from room to room clad only in a towel having different bits of me looked at by different doctors. One of them looked up my bum with a torch which seemed a bit cheeky to me. He didn't even say excuse me. Anyway, the whole thing came to a halt when they flicked all these charts of coloured spots in front of me. I was supposed to see lots of little numbers but all I saw was lots of little coloured spots. This was serious. I was called before the head doctor. No, no, I mean the senior doctor. He invited me to tell him what colour the leather top of his desk was. Muddy brown was not the right answer. So you see, that is how I didn't become a policeman.

I was also once an applicant for a job as an insurance inspector with the Lawful and Gentle Insurance Company. 'Insurance Inspector' was the title that insurance companies used to give their salesmen. It was a genteel euphemism which has probably now been overtaken by something even more obscure. If the American hospitals can use 'negative patient output' to describe dead patients, then the sky's the limit.

Be that as it may the agency manager of the Lawful and Gentle invited me to an interview at his London club. Near St James's, I think it was. It was the first time that I had ever been in a gentlemen's club. Come to think of it, it was also the last time, except for the National Liberal Club and that doesn't really count, does it? Anyway, I was totally and irretrievably intimidated. Not surprisingly, I can remember little of the interview beyond the fact that with great courtesy and over a cup of quite dreadful coffee my interviewer made it clear that his sales force was not yet ready for me. He did, however, give me the benefit of his advice. He suggested that I should join a rugby club and sell personal accident policies to all the members. This would have the double benefit of proving my worth as an insurance salesman to any potential employer and at the same time earn me commission on the premium income at the then going rate of fifteen per cent. The thought of all that mud and shoving and communal baths and beer drinking and rude songs totally unnerved me and I did not pursue a career in insurance sales.

Whilst pursuing my career in the probation service I applied to attend a special seminar group run by an eminent psychiatrist. Now I was used to working with psychiatrists and generally I found them a pleasantly nutty lot but being interviewed by one for a place on a elite group was a bit confusing. How should I present myself? I attended for interview at this rather plush clinic in one of the more affluent bits of London. The eminent psychiatrist was in a very eminent sort of mood. I had arrived in a relaxed frame of mind wearing my corduroy jacket and Hush Puppies, ready to share my psyche with anybody. It was a mistake. Too late I realised that this was an intellectual conversation and dark suit job. Never mind. Bloody psychiatrists. What do they know anyway?

After some six years in the probation service the urge to become a senior probation officer overtook me. Don't ask me why. It certainly wasn't the money. The first time I applied I didn't get an interview. The second time the interview board turned me down but suggested that I should apply again. The third time they turned me down without comment. The fourth time they gave me the job. I think that they had decided that it was the only way they could stop me bothering them.

Some years later I applied for the job of senior court welfare officer in Worcester. Another mistake. The interview panel seemed to take quite a shine to me. In fact they were so taken with me that I thought that they must be looking at the wrong set of papers. It was just my luck that after having been shortlisted and offered an interview I discovered that I could never have afforded to live in Worcester. I spent most of the interview trying to persuade them that I was unsuitable for the job. I didn't have the nerve to tell them that I had discovered that I couldn't afford it.

Being a glutton for punishment, I then applied to be the director of a new experimental Home Office-sponsored special treatment centre for recidivists. I read all the relevant material on special treatment projects, visited the premises that had been acquired and talked with the relevant assistant chief probation officer. The post was so important that they had a special appointments panel. I gave them the benefit of my ideas. It turned out that they preferred their own. Still, the chief probation officer wrote me a very nice letter. As it happened, the director who was appointed only lasted a year.

Then there came a point when I really began to get ideas above my station. I have only recently remembered this incident. Probably it was so painful that it induced temporary memory loss. Well, temporary as in twenty-four years. By this time I had been working as a probation officer for about twelve years and six of these were as a senior so I was beginning to think I knew a bit about the business. I saw this advertisement for probation inspectors in the Home Office and sent for details. In true Home Office style they sent me sufficient paper to give my postman a hernia. I drafted what I hoped was a suitably persuasive application and waited. Eventually I was invited to an interview on the ninth floor of an anonymous government office block just off Whitehall. The memories of the interview are mercifully clouded. I know that I was trying to make the most of my experience in probation and my tormentors who were clearly in love with their own cleverness patronised me heavily whilst carefully exposing my lack of academic success. Well, virtually none really. The rejection letter ran to three and a half lines and was signed by someone I had never heard of.

After this, the only thing to do seemed to be to get a qualification that would impress the Home Office. I decided to apply for the full-time course of high-powered academic social work training. I regret to report that I was rejected.

Of course, even Edom's life has not been a totally unmitigated disaster. I have in fact remained in gainful employment for most of my life although even that is a mixed blessing and only means that I shall have to pay my own fees in the old people's home. Still, it has meant that even I have managed to get some jobs. Of course, this means that the urge to better oneself is ever present. The most senior job to elude me was the post of deputy chief probation officer for Blankbury. It was all a bit of an ordeal. I had to travel to the county town and was interviewed in the old Guildhall. The entrance was so imposing that I thought that I would have to pay to go in. Inside it was all oak panelling and sombre oil paintings of venerable public officials. There were pictures of Lord Lieutenants and High Sheriffs peering down at me disapprovingly. Even the waiting room had stained glass windows. I was clad in my best blue pinstripe and a new Liberty tie but it was not enough. You would have needed an old Etonian tie and a suit from Saville Row to have felt at ease in there. A double first from Oxbridge would have helped as well.

What looked like the entire probation committee had turned out to interview me. I kept telling myself that the

Home Office had given their approval to me being shortlisted so that I must be in with a chance but this didn't help my crisis of confidence. Perhaps the Home Office had been looking at the wrong file. And did the Blankbury probation committee know that I had failed my School Certificate in woodwork? Each member of the committee asked a question. Some were carefully rehearsed and predictable whilst others seemed original to say the least. There was one questioner who seemed to be under the impression that I was being interviewed for the post of chief weights and measures officer. The elderly lady at the end missed her turn altogether but I think that she had nodded off. Nobody seemed to notice.

Of course, I wouldn't want you to think these were my only failures. We all have our pride. I have been turned down for lots more jobs. I wish I had kept all those letters that said that I hadn't been selected for interview. I should really have kept a scrapbook of them. They would have made interesting reading in the old people's home. Assuming that they will let me in. Perhaps I will fail the interview.

Summon Up the Blood

The Royal Air Works has a lot to answer for. It was another of those volunteering situations. One was always getting volunteered for something in the Air Works. Flight Sergeant Griffin announced to all us erks in his slightly apologetic style that we were required for special duties. Oh God, what was it this time. Fire picket? Special kit inspection? Outbreak of World War Three? No, it was blood. They needed our blood and apparently we had just volunteered.

We reported to the sickbay, jacket off, sleeve rolled up. Then we waited a bit impatiently whilst the blood dripped into the bottle, then ten-minute breather, a free bottle of pale ale and then back to duty. Oh, I forgot, they gave me a little certificate as well.

Well, that was the way it was back in 1952 but a lot of blood has trickled down the tube since then. You see, it didn't seem all that complicated so it became a bit of a habit. Back in civvy street again I continued to surrender small quantities of my life's blood at slightly irregular intervals. It was a bit like going to church. It was a trifle tedious at the time but once you had been there was this warm glow of self-righteousness.

The blood transfusion service had by now given me a small passbook a bit like a driving licence in which they stuck my little certificates each time I bled.

As the years rolled by I donated blood in all sorts of places but the process seemed to get steadily more complicated. As people began to travel abroad on holidays the blood collectors got more and more suspicious about the sort of strange bugs we might be bringing back.

There came this terrible time when I noticed that all the questions about foreign travel included something about visits to South America. Now I never thought that I had been to South America but I suddenly remembered that whilst on a visit to Texas in 1974 my hosts had driven me over the Rio Grande and through the border into Mexico to visit a little town called Matamoros. It was only two miles over the border and we only stayed there for about three hours. I remember buying three ethnic cushion covers and a chunky necklace for my wife that made her neck go green. My only other memories are of a very small goat being roasted on a spit in a shop window, lots of Mexican flies and street gutters running with evil-smelling liquids, the origins of which I preferred not to know.

Anyway, when I casually mentioned my visit to Mexico to the blood people they went potty. I pointed out that my visit had been fifteen years before but it was of no avail. They were nearly wetting themselves. Apparently there was nothing worse for your blood than an afternoon visit to Mexico. They went into a huddle. Eventually after long and scientific deliberations they decided that since I was still around to tell the tale it was probably all right. I had already reached much the same conclusion.

Oh dear, then there was Kenya. The blood people didn't like Kenya either. I had never thought of Kenya as particularly foreign. Any country that gives you egg and bacon for breakfast can't be all that foreign. I went to Kenya in about 1986 but it still throws the blood people into a tizzy every time I mention it. Mind you, there was that pretty dusky maiden on the beach in Mombassa who walked up to me with a happy smile and slipped her hand into mine. I thought that she was just a friendly native or maybe she wanted to take me to view some cut price wood carvings of water buffalo. By the time I realised what she was actually selling she had given me up as a bad job and had wandered off elsewhere. I think she thought that I was subnormal. Anyway, I never mentioned her to the blood merchants.

Blood merchants do not like Morocco or Tunisia either but then come to think of it, neither do I. I have never forgiven the Moroccans for that couscous they served me in Marrakech and as for that camel ride in Hammamet, least said soonest mended.

Over the years I have accumulated a bundle of tattered certificates. After the first ten they gave me a badge but I was too shy to wear it for fear it would be showing off, like wearing a Rotary Club badge. After I had given thirty-seven lots they gave me a silver card to store the certificates in. No explanation, just silver card. More recently they gave me a gold card to mark my half-century. They didn't tell me what the benefits are. Perhaps it is like a Forte gold card. Maybe you get a discount if you ever need blood.

Over the years I have given blood in all sorts of venues: drill halls, community centres, schools, church halls, the co-op hall, the town hall, you name it I have bled in it. Bleeding under a graphic painting of the crucifixion in St Jim's Church hall was probably the worst. The last church hall just had a banner proclaiming 'Trust in the Lord'.

Giving blood has now become really hard work. You really need a degree or at least several A levels. Gone are the days when you just wandered in and they took a pinprick of blood and dropped it in a bottle and if it sank to the bottom you were okay. Even then you had to sign a little form to say that you hadn't had jaundice or glandular fever and I expect that the black death was also regarded with some disfavour. But once you had signed the little form it was chocks away, sleeve rolled up, hop up on the couch, do a quick bit of bleeding and you were ready for your free cup of tea.

Those days are long gone. These days they send you an invitation to attend, then a week later a reminder accompanied by a long list of things you mustn't have done if you want to give blood. It makes me go hot and cold just reading about all these hazards and misfortunes. The warning note also reminds me that I mustn't drive a train or fly a plane after giving blood. Fortunately it doesn't say anything about not driving a six year old Renault. Then the documents suggest that you might like to bring a friend although they make it clear that certain types of friend would not be welcome. When you eventually get to the session, assuming that you have not been deterred already, the going really gets tough. First of all they have a receptionist to screen you. She is invariably unhappy in her work and gives the impression that she would get more fulfilment from setting out traffic cones on the M25. The first thing she does is give you a number. (There is nothing better than a number to put you in your place.) On one visit in 1995 I was blood unit number seventy-two. It's nice to know that I am helping someone to achieve his performance contract.

Then the receptionist gives me a four-page question-naire. Get any of those wrong and it is straight to the bottom of the class. Am I pregnant? Have I had any acupuncture, tattooing or body piercing? Have I been with a lady of easy virtue? Or, even worse, a gentleman of easy virtue? Say anything at all about HIV or AIDS and you are straight out the door.

My problem is more mundane. I take pills for my gout. Every time I have to declare this. Every time I am marched off to see the doctor whilst everyone else stares at me and speculates about what dread disease or dirty habits I have revealed. Each time the doctor looks up my pills in his little book and eventually pronounces me fit to give blood.

I have been giving blood on and off now for over forty years but still they worry about me. Why they can't put my gout pills and my foreign travel on their bloody computer, I'll never know. The AA and the *Reader's Digest* and everyone else who wants to sell me anything seem to have every last detail about my lifestyle on their computers.

Anyway, once cleared by the doctor they take more particulars. Then they take the blood sample, I sign another declaration and they give me some more bits of paper. Two people have done this bit of the process. Smiling is clearly not in their job descriptions. They operate rather like a serious crimes squad interrogation team.

Then I sit and wait. And wait. Eventually someone calls my number. The nurse is not happy in her work either. Anyone would think that I had asked her to give blood. If the nurse talks to me at all it is to complain about the long hours and the low pay. Then the doctor comes to put the needle in. I don't know where the blood transfusion service gets its doctors but they are not at the summit of the profession. One time the lady doctor was shaking so much I thought that she had DT's. It is a wonder she found my arm, let alone my vein. In fairness, most of the doctors can find my vein without too much difficulty but then my vein stands out like Hadrian's Wall so this is no great achievement, especially since they can practise doing it at least seventy-two times a day to my knowledge.

Times change. They used to collect the blood in glass bottles and then place them carefully in containers like milk crates. Nowadays the blood goes into plastic containers like large sachets of tomato sauce at a Happy Eater. Seeing it like that doesn't give you any pride in achievement any more.

Once the blood is extracted and you have had a little rest they give you your certificate and you go and get your free cup of tea and a digestive biscuit if they haven't run out.

You used to be able to sit in quiet contemplation but these days you have to read their business plan, their annual report and their corporate strategy. You can also have some pamphlets if you are that silly. The pamphlets tell you that the aim of the blood transfusion service is to collect blood. They also tell you that this is a good thing. Personally I am beginning to wonder.

In about 1995 they started sending me extra bits of paper through the post. They are usually addressed 'Dear Donor', have a facsimile signature and are written on a word processor. Apparently there is now a National Blood Authority. They have somebody with a knighthood and an OBE to chair it. Surprise, surprise – they planned to reorganise it. This would make everything better for everyone. There were, of course, to be consultations. Would I like a copy of the consultation document? Would I like to recruit some new donors? And by the way, do keep bleeding.

The last few times I have been summoned to bleed there has been yet another change. In addition to all the other gubbins there is a bar code at the bottom of the letter. I am asked to bring this with me to the session; the bar code will help to speed up my registration. Is there no dignity? Have I been a donor all these years to end up being processed like a packet of streaky bacon at a Tesco checkout?

There was an occasion in 1995 when I attended to bleed which turned out to be a total surprise. Every time I attend I find they have changed the procedure in some way or another. I think this is just to maintain the initiative and to confuse all the regular bleeders. But this particular time was totally confusing. They were all really, really nice. This quite upset me. After all, I like to know where I stand. Besides, if this goes on it will spoil my little essay, won't it?

I only recently discovered that the blood transfusion service has been flogging off its surplus stocks to foreign hospitals. I notice that they do deliveries to private hospitals here as well. I wonder how much they charge for it. If I had known all this forty years ago I could have gone into business on my own account and cut out the middle man. Or maybe I could try sending the National Blood Authority an invoice for all the blood they have had over the years; with accrued interest, of course. Everyone understands that we are in a market economy these days.

Still, never mind. They won't take your blood after you are sixty-five so it will soon all be over. It will be a bit of a relief really. I can't cope with all the paperwork and a Blood Donor's Charter will only make my head hurt.

Animals

People tell me that I am sentimental about animals. Sometimes when faced with a couple of juicy rashers of best back I get a vision of lots of little porkers snuggling up to their mum and mum hoping that they are all going to grow up to be brain surgeons.

One vision that really haunts me is the face of a frightened sheep peering out of a vast lorry packed with hundreds of his compatriots and thundering round the M25 on its way to a slaughterhouse hundreds of miles away somewhere in Europe. Silly Billy that I am, it always conjures up for me those old newsreel pictures of human beings being herded into cattle trucks on their way to Auschwitz or Belsen.

Then there are those battery hens all cooped up in little cages unable to move around and denied all freedom. Still, I mustn't be fanciful, must I? I don't expect they mind. Maybe they like being debeaked. Then there is all that fox hunting and deer hunting and hare coursing and otter hunting and badger digging. It is well known that they all enjoy it and enter into the spirit of the thing. Besides, the Good Lord wouldn't have put them here if they weren't to be hunted, would he?

Mind you, if you were expecting to be reincarnated as a hedgehog in your next life you probably wouldn't be nearly so heavy on the throttle when you next roar down that country road at dusk in your two-litre Volvo. Just one further thought: if for one moment you thought that you were going to be a veal calf in your next life I suspect that your veal marengo might stick in your throat a bit.

Sentimental or not, my attitudes to animals were probably shaped by two elderly family retainers, Layton and Johnstone. These were two large black tom-cats named after the popular singers of the thirties. The real life Johnstone was cited in a divorce action and our Johnny was a bit of a one with the ladies as well. Our Latey died whilst I was quite young but Johnny shared most of the war years with me although he was never entirely happy with our air raid shelter and preferred to continue his nocturnal tom pussy activities whenever possible. Not even the Blitz, I learned, can come between a tom pussy and his love life. Although Johnny guarded his territory with tooth and claw and became increasingly battle-scarred, he eventually died of old age.

I buried him wrapped in my old blazer at the top of the garden. I made a little wooden cross and carefully inscribed on it 'Johnny – Died January 1944' in pokerwork. The circumstances of his birth could not be recorded for posterity since they were shrouded in mystery. Anyway, the little cross rotted away long ago but I like to think that perhaps sometimes on a still and moonlit night a phantom Johnny may be seen lifting his tail defiantly up against the dustbin at number eight Springhurst Avenue just as he used to do all those years ago.

Then there was Tuppence who joined us uninvited during the Blitz. We assumed she was a refugee from some other theatre of war and took her in. She rewarded us by a regular supply of fluffy kittens for the next five or six years. Tuppence had her kittens at various venues according to mood and her labour ward included the space behind the copper under the draining board, the airing cupboard in the bathroom, the cupboard under the stairs and the toy-box in the back bedroom. If the mood took her she would move them from one site to another, one by one, by the scruff of the neck. It was not unknown for her to move a brood of five from the kitchen to the airing cupboard bumping them up thirteen stairs in the process. If you put them back she would do it again. She was a very determined pussy cat.

One of Tuppence's offspring was a long-haired tabby called Chris. Like most of the Edom household he was eccentric. He eventually disappeared without trace but then turned up a year later. He gave no explanation for his sabbatical but just began miaowing for his supper as if nothing had happened.

Tuppence also produced one particularly plain short-haired black cat. He was one of her few failures. He was so plain that no one would have him so we kept him. He took up where Johnny had left of and became the scourge of the neighbourhood. We called him Jimmy. He had a permanently torn ear and at least one eye was usually closed. He was heavily into howling, spitting and fighting. Frankly, he was horrible. But you had to admire him. There were no half measures about Jimmy. He could have won prizes for horribleness.

The Edom household was, as you will have gathered, heavily into cats. The only other animal influence in my childhood was Goldie the goldfish who went a nasty colour and floated to the surface of his bowl in about 1943. Oh, and I almost forgot. There was also Göring the resident rat who lived under the garden shed. He was large, lethargic and had a shaggy coat. Göring didn't often come out during the daylight hours but he was of uncertain disposition and even Johnny pretended not to notice him when he did come out.

Having had such a powerful pussy presence in my early life I have always prided myself on my way with cats. Unless I tease them, I find that cats seldom whop me except (a) when they are feeling playful, (b) when they are feeling irritable, or (c) when they are bored or out of sorts or if I try to remove them from my favourite armchair. Anyway, the loss of blood is usually minimal.

It is part of my conceit as an animal lover that all animals must know that I am on their side. I like to think that they sense my identification with them and my very special understanding of their uniqueness and their right to be recognised as independent beings with their own individual identities. Then I visited an urban farm. Specially designed it was so that we could relate to the animals – to sort of commune with them. I bought my bag of multi-purpose feeding material. (I bought the jumbo size bag so that I could do a lot of communing.) We went and looked at the pigs first. The notice suggested that we were welcome to enter the sty and, well, sort of commune. The moment I got in there this piggy Mafia rushed me mob-handed. Muddy snouts surrounded me and played havoc with my light blue strides. I retreated rapidly.

The goats were next. I offered the senior goat a handful of tasty bits from my jumbo bag of approved feeding material. He ignored my offering, made a quick feint movement and snatched the bag from my hand. He ate the contents and the bag as well whilst his compatriots stood around leering menacingly.

I had an apple for the horses. Everyone knows that with an apple a horse is your friend for life. I picked the wrong horse. He ate my apple all right but once it was consumed he turned really nasty and bit my arm when I was least expecting it. How was I to know that he was suffering from a personality disorder?

Mind you, they were supposed to be domestic animals. It was worse at the Wildlife Park. I only had to look at the Indian elephant and he started doing big jobs in very large round dollops. Then when I went to the white rhino enclosure it got totally out of control. I scarcely like to tell you what the gentleman white rhino started doing to his lady friend; at least I hope it was his lady friend. When I went through those drive-through enclosures the baboons bent my windscreen wipers and one of the lions chewed my wing mirror. The notice said that you could get out of your car in the giraffe enclosure but the giraffe hadn't read the notice. It was touch and go, I can tell you.

My special affinity with animals extends to foreign animals as well. Mind you, that camel in Hammamet was obviously suffering from stress or premenstrual tension or something. In fairness I have to say that if I spent all day and every day plodding up and down the same wadi with a tourist on my back I might have become a bit tetchy myself. Still, the way he, she or it kept turning round and trying to bite my kneecap was, I felt, a bit extreme. After all, we all have our problems and I was a member of the RSPCA.

Then there was that horse in Malaga. He pulled a carriage into which the owner tried to inveigle tourists for a ride round the town. It was late in the evening and we had been in a nightclub. The horse's whole attitude conveyed that he would like to be back in a cosy stable with his hooves up but we silly billies insisted. That horse took us on the slowest tour of Malaga that you could imagine. Every so often he stopped altogether and turned and stared at us reproachfully. Oh, and he also wheezed heavily as if he had terminal bronchitis. I would have welcomed at least a little enthusiasm – after all, he was a part of the tourist industry. But he succeeded in making me extremely guilty even to this day.

Personally I remain heavily into cats as they don't give you any opportunities for delusions of grandeur. You know where you are with a cat; nowhere. It's a very useful preparation for the realities of life and for engendering a sense of humility. Have you ever thought how much better Mrs Thatcher might have been if she had had a cat in her

494

family?

Mice are a bit tricky. I have always been a bit uncertain about mice ever since I opened the dustbin and found a little furry face peering up at me. I put the lid back. I went back later, feeling guilty and determined to rescue him but he had gone. Heaven knows how. There must have been an emergency exit in that dustbin. Then when I moved in to my office in Plumstead I found to my surprise what looked like a mouse hole in the wainscoting. I peered into the hole only to find a face and whiskers peering out. It was singularly unnerving. Then there was my bedsit in Balham. The resident mouse there was a tyrant. That mouse had been on assertiveness training. He used to do balancing tricks on my bedhead in the middle of the night and would then use the coffee table as a skating rink. I used to throw coins at him but he took no notice. In the end I put down poison. When he disappeared I had to have counselling to cope with my feelings of guilt.

I tried some pet white mice for a while but I was always afraid that their breeding habits would get out of control and I would suffocate beneath a surfeit of white mice. I also have to say that pretty though they were they didn't half pong. I gave them away in the end.

I did have an ongoing relationship with a flock of geese for a while. Well, actually it was three but it seemed a lot more. Our neighbours were heavily into self-sufficiency at the time but when they went off on their holidays they used to ask me to look after their geese. Having my local reputation as an animal lover to preserve, I weakly agreed. Now these geese were already known for their antisocial qualities. They had a penchant for loud early morning conversations amongst themselves which meant that no one in Larches Close Addlestone ever slept late.

My neighbours showed me what was required before they went away. It was simple really. I let the geese out of their hut in the morning, changed their water, gave them some grain and let them get on with it. In the evening I merely had to herd them into their hut and lock the door so that the local fox was denied a late supper.

The first evening when I went to herd them into the hut was a disaster. It was like the gunfight at the O.K. Corral. They attacked me mob-handed. I tried to explain about the fox and how it was for their own good but they were in no mood for rational argument. Eventually they lost interest and I was able to coax them into the hut but they made it clear that it was only force of habit and not my powers of persuasion that won the day.

The next day I adopted a new strategy. I put on heavy wellies, shoved rolled-up newspapers down my trouser legs and armed myself with a kiddies' plastic baseball bat. The geese complained bitterly about this overreaction but they went honking into the hut.

I have been a serious frog breeder and hedgehog fancier for a good many years now. In fact, if I decide to weed my heather garden, which I don't do all that often, I usually find an aggrieved frog who clearly resents my interruption of his domestic life.

Hedgehogs tend to be a bit more elusive, but on a spring evening as dusk falls mum often brings her babies out for a stroll and a worm or two.

More recently we seem to have adopted an urban fox. We provide him with a sort of takeaway service. We put all our scraps out in a foil tray for the birds and he takes them away. Recently when I inspected the farthest environs of the garden I found about six foil trays under the laurels at the bottom of the garden. They were all licked clean.

I had budgerigars once but I made the mistake of having a cat as well. Hamish turned out to be partial to poultry. So since then I have stuck with cats. After Hamish came Penny, and Sue and Simon and Sophie and Samantha and

Barley and Duffy and Rosie. Like I said, you know where you are with cats.

Mind you, Samantha went a bit odd in her later years. Do you think that cats can get Alzheimer's disease? She also went stone deaf and developed a penchant for midnight howling and pulling her fur out. When she had been out to do her whoopsies she would return in a state of great exhilaration and race up and down the hall with her tail in the air.

Tagalong Plum Duffy, to give him his full name, is a British Blue although he looks grey to me. He is a very amiable cat but not noted for his intellectual qualities. Well, in fact he is as near brain-dead as makes no difference. His sister Tagalong Rosie Lee is a fluffy colour point. She is very pretty, and like many pretty females is totally egocentric. Unlike any other pussy cat I have ever known, she sleeps late in the morning and never has breakfast before nine thirty. Sometimes she decides to give a display of her prettiness. To do this she lays on her back with all four paws in the air and displays her fluffy white tummy. If this fails to evoke admiring comments she goes and sulks behind the sofa.

The other problem with cats is that they are inclined to bring all their little friends home – dead or alive. Our large fluffy Persian tom-cat was the best. He didn't know that he was a show cat. He thought that he was a hunter. He brought ever more exotic trophies home. He started with mice then moved on to starlings, blackbirds and pigeons. The first starling seemed totally unmoved by having been taken prisoner and dragged through two successive cat flaps. He settled down to eat Barley's tea much to Barley's chagrin. Then Barley brought home a baby rabbit (alive), and then half an adult rabbit (dead). God knows what happened to the other half. Barley became ever more eccentric. We had live mice behind the refrigerator, dead mice behind the sink unit and a dead rat on the patio. Sometimes Barley brought frogs and once, just for a change, a dragonfly. The dragonfly, I have to tell you, was not well pleased.

Well, I saw old Barley go quite a few years ago now. In my dotage I look back on a long line of pets who have passed on, gone over, have gone to meet that great animal lover in the sky… Unfortunately, all this inspires in me the thought that it may soon be my time to be mercifully put down. Fanciful? Not, I suspect, if the new order has its way.

The Author

I first became an author in about 1938. My joined-up handwriting and spelling were giving me some trouble at the time so my dear old mum wrote it all down for me at my dictation. I remember that it was written out most carefully in her small neat handwriting in a penny Woolworth's notebook. The story was of the 'Once upon a time' variety and each new paragraph started either 'And then…' or, 'What happened next was…' I seem to remember that there was a handsome prince and a number of elves but the storyline eludes me. The book was never finished but I seem to recall that it reached about three pages before inspiration failed me. My mum kept it in her handkerchief drawer for some years so I knew she thought that it had literary merit.

In about 1947 I wrote an article entitled 'By Car to the Coast'. This was inspired by the fact that it was the first time that I had been in a car, or to the coast, since 1939. At the time, the experience of travelling to Herne Bay in a motor car seemed unusual enough to record for posterity. Sadly, posterity will have to do without it since I threw it out by accident in about 1955.

I wrote another book in 1959. I wrote it out in exercise books in my best handwriting and a kind and generous girlfriend typed it out for me. It was a searing exposé of the world of insurance and the virtuous and upright insurance clerk hero bore a remarkable resemblance to the author. I never submitted the book for publication for two reasons.

One, because I feared the hurt of rejection and two, because I couldn't afford the postage.

In 1964 a friend gave me a copy of *The Writers' and Artists' Year Book*. This was quite a revelation, even if it was the 1962 edition. It was full of wonderful opportunities for a budding author like me. There were people who offered advice and criticism, and people to type your work and agents to sell it for you and courses to improve your writing and people who would revise it, people who would suggest plots and hundreds of publishers who were clearly just itching to publish my next novel. It was very encouraging. All I had to do was get on and write it. The trouble was that I could never get around to starting it. Inspiration just would not come and I feared that I might be burnt out.

In 1966 the writing urge overcame me again. I decided to be a serious and dedicated author. First I bought a second-hand portable typewriter and lots of paper. I planned to do a lot of writing you see. I still didn't fancy writing another novel so I decided I would be a short story writer instead. The typewriter cost £11. 10s. so you could tell that I was in deadly earnest. The portable had a very positive image and was just like the sort of machine that journalists and authors used in B movies. I liked to imagine myself as a newspaperman on a hot story hunched over my typewriter late at night, chain-smoking between slurps of black coffee. Still, just in case I didn't get a scoop immediately, I didn't give up my day job.

In those days the *Evening News* published a short story every day. I studied the format carefully and began my story writing. The stories had to be of the type that could be started at Waterloo and finished by Surbiton and preferably with an unexpected twist at the end. Just to be sure, I wrote stories with two twists at the end. Even I was confused. Ah well, never mind.

I did manage to get a short, rather self-righteous article

published in an obscure social work magazine in about 1965. This profound and thought-provoking article stimulated a deluge of fan mail. Well, three letters actually. I suspect that the writer of one of them was irredeemably potty and one of the others seemed to have written to the wrong address.

I first got into poetry writing in about 1975. I never really understood poetry. What is the difference between poetry and a rhyme and what makes blank verse verse? Or blank, come to that. Anyway poetry or rhyme, I wrote a lot of it. I bought a rhyming dictionary and sent my little efforts off to all those modest publications that published new poets. I must say they were all remarkably kind to me. Some even offered constructive criticism. None of them volunteered to print my efforts. Still, one of them told me that the last two lines of one of my poems were quite moving. No comment was offered on the remainder.

Then came a brief moment of success. The *Evening Standard* published one of my poems. I was beside myself with excitement. Unfortunately, no one I knew seemed to have seen it so I had to find ways of drawing it to their attention. This I found rather difficult. How do you casually introduce a sentence like, 'By the way have you a copy of last Thursday's *Evening Standard*?' I am tempted to set out the poem here but you haven't done me any harm so I won't.

In desperation I tried my hand at what can best be described as erotic poetry. Although I quite enjoyed writing it there didn't seem to be any market for it. Not for the first time I discovered that whilst there may be a lot of sex about there is also a good deal of hypocritical prudishness. In the end I tore the poems up.

Of course, throughout my working life I had to write items for my employers' annual reports and similar publications and occasional pieces for related organisations.

The trouble is that anyone will publish something if it is sufficiently flattering or adulatory or tells them just what they want to hear but I saw that not as creativity but more like grovelling. Not that I haven't done plenty of that in my time.

More recently I have concentrated on humorous essays. Well, they are meant to be humorous anyway. I am planning to leave my collection of rejection slips to the nation. I once received a rejection slip from the original *Punch* which commented in quite a kindly way about my writing. 'A well written piece but too esoteric for us,' it said. I had to look up what esoteric meant. Still, look what happened to *Punch*.

Every now and then the urge to be a famous author re-emerges, usually when some record-breaking new book is published. The books that appear to succeed seem to fall into three main categories which I have carefully analysed:

(a) Literary masterpieces. These have usually won a literary prize and been praised by *The Times Literary Supplement* with words like 'intricately plotted', 'beautifully written', 'skilfully assembled' and 'rare qualities of intellectual scope and imaginative understanding'. Sometimes I don't even understand the reviews, let alone the books. I think my chances of writing a book of this type are not good.

(b) Books of adventure and bravery. Accounts of crossing the Atlantic on a raft made of an old Dutch dresser reinforced with parcel tape or surviving for three months on a diet of husky dog biscuits in an igloo in the Antarctic spring to mind. My days of bravery and derring-do have yet to arrive so reluctantly this route to literary fame seems closed.

(c) Books of autobiography by those who are famous either in their own right or by association. My only hope would have been to have had a rampant affair with Lady Thatcher or to have been found not guilty at the Old Bailey of trying to blow up Okehampton. Regardless of inclination, I think I lack the nerve for this type of literary opportunity.

When all else fails I write letters. I specialise in indignant letters. The more they are not published the more indignant I get. The *Guardian* did publish one of my letters once. It was all about divorce law reform. That was in about 1962 when it certainly needed reforming. When I can't get my views published I write to MPs and Cabinet ministers instead. I don't expect they read the letters but at least they feel they have to get their minions to reply.

My recent campaigns have been about the M25 which is always good for a laugh and about animal cruelty which isn't. When all else fails I write about the future of the railways or the National Health Service. Pretending they have a future is all part of my odd sense of humour.

A few years ago I managed to master the use of a word processor. I don't have a very sophisticated machine but going at my present rate I don't expect to exhaust its capacity until 2022. I shall be eighty-nine by then.

But now a stop-press note. In 1996 a magazine published one of my little essays and paid me £20 for it. They censored all the rude bits that I had thought were the funniest and reduced its length by nearly a quarter but nonetheless it was the nearest to fame up to then. Then in 1997 they published another one. This time they changed the title but paid me £25. I will keep you posted of any further developments but you would be well advised not to hang around in breathless anticipation.